CW00972295

Church of England Record Society

Volume 16

THE BACK PARTS OF WAR:
THE YMCA MEMOIRS AND LETTERS OF BARCLAY BARON,
1915 to 1919

The record of the British churches in the First World War is still mired in caricature and controversy. While most of the historiography on the British churches and the British soldier of the First World War centres on army chaplains, the critical work of civilian religious welfare organisations has been largely ignored. This volume represents an account of the work of the Young Men's Christian Association with the British army in France, Belgium and occupied Germany from 1915 to 1919. Barclay Baron, the author of these memoirs and letters, was a committed Anglican layman who was dedicated to the cause of Christian social work throughout his adult life. Before 1914 he played a prominent role in the development of the Oxford and Bermondsey Mission and, after the war and his work for the YMCA, he became a major figure in the Toc H movement. The story that Baron tells through his memoirs and letters is as salutary as it is unfamiliar; far from being ineffectual onlookers, through the YMCA in particular the churches provided a ubiquitous, unstinting and even heroic service to the British soldier in the months and years of the First World War.

Dr MICHAEL SNAPE is Senior Lecturer in History at the University of Birmingham.

THE BACK PARTS OF WAR:
THE YMCA MEMOIRS AND LETTERS
OF BARCLAY BARON, 1915 to 1919

EDITED BY

Michael Snape

THE BOYDELL PRESS
CHURCH OF ENGLAND RECORD SOCIETY

© Michael Snape 2009

All Rights Reserved. Except as permitted under current legislation
no part of this work may be photocopied, stored in a retrieval system,
published, performed in public, adapted, broadcast,
transmitted, recorded or reproduced in any form or by any means,
without the prior permission of the copyright owner

First published 2009

A Church of England Record Society publication
Published by The Boydell Press
an imprint of Boydell & Brewer Ltd
PO Box 9, Woodbridge, Suffolk IP12 3DF, UK
and of Boydell & Brewer Inc.
668 Mt Hope Avenue, Rochester, NY 14620, USA
website: www.boydellandbrewer.com

ISBN 978-1-84383-519-6

ISSN 1351-3087

Series information is printed at the back of this volume

A CiP catalogue record for this book is available
from the British Library

This publication is printed on acid-free paper

Typeset by Tina Ranft
Printed in Great Britain by
CPI Antony Rowe, Chippenham and Eastbourne

For John Bourne, David Baron and in memory of my parents

Contents

Letters

Note * Indicates letter discovered in autumn 2008 and now in the possession of the Baron family. See Introduction, Barclay Baron, p. 14.

APPENDIXES

Illustrations

Acknowledgments

I remember my grandfather telling me a story – on more than one occasion – of his experiences while on leave from France during the First World War. He arrived in London en route for Lancashire, still desperately seasick after a wretched Channel crossing. Groggy and unable to make his own way, he sat down on the kerbside and was rescued by a stranger – 'a decent chap' – who took him to Euston station, carrying his rifle and pack for him. Once there, this Good Samaritan fetched him a mug of beef tea, which unfortunately made him sick, before putting him on a north-bound train. Although he never remarked on this, there is a strong possibility that, like untold thousands of soldiers who passed through London in the war years, my grandfather was a beneficiary of the good offices of the Young Men's Christian Association. On more certain ground, in June 1917 my great-grandfather received a letter from the matron of a ward in a military hospital at Etaples. My grandfather's eldest brother had been badly wounded and her letter urged my great-grandfather to come and see him. Although my great-uncle died before any visit could be arranged, for years I wondered how, in the midst of that terrible war, it would have been at all possible for an elderly civilian to visit a wounded relative in a French hospital, especially as this story was no hazy anecdote but was soberly reported at the time in the local press. Once again, the war work of the YMCA, this time for the families of dying soldiers, suggests an answer, although it was many years after becoming interested in Britain and the First World War that this became apparent to me. For personal reasons therefore, and even at a distance of ninety years, it is a source of some satisfaction to requite the kindness of the YMCA by taking the story of their forgotten war work, as related in the memoirs and letters of Barclay Baron, to a wider readership. In this I have been greatly helped by the notes and comments of Mr David Baron and Mrs Josephine Tennent, by Prof. Clyde Binfield, Prof. John Briggs, Dr John Bourne, Prof. Gary Sheffield, Prof. Hugh McLeod, Mr Rob Thompson, Dr Steffen Prauser, Dr Armin Grünbacher, Dr Angela Kershaw and also by the staff of Special Collections at the University of Birmingham, where the archives of the British YMCA are now lodged. I am also immensely grateful to the Council of the Church of England Record Society for agreeing to publish this volume and to Prof. Stephen Taylor for being a constant source of advice and support. My thanks are also due to Lord Remnant and to Colin Williams for their generous financial assistance towards the costs of publication. Lastly, my warmest thanks are due to my heroically supportive wife, Rachel, and to my daughters Katy and Helena for once again indulging my incurable fascination with the First World War.

Abbreviations

ACG	Assistant chaplain-general
ADS	Advanced Dressing Station
AEF	American Expeditionary Force
AOC	Army Ordnance Corps
APM	Assistant provost marshal
AQMG	Assistant quartermaster-general
ASC	Army Service Corps
BEF	British Expeditionary Force
CB	Companion of the Order of the Bath
CLC	Chinese Labour Corps
CMS	Church Missionary Society
CRE	Commanding Royal Engineers
Crockford's	*Crockford's clerical directory*
CWL	Catholic Women's League
DCG	Deputy Chaplain-General
DSO	Distinguished Service Order
FAU	Friends' Ambulance Unit
GHQ	General Headquarters
KBE	Knight Commander of the Order of the British Empire
KCMG	Knight Commander of the Order of St Michael and St George
KCVO	Knight Commander of the Royal Victorian Order
MAC	Museum of Army Chaplaincy
MC	Military Cross
MMG	Motor Machine Gun Corps
NCO	Non-commissioned officer
OBE	Officer of the Order of the British Empire
ODNB	*Oxford dictionary of national biography*
OMM (OBM)	Oxford Medical Mission (Oxford and Bermondsey Mission)
PEF	Portuguese Expeditionary Force
RAMC	Royal Army Medical Corps
RE	Royal Engineers
RFA	Royal Field Artillery
RP	Rawlinson Papers
SCA	Soldiers' Christian Association
SCM	Student Christian Movement
TF	Territorial Force
VC	Victoria Cross
WAAC	Women's Army Auxiliary Corps
WEA	Workers' Educational Association
WEC	War Emergency Committee
YHA	Youth Hostels Association
YMCA	Young Men's Christian Association
YWCA	Young Women's Christian Association

PART 1

INTRODUCTION

Barclay Baron (1884–1964)

'This was the watershed of our lives, the tremendous ridge of effort and suffering which we climbed from one world and from which, if we survived, descended into another which can never be the same.'[1] Thus was the First World War described and remembered by Barclay Baron, who served with the Young Men's Christian Association in France, Belgium and Germany from 1915 to 1919. Barclay Baron was the only son and eldest child of a leading throat surgeon, Barclay Josiah Baron (1857–1919), founder of 'a department for the treatment of diseases of the nose and throat' at Bristol General Hospital, a department he ran for eighteen years. In 1913, however, Barclay Josiah became a member of the city council and was elected lord mayor of Bristol in 1915. He held this office for two consecutive annual terms, hosting King George V during a royal visit to the city in 1917. Knighted the following year for his services to Bristol, in the last months of his life he also held an important regional post in the newly created Ministry of Labour, in which office 'he won the confidence of his colleagues by his ready grasp of intricate questions, his broad-mindedness and impartiality'. However, his public career was brought to an end by his sudden death in June 1919 following a fall at his home in Clifton.[2]

Barclay was one of four children and, although his father was known as 'a keen man of business, with a considerable knowledge of accountancy' (who, moreover, 'had made statistics a hobby')[3] his was a more artistic temperament and he pursued his interests in art, literature and the natural world from an early age. Born into a Quaker family (Baron always took pride in the fact that at least four of his ancestors 'lay in West Country jails, not languishing but rejoicing to stand for the faith of the Society of Friends')[4] when Baron was thirteen his entire family were baptized into the Church of England. The reasons for this transfer of allegiance (whether social, theological or perhaps a mixture of the two) are unclear but around this time Baron began to evince signs of a liberal religious outlook that he was to retain for the rest of his life. One formative influence was Charles Kingsley's *Glaucus* (1855), which he read during an adolescent crisis of

---

[1]   B. Baron, *One man's pattern* (London, n.d.), pp. 15-16.
[2]   *Times*, 9 June 1919, p. 12; *Who was who: a companion to 'Who's who' containing the biographies of those who died during the period 1916–1928* (London, 1929), p. 57; T. Wilson, *The myriad faces of war* (Cambridge, 1988), p. 533.
[3]   *Times*, 9 June 1919, p. 12.
[4]   Baron, *One man's pattern*, p. 1.

faith prompted by reading his father's copy of *The origin of species*. As Baron remembered, Kingsley seemed to reconcile Christianity with Darwinian science and he was thereafter content 'to see all natural creation, enhanced not clouded by the idea of evolution, as "the garment and the speech of God"'.[5]

Although they were not contemporaries, like Field Marshal Sir Douglas Haig Baron was educated at Clifton College. Here, and at variance with the school's bias towards cricket, he continued to nurture his interests in art and literature. As he later remembered:

> Drawing and writing, neither of them reckoned at school as front-rank subjects, were the only ones which brought me calf-bound prizes to put on my shelf. When I confronted our dreaded headmaster in his study to receive the last of these he shook me by the hand with his final word of advice – 'Always go on writing, but nearly always burn it.'[6]

In 1902 Baron entered University College, Oxford, where he was a contemporary of Clement Attlee. With his conscience already stirred by Kingsley's 'social' novels, Baron was further influenced at Oxford by the Christian socialism of Henry Scott Holland, as propagated by the Christian Social Union and his monthly *Commonwealth*. Hence, in a campaign against 'sweated labour in the clothing trade', Baron lobbied among his friends 'to buy only at shops on [Holland's] limited "white list" – and it did not include the best tailors in the town'.[7] Baron's growing interest in social questions also meant that he began to visit 'the dismal slums of Oxford' in the company of a fellow undergraduate, Alec Paterson, whom he befriended during his first hours as an undergraduate. Of their visits Baron remembered:

> There in a fourpence-a-night doss-house we came week by week to know a hopeless, happy-go-unlucky kitchenful of men, a disregarded sample of what writers of the time termed 'the Submerged Tenth'. We could do nothing for them but we were welcomed to share with them their tea out of a common bowl, their shag and dominoes, and to give them a simple service on Sunday night; as friends we tried to understand the cause, to guess the cure of their condition. It was our earliest, tentative incursion into the abyss of poverty.[8]

In his first year at Oxford Baron also fell under the spell of Dr John Stansfeld, a civil servant who had studied medicine part time and who was the founder of the Oxford Medical Mission (an institution that was renamed the Oxford and Bermondsey Mission in 1910 after Stansfeld, its only medical practitioner, left to take holy orders).[9] Drawing on the model of medical missions overseas, which were usually established in areas 'where evangelistic progress was slow and where the Church was unwelcome, as in China',[10] the OMM was very much an

5   *Ibid.*, p. 4.
6   *Ibid.*, p. 5.
7   *Ibid.*, p. 6.
8   *Ibid.*, p. 7.
9   B. Baron, *The doctor: the story of John Stansfeld of Oxford and Bermondsey* (London, 1952), pp. 62–4.
10 A. B. Bartlett, 'The churches in Bermondsey 1880–1939', Ph.D. dissertation, University of Birmingham, 1987, p. 142.

evangelical initiative seeking to make headway in one of the poorest areas of London.[11] Its founder, who began his work in Bermondsey in 1897, was closely associated with Wycliffe Hall (of which he was a part-time student) and with the Oxford Pastorate, a fellowship inaugurated in 1893 as 'an unofficial chaplaincy in the University of Oxford' and which Baron saw as being 'an Evangelical counterblast to the strong influence on undergraduates of the Oxford Movement'.[12] Indeed, and as Baron also perceived, the OMM was a very clear rival to Oxford House in Bethnal Green (an Anglo-Catholic foundation opened some years earlier, which was then booming under the leadership of a future bishop of London, Arthur Winnington Ingram)[13] and as a direct 'counter-attraction for the undergraduate's service'.[14] In 1901, the evangelical identity of the OMM was confirmed when Stansfeld became a Pastorate chaplain and Francis Chavasse (the founder of the Pastorate, a former principal of Wycliffe Hall and now bishop of Liverpool) was appointed Visitor to the mission.[15] Although the OMM had begun as a medical practice (with Stansfeld working from a consulting room in his house in Abbey Street after a day's work in the City)[16] with the arrival of volunteers from Oxford the mission quickly branched into boys' clubs, in which field it was to make its most lasting mark. Initially, Stansfeld invited young men and boys to attend a Bible Class in return for their medical treatment. While this invitation was at first resisted by its intended beneficiaries, these Sunday afternoon classes soon became the nucleus of a growing network of local boys' clubs.[17] Indeed, such was the success of the OMM that it was paid the flattery of imitation when, in 1906, the Cambridge Medical Mission was established nearby, a venture that became 'the home mission of the Cambridge Inter-Collegiate Christian Union'.[18]

That Baron, whose religious views were essentially broad and liberal, should have been drawn so strongly to the work of the OMM was testimony to Stansfeld's manifest integrity and charisma. While, even as a young man, Baron eschewed dogmatic religion and 'the controversies of Christendom',[19] even those who did not share Stansfeld's evangelical churchmanship and unbending moral Puritanism were inspired by his single-mindedness and 'wonderful *directness*'.[20] As Baron recollected of his first encounter with Stansfeld, it was 'on an unforgettable evening in a college room [that] a whirlwind visit from John Stansfeld, "The Doctor", snatched Alec and me – and a succession of others – into Bermondsey, the poorest corner of all London'.[21] On that evening, their

[11]   Baron, *The doctor*, pp. 4, 11; Bartlett, 'The churches in Bermondsey', pp. 35–6, 45 n. 53.
[12]   Baron, *The doctor*, p. 4.
[13]   *ODNB*, A. F. Winnington-Ingram; *Crockford's*, 1913, p. 937.
[14]   Baron, *The doctor*, p. 4.
[15]   *Ibid.*, p. 5.
[16]   *Ibid.*, pp. 7, 16.
[17]   *Ibid.*, p. 17.
[18]   Bartlett, 'The churches in Bermondsey', p. 143.
[19]   B. Baron, *The growing generation* (London, 1911), pp. 183–4.
[20]   Baron, *The doctor*, pp. 144–8.
[21]   Baron, *One man's pattern*, p. 7.

visitor sat on the edge of an armchair munching biscuits and issued a brief but compelling appeal:

> He talked in staccato sentences about a dispensary and a boys' club in South London. He turned to these new members of his old University for help, in terms that shocked them. Other speakers had already put to them the claims of University settlements in poor parts and had even touched them for a facile half-crown. But this man asked for no money: he simply said, 'Come and live the crucified life with me in Bermondsey.' Then he was gone, on his way to the station.[22]

The flow of undergraduate visitors to the OMM increased (particularly during university vacations) with the acquisition of new and larger premises in a former corset factory.[23] These visitors were accommodated on the second floor, the ground floor serving as Stansfeld's dispensary and the first as the home of the boys' club.[24] As Baron remembered, conditions for resident undergraduates were spartan to say the least:

> The second floor of 134 Abbey Street, with the attics above, was the domain of 'the residents' but was apt to be invaded at almost any hour by problems and noise from the floor below. The square factory-floor space had been divided, rather oddly, by amateur carpenters with matchboard partition walls, far from sound-proof...The rule of the house had a monastic simplicity. No floor coverings were permitted, no armchairs or cushions and no window curtains.[25]

Food was plain (bread and treacle was something of a staple) and smoking was, officially at least, forbidden. Visits to the theatre were discouraged, especially to the nearby 'Star' musical-hall, which Stansfeld was wont to portray as 'the Devil's particular playground'.[26] Furthermore, 'Eating sweets, lying late in bed, wearing slippers to breakfast and other small indulgences by residents were frowned upon; they were all classed roundly by the Doctor as "the pig life". He said it with his delightful smile, but he was known to be in earnest.'[27] Not surprisingly, Baron remembered that 'Mothers and aunts, when they heard rumours of this *ménage*, were apt to feel anxious but a little proud of their boy's self-sacrifice and hardship.'[28]

The main task of these occasional residents was to assist with the running of the boys' clubs and their activities – namely sports, evening prayers and regular camps.[29] However, there were also different but related duties to undertake at a nearby mission church:

> A weekly activity of St Andrew's took place very late on Sunday evening and was known simply as 'the drunk service'. In this the Doctor expected some of

[22] Baron, *The doctor*, p. 29.
[23] *Ibid.*, p. 20.
[24] *Ibid.*, pp. 20–3.
[25] *Ibid.*, p. 30.
[26] *Ibid.*, p. 146.
[27] *Ibid.*, p. 32.
[28] *Ibid.*
[29] *Ibid.*, pp. 23–4, 36–44, 146.

his undergraduate helpers to take a hand. Their duty began with walking down Abbey Street at closing-time and collecting a congregation from the public-house doors. Sometimes they received their man direct from the hands of the 'chucker-out', sometimes they linked arms with a customer who was clearly uncertain of the way home. Their captures were then steered, in some cases almost carried, to the benches in the bare little mission church, where they either sang with maudlin fervour old favourites from *Golden Bells*, relapsed into a coma, became abusive or were sick.[30]

Thus did a remarkable roll call of Oxford men spend their university vacations. A single photograph of a group of helpers at an OMM camp in 1907 includes Barclay Baron, Alec Paterson, Neville Talbot and Geoffrey Fisher;[31] however, at other times and on other occasions, the mission's helpers included Clement Attlee, William Temple, 'Tubby' Clayton and Donald Hankey.[32] While Baron counted his Oxford education as his parents' 'crowning gift' to him,[33] it is clear that his heart was in the slums of south London and he later echoed Donald Hankey's words:

When I go to Bermondsey I feel a warmth all over. There I am at ease. There I am at home...Bermondsey showed me what is better than beauty. I went to give and stayed to receive, and what I learned and what I received were the three gifts of which the Apostle tells – faith, hope and love.[34]

On leaving Oxford in 1905, Baron trained as an artist in Germany, London and Italy, acquiring German and Italian in the process. In Germany Baron studied at the universities of Berlin and Munich and learnt to appreciate 'the warmth and order of a German family and the paradox of the earnest, frugal but uninhibited fashion of student life'.[35] However, it would seem that he also encountered a much less attractive face of imperial Germany. As his son, David Baron, recounted:

He once told me how, coming out of a Berlin restaurant one evening with an officer friend in uniform, he had slapped him on the back in the course of conversation. 'Lucky nobody saw that', said his friend, 'or I should have been obliged to run you through with my sword for insulting the Kaiser's uniform'; and he meant it.[36]

While studying for a year in London, Baron lived on the proceeds of free-lance journalism and private tutoring, consoling himself with the proximity of the OMM and with the knowledge that 'the joyful welcome of Bermondsey awaited me for the weekend'.[37] Later, during eighteen months as a private tutor in Verona, Baron developed a strong sympathy for Catholic modernists, who were then

---

[30] *Ibid.*, pp. 17–18.
[31] *Ibid.*, p. 42, Plate III.
[32] *Ibid.*, pp. 22, 167–71, 205.
[33] Baron, *One man's pattern*, p. 6.
[34] *Ibid.*, p. 8.
[35] *Ibid.*
[36] D. Baron, 'Some recollections of my father Barclay Baron', unpublished paper, n.d.
[37] Baron, *One man's pattern*, p. 11.

being hounded by Pope Pius X, and fed his lifelong passion for art history which issued in a study entitled *Girolamo Mocetto, painter-engraver* (1909).[38]

However, in 1909 Baron returned to England and to Bermondsey. Although there was scant hope of earning a living as an art historian, he was nevertheless able to find an outlet for his interests by lecturing at the National Gallery for the Workers' Educational Association.[39] Furthermore, and with the election of a socially reformist Liberal government in December 1905, there was an important demand for the kind of experience that he and his well-connected Bermondsey colleagues had accrued. Both Alec Paterson and Barclay Baron were close to Herbert Samuel, a leading proponent of the 'new Liberalism' and an under-secretary at the Home Office from 1905 to 1909;[40] Paterson played a major *rôle* in drafting the Children Act of 1908 while Baron worked as Samuel's private secretary.[41] Furthermore, in 1911, and after working for some years in Bermondsey as an unpaid teacher in an elementary school, Paterson published *Across the bridges*, a personal account of life and conditions in Bermondsey that was prefaced by Edward Talbot, then bishop of Southwark, who saluted the work of the OBM as 'the best work in London'.[42] *Across the bridges* made a considerable impact, running through eleven printings between 1911 and 1928.[43] In this book, Paterson dealt primarily with youth issues (including the subject of youth religion) but he also discussed family life, marriage, living conditions and the situation of the working man; he concluded by calling for greater understanding and mixing between the social classes.[44] For his part, Baron wrote occasional articles (and penned the odd cartoon) for the Liberal *Daily News*,[45] he lobbied London County Council for the provision of school meals and in 1911 wrote *The growing generation: a study of working boys and girls in our cities*, which was published later that year by the Student Christian Movement for the benefit of church 'Social Study Circles'.[46] Styling himself a 'Worker at the Oxford and Bermondsey Mission', *The growing generation* was an early manual of youth work (including book lists and a summary of relevant legislation) in which Baron addressed issues such as the physique, education, work, recreation, family life and religion of the adolescent.[47] Building on his reputation as a Christian social analyst and commentator, from 1914 to 1915 Baron was one of the principal editors of *The Challenge*. This was a progressive, illustrated Church of England newspaper which appealed to a younger readership; it espoused 'a liberal tone in its theology, in its general

---

[38]   *Ibid.*, pp. 12–13.
[39]   *Ibid.*, p. 14.
[40]   *ODNB*, Herbert Samuel.
[41]   Baron, *The doctor*, pp. 14, 163–4.
[42]   A. Paterson, *Across the bridges* (London, 1911), p. viii.
[43]   Baron, *The doctor*, pp. 163–4.
[44]   Paterson, *Across the bridges, passim*.
[45]   Barclay Baron to Jane Baron, 8 January 1910.
[46]   Baron, *One man's pattern*, p. 14; Baron, *The growing generation*, p. v.
[47]   Baron, *The growing generation, passim*.

intellectual outlook, and in church politics', standing for ecumenism, church reform and the cause of the social gospel.[48]

However, Baron's first commitment was always to the OBM and he became its warden in 1911, working from its new headquarters in Riley Street and sharing rooms nearby with Donald Hankey.[49] The following year he met Rachel Abel Smith, who was then working for the evangelical Time and Talents Settlement which had established itself next door to Bermondsey rectory in 1896, the year in which Henry Lewis (a former Indian missionary of the Church Missionary Society) became rector.[50] The settlement's non-resident female volunteers worked with girls and young women, principally through girls' clubs and district visiting, and they proved a rich source of wives for the denizens of the OBM.[51] Somewhat older than Baron, Rachel Abel Smith was the daughter of a deceased Conservative MP and her mother had been a founding member of Time and Talents. She was also related to Sir Thomas Fowell Buxton, a longstanding vice-president of the YMCA, who shared her late father's evangelical sympathies, his social conscience and his support for the CMS.[52] While her work in Bermondsey had not met with the wholehearted approval of her wider family,[53] the couple's engagement was announced in *The Times* in May 1914 and they were married by Stansfeld in Southwark Cathedral on 25 July, with Alec Paterson acting as Baron's best man. Naturally enough, the guests at the wedding reception represented the extremes of wealth and poverty, with 'top-hat and cloth cap coming together' for the happy event. Nevertheless, and despite the unlikely success of their wedding day, the couple's honeymoon in the Scottish Highlands was to be shattered by the outbreak of war with Germany ten days later.[54]

Among his many interests, Baron's first-hand experience of Germany and his knowledge of German meant that he had been active in attempts to improve Anglo-German relations through the churches, bilateral efforts that had issued in exchange visits by leading British and German churchmen in the years 1908–14.[55] While this background contributed towards his loathing of wartime hate-mongering, his reaction to the war when it came was unambiguous: he returned to London in order to enlist. Quite apart from his antipathy towards Prussian militarism, Baron's desire to serve in the army was driven by his conviction that the war offered the ultimate consummation of the OBM ideal of Christian brotherhood between social classes. Despite the mission's best efforts and intentions, there had always been an obvious gulf between its Oxford and

[48] F. A. Iremonger, *William Temple* (Oxford, 1948), pp. 182–3; Appendix II, p. 265.
[49] D. Baron, 'Some recollections'; Barclay Baron to Jane Baron, n.d. 1913.
[50] *Crockford's*, 1899, p. 826.
[51] www.infed.org/socialaction/time_and_talents.htm. Consulted 20 October 2008; Baron, *The doctor*, pp. 12, 161.
[52] *Times*, 1 June 1898, p. 8; *ODNB*, Sir Thomas Fowell Buxton; *Year book of the National Council of Young Men's Christian Associations of England, Ireland and Wales*, 1914, p. 5.
[53] Barclay Baron to Jane Baron, 21 April 1914.
[54] *Times*, 18 May 1914, p. 11; Baron, *One man's pattern*, pp. 7, 15; Appendix II, pp. 269–70.
[55] J. A. Moses, 'The British and German churches and the perception of war, 1908–1914', *War and Society*, V (1987), 23–44 at 28–37.

Bermondsey elements and it was only occasionally 'in the life of the club, in camp or on the cricket field that they reached common ground and could be rivals and partners on the level'.[56] The coming of war, on the other hand, and the prospect of serving together in the ranks, seemed to offer the means of finally bridging this chasm. As Donald Hankey remembered:

> To understand the working man one must know him through and through – live, work, drink, sleep with him. And the war gave us a unique opportunity of doing this. We knew that we could never become working men; but no power on earth could prevent us from enlisting if we were sound of wind and limb. And enlisting meant living on terms of absolute equality with the very men whom we wanted to understand. Filled anew with the glamour of our quest, we sought the nearest recruiting office.[57]

With the benefit of hindsight, Baron viewed the results of this impulse rather differently; it was, he stated, 'in the ultimate, elemental affair of living and dying together' that their elusive union 'reached its completion'.[58] Although the Christian socialist R. H. Tawney (a veteran of Toynbee Hall, Oxford's settlement in Whitechapel) felt a similar compulsion to eschew a commission in order to serve in the ranks of the 22nd Manchester Regiment,[59] for many involved with the OBM the immediate precursor of this fusion in khaki was their membership of the Stansfeld Club, an organization formed in 1911 to keep young men 'in the family circle of the Mission'.[60] As Baron remembered:

> The great majority of its members, among them the very best, left at once to join up. Many of them, from Oxford as well as Bermondsey, enlisted in the local Territorial battalion of the London Regiment, the 22nd (The Queen's) [and] the pale ghost of the men's Club faded out of existence.[61]

While Paterson enlisted in the 22nd London Regiment and Hankey found himself in the 7th Rifle Brigade, a battalion of Lord Kitchener's volunteer New Army, it was Baron's unhappy lot to be rejected for military service on medical grounds. Despite his vigorous outdoor interests (he had hiked across the Pyrenees in 1913 and cycled over the Alps four years earlier),[62] for the war's first months he found himself languishing among the 'two or three men unfit for active service' who were left to run the mission's junior clubs, ventures that staggered 'on through the war years in mounting difficulties'.[63] While tempered by the birth of his eldest child in the spring of 1915, Baron's urge to serve despite his rejection by the army remained undiminished and at this point his membership of the Cavendish Club came to the rescue. Created in 1911 and lavishly supported

[56] Baron, *The doctor*, p. 35.
[57] D. Hankey, *A student in arms* (London, 1918), p. 93.
[58] Baron, *The doctor*, p. 35.
[59] *ODNB*, R. H. Tawney.
[60] Baron, *The doctor*, pp. 172–4.
[61] *Ibid.*, p. 174.
[62] Baron, 'Some recollections'; Baron, *One man's pattern*, p. 13.
[63] Baron, *The doctor*, p. 174.

by the duke of Devonshire, the Cavendish Club was a West End club with a strong social conscience where Baron had entertained a native officer of the OBM in 1913 just 'as Oxford men have been to see him in Bermondsey'.[64] In the summer of 1915, and with the assistance of the Cavendish Association (an offshoot of the club that was dedicated to promoting the ideal of social service in Britain's public schools and universities)[65] Baron volunteered to serve with the YMCA in France, originally with the aim of establishing a club for army officers in Le Havre.

As his four-year career with the YMCA went on to demonstrate, Baron was ideally suited to this type of war work. Although he was not an evangelical and had no formal connection with the organization, he was not untypical of the men who comprised the majority of the YMCA's overseas workers during the First World War. While he had met Lord Kinnaird at the home of the Fowell Buxtons at the time of the Anglo-German exchanges (where he had formed the impression that the president of the Association's National Council was 'the greatest old bore alive')[66] the wartime work and ethos of the YMCA was much more to his liking; indeed, in December 1916 he even told his mother how his Red Triangle work was really 'just the OBM on a huge scale'. If he found his work congenial and even familiar in certain respects, he also had the advantages of youth and (despite the army's reservations) of robust health. Furthermore, Baron had grown attuned to evangelical sensibilities in Bermondsey, he had the common touch and he had roughed it in Bermondsey and as a would-be artist; he was also articulate, self-assured and well connected and had acquired considerable organizational and administrative experience through his work for the OBM. All of these factors help to explain why he rose to such prominence in Red Triangle work while never actually being a member of the YMCA. They also help to account for his comfortable accommodation to military life and culture, a photograph of Baron in Cologne in 1919 showing him fully at ease in khaki and with the confident bearing of the veteran officer that he could so easily have been.[67]

However, despite his long association with the YMCA, its changing ethos, the support of the whole Baron family for YMCA war work and his fleeting interest in its post-war future, Baron did not choose to continue his involvement with the Association after his return to England in 1919. Although he never made the reasons for this decision clear, it could be that the YMCA was too well established, too Free Church and perhaps too tainted by commerce for his liking and that, after the war, he sought to make his home in a newer, more comfortably Anglican and fraternal organization such as Toc H. Evidently, the younger movement completely eclipsed the YMCA in Baron's affections; in his memoirs he wrote how the YMCA, even at its best, could not match the spirit of Talbot House in Poperinghe, the source of the later Toc H movement. Moreover, and

[64] Barclay Baron to Jane Baron, n.d. 1913; B. Baron, *The birth of a movement 1919–1922* (London, 1946), pp. 115–16.
[65] Baron, *One man's pattern*, p. 16; Baron, *Birth of a movement*, pp. 116–18.
[66] Barclay Baron to Jane Baron, 5 June 1914.
[67] See Illustration 1.

despite being appointed an OBE for his work with the YMCA, his service with
the Red Triangle was not even mentioned in his short autobiography *One man's
pattern*. Such an omission is, indeed, all too illustrative of the place of Talbot
House in the popular memory of the war and of the general amnesia that has
obscured the Association's contribution. At the time, and rather ironically,
leading figures in the YMCA were wont to equate Red Triangle work with that of
Talbot House, one of their number writing with confidence in October 1918:

> Of [our] centres [in Flanders] probably the most interesting was an old
> Belgian club at Poperinghe…This old club, with another organized by the
> Church of England, called Talbot House, will no doubt figure in history for
> the part played in providing a 'home from home' to the surging masses of
> troops which thronged this town during those memorable months of the
> Flanders battles. And a [YMCA] hut always open day and night in the Station
> Square did yeoman service for the many divisions of troops, odd units, and
> individual officers and men detraining and entraining at Poperinghe Station,
> always a hot spot.[68]

Whatever his other feelings may have been, what was probably decisive in
ensuring that Toc H supplanted the YMCA in Baron's affections was the fact that
he came to see it as the direct spiritual successor of the OBM. In 1946, and in his
history of the early years of Toc H, Baron wrote:

> What our members constantly call 'the Toc H spirit' was as constantly known
> to their spiritual ancestors in Bermondsey as 'the OBM spirit'…Bermondsey,
> by no accident, has given many men to Toc H – Alec Paterson, Charlie
> Thompson, Hubert Secretan, Barclay Baron and others – and has received
> some men back from Toc H in return. Its 'pre-natal' influence on Toc H was
> quite direct and vital. Two principles, every day repeated in a thousandfold
> variety of words and deeds, made up the gospel of John Stansfeld, 'the
> Doctor': they were 'We *are* one family' and 'Remember, as you do this, you
> do all to the glory of God.' These are surely the whole gospel of Toc H –
> Fellowship and Service, in all its relationships, human and Divine. As for the
> word 'family', which from early 1922 onwards is found in Toc H literature
> and on the lips of its members, it came direct from 'the Doctor's' mouth and
> heart and was merely imported by one of his disciples at Toc H
> Headquarters.[69]

Six years later, Baron reprised this theme in his biography of John Stansfeld, in
which he stressed that the prime movers of Talbot House, namely Neville Talbot
and 'Tubby' Clayton, were 'both of them "the Doctor's men" in years past' and
that the spirit and ethos of the OBM was very much that of the 'soldiers' club of
a unique character on the edge of the dreaded Ypres battlefield'.[70] Moreover, he
dwelt on how Stansfeld had sought membership of the new movement, on how

---

[68] YMCA Archives, University of Birmingham, K26 YMCA War Work No. 13. France. H. A. Down,
    'Pioneering on the Western Front. 3½ years with the YMCA', p. 20.
[69] Baron, *Birth of a movement*, p. 4.
[70] Baron, *The doctor*, p. 207.

Clayton had remarked 'that Bermondsey was the true cradle of Toc H' and on how 'from the first days of its getting together leadership began to come to the new movement from "across the bridges"'.[71]

Although not present at its inaugural meeting in November 1919, Baron was a key figure in the early Toc H movement, especially after it incorporated the Cavendish Association, for which he was then working as travelling secretary, in 1921.[72] Over a period of decades he edited the Toc H journal, designed the distinctive Toc H 'Lamp of Maintenance' (choosing its inscription '*In lumine tuo videbimus lumen*'),[73] chronicled the movement's history and served as its vice-president and travelling secretary. Furthermore, his artistic talents found expression in the composition of a number of Toc H masques, some of which were performed in the Albert Hall.[74] After Baron's death, and in honour of his contribution to the movement, a room at Talbot House was named in his memory.[75]

However, Baron's interests were not confined to Toc H. While he remained very much involved in the affairs of the OBM (which was renamed the Oxford and Bermondsey Club in the aftermath of the First World War)[76] he also wrote a number of hymns, including the club's hymn[77] and 'Go forth with God!', which was published as one of *The Oxford choral songs* in 1937. In a more secular vein, he was also an early pioneer of the Youth Hostels Association (which was inspired by similar institutions in Germany) and he served as the YHA's first chairman from 1930 to 1937.[78] During the Second World War, in which his flat in Earl's Court fell prey to a German incendiary bomb, Baron served in the Home Guard and he partly relived his younger days by running an Allied servicemen's club in Westminster.[79] Despite the loss of his artwork and extensive art history notes to the *Luftwaffe*, Baron's interest in the natural world continued unabated, and in the last years of his life he assembled an impressive collection of ferns.

The manuscript

If he was remarkably reticent in public about his service with the YMCA during the First World War, Baron's recollections of these years and his surviving letters are invaluable sources of information on Red Triangle work in France, Belgium and Germany from 1915 to 1919. At the core of this volume are Baron's memoirs of his YMCA war work, memoirs which are now deposited in the YMCA

[71] *Ibid.*, p. 208.
[72] Baron, *One man's pattern*, p. 16; Baron, *Birth of a movement*, pp. 10–13, 118.
[73] 'In thy light shall we see light', Psalm 36:9.
[74] Baron, *One man's pattern*, p. 18; Baron, 'Some recollections'.
[75] www.talbothouse.be. Consulted 12 January 2009.
[76] Baron, *The doctor*, pp. 174–5.
[77] *Ibid.*, p. 212.
[78] *Times*, 15 January 1932, p. 9; Baron, 'Some recollections'.
[79] Baron, *One man's pattern*, p. 13; Baron, 'Some recollections'.

Archives at the University of Birmingham. These represent chapters of an uncompleted war memoir (or possibly even a larger autobiography), the residual part of which – entitled 'The edge of the storm' – is published in a lightly edited form as Appendix II. This chapter, which covers Baron's marriage and earlier career at *The Challenge*, is still in the possession of the Baron family and, while separate and distinct from his YMCA papers, has been published in order to shed further light on Baron himself and on the early months of the war as he experienced them. Whatever its parameters, the larger work had clearly not been finished by the time of Baron's death. His memoirs peter out with some impressions of German character formed while he was serving in the Rhineland, the pagination of the manuscript is erratic throughout and the surviving version of Chapter three is not in Baron's hand but appears to be a typed copy of the lost original.

However fractured and incomplete, Baron's memoirs appear to date from the early 1960s, years that in Great Britain saw the beginnings of a huge resurgence of interest in the First World War. This phenomenon was fuelled by a succession of fiftieth anniversaries and by the massive impact of the BBC television series *The Great War*, a series that was first broadcast between 30 May and 19 November 1964.[80] As Baron died some weeks before broadcasting commenced, it appears that he may have been moved by a simple sense of history; nevertheless, his loose rendering of quotations, his occasional inaccuracies (especially regarding military operations and units) and a number of points that conflict with details in his correspondence suggest that he wrote largely from memory and without reliance on reference works or the aid of his wartime letters.

Of the twenty-four letters, which comprise the balance of Baron's surviving YMCA papers, eighteen were written to his mother, Jane Baron (née Robinson) and are kept in the Department of Documents at the Imperial War Museum in London. However, while the present volume was being prepared in the autumn of 2008, six further letters came to light at the home of Baron's son, David Baron, comprising another four letters to his mother, an illustrated letter to David Baron (which, as it was written as a fairy story for a three-year-old, has not been included in this volume) and, finally, a letter to Rachel Baron from William Wilson, one of Baron's co-workers at Le Havre, which has been included as Appendix I.

While Baron's memoirs and letters have the clear advantage of being engagingly written by an informed and educated observer, in addition to some discrepancies in detail, there is also a certain dissonance between them. Baron's letters were remarkably candid and, although written to his mother, he certainly did not spare her some of the more shocking details of the war on the Western Front, a fact evidenced by his descriptions of the Somme battlefield and of the human and animal detritus of war in Bailleul in September 1918. Nevertheless, and despite its horrors and discomforts, his letters show that his personal commitment to the war remained clear and unshaken. On 21 December 1916, Baron wrote:

---

[80] D. Todman, *The Great War: myth and memory* (London, 2005), pp. 29–35; *The Great War: viewing notes* (North Harrow, 2001), *passim*.

These are unmistakeably terrible days but also unspeakably grand. I often say, from the platform, to soldiers 'The war has shown us the Devil in men – in ourselves as well as in our enemy. War has also shown us, what many of us never suspected, God in men also! Let that be clear, as it becomes every day clearer to me, and what is there not possible for our chastened world in the future?'[81]

If anything, his resolve seems to have been strengthened in 1917–18 by the exalted but uncompromising diplomacy of President Wilson and by the evidence he saw of German conduct in occupied France, most notably in Péronne, Bailleul and Lille. Indeed, and with reference to these depredations, Baron could write in October 1918:

I wish to God every striker in England could be pushed through this country and lie in this mud and taste this unspeakable bitterness which the French know so well. He would – if he was a sensible man – go away quietly to work or to shoot himself in a corner hiding.[82]

However, for much of British society the inter-war years were a period of lengthy reflection and growing recrimination, a tendency that reached its height around 1930 with the craze for so-called 'war books', memoirs and novels that were generally characterized by their lurid and negative depictions of the war.[83] This craze was strongly deplored by its critics (not least among whom was 'Tubby' Clayton, whose Toc H movement represented a more positive legacy of the war experience)[84] and it was illustrated by the popularity of Robert Graves's fictionalized autobiography *Good-bye to All That* (1929) and, still more strikingly, by the dazzling success of Erich Maria Remarque's novel *All quiet on the Western Front*, which appeared in English earlier that year.[85] By the time Baron wrote his memoirs in the early 1960s, a failed peace, another world war, the poetry of Siegfried Sassoon and much inter-war criticism of the British high command (not least by fellow Liberals such as C. E. Montague and David Lloyd George)[86] had plainly made their mark upon him. In his memoirs, this translated into some impassioned outbursts against war and its attendant hysteria, as well as into some strong criticism of the military hierarchy (most notably of Generals Asser, Rawlinson and the unnamed hero who taunted German prisoners of war in Le Havre). Nevertheless, the overall tone of his memoirs is one of ambivalence, for juxtaposed with these sentiments are an interest in military history, a profound regard for General Plumer, an immense pride in the British soldier and an abiding animus against German (or, perhaps more properly, 'Prussian') militarism, an animus that still led him to savour the humiliation of Cologne upon its occupation

81 See p. 227.
82 See p. 256.
83 C. Falls, *War books*, 2nd edn (London, 1980), pp. xiv–xvii.
84 P. B. Clayton, *Plain tales from Flanders* (London, 1929), p. 143.
85 M. Seymour-Smith, *Robert Graves: his life and work* (London 1982), pp. 191–4; B. Bond, *The unquiet Western Front* (Cambridge, 2002), pp. 35–8.
86 K. Grieves, 'C. E. Montague and the making of *Disenchantment*', *War in History*, IV (1997), pp. 35–59, *passim*; Bond, *The unquiet Western Front*, pp. 46–8.

in December 1918. In short, and in the later years of his life at least, Baron seems to have belonged to that intriguing majority of British veterans who neither relished nor loathed the war but who, as Denis Winter has argued, simply lived with their conflicting experiences and emotions and who 'were never able to reach a final judgement' upon it.[87] Indeed, taking stock of the impact of the war in the early 1950s, Baron had written simply that it had 'immensely quickened the tempo of social change, with much eventual benefit and some disadvantage'.[88]

Despite this ambivalence, in historiographical terms Baron's memoirs and letters tend to support an emerging revisionist consensus on the *rôle* of the churches in the First World War.[89] Pilloried by Christian pacifists in the inter-war and Cold War periods, the conduct of the British churches in the First World War has long been associated with the image of bellicose bishops, compromised clergy and ineffectual chaplains, an image popularized, above all, by the poetry and prose of Siegfried Sassoon and Robert Graves. However, while Baron clearly deplored wartime Germanophobia in the churches,[90] the work of the YMCA in the conflict, so vividly related in his memoirs and letters, underlines another, untold side of the story – one of unstinting and courageous service by thousands of church people, clergy and laity alike, to those who bore the brunt of a terrible war that was steadfastly held to be just by the vast majority of the British people.[91]

---

[87] D. Winter, *Death's men: soldiers of the Great War* (London, 1979), pp. 224–6.

[88] Baron, *The doctor*, p. 213.

[89] M. Snape, 'The Great War', in *The Cambridge history of Christianity*, IX: *World Christianities c. 1914 – c. 2000*, ed. H. McLeod (Cambridge, 2006), pp. 131–50; M. Burleigh, 'Religion and the Great War', in *A part of history: aspects of the British experience of the First World War* M. Howard (London, 2008), pp. 74–81; A. Wilkinson, 'This was a battle for true freedom', *Church Times*, 7 November 2008, p. 13.

[90] See Appendix II, pp. 273–4.

[91] A. Gregory, *The last great war: British society and the First World War* (Cambridge, 2008), pp. 294–6.

The YMCA and the British army in the First World War

Introduction

The enormous significance of the work of the Young Men's Christian Association for the British army of 1914–18 has been largely overlooked in the historiography of Christian philanthropy in modern Britain and in the vast historiography of Britain and the First World War.[1] Historians of British religion and the First World War have tended to focus their attention on the experience of individual denominations and, in common with military historians, have usually confined their studies of the churches' direct involvement with the army to the commissioned clergymen of the Army Chaplains' Department. As a civilian and interdenominational organization the YMCA has therefore been neglected, notwithstanding the confident contemporary claim that its wartime work for British soldiers 'will never be forgotten so long as human gratitude counts for anything'.[2] However, J. S. Reznick's recent study of Britain's wartime 'culture of caregiving' has rightly drawn attention to YMCA hut work as a prime example of practical care for the British soldier. Furthermore, Reznick has stressed the domestic atmosphere of many Association huts (an atmosphere that was embodied in their female workers) and has emphasized the secular tone of much of the Association's army work, the controversial nature of its trading practices and the public suspicions of wartime profiteering to which they gave rise.[3] However, Reznick's contribution, valuable though it is, still represents a very partial picture of the Association's work with the British army during the First World War. As the rest of this introduction will show, the multifaceted war work of the YMCA extended far beyond the confines of its huts, men predominated among its overseas workers and the deeper and manifold significance of this work for the army, the soldier and the Association itself deserves much fuller consideration.

[1] See, for example, F. Prochaska, *Christianity and social service in modern Britain: the disinherited spirit* (Oxford, 2006), *passim*.

[2] Ian Hay, 'Home on leave', in *Told in the huts: the YMCA gift book*, ed. A. K. Yapp (London, 1916), pp. 133–4.

[3] J. S. Reznick, *Healing the nation: soldiers and the culture of caregiving in Britain during the Great War* (Manchester, 2004), pp. 17–41.

Origins

A host of religious organizations plunged themselves into army work between 1914 and 1918. By 1917, those working with the British Expeditionary Force (BEF) in France included the Church Army, the Salvation Army, the Catholic Women's League, the Friends Ambulance Unit, Catholic Huts for Soldiers Abroad, the Scottish Churches Huts Joint Committee, the Army Scripture Readers' and Soldiers' Friend Society, the Navvy Mission Society and the British Soldiers Institute.[4] However, none of these attained the size, prominence or efficiency of the YMCA. In 1916, and in appealing for donations towards the hut work of the CWL, a Jesuit priest admonished his Farm Street congregation that 'The work of the Young Men's Christian Association shows us what we ought to do, and shows us how to do it.'[5] Likewise, and in opening a YMCA hut at Folkestone that year, the archbishop of Canterbury declared that the YMCA was 'first and foremost among societies working for the well-being of soldiers'.[6] As these endorsements suggest, most contemporaries would have agreed, however reluctantly, with a journalist's verdict that 'The Young Men's Christian Association stepped at the beginning of the war to the very foremost place in work for the soldiers, and retained its lead along.'[7]

In part, the pre-eminence of the YMCA was due to the fact that it had already acquired considerable experience of working with soldiers in the field. During the Boer War (1899–1902), its army auxiliary, the Soldiers' Christian Association, had furnished and maintained a number of 'Writing Tents' for the troops in South Africa. These supplied reading and writing materials free of charge and served as venues for religious services. Furthermore, since the 1890s many local associations had undertaken similar work with the Volunteers (then part of the army's reserve forces) at their annual summer camps.[8] Given its extensive experience of camp work with the Volunteers (who were incorporated into the new Territorial Force in 1908) and also the work of the SCA in South Africa, the YMCA in Britain possessed the expertise, the equipment and the organization to develop its work with the British army from the earliest days of the First World War. In fact, and with the benefit of hindsight, Sir Arthur Keysall Yapp construed the Association's prior work with the Volunteers and Territorials in providential terms, arguing that:

[4] YMCA Archives, University of Birmingham (hereafter YMCA), K27 YMCA War Work No. 14. France. 'Re-organisation of the administration of voluntary institutions working for the benefit of the British armies in France', 7 May 1917; RP, Downside Abbey, correspondence relating to Catholic huts and clubs for troops in France 1916–19; M. Snape, *God and the British soldier: religion and the British army in the First and Second World Wars* (London, 2005), pp. 207–16.

[5] *YM. The British Empire YMCA Weekly*, 24 November 1916, p. 1098.

[6] YMCA, J7 National Council signed minutes, 5 May 1916.

[7] F. A. McKenzie, 'Welfare work for the soldiers from base to battlefield: a record of splendid achievement', in *The Great War*, ed. H. W. Wilson and J. A. Hammerton (13 vols., London, 1914–19), XI, 401–24 at 404.

[8] M. Snape, *The Redcoat and religion: the forgotten history of the British soldier from the age of Marlborough to the eve of the First World War* (London, 2005), pp. 108–9; Snape, *God and the British soldier*, p. 208.

Institutions as well as individuals are prepared all unconsciously for the tasks which God has in store for them...In those camps of citizen soldiers we learned to know the soldier and to understand his needs when on active service...It was owing to the experience we had gained in Volunteer and Territorial camps that we were able to take the field in the Great War as soon as hostilities began.[9]

Significantly, Yapp was speaking as the prime mover and chief architect of the Association's wartime work. Born the son of a Herefordshire farmer in 1869, Yapp was a keen temperance man and part-time evangelist who worked as an agricultural engineer before becoming the full-time secretary of Derby's YMCA in 1892, only two years after joining the Association. However, even before the war Yapp had distinguished himself as an innovator; from 1898 he had overseen the expansion of YMCA work in Lancashire (where he was an early pioneer of YMCA camp work with the Volunteers) and he had served as the first salaried secretary of the Manchester YMCA from 1907 to 1912, at which point he became the general secretary of the National Council of Young Men's Christian Associations, Incorporated, a body to which English, Welsh and Irish associations were affiliated.[10] With the outbreak of war in August 1914, Yapp swiftly convened an emergency meeting of the National Council,[11] perceiving the new conflict in Europe to be an unprecedented opportunity for the Association to serve the British Empire and to broaden its appeal among the young men of the nation. In grasping this opportunity, he also adopted the 'Red Triangle' device (symbolizing spirit, mind and body) as 'the emblem and badge' of the Association's war work. Among Yapp's admirers at least, his grand vision earned him the reputation of being an invincible and appealing optimist, a man for whom the term experiment was 'a blessed word'.[12] However, when faced with opposition on the National Council, it was probably the Association's existing links with the army and with the royal family (George V being patron of the National Council) that served to clinch Yapp's case for a major expansion of YMCA army work. In an early exchange with the council's more cautious and conservative president, Lord Kinnaird, Yapp made the passionate plea that 'everything was at stake...the YMCA, by keeping up the morale of the army could help the country to win the War [and] if we lost the War everything would be lost'.[13]

However, a further (and unspoken) imperative seems to have been the poor public image of the Association in the pre-war years. While Thomas Hughes had lambasted the 'religious Pharisaism' of the early YMCA in his hugely influential *Tom Brown's schooldays* (1857),[14] half a century of development had seen the image of the Association progress from the obnoxious to the insipid. Writing in

[9] A. K. Yapp, *In the service of youth* (London, 1927), pp. 52–3.
[10] *ODNB.*
[11] YMCA, J7 National Council signed minutes, 7 August 1914.
[12] Yapp, *In the service of youth*, p. 60; *The Red Triangle Bulletin*, 31 August 1917, p. 1.
[13] Yapp, *In the service of youth*, p. 61.
[14] G. W. E. Russell, 'Comradeship', in *Told in the huts*, ed. Yapp, p. 157.

the *Daily Mail*, F. A. McKenzie observed that at the beginning of the war 'the average citizen regarded the YMCA as a somewhat milk-and-waterish organization, run by elderly men, to preach to youth'.[15] In 1915, an Anglican clergyman agreed that 'There was a time when no one took the YMCA quite seriously, and every schoolboy knows the story of the [YMCA] young man who pretended that he dare not go home in the dark.'[16] Returning to the subject in 1918, McKenzie remarked that 'Up to the outbreak of war the YMCA in England was openly regarded by the outside public as a narrow, purely religious organization. [W. S.] Gilbert's sneer at "the YMCA young man" represented the common attitude.' This attitude, he argued, was not without foundation for 'The YMCA had for some years been controlled by a group of men who had not kept fully in touch with the younger generation. They carried the narrower religious practice of the middle of the nineteenth century into the twentieth century.'[17]

Certainly, the structures and finances of the Association had helped to impede innovation and, arguably, expansion as well. In 1910, a year in which YMCA funds and membership appeared to be on the point of decline, the 399 associations of England, Wales and Ireland counted only 30,000 full members, although further categories of club, junior and honorary members raised their total membership to just over 92,000.[18] Despite their common evangelical ethos, local associations still varied considerably in character and emphasis. As an internal memorandum recognized in 1916:

> Some Associations have been dominated by enthusiastic members of one section of the Church of England. Others have been predominantly Free Church Associations. Others have been led by earnest men who have maintained that what was most needed was for us to ignore our denominational differences and unite in aggressive evangelistic work, never realizing that without the Church their converts could not be built up in faith and character.[19]

Furthermore, their most established, influential and affluent members tended to be products of an earlier and more staid generation, a point that was not lost on F. A. McKenzie:

> Each YMCA was a separate unit in itself, with complete self-governing powers inside the constitution of the movement. There were district councils and a National Council, but the National Council had no power to control the smallest local body. Each YMCA was administered by a committee, and these committees were usually composed of prosperous older men, more or less imbued with the ideas of their generation.[20]

---

15   T. W. Koch, *Books in camp, trench and hospital* (reprinted from the *Library Journal*, 1917), p. 12.
16   Anon., *YMCA war work in Britain and Flanders by two Oxford men* (London, 1915), p. 13.
17   McKenzie, 'Welfare work', p. 405.
18   *Year book of the National Union of YMCAs*, 1910, 'Summary of statistics (1909–10)'.
19   YMCA, K24 YMCA War Work No. 4. Religious. 'Memorandum regarding the interdenominational position of the YMCA', December 1916.
20   McKenzie, 'Welfare work', p. 405.

Still, even McKenzie conceded that a new and more progressive generation of leaders was in the process of asserting itself, a generation that was very much influenced by the example and success of YMCA work overseas:

> In other lands, notably in America, in India, and Burma, and in the Dominions, the YMCA had focused the social activities of the general community for the young man. In England this was not the case…But young men in touch with youth were rising up in the association itself…They gradually acquired larger power in the committees, which had hitherto been dominated by the rich seniors. Some of the older leaders passed away, full of years and honours [and] some of them saw the necessity of new ways for new times.[21]

The attitudes of many of these younger men were clearly conditioned by the concerns of the social Gospel, which was then at the height of its appeal,[22] and by a strong conviction that the Association's unenviable public image was all too apposite. In 1916, a survey of 'The work of the YMCA' remarked that

> The movement, as originally started in England – from whence it spread throughout the world – came from an evangelical source…The founders were good men, for the greater part trained in a somewhat narrow mould…Its social features were developed cautiously – if not jealously – because its leaders feared that the religious side of the work might be jeopardized. Smoking was prohibited in YMCA buildings and the members were advised to abstain from athletic contests. Naturally such points were criticized by the younger men who gradually came into their own on the committees, and presently a broader and more catholic policy found expression.[23]

However, despite clear signs of change (by 1914 most local associations seem to have possessed either athletic clubs or gymnasia)[24] older perceptions of the YMCA lingered on. Hence, in 1914 public opinion still held that 'the Association created a particular type of young man supposed to be addicted to personal introspection and lacking virility and commonsense'.[25] This perception certainly troubled Yapp, who fully accepted that the pre-war YMCA was too widely viewed as 'effeminate and namby-pamby'.[26] Indeed, when reflecting on the impact of the war on the YMCA, he even contested that it had found its salvation in this ordeal:

> I am convinced that those who write the history of the Association in days to come will date the renaissance of the YMCA from 1914…Throughout its earlier years the YMCA had confined itself mainly to religious work, though not without provision for recreation and education. In many Associations the

21 *Ibid.*
22 D. Bebbington, *Evangelicalism in modern Britain: a history from the 1730s to the 1980s* (London, 1995), p. 212.
23 Anon., 'The work of the YMCA', in *The Times history of the war* (21 vols., London, 1914–21) IX, 179–200 at 180.
24 *Year book of the National Council of Young Men's Christian Associations of England, Ireland and Wales*, 1914, pp. 126–57.
25 Anon., 'The work of the YMCA', p. 180.
26 Yapp, *In the service of youth*, p. 57.

spiritual interest had dominated, or even dwarfed, the physical and intellectual. The leaders and guides of the movement clung to the Puritan traditions of their own early days. And in tone and temper not a few YMCA members incurred the reproach – often an unjust reproach – of being pietists or prigs.[27]

Finances

As we have noted, in grasping the opportunities he saw in the new European war, Yapp was obliged to defy a strong body of more conservative and circumspect opinion on the National Council, a bold course of action given that he had served for only two years as its general secretary.[28] Its president, Lord Kinnaird, though not present at the emergency meeting of 7 August,[29] was strongly opposed to the idea of the YMCA 'embarking on a big programme of war work'.[30] In addition to the internal (and largely generational) politics of the Association, there was also a fundamental question of finance to resolve. The outbreak of war coincided with many of the annual camps of the Territorial Force and their abrupt cancellation involved the YMCA in heavy financial losses before the army had even fired a shot in anger.[31] Although the emergency meeting of 7 August 1914 sanctioned Yapp to incur 'all necessary expenditure' for army work, this licence obtained only for as long as existing funds lasted and Kinnaird flatly refused to put his name to a public appeal for a further £25,000. In fact, three days later he sought to check Yapp's enthusiasm by informing him that he had been in touch with the Scottish National Council 'and that they had decided against an appeal for money because of the financial difficulties of the country'. Undaunted by this pessimism, Yapp took the audacious decision to sign the appeal himself and the £25,000 was duly raised within a few days.[32] The signal success of Yapp's decision had a double significance. First, it transformed the financial basis of the Association's work; hitherto, its principal financiers had been a group of leading supporters known as the 'Big Six', patrons who had underwritten the costs of those initiatives that met with their approval. However, Yapp's plans for the army in August 1914 were not to their taste, a fact that pushed Yapp towards rebellion, knowing that the failure of his unilateral appeal would mean an abrupt end to his YMCA career. However, when his gamble paid off, it seemed to him as if the Association had been set free – financially emancipated 'in spite of itself'.[33] Second, its success seems to have inspired a certain confidence, even a certain faith, among the membership of the YMCA's War Emergency Committee that it would invariably find the means to finance its new and ever expanding army work.

[27]   *Ibid.*, pp. 53–4.
[28]   *Ibid.*, pp. 26, 35–41.
[29]   YMCA, J7 National Council signed minutes, 7 August 1914.
[30]   Yapp, *In the service of youth*, p. 28.
[31]   *Ibid.*, p. 60.
[32]   *Ibid.*, p. 62.
[33]   *Ibid.*, pp. 56, 62.

The WEC, which was essentially the National Council's Finance Committee in another guise, was appointed 'to deal with all matters requiring immediate attention'[34] and chiefly consisted of 'business men over military age', its key figures being its chairman, Colonel Sir Thomas Sturmy Cave, its treasurer, Sir Henry Procter, and Yapp himself, who served as the committee's secretary and 'chief organizer'.[35] In due course, the growing scale and complexity of the Association's war work required the formation of several sub-committees of the WEC; by the end of 1917 they included committees for Finance, Religious Work, Buildings, Work for Discharged Sailors and Soldiers, Staff and Trading.[36] Following its emergency meeting on 7 August 1914, the National Council did not meet again until early October.[37] However, in the intervening period the WEC took on massive commitments on its behalf. As Yapp later reflected:

> [T]he Council would assuredly have suffered from 'cold feet' had they faced the problems I had to face, and had they been called upon to run the risks we had to run. In those early days we adopted the maxim, 'No urgent appeal for a tent or hut must be refused if on investigation it proves to be really needed by the men', and to this maxim we adhered right through the War.[38]

However, this policy bordered on recklessness, especially when its practical corollaries became apparent. While scores of YMCA marquees were erected at training camps in England during the late summer and early autumn of 1914, a stormy autumn followed by 'an exceptionally wet winter' meant that better facilities were soon required. Whereas the original canvas marquees had been 'comparatively cheap and portable', the prefabricated wooden huts that replaced them cost up to £700 each. Many had their own kitchen facilities and, in larger camps, 'a double hut' was sometimes required which comprised 'a special room for concerts, lectures and services apart from the common room used for games, correspondence, and the serving of refreshments from the counter'.[39] In London (where many huts were erected in or near railway stations to serve the needs of troops in transit) their facilities could be even more elaborate, with the Aldwych and Gower Street huts costing over £7,000 each. The latter, christened the Shakespeare Hut, was regarded as 'the best of its kind' and had its own 'canteen, billiard room, quiet room, verandah and sleeping and bath room accommodation'.[40] Not surprisingly, monthly expenditure quickly outstripped monthly donations to the War Emergency Fund. By February 1915, the Fund's deficit was running at more than £16,000;[41] twelve months later, this deficit had more than doubled.[42]

---

[34] YMCA, J7 National Council signed minutes, 7 August 1914.
[35] Anon., 'The work of the YMCA', p. 179; McKenzie, 'Welfare work', p. 406.
[36] YMCA, J115 War Emergency Committee copy minutes, 11 December 1917.
[37] YMCA, J7 National Council signed minutes, 2 October 1914.
[38] Yapp, *In the service of youth*, pp. 60–1.
[39] Anon., 'The work of the YMCA', p. 182.
[40] *Ibid.*, p. 190.
[41] YMCA, J7 National Council signed minutes, 5 March 1915.
[42] *Ibid.*, 7 April 1916.

As a result of its munificent policy on huts, by 1918 the Association had spent more than £1,000,000 in erecting them at home and abroad and their running costs amounted to over £1,800 per day.[43] Stationery expenses were particularly heavy for, as in South Africa, a key function of these centres was to serve as soldiers' writing rooms, with paper, envelopes and postcards being available free of charge. Given the unprecedented size of the British army in the First World War, YMCA stationery was consumed on a prodigious scale. As two YMCA lecturers, recently returned from France, reported in the *Birmingham Daily Post* in April 1917, 'In one hut we visited on Sunday, March 18, 3,500 pieces of writing paper were used between 3 and 8.15 p.m., and in the same hut 120 tables were in use by the Tommies writing home.'[44] Two years later, it was estimated that well over a billion pieces of stationery had been issued during the course of the war at a total cost of £233,115.[45] Other acts of munificence also came to involve heavy expenditure, especially the routine distribution of free refreshments to the wounded, to troops in transit and to soldiers in or near the front line. In the first fortnight of the battle of Arras in April 1917, £4,000 worth of goods – chiefly biscuits, chocolate, tobacco and hot drinks – was distributed among the walking wounded; similarly, according to Brigadier-General J. E. Edmonds (the official historian of the war on the Western Front) in February–March 1918 '5,000 to 6,000 gallons of hot drinks, chiefly cocoa, were given free to the men each week' by YMCA workers in the Ypres salient alone.[46] In addition to all of this, the WEC stepped up to meet unforeseen crises. With the signing of the Armistice, for example, the YMCA proved to be an important source of relief for British prisoners of war returning from captivity in Germany, whose population was now on the brink of starvation. As Yapp remembered:

> Repatriated British prisoners of war returning from different parts of Germany, and arriving half-starved and in ill-health across the French and Belgian frontiers, usually came across a YMCA centre before making contact with other British posts. We rushed up supplies to these centres to supplement the stores already there; and, of course, everything had to be given free of charge. That single piece of practical service cost the Association more than £50,000.[47]

Much of this work was funded by a torrent of donations and subscriptions from the general public, giving that was partly solicited by the Association's innovative use of full-page advertisements in national newspapers and by special postcards from which miniature huts could be assembled and displayed.[48] The

43 McKenzie, 'Welfare work', pp. 404, 406.
44 YMCA, K26 YMCA War Work No. 13. France. *A tribute from two Birmingham citizens. Reprinted from the 'Birmingham Daily Post', April 18th, 1917*, p. 3.
45 YMCA, K27 YMCA War Work No. 14. France. 'The latest YMCA statistics', 20 January 1919.
46 E. Dunkerley, *The Red Triangle circle* (London, n.d.), p. 14; J. E. Edmonds, *History of the Great War based on official documents. Military operations France and Belgium, 1916: Sir Douglas Haig's command to the 1st July* (London, 1932), p. 140 n. 1.
47 Yapp, *In the service of youth*, pp. 135–6.
48 A. K. Yapp, *The romance of the Red Triangle* (London, n.d.), p. 42; Reznick, *Healing the nation*, pp. 21–2.

YMCA was also prolific in its other fundraising publications. Besides a regular series of pamphlets known as the *Red Triangle Papers*, these included *Told in the huts: the YMCA gift book* (a 'Book of romance, thrilling deeds and heroism' which sold for 3s 6d at Christmas 1916),[49] Arthur Copping's *Tommy's Triangle* of 1917 (which came replete with perforated postcards for donations and a note asking that the book be passed on)[50] and Erica Dunkerley's *The Red Triangle circle*. The latter included a foreword by Dunkerley's father, John Oxenham, a Congregationalist and 'the most popular poet of his day',[51] who admonished: 'Can you imagine what it would mean to all the boys out there and at home if the YMCA were to stop? It is unimaginable. It would be a national catastrophe.'[52] In addition, he offered a poem on what he termed 'the Great Wheel of the YMCA'. It was, perhaps, memorable for the wrong reasons:

> The work goes on like a Mighty Wheel,
> Which may not stop in the public weal,
> But, remember this – and respond with zeal –
> The Wheel needs constant oiling!

> It is doing God's good work below,
> It is helping to break down the foe:
> If you pay a tithe of what you owe,
> The Wheel will not lack oiling.

> It is helping to transform the earth,
> It is bringing Life to nobler birth,
> Can you – dare you – let it suffer dearth,
> For lack of constant oiling?[53]

Besides all of this, an army of local supporters mounted an endless succession of flag days and street collections. In January 1917, for example, and in Barclay Baron's home town of Bristol, one thoroughfare played host to a full-sized 'replica of a YMCA dug-out in France', this sand-bagged edifice being intended to show passers-by 'what is being done at the front'.[54]

These combined efforts ensured that £830,000 was raised for the YMCA's war work between 1914 and 1916, a sum that had risen to around £3,000,000 by the end of the war.[55] If this seemed to justify on a national level the Association's Derbyshire nickname of 'Yapp's Money Cadging Association',[56] funds were also forthcoming from other sources. From the apex of the military hierarchy, the Army Council helped with 'two big loans', and a government grant of £25,000 was made

49 *YM*, 17 November 1916, p. 1088.
50 A. E. Copping, *Tommy's Triangle* (London, 1917), p. 190.
51 J. M. Bourne (ed.), *Who's who in World War One* (London, 2001), p. 225.
52 Dunkerley, *The Red Triangle Circle*, pp. 4–5.
53 *Ibid.*, p. 5.
54 *Red Triangle*, 19 January 1917, p. 45.
55 McKenzie, 'Welfare work', p. 406; Yapp, *In the service of youth*, pp. 57, 138.
56 Yapp, *In the service of youth*, p. 35.

'towards the erection of new YMCA huts that were urgently needed by the troops'.[57] Furthermore, in December 1919, and on the strength of its work among American troops in Europe, the American YMCA made a handsome donation of £250,000 to its British counterpart – a sum it could well afford given that it received more than £33,000,000 worth of donations in only eighteen months of war.[58]

However, given that the overall cost of its war work was eventually placed at over £8,000,000,[59] there was clearly a significant shortfall in the Red Triangle's finances. While the Army Council duly wrote off part of the money it was owed, an issue that would return to haunt the YMCA was the key *rôle* its trading surpluses played in funding its war work. Given the number, nature and ubiquity of its centres, the Red Triangle's canteen receipts were enormous and the Association even came to gauge the progress of its work by the scale of its turnover. As Oliver McCowen noted of the growth of its work in France in 1917: 'The trading account for the six months ending November 30 amounted to £975,000, which represents 40 per cent. of the total account since the beginning of the war. This shows better than any words could do the astonishing development of the work during the last half-year.'[60] The YMCA's canteen receipts for the period August 1914 to June 1920 totalled over £17,000,000, from which the Association made a gross profit of just over £3,600,000.[61] Aware of the growing turnover of YMCA centres (and in keeping with its policy towards the civilian contractors who ran the army's own canteens, who were required to pay a proportion of their takings into regimental funds)[62] in the early months of the war the War Office attempted to impose a 10 per cent levy on Red Triangle huts.[63] However, this bid was defeated by the Association's claim that its canteen profits were essential to its other work:

> The canteens are professedly run for profit. No canteen manager is entitled to give anything to his clients, everything must be paid for, and he must render a strict account. [However, the YMCA], though run on strict business lines, was not a business undertaking...the whole of the profits were spent for the direct and immediate benefit of the troops.[64]

While this reasoning persuaded the prime minister, Herbert Asquith, to rule in favour of the YMCA in 1915, the matter was reopened later in the war. Hence, from March 1918 many YMCA huts were subject to a financial levy: all those located on government land were required to pay a 6 per cent rebate of their gross takings on refreshments 'to such authority as the War Office may appoint, for

---

[57] *Ibid.*, pp. 149, 134–5.
[58] *Ibid.*, pp. 138–9.
[59] H. McMahon, 'The YMCA and the war', *Hutchinson's pictorial history of the war* (26 vols., London, 1939–45), III, p. 308.
[60] *The Red Triangle Bulletin*, 8 March 1918, p. 3.
[61] *Times*, 28 May 1921, p. 7.
[62] Reznick, *Healing the nation*, p. 32.
[63] Yapp, *Romance of the Red Triangle*, pp. 58–9.
[64] *Year Book of the National Council of Young Men's Christian Associations of England, Ireland and Wales (incorporated...containing a report of the War Emergency Work of the Association from 1914 to 1920*, 1921, p. 9.

expenditure...in connection with the camp where the Hut is situated'.[65] While this decision rankled with Yapp, who complained that most of the huts were 'loaned free to the Military for church parades and military lectures' in any case,[66] given that it only applied to YMCA huts in Great Britain the exaction hardly undermined its finances. Indeed, given the enduring scale of its trading surpluses, in the aftermath of the war the Association could still maintain that this revenue had funded half its work – 'but for this profit the work would have had to be curtailed by one-half, unless public subscriptions had been doubled'.[67]

Despite backroom wrangling over rebates, public controversy over the Association's profits was largely confined to the post-war period, as we shall see. What was more remarkable in the meantime was the fact that the YMCA succeeded in gaining the general support of the nation at large. Donors to the War Emergency Fund included the king, Queen Mary and other members of the royal family. While Queen Alexandra, the queen mother, was among the first to pay for an entire hut in November 1914,[68] 'Livery companies and railway, banking and commercial undertakings added their share to the funds, while humbler people brought their shillings.'[69] In one instance, a farm labourer (rejected by the army on medical grounds) gave £50 – 'practically the whole of his savings' – to the president of his local YMCA as it was 'the only thing he could do to help the men at the Front'.[70] The Red Triangle even attracted cross-species support. In 1915, and in response to the Kaiser's reported boast 'that, if need be, he would arm every cat and dog in Germany in defence of the empire', a Miss Maud Field appealed to a similar spirit of patriotism among the cats and dogs of Britain, 5,000 of whom 'contributed sums ranging from £5 to a penny' in order to build and furnish a hut at Rouen. In this instance, notable benefactors included a moggy named Alma, a Jack Russell called Tom, a bulldog called Bunty and a Highland terrier who gloried in the name of MacPeach.[71]

On a more poignant note, growing casualty lists meant that many benefactions were made in memory of loved ones; from 1915 entire huts were being donated 'in memory of officers and men who have died in action'.[72] More typically, these gifts were much smaller. For example, William Hynes of Whitworth Park, Manchester, wrote to the YMCA in 1916:

> I have great pleasure in sending £1 enclosed, and I do so in memory of my son Douglas, who was killed on the 1st July in France; but while in the Army and in training he received benefits from you – which I feel cannot be repaid in kind, but demands my prayerful commendation of your good work, which should commend itself to all parents.[73]

[65] YMCA, J7 National Council signed minutes, 1 February 1918.
[66] Yapp, *Romance of the Red Triangle*, p. 59.
[67] *Times*, 28 May 1921, p. 7.
[68] *Ibid.*, 7 November 1914, p. 4.
[69] Anon., 'The work of the YMCA', p. 179.
[70] Yapp, *Romance of the Red Triangle*, p. 50.
[71] *YM*, 12 March 1915, p. 207, and 26 March 1915, p. 256.
[72] *YM*, 12 March 1915, p. 207.
[73] YMCA, K40 Typescript extracts of letters of appreciation. William Hynes, 1916.

As the varying size of such gifts serves to illustrate, the sheer breadth of the Association's support was striking in itself. As F. A. McKenzie wrote:

> Perhaps the most remarkable feature of the support given to the YMCA was not so much the amount raised as the way in which it represented the entire nation. Every class of the community subscribed to it. The King, its patron, sent a message saying how the organization had 'worked in a practical, economical, and unostentatious manner, with constant knowledge of those with whom it had to deal'. Army commanders wrote urging its claims. Some ragged boys, pushing themselves into the Euston Hut, when asked what they were doing there, said that they had come to see how their money was spent...Between King and street-boys the whole community joined in, the heads of the universities, the chapters of cathedrals, the lord mayors and mayors of cities, the heads of the Navy and the Army, the theatrical and musical professions – all made common cause.[74]

Workers

In addition to funding, the recruitment of workers also posed a formidable challenge. On the Western Front alone, at one point the number of those working for the Red Triangle rose to as many as 1,750 and, although volunteers could serve for as little as three or four calendar months, they were not easily found.[75] While many Anglican clergymen eventually came forward, they were initially reluctant to do so. As one of their number wrote in 1915:

> [T]he fact remains that the Church of England has not contributed her fair share of workers – at any rate of men workers – to the YMCA...In the minds of some, the YMCA is identified with a vague undenominationalism against which we are right to protest; but, whatever may have been the case in the past, this is not true today.[76]

Although this reluctance had dissipated by the end of the war (by which time even Anglo-Catholic bishops were happy to give the work of the YMCA their enthusiastic blessing)[77] the parallel and even competing activities of the Church Army and the evangelical traditions of the YMCA meant that the Free Church and Scottish Presbyterian clergy proved a richer source of clerical manpower. According to one estimate, around 260 Free Church ministers served overseas as YMCA workers while nearly 170 more worked at centres in the British Isles.[78] The changing ethos and widening remit of the Association during the war years

---

[74] McKenzie, 'Welfare work', p. 406.
[75] Edmonds, *History of the Great War*, p. 139; *Times*, 14 September 1917, p. 9.
[76] Anon., *YMCA war work in Britain and Flanders*, p. 18
[77] YMCA, K40 Typescript extracts of letters of appreciation. The bishop of Winchester, 24 October 1918.
[78] J. H. Thompson, 'The Free Church army chaplain 1830–1930', Ph.D. dissertation, University of Sheffield, 1990, p. 377.

may have held a particular appeal for more liberal churchmen who were unable or unwilling to seek commissions as army chaplains. Men of this stamp included the famous (or notorious) R. J. Campbell of London's City Temple and D. S. Cairns of the United Free Church College, Aberdeen, who later distinguished himself as the author of the *Army and religion* report.[79]

Initially, those clergymen who embarked for France went 'by individual arrangement with the YMCA'.[80] However, in the winter of 1916–17 its chronic shortage of manpower obliged the Association 'to approach the authorities of the principal denominations in England and Scotland, with a view to securing a large number of young clergymen and ministers for YMCA service'. This appeal met with a sympathetic response, especially from north of the border, the United Free Church producing more than 100 volunteers and 'a generous financial grant' with which to release them for work with the Red Triangle.[81] While they temporarily eased the problem of recruitment, these negotiations also forced the Association to clarify and reassert its interdenominational nature and to disavow any suggestion of competition with the churches themselves. Increasingly beholden to the latter for funds and for workers, in a meeting with the archbishop of Canterbury, who was nominally a vice-president of the Association,[82] Oliver McCowen, the organizing genius of its work on the Western Front, reassured Randall Davidson that

> [A] majority of the responsible leaders in the YMCA were determined that the Association should not become another denomination, but should become as truly interdenominational as the Continuation Committee and the Student [Christian] Movement. I said that we recognized that all that was vital in the spiritual life of the YMCA had its origin in the Churches, and that a large majority of the most thoughtful secretaries in the Association Movement of all countries would break their connection with the Association if they felt that the Association was growing up outside of the Church, and a rival to it.[83]

In consequence, McCowen appealed to his hut leaders to 'go more than half way in doing all they can to serve the chaplains'; furthermore, in emphasizing the need to co-operate with the Army Chaplains' Department, he stressed that:

> All of our workers should understand that a large proportion of the clergy and ministers who go out to France in the future go at the joint invitation of the YMCA and their own Churches, and that this dual arrangement obliges us to be even more careful to ensure that they are given the largest opportunity for service...All I want is that those who are responsible for their work realize the circumstances under which they have to come, and the necessity of so

[79] Yapp, *In the service of youth*, pp. 169–72.
[80] YMCA, K24 YMCA War Work No. 4. Religious. 'Memorandum regarding the interdenominational position of the YMCA', December 1916.
[81] *Ibid.*
[82] *Year book*, 1914, p. 4.
[83] YMCA, K24 YMCA War Work No. 4. Religious. 'Memorandum regarding the interdenominational position of the YMCA', December 1916.

arranging their canteen work that they will have time for personal religious interviews, study circles, and occasional speaking.[84]

Even towards the end of the war, the author E. W. Hornung was struck by how many ministers there were among his fellow YMCA workers.[85] However, by this point it had been clear for a long time that the clergy alone could never supply the requisite manpower. In 1917, the nature of its work on the Western Front demanded a huge increase of YMCA workers, their numbers rising by 50 per cent between April 1917 and April 1918 from 981 to 1,423.[86] Although clergymen comprised more than a third of the Association's workers in France in July 1917,[87] this proportion fell to less than a quarter in the course of a year in which the Association sent nearly 2,000 male workers overseas.[88] With the YMCA and the Army Chaplains' Department in competition for volunteers among the clergy from the outset, as the war lengthened the YMCA became locked in a losing battle with the army over dwindling resources of lay manpower as well. In the autumn of 1915 Oliver McCowen was perturbed by the introduction of the Derby Scheme, a prelude to conscription whereby eligible men could attest for service without being immediately enlisted. As he wrote with an air of relief to Yapp that November:

I saw the [Inspector General of Communications] this morning and told him that our men were ready to offer in every instance; that ninety per cent of our men in France were either medically unfit, or ministers, and that I wanted to have his opinion as to whether the work of the remaining ten per cent, as YMCA secretaries, would not mean more for the country at this time than if the men went into Khaki. He said that, in his opinion, this proportion of fit men was necessary to our work out here, and the [Assistant Adjutant General] – Col. Burden – said that, in his opinion, they were much more useful to the Army in their present capacity than if they went into Khaki.[89]

With the coming of conscription in January 1916, the situation deteriorated and, in May, Yapp made the following appeal after a visit to France:

As to the future, humanly speaking, everything will depend on the personal element. Without a sufficiency of men and women of the right sort the work will be crippled and limited, and where the men are to come from it is not easy to see. We would appeal in the strongest possible way for the help of men between the ages of 41 and 48, also for the co-operation of an increasing number of the younger clergy and ministers.[90]

As the dragnet of conscription grew tighter, the shortage of male workers grew ever more acute, especially during the winter of 1916–17. In a confidential

[84] Ibid.
[85] E. W. Hornung, Notes of a camp-follower on the Western Front (London, 1919), pp. 240–1.
[86] YMCA, J116 War Emergency Committee copy minutes, 21 May 1918.
[87] Ibid.
[88] Ibid.; YMCA, J7 National Council signed minutes, 1 February 1918.
[89] YMCA, K26 YMCA War Work No. 13. France. Oliver McCowen to A. K. Yapp, 13 November 1915.
[90] YM, 19 May 1916, p. 451.

report to Yapp dated 12 February 1917, R. G. MacDonald, who was then responsible for YMCA work in Third Army Area, wrote:

> Our minimum staff is supposed to be two workers for each centre, except those open day and night which are allowed at least six. This at present would allow us 60 workers in all. Our last return to the [assistant provost marshal] showed that we had only 31, two of whom were on leave, whilst the usual percentage of the remainder were sick. Thus we are more than 50% below strength, which is a very serious handicap. This has been considerably aggravated by the action of the Army Commander ten days ago in withdrawing without warning all our [army] orderlies in accordance with the policy that all possible men should be available for the firing-line. This threatened to cripple our work most gravely, and to make much of it impossible...To bring ourselves up to strength, staff our new centres, and take the place of workers returning to England on the termination of their engagement, we shall require at least 50 new workers in the immediate future. As most of our work is near the line, they should be as strong and virile as possible, of good nerve and with a real sense of the call of God.[91]

However, these were increasingly unrealistic desiderata. On the eve of the German spring offensive of 1918, the Association's greatest trial on the Western Front, the situation in France was such that more than a quarter of the Red Triangle's male workers were overage.[92] As Yapp remembered:

> [F]or years we could only recruit men of forty or over, unless they had been rejected for military service. The Director-General of Recruiting had before him a complete list of our male workers; and as year after year the age limit was raised our ranks were combed out again and again. I can never express adequately my respect for the men, over military age or physically unfit, who served the YMCA on the various fronts; no risk was too great for them to undertake, and no work too hard.[93]

Given these constraints, the profile of the Association's male overseas workers became increasingly diverse.[94] In 1917, Arthur Copping noted that the motley staff of a YMCA officers' club at Albert consisted of a country gentleman, Congregationalist minister and a commercial traveller.[95] While Yapp consoled himself with the thought that at least some of these workers (who often faced the dangers of the front with no military training) were at least former soldiers,[96] a YMCA worker killed at Vlamertinghe in 1917 was mourned as 'a splendid old man, a retired Patagonian sheep farmer, who had come over but recently, keen to do his bit for the boys. He was 60 years of age, but full of energy and enthusiasm

[91] YMCA, K26 YMCA War Work No. 13. France. 'Report on YMCA work in Third Army area', 12 February 1917.
[92] YMCA, J116 War Emergency Committee copy minutes, 21 May 1918.
[93] Yapp, *In the service of youth*, p. 64.
[94] *Ibid.*, pp. 102–3.
[95] Copping, *Tommy's Triangle*, pp. 165–6.
[96] Yapp, *In the service of youth*, pp. 102–3.

for his new work.'[97] However, from a very early stage it was clear that many of its wartime workers had no experience of, or even sympathy with, the pre-war YMCA. By 1915, its workers in France were already being described as of 'all sorts and conditions, young men and maidens, old men and parsons, and of all denominations, a veritable "farrago", including Roman Catholics and Quakers'.[98] In fact, so pressing was the need for men that even a religious commitment came to be seen as non-essential for Red Triangle work; as one volunteer testified for *The Times* in September 1917, 'As I know from personal experience, a purely secular worker will receive a warm welcome, and can find his sphere of usefulness.'[99]

Besides facilitating the involvement of non-believers, the Association's manpower problems also dictated one of the most obvious changes in YMCA policy, overturning its governing principle that its work should be done 'for young men by young men'.[100] At its wartime peak, 40,000 women were doing some form of work for the Association but such was the shortage of male staff overseas that a Ladies' Auxiliary Committee for France was established at Yapp's instigation in the autumn of 1914.[101] Under the presidency of Princess Helena Victoria of Schleswig-Holstein, the 'Ladies' Committee' was responsible for engaging the services of the celebrated actress and theatre manager Lena Ashwell (who organized her first concert party for the army's French bases in January 1915), for collecting sundry articles 'for the use of the men' and also for the recruitment of 'lady helpers', whose assistance 'saved the necessity of employing men required for the fighting line'. Around 300 female workers had been recruited by 1916 and, in the French bases of the BEF, they remained an important and conspicuous element of the Red Triangle's staff until the end of the war. By January 1918 they comprised 499 (or 40 per cent) of its 1,236 workers in France.[102] However, the distinguished and eminently well-connected members of the Ladies' Committee also played a vital, if less obvious, *rôle* in facilitating the Association's work in France. While the Ladies' Committee included Lady French, the wife of the commander-in-chief of the British Expeditionary Force,[103] it was Princess Helena Victoria who, in November 1914, secured the agreement of the Army Council for the free transportation of 'equipment and workers from the English ports to [their] destination' in France. Furthermore, among the first women to volunteer for service overseas was Lady Henderson, the wife of the commander of the Royal Flying Corps, Sir David Henderson, who was temporarily commanding a division in France.[104]

---

[97]   YMCA, K26 YMCA War Work No. 13. France. H. A. Down, 'Pioneering on the Western Front. 3½ years with the YMCA', p. 21.

[98]   Anon., *YMCA war work in Britain and Flanders*, p. 18.

[99]   *Times*, 14 September 1917, p. 9.

[100] Yapp, *Romance of the Red Triangle*, p. 63.

[101] Yapp, *In the service of youth*, pp. 64–5; C. Messenger, *Call-to-arms: the British army 1914–18* (London, 2005), p. 467.

[102] Anon., 'The work of the YMCA', p. 185; *YM*, 15 October 1915, p. 943; Edmonds, *History of the Great War*, p. 139; YMCA, J116 War Emergency Committee copy minutes, 21 May 1918.

[103] *Times*, 10 December 1914, p. 6.

[104] YMCA, K26 YMCA War Work No. 13. France. A. K. Yapp to Oliver McCowen, 18 and 24 November 1914.

It was thus with pardonable exaggeration that Edmonds could claim that the YMCA's staff on the Western Front consisted of 'lady workers and men of low medical category or over service age'.[105] Given the constituencies from which they were drawn and the rigours and dangers of their work, the war exacted a steady toll of YMCA workers. Whereas the number of British soldiers who were killed by enemy action far exceeded those who died of disease during the First World War,[106] this disparity was reversed among YMCA personnel, individuals who were not, by definition, recruited from among the most robust elements of the population. According to the Association's own figures, fifty of its workers 'Died through illness while on service' (a total that included a dozen women)[107] and a further eighteen were either killed or died of wounds received. Significantly, among the latter were two women, namely Emily Pickford and Betty Stevenson. While the details of Pickford's death are unclear, Stevenson, aged only twenty-one, died during a German air raid on Etaples in May 1918, an incident in which two Red Triangle workers were also badly wounded.[108] Her life and death became the subject of a substantial memorial volume.[109] In addition to the danger of air attack on the army's French bases, YMCA centres in forward areas on the Western Front were frequently within German artillery range. In early 1917, R. G. MacDonald wrote to Yapp:

> No impression of all our work stands out more strong and clear than that of the Everlasting Arms which have enfolded us all, warding off all harm. Well nigh legion are the instance of wonderful escapes; and the term 'providential' becomes luminous with meaning when used of them...At D—e our Leader of five weeks ago had just risen and gone for a morning sprint, when a shell plunged through the roof on to his bed, making short work of it and his pyjamas and the floor beneath. The induction of his successor was signalized by a chunk of shrapnel tearing through the roof.[110]

Despite MacDonald's gratitude for such narrow escapes, in 'one black week'[111] in August 1917 two YMCA workers were killed in separate incidents near Ypres. The first, Alfred Wilcox, 'a promising young minister',[112] died at Reninghelst on 18 August while the second, Cecil Withers, was killed at Vlamertinghe a few days later. As *The Red Triangle Bulletin* reported their deaths:

> It is with profound regret that we record the death of two of our workers in France. They have been 'killed in action' as truly as any soldier, for they have fallen nobly while engaged in their dangerous work of ministering to the wants of the troops in a forward area. The Rev. A. Wilcox, who was in charge of a group of huts at R-, was struck by a piece of shrapnel, and after lingering

---

[105] Edmonds, *History of the Great War*, p. 139.
[106] G. Corrigan, *Mud, blood and poppycock: Britain and the First World War* (London, 2004), pp. 58–9.
[107] *Year book*, 1921, p. 90.
[108] *The Red Triangle Bulletin*, 7 June 1918, p. 4, and 14 June 1918, p. 4.
[109] 'CGRS' and 'AGS', *Betty Stevenson, YMCA Croix de Guerre avec Palme* (London, 1920).
[110] YMCA, K26 YMCA War Work No. 13. France. Undated report, 1917.
[111] *Ibid*. H. A. Down, 'Pioneering on the Western Front. 3½ years with the YMCA', p. 21.
[112] *Ibid.*, p. 20.

for twenty-four hours, was buried with military honours. In another part of the same area Mr. Cecil Withers was killed, almost instantaneously, by the explosion of a bomb, which fell near his tent. Mr. Withers had been out only a few weeks, and was doing very promising work in a new centre. The sympathy of the Association will go out to the widows and children of our comrades who have fallen at the post of duty.[113]

It was symptomatic of the courage and indefatigability of so much YMCA war work that a replacement was very shortly at Withers's post. As Harold Down, a senior YMCA secretary in Fifth Army, remembered:

At this time our workers were all too few, and I asked to be allowed to take his place until another worker arrived. I shall never forget that night taking over from a dead man, sleeping in the little tent in which he met his death, and gazing up at the spot where the missile of death had pierced the canvas.[114]

What helped to inspire such dedication – even recklessness – among YMCA workers was a close identification with the men, the units and even the positions to which they were attached. This devotion was partly fed by the fact that many had volunteered out of a sense of obligation to one who was serving or one who had been killed. As a certain visitor to the Western Front remarked, of five 'elderly volunteer workers' of the YMCA he had encountered in France 'three had sons up in the trenches' while the other two 'had sons lying in the soldiers' cemeteries behind the lines'.[115] This was certainly true of E. W. Hornung, who lost his only son Oscar, 'A simple-minded and religious boy', on the Western Front in July 1915.[116] However, Hornung stressed that his was a common plight and that 'The YMCA is the refuge of those consciously or unconsciously in quest of this anodyne.'[117] While not falling into this category, months of service alongside them meant that Barclay Baron came to identify very strongly with the soldiers of Second Army; furthermore, even after a serious accident and the ordeal that Fifth Army went through during the German spring offensive of that year, in the autumn of 1918 Harold Down's driving ambition was to be back with the British troops taking part in the Allied counter-offensives. With victory now in view, Down claimed to be

[S]training at the leash to be again with my colleagues who are daily following in the wake of the Army...Once again I sigh for adventure and yearn for romance, for I see a vision of the greatest adventure of all – the Boche is on the run, we are breaking through, and I want to be in at the finish with the boys we came to serve.[118]

[113] *The Red Triangle Bulletin*, 31 August 1917, p. 2.
[114] YMCA, K26 YMCA War Work No. 13. France. H. A. Down, 'Pioneering on the Western Front. 3½ years with the YMCA', pp. 20–1.
[115] Koch, *Books in camp, trench and hospital*, p. 15.
[116] S. R. Chichester (ed.), *E. W. Hornung and his Young Guard 1914* (Crowthorne, 1941), pp. 50–1.
[117] Hornung, *Notes of a camp-follower*, p. 252.
[118] YMCA, K26 YMCA War Work No. 13. France. H. A. Down, 'Pioneering on the Western Front. 3½ years with the YMCA', p. 37.

Clearly, workers in forward areas were liable to go to extreme lengths in order to maintain their presence among the troops. The best illustration of this was the case of Dr C. Magrath who, throughout the fighting near Ypres from June to November 1917, 'carried on in his quaint little system of dug-outs in the bowels of the earth near the historic Lille Gate, right through Messines, and "the Battles of the Ridges" and organized a number of dug-outs in front of Ypres after the Flanders battles'. Acclaimed by Harold Down as 'the YMCA hero of Ypres',[119] Magrath was unmoved by Barclay Baron's entreaties to evacuate his post in the midst of the German spring offensive in Flanders. As Baron reported to McCowen on 17 April 1918, 'Magrath holds on at Ypres. I was there today under very trying conditions to move him, but he refuses to go and prefers to wait two days unless things get much worse. All his stuff is cleared and he is carrying on with a small stock and three orderlies.'[120] Significantly, Magrath's exploits in the Ypres Salient even found their way into the British official history of the war, with Edmonds noting how a certain YMCA worker had 'carried on in Ypres for 2½ years, living all the time in a small dug-out'.[121] However, Magrath's conduct differed only in degree from that of many of his Red Triangle colleagues. Writing of his fellow workers in Third Army in the spring of 1918, E. W. Hornung maintained that 'Chief...among the virtues of my comrades, I think any unprejudiced observer would have placed that of Courage...I never saw a man among us outwardly the worse for nerves.'[122] In part, Hornung ascribed this stoicism to a determination among clergymen in particular to show neither 'shaken nerves' nor 'a shaken faith' and in that, he claimed, 'they were not only worthy of the men they had served so devotedly to the end, but of the sublime tradition it was theirs to uphold'.[123] Illustrative of such behaviour was an incident in June 1917, when Lieutenant-Colonel Rowland Feilding of the 6th Connaught Rangers met a YMCA worker amidst the ruins of the recently captured village of Wytschaete:

> The only structures that have resisted our bombardments are the steel and concrete emplacements built by the enemy among the foundations of the village [and] I found a YMCA man in one of these emplacements. He had actually established a forward canteen in it, and had a few packets of cigarettes and other things to sell to the troops...It turned out that this fine sportsman was a Nonconformist minister. We shook hands and I congratulated him on his effort. For his cash-box he had a German machine-gun belt box.[124]

---

[119] *Ibid.*, p. 22.
[120] YMCA, K27 YMCA War Work No. 14. France. Barclay Baron to Oliver McCowen, 17 April 1918.
[121] Edmonds, *History of the Great War*, p. 140.
[122] Hornung, *Notes of a camp-follower*, p. 241.
[123] *Ibid.*, pp. 245–6.
[124] R. Feilding, *War letters to a wife* (London, 1929), pp. 194–5.

36

INTRODUCTION

The YMCA and the BEF

Bases

Despite the admiration it could arouse, the Association's presence in such forward areas was a relatively late development. In the early weeks of the war, the most urgent need to be addressed was that of the troops at home. Within a week of the outbreak of war, the YMCA was active among the regular soldiers of the BEF who were preparing to cross to France. On 10 August 1914 General Sir Horace Smith Dorrien, who had made his mark as 'a fine soldier and a God-fearing gentleman',[125] thanked the Association in the following terms:

> No one appreciates more than I do the enormous amount of good work done by the YMCA and how that Association is always ready to come forward in the most unselfish way in peace and war to look after the comforts and happiness of the soldier. Not only do I give you permission to carry on your good work for the troops in the Southern Command, but I thank you very much for having come forward.[126]

Besides the mobilization and deployment of the army's regular and Territorial forces, Lord Kitchener's recruitment campaign of 1914–15, launched within days of the outbreak of war, produced 500,000 new recruits by mid-September 1914 and had yielded more than 1,500,000 by September 1915.[127] Given the acute shortage of barrack accommodation for the men of Kitchener's 'New Army' in particular, the War Office authorized the hasty construction of vast new training camps and the billeting of soldiers upon civilians.[128] However, if the former policy created a large number of isolated, uncomfortable and unhealthy encampments, the latter had serious implications for the moral welfare of the army and of the nation at large. The gradual confinement of the regular army to its barracks during the nineteenth century had brought an end to billeting as a normal military practice and it also meant that the moral hazards usually associated with large concentrations of young men free of the restraints of home had been largely confined to garrison towns. However, from the late summer of 1914 the huge expansion of the British army meant that the moral perils connected with soldiering once again became widespread, a fact that was reflected in a rising tide of illegitimate births in 1916.[129] Practised as it was in raising the tone of Territorial camps and in providing amenities for their inhabitants, the YMCA quickly mobilized against the physical discomforts and moral dangers of the hour by opening more than 250 centres in Great Britain within ten days of the outbreak of war.[130]

---

[125] Bourne (ed.), *Who's who in World War One*, p. 268; E. Paice, *Tip and run: the untold tragedy of the Great War in Africa* (London, 2007), pp. 152–3.
[126] YMCA, K40 Typescript extracts of letters of appreciation. General H. Smith Dorrien, 10 August 1914.
[127] A. Rawson, *British army handbook 1914–1918* (Stroud, 2006), pp. 23–4.
[128] P. Simkins, 'The four armies 1914–1918', in *The Oxford illustrated history of the British army*, ed. D. Chandler and I. Beckett (Oxford, 1994), pp. 252–3.
[129] *Ibid.*, p. 253.
[130] Yapp, *In the service of youth*, p. 58.

Although 'public halls, mission rooms and other suitable buildings were hired in centres occupied by thousands of troops',[131] the greatest need of all was felt in the new training camps on Salisbury Plain and elsewhere. As one source put it:

> Neither barracks or temporary buildings were sufficient at first to house the hundreds of thousands of recruits who joined the new armies. Away on lonely commons, under canvas, in barns, halls and schools, billeted in private houses, or in many cases occupying empty ones...their accommodation taxed all resources to the breaking point. Moreover, coming straight from civilian life, many from middle-class families, the men found the social amenities in camp less than those usually enjoyed by the soldier in barracks. It was at this point that the YMCA came to the assistance of the New Army. The methods adopted appeared exceedingly simple. In the early days of the war marquees were erected... Tea, coffee and refreshments were supplied during the soldier's off-duty hours. He could obtain an early cup of tea before going on duty at six o'clock on an autumn morning, and when he returned after a night march he usually found hot refreshment before he turned in for the night. Cigarettes, matches, boot-laces, buttons and other sundries could be obtained at the YMCA counter. The Association never coveted the position of haberdasher and tobacconist to the troops, but when the camp was situated miles away from a town the soldier appreciated this service.[132]

Given the manifest value of its contribution and the Association's record of working with citizen soldiers, the military authorities were accommodating in every way: 'They smoothed away difficulties, provided facilities for transport, and detailed orderlies for pitching the marquees and other heavy work. The marquees were usually within the camp boundaries, and became a part of the life of the camp.'[133]

In view of Boer War precedents, the proximity of the Western Front and the primacy of this theatre of war, it was not long before the work of the YMCA followed the BEF to France. While this idea was raised as early as the National Council meeting of 7 August 1914,[134] by October plans were clearly in hand to carry this forward. With the lengthy retreat of the BEF from southern Belgium towards Paris following the battle of Mons (23 August), serious thought was given to basing Red Triangle work in Paris, building on the Association's existing organization in the city. However, the Allied victory at the battle of the Marne (4–10 September) and the fluid nature of the fighting on the Western Front in the early autumn had taken the BEF northwards; to the river Aisne by mid-September and to Flanders by early October. As S. Hyde-Coleman (secretary of the Anglo-American YMCA in Paris) wrote to Yapp later that month, due to the current situation on the Western Front and the sensitivities of the French authorities there was now very little scope for work based in the capital:

[131] Anon., 'The work of the YMCA', pp. 182–3.
[132] *Ibid.*, p. 181.
[133] *Ibid.*, p. 182.
[134] YMCA, J7 National Council signed minutes, 7 August 1914.

There is very little to be done amongst the wounded in Paris as they have numerous visitors and the clergy go round all the hospitals every day. No more British wounded are being brought to the City, so that with the exception of serious cases they will all be away shortly. Away from Paris the difficulty arises of obtaining permission from the French Authorities. For example, to go into a Town five kilometres from my home I am supposed to obtain a 'laisser passer'. To be with the troops is therefore no easy affair, as so much secrecy is being maintained that a party of Tommies who were in here on Saturday would not tell us the name of their regiment…Perhaps when the permanent British base is established our secretaries will be allowed over, but this camp is not yet a fait accompli. The base of operations is moved every few days, and I am quite sure that we would not be allowed anywhere near their locality…The situation is novel, for although we are a friendly Power operating in conjunction with France we have to avoid giving offence by doing things which to us seem quite feasible.[135]

However, there remained the possibility of work at Le Havre, a major Channel port and (despite its temporary closure during the German advance on Paris) the hub of the BEF's lines of communication in 1914.[136] On 14 November Yapp was able to inform Hyde-Coleman that

I have at last received permission to begin work with the Expeditionary Force, and Mr. Oliver H. McCowen with two other workers, will leave for Havre tomorrow morning. Mr. McCowen will, no doubt, communicate with you and I shall greatly value your co-operation. I hope that very soon you will be able to meet and confer together on our plan of campaign. We have a most cordial letter from the Commanding Officer at Havre welcoming our help.[137]

Oliver McCowen, who was to act as the YMCA's organizing secretary in France for the duration of the war, was a congenial choice for Yapp. The son of a wealthy Irish businessman, he had trained as a laywer and had developed a practice in his native Tralee before becoming a full-time YMCA secretary. Though organizing secretary in Burma, McCowen had been home on leave when war broke out and he was charged with developing Red Triangle work with the BEF after a short stint of camp work in Ireland. Very much a progressive within the Association, his energy and dynamism was to play a major *rôle* in securing its pre-eminent place among civilian welfare agencies in wartime army work. By 1917, *The Red Triangle Bulletin* could fairly claim that McCowen had gained 'the confidence equally of the YMCA staff in France, our own Headquarters, and the military authorities'.[138] According to Yapp, who had actively sought McCowen's appointment, 'Under his capable direction our work in France grew by leaps and bounds, and in his dealings with the military authorities and in the direction of

---

[135] YMCA, K26 YMCA War Work No. 13. France. S. Hyde-Coleman to A. K. Yapp, 27 October 1914.

[136] M. Brown, *British logistics on the Western Front 1914–1919* (Westport, CT, 1998), pp. 59–60.

[137] YMCA, K26 YMCA War Work No. 13. France. A. K. Yapp to S. Hyde-Coleman, 14 November 1914.

[138] *The Red Triangle Bulletin*, 26 October 1917, p. 4.

our whole plan of campaign he evinced unusual gifts of organization and leadership.'[139] McCowen's 'small party' on his original fact-finding visit to France also included Barclay Baron's future boss, L. G. Pilkington, who had the distinction of being fluent in French. As Yapp wrote to him that November, 'I am inclined to think we may have an exceptional opportunity for service with our men now in France; also possibly amongst the French troops.'[140]

On his arrival in Le Havre, and with the assistance of the local military authorities, McCowen swiftly took matters in hand. On 15 November he reported to Yapp that

> We were cordially received by Col. Money whom we called on at once and arranged to go around Havre with him this morning. Col. Money placed a car at our disposal and his adjutant Capt. Hughes spent the morning driving us round to the six camps.
>
> I am not allowed to state the numbers in the camps but they are large enough to warrant the immediate erection of four huts and you may interpret this liberally.
>
> The position here is full of need and of opportunity. We shall want at least 12 workers later on and we ought to have a man with a car as soon as possible – there is no danger of its being commandeered.[141]

Within a few days, Pilkington was able to report on further progress:

> I have proposed to Col. Money, and he is strongly in favour of the scheme, that a Soldiers' Welfare Committee be formed and on it represented all those who are working here for the benefit of the soldiers. It will save endless trouble…Everybody here is full of admiration and respect for what the YMCA did for the troops in England when they were there, and so they expect a tremendous lot of us.[142]

In keeping with its traditions, the first YMCA facilities to open at Le Havre were 'a reading and recreation room for the troops' (which was based in a Methodist chapel and which also served afternoon refreshments) and a couple of writing tents. All were open by the end of November and the flow of correspondence that issued from them grew to the extent that the military authorities soon – and rather deftly – handed the duty of censoring it to the Association's workers.[143] By mid-December, the first batch of lady helpers had arrived, the first huts had been erected and the delivery of further huts for the base at Rouen was impending.[144] The speed of the development of YMCA work at Le Havre and elsewhere was more than matched by the need, for in the winter of 1914–15 the camps of the army's French bases very much replicated the dreary and demoralizing conditions of life in the home camps. According to one visitor

---

[139] Yapp, *In the service of youth*, p. 69.
[140] YMCA, K26 YMCA War Work No. 13. France. A. K. Yapp to L. G. Pilkington, 9 November 1914.
[141] *Ibid.*, O. McCowen to A. K. Yapp, 15 November 1914.
[142] *Ibid.*, L. G. Pilkington to A. K. Yapp, 23 November 1914.
[143] *Ibid.*, P. H. S. Sitters to A. K. Yapp, 24 November 1914; O. McCowen to A. K. Yapp, 1 December 1914.
[144] *Ibid.*, O. McCowen to A. K. Yapp, 16 December 1914.

to France in 1915, all through the previous winter men had 'roughed it under canvas amidst more or less continuous rain for days together. For months the camps have been covered with slush and mud'.[145] Some years after the war, George Ashurst, a soldier of the 2nd Lancashire Fusiliers, wrote with some feeling on the wretched conditions of a camp at Le Havre in November 1914:

> The camp was under canvas and six inches deep in mud. Food was rotten and insufficient, Woodbine cigarettes were sixpence a packet, and one had to queue up for a packet even when they were to be got at all. Only one blanket per man was issued, and we had to keep warm at night by sharing each other's blankets and sleeping in our uniforms. Life was just terrible, the route marches were almost killing, and one was delighted to see one's name on the list of a draft for the front line.[146]

Still, in addition to the front-line troops who passed through them during the course of the war, the French bases of the BEF were also home to a large and more sedentary population of 'Permanent Base' men. Completely overlooked in the popular mythology of Britain and the First World War, as early as October 1915 Lena Ashwell complained how the public too easily forgot the vital *rôle* and unenviable situation of the thousands of men 'doing the monotonous work behind the lines – the transport workers, bakers, [Army Service Corps] men, motor repairers, &c. – the multitude of workers who feed and supply the armies in the field, and whose strenuous work is as dreary as it is necessary'.[147] For such men in particular, who comprised around a third of the BEF by 1918,[148] it was thought that the YMCA had a special *rôle* to play. As one sympathizer put it:

> On the outskirts of the large towns, where the Army Auxiliary Forces are camped, groups of huts provide for crowds of men daily and nightly, and thousands of men whose work keeps them permanently at such Bases have made it a regular habit to spend every night in the local YMCA centres. Many of these men are middle-aged and elderly, skilled in some form of work upon which armies nowadays depend; bearded men, fathers of families, looking not for excitement, but for quiet homeliness, and these men have simply made the YMCA their home for the time being.[149]

However, this was not the whole story. As one YMCA worker conceded, base work among soldiers of all kinds was as prudential as it was altruistic for 'Men withdrawn from the influences of home, herded together, either in – or on the outskirts of – a large town in a foreign country, with no restraints save those of a severe military discipline, need protection from the obvious temptations which attack their scanty hours of leisure.'[150] In 1915, this theme was taken up by a

[145] *Ibid.*, 'The YMCA at the Front. Lure of the drink', 1915.
[146] R. Holmes (ed.), *My bit: a Lancashire fusilier at war 1914–18* (Marlborough, 1987), pp. 32–3.
[147] *YM*, 15 October 1915, p. 943.
[148] *Statistics of the military effort of the British Empire during the Great War 1914–1920* (London, 1922), p. 65.
[149] YMCA, K26 YMCA War Work No. 13. France. 'GRC', *Memoranda of a visit to France*, undated, p. 3.
[150] Anon., *YMCA War work in Britain and Flanders*, p. 16.

visitor to France who, while skirting round the delicate issues of prostitution and venereal disease, invited his readers to consider other consequences of leaving so many troops to their own devices:

> Imagine thousands of men encamped four or five miles away from a French town and after their duty possessed of not a single facility for recreation or any meeting place except the canteen... Some of these men would inevitably get out of camp but for the YMCA. They would trudge off to the French cafe and unaware of the quality of the drinks would become intoxicated...Men who wanted a bit of a change from the dreariness of the camp in France have time after time been punished by the military authorities on account of drunkenness contracted through ignorance. The lure of the drink is strong with some men and if you cannot provide counter attractions they are sure to succumb. Being at War their punishment is naturally heavier and as a natural corollary the man who may otherwise be a good soldier is demoralized.[151]

Spurred on by the needs of the times, throughout 1915 YMCA work mushroomed in this milieu. As early as New Year's Day, Yapp was able to inform the Royal Army Temperance Association that 'We are erecting seven huts at HAVRE, five at ROUEN and others at Boulogne.'[152] By the end of the year, and in Le Havre alone, the YMCA had opened no fewer than thirteen centres. These comprised two huts in the Remount Camp; a hut and an attached quiet room in Number 15 Camp and in numbers 1, 2 and 3 Docks and in Number 9 Stationary Hospital; a hut in Number 4 Dock and in Number 18 Camp; a marquee in Number 2 Camp and, lastly, a reading room, an officers' club and a 'Central Town Institute and cinema' in Le Havre itself, the latter being described as 'a very formidable opponent to places of ill-resort'.[153] Moreover, the dynamic of expansion continued into 1916. In April, a second hut was allocated to Number 9 Stationary Hospital and another hut was allotted to replace the marquee in Number 2 Camp. The need for the latter was particularly acute as the camp was a rest camp, at times home to thousands of men recuperating from the stresses of the front line, and there was nothing available to them except the YMCA and 'several low class cafes and estaminets'. Additional resources were, on that account, also allocated to the Central Town Institute which, with its daily cinema shows and cheap meals, was deemed to be 'the very best counter attraction to the low-class cafes and estaminets and places of bad repute' in which the port abounded.[154] Despite the scale of this provision, subsequent months saw further growth, with Barclay Baron writing to Yapp in January 1917: 'We have three new huts building in

---

[151] YMCA, K26 YMCA War Work No. 13. France. 'The YMCA at the Front. Lure of the drink', 1915.

[152] *Ibid.*, A. K. Yapp to C. White, 1 January 1915.

[153] *Ibid.*, 'Memorandum of interview with Mr. Oliver McCowen re centres in France', 31 December 1915.

[154] YMCA, K27 YMCA War Work No. 14. France. 'Memorandum re newly allotted huts in France', 6 April 1916.

this area and the prospect of having to take over eight coffee stalls and other institutions from private workers in Havre before the beginning of March.'[155]

Two important ventures in Le Havre that directly involved Baron were the Association's officers' and young soldiers' clubs. Although the YMCA had not previously catered for the specific requirements of regular or Territorial officers, the wartime expansion and social diversification of the officer corps[156] presented the YMCA with a new field of opportunity. In 1915, and with a view to keeping wayward young officers away from the fleshpots of Le Havre, a well-appointed officers' club was opened in the centre of town. As explained in a memorandum of 1916:

> It is situated within a few hundred yards of Base Headquarters in commodious premises which include 5 reading and writing rooms, and lounge, dining rooms, bedrooms and bath rooms. As many as 80 breakfasts are served after the arrival of the morning boat, and often similar numbers of lunches and dinners. For the large number of young officers waiting between boats and trains, this Club has been a very great boon.[157]

Indeed, the success of the officers' club was such that a second was soon open for business in Number 1 Camp as well. Situated in another rest camp, in addition to serving meals the attractions of this facility included 'large mess and smoking rooms, drying rooms and baths'.[158] Despite some wrangling over these ventures, to which we shall return, in February 1917 McCowen was able to deliver an encouraging report on the continuing success of Le Havre's original officers' club:

> The daily turn over exceeds one thousand francs; every bedroom in the place is booked, and with it all, the quiet home atmosphere is maintained. Since the 1st of January no less than forty-three young subalterns have given subscriptions, as a token of their gratitude, to the funds of the YMCA, and numbers of Generals and Staff Officers have paid all kinds of tributes to the success of the Club.[159]

As a result of these experiments in Le Havre, by the end of 1916 further clubs and rest rooms for officers had been established in St Omer, Calais, Etaples and Abbeville as well as in more forward locations such as Amiens, Albert and Reninghelst.[160]

Besides young officers, another vulnerable group to which the YMCA in Le Havre paid special attention were those early war, under-age volunteers who were sent back to base from their units on the discovery of their pretence. As a result of careful lobbying by Barclay Baron and Canon J. O. Hannay, an Anglican army

[155] *Ibid.*, B. Baron to A. K. Yapp, 22 January 1917.
[156] K. Simpson, 'The officers', in *A nation in arms: a social study of the British army in the First World War*, ed. I. Beckett and K. Simpson (Manchester, 1985), pp. 88–9.
[157] YMCA, K27 YMCA War Work No. 14. France. 'Officers' clubs and rest rooms run by the YMCA', 1916.
[158] *Ibid.*
[159] *Ibid.*, O. McCowen to A. K. Yapp, 5 February 1917.
[160] *Ibid.*, 'Officers' clubs and rest rooms run by the YMCA', 1916.

chaplain, permission for a young soldiers' club was eventually extracted from the military authorities. In May 1916, *YM. The British Empire YMCA Weekly* announced that:

A Young Soldiers' Club has been formed in one of the big base camps. It is used almost entirely by lads who have joined the Army, but who are not of the prescribed age. Several hundreds of them are in camp around our hut, which is a great boon to them, and will, we believe, exercise a strong influence for good.[161]

In addition to the wholesome home environment and the various creature comforts offered by YMCA centres in base areas, a key factor in their success was a rich and varied schedule of entertainments and activities. In 1915, an Anglican clergyman and Oxford don described those provided by the staff of a larger hut at Le Havre:

Here, every evening, there are entertainments and 'full houses', sometimes a sing-song, sometimes a lecture, sometimes an amateur dramatic performance... Sometimes, too, we have French classes, and sometimes debates...Outside recreations, too, are provided – cricket matches, sports, football cup ties. For the moment I am acting as 'O.C. Games', and spend part of my time negotiating with farmers for the hire of football fields and in securing volunteers to level the ground and erect goal posts.[162]

In marked contrast to the miserable conditions that prevailed during the previous winter, the YMCA in Le Havre marked Christmas 1915 in lavish style. As L. G. Pilkington wrote to Yapp on New Year's Eve:

I feel driven to use all the superlatives I can lay my tongue to in describing the conduct of our workers. They were simply magnificent in the way they rose to the occasion. Every hut was thoroughly decorated and the best of it was they got the men themselves to join in the majority of the decorating, and the men enjoyed this most thoroughly...[W]here the population was at all permanent they provided teas every night during the week. We had 300 or 400 men sitting down to tea every night in each hut. The tables were laid and decorated by the ladies. After tea there was always a concert or some sort of special entertainment. The men, thanks to the spirit of the workers, rose to the occasion splendidly...They took the teas simply as they were meant, as a reminder of home, and I feel confident that they did prevent a very large number of men from going astray. At the re-inforcement camps a series of entertainments were given every night during the week, including games, competitions and pillow fighting, etc. On Christmas Eve and Christmas Day in two of the huts presents were given to something like 2,000 men who were in the hut at that moment.[163]

[161] *YM*, 19 May 1916, p. 448.
[162] Anon., *YMCA war work in Britain and Flanders*, p. 15.
[163] YMCA, K26 YMCA War Work No. 13. France. L. G. Pilkington to A. K. Yapp, 31 December 1915.

While such largesse was unusual, a regular attraction of YMCA centres were the concerts given by Lena Ashwell's touring concert parties, events that supplemented the in-house affairs organized by hut leaders and high-profile concerts given by stars such as Harry Lauder, who in June 1917 played to a crowd of more than 2,000 in a YMCA hut in Boulogne.[164] Much to Ashwell's surprise, the tour of her first concert party (which took place early in 1915 and which was privately funded) turned out to be a phenomenal success. As Ashwell recalled:

> The experiment succeeded beyond all expectations; the men were longing for music and cheerfulness, and for a breath of home, and when it was seen how eagerly the concerts were welcomed, not only by the rank and file, but by C.O.'s, chaplains, and doctors, on behalf of their charges, we undertook the work of organizing a regular series of concert tours, and a campaign to raise funds to cover the expenses entailed.[165]

By the autumn of 1915 two parties were 'continually at work' touring the French bases, their artistes performing to gruelling schedules. According to Ashwell, in a single twenty-four-day period in 1915 one of her parties gave no fewer than 'nineteen hospital and forty-three camp concerts'.[166] However, the demand for these entertainments grew rather than diminished. In subsequent months, all male troupes were admitted 'right up to the firing line' in France and mixed concert parties were despatched to Malta and Egypt.[167] In January 1919, when no fewer than twenty-five of Ashwell's parties were at work, the YMCA claimed to have hosted no fewer than 20,000 of their concerts and to have borne all of the costs involved.[168] While it also fostered a rather unlikely craze for country dancing in the latter months of the war,[169] straddling the boundary between entertainment and evangelism was the work of Bradford-born ventriloquist Arthur Feather, whose evening shows invariably concluded with 'family prayers'. Having performed in camps in England, Feather arrived in France in 1915, working in Le Havre and Rouen before going into army areas where 'he continued his service, sometimes in the open-air, at other times in barns, and most evenings in the YMCA marquees and buildings'. Indeed, for some weeks Feather and his inseparable wooden 'pal' lent the YMCA centre at Poperinghe railway station an air of the surreal, performing between 11.00 p.m. and midnight to men fresh from the trenches and awaiting the departure of the leave train.[170]

According to contemporary sources, Red Triangle work in the bases of the BEF was widely appreciated by its beneficiaries. A YMCA worker at Le Havre penned the following description of a typical hut scene:

[164] H. Lauder, *A minstrel in France* (London, 1918), pp. 142–3.
[165] *YM*, 15 October 1915, p. 943.
[166] *Ibid.*
[167] L. Ashwell, 'Concerts at the Front', in *Told in the huts*, ed. Yapp, p. 148.
[168] YMCA, K27 YMCA War Work No. 14. France. 'The latest YMCA statistics', 20 January 1919; *Times*, 15 March 1957, p. 13.
[169] D. C. Daking, 'The very best job in France', *The Red Triangle*, July 1918, pp. 446–8.
[170] *YM*, 21 January 1916, p. 44.

At one end there is the canteen...where at all hours of the day, from 6 a.m. to 9 p.m., there is an endless stream of men, waiting their turn for a cup of coffee, a slab of 'dolly cake', or it may be for 'fags', bootlaces, or bachelor buttons; some of them after a long day's work – 'fatigues' they rightly name them – down at the Docks: others just arrived from England, ('Blighty' they soon learn to call it), staying for a few hours in a 'rest camp' before they go up the line: others, again, back from the Front, waiting a few days for the order to return. And a cup of hot coffee is a good thing on a cold, wet night, when one is drenched with rain and covered with mud [and] it is long past tea-time and no more rations can be issued.[171]

Moreover, in a breezy letter of appreciation written in April 1916, a J. R. Parker related how 'When I visit Le Havre I always partake of tea at the YMCA Central. It is quiet, yet attractive, and one can depend on having a good tea (same as mother used to make) at quite a modest price.' He was particularly appreciative of the 'gentle, dainty creature' who served him on one of these occasions and who seemed unperturbed by her clients' banter.[172] Indeed, it was a testimony (however tactless) to the popularity and efficiency of the YMCA more generally that one South African chaplain based in Le Havre wrote:

The YMCA really does, on a well-organized and much more efficient scale, all that the Army asks of the Chaplains' Department – with the exception, perhaps, of funerals, which could, of course, be arranged easily. It keeps the men's spirits up; it provides them with amusements; it offers a flavouring of religion, sufficiently toned down so as not to hurt anyone's feelings...the YMCA is amazingly successful. Everyone speaks well of it. We are all welcomed into it. It even smiles on a person like myself, and gives me tea and biscuits because I wear a Maltese Cross, and utterly disarms me...Abolish the Chaplains' Department and establish the YMCA.[173]

However, the most striking and challenging indication of the resourcefulness and adaptability of the YMCA in base areas came in the high summer of 1916, when the docks at Le Havre were swamped by hospital trains conveying wounded men from the Somme battlefield to hospital ships bound for England. Baron's account of the *ad hoc* work that took place as they unloaded at Le Havre is probably the most vivid and compelling part of his memoirs. However, a corresponding record of this work was provided in 1917 by another YMCA worker, who remembered how

The Big Push on the Somme had just begun when I arrived at [Le Havre], and was put in charge of one of the shifts working among the wounded arriving in long trainloads at the Quai, sometimes straight from the front, sometimes from base hospitals up the line, to be put on board the hospital ship for England.[174]

---

[171] Anon., *YMCA war work in Britain and Flanders*, pp. 14–15.
[172] *YM*, 14 April 1916, p. 328.
[173] R. Keable, *Standing by: wartime reflections in France and Flanders* (London, 1919), pp. 34–5, 41.
[174] Anon., 'Work among the wounded at the Quai d'Escale', *The Red Triangle*, 2 February 1917, p. 91.

In the event, a system was rapidly perfected to ensure the maximum possible distribution of comforts and writing materials to their human cargo:

> As the long hospital train nears the station on the Quai it pulls up for a moment to divide into two portions, and thus comes into the station beside both platforms. The moment it stops, four YM workers make a dash for the front and rear of each portion…As the YM workers pass swiftly out and in among the walking wounded, or pick their steps carefully through the train wards, lest a sudden jolt should cause them to tread upon a wounded man, they distribute postcards, pencils, copies of *Blighty*, cigarettes and tobacco, and speak a kindly, cheery word to the men. By the time the workers have met, the train is usually in the station, and the walking cases are pouring from the train.[175]

From this point onwards, the workers were engaged in assisting the badly wounded:

> Meanwhile the orderlies are busy unloading the stretcher cases for the bearers to carry on board, and very soon the long platforms are covered from end to end with a load of suffering, broken humanity, which partly represents the tragedy and wastage of war. But the YM worker has no time to moralize. He is busy passing from stretcher to stretcher, collecting the postcards from those who have written home themselves…or he is kneeling beside those who long to write but cannot, to do it for them. I kneel beside a big, brawny man from Kent, wounded just beneath the nose and in several other places, unable to write, but eager to let his wife and children know that he is doing well…But when he thinks of home, his chin begins to work, his lips to quiver, and his eyes to fill, and he cannot utter a word. The moment he can command his voice he explains carefully that this wound under his nose causes his eyes to water every little while. I assure him I understand. That is just the kind of dirty trick that such a wound would be sure to play a man. Then I write the postcard myself, read it over to him, and on hearing that it is more than satisfactory, I pass on.[176]

Army areas

Difficult and distressing as this work must have been to its unprepared workers, by the summer of 1916 the YMCA was acquiring a grim familiarity with front-line conditions, a familiarity that was to deepen as the war went on. Significantly, the first senior commander to welcome the extension of Red Triangle work into forward areas was General Sir Douglas Haig of First Army, who would go on to supersede Sir John French as commander-in-chief of the BEF in December 1915.[177] The timing of the commencement of YMCA work in First Army area (namely July 1915) is notable in itself. The regular and Territorial divisions of First Army had already participated in three major – and unsuccessful – offensives (at Neuve Chapelle, 10–13 March; Aubers Ridge, 9 May; and Festubert, 15–25 May) since the beginning of the year and First Army, duly

---

[175] *Ibid.*
[176] *Ibid.*
[177] *Red Triangle*, 23 February 1917, p. 159.

reinforced by several divisions of the New Army, which began to arrive in France that May, was earmarked to undertake a fourth and much larger offensive at Loos.[178] Significantly, the divisions of Kitchener's New Army, the archetypal citizen soldiers of the First World War, would play a major *rôle* in the fighting at Loos and it seems quite likely that the opening of Red Triangle centres in First Army area was partly intended to ease their transition to front-line conditions by maintaining the amenities to which they had become accustomed. In any event, the work in First Army area began in a deserted convent at Aire, then home to army headquarters, in July 1915.[179] As J. H. Hunt, the YMCA secretary at Aire and a veteran of Territorial work in England,[180] soon informed McCowen:

> You will be pleased to know that the work here is still being maintained successfully – there are no signs of a re-action. The rooms are packed every night...After the Church Parade on Sunday Sir Douglas Haig, Gen. [Percy] Hobbs [the deputy-adjutant and quartermaster-general] and the Staff came in. Sir Douglas was intensely pleased and with a hearty handshake wished us all success.[181]

However, such was the demand for the services of the Red Triangle that the initial centre at Aire soon found it hard to cope. As McCowen wrote to Yapp on 24 July, 'I motored...up to Aire yesterday and found things going very well. Sir Douglas Haig and his whole staff were in on Sunday morning. He complimented Hunt very warmly on the work and said how grateful he was that we were doing this for the troops.' Nevertheless, he went on to relate that

> The problem of supplies at Aire is becoming a big one. Men are coming very great distances, with huge orders, for their units and we are saying that it is very difficult, from one Centre, to supply all these, but that if we could only get established in other Centres, the problem would become much easier.[182]

In other words, the logic of expansion proved irresistible. The first YMCA centre in Second Army area in Flanders opened at Reninghelst that August, access that may have been helped by the fact that the wife of the army commander, Sir Herbert Plumer, was the lady superintendent of the Aldwych Hut in London.[183] In mid-September McCowen announced to Yapp that

> The whole front is now open to us and we are going to have a tremendous task to meet the emergency adequately...I have just returned from a visit to the three Armies from Ypres [in] the North to Albert [in] the South, and find doors open everywhere and officers and men alike clamouring for us before the Winter closes in.[184]

---

[178] G. Sheffield and J. Bourne (eds.), *Douglas Haig: war diaries and letters 1914–1918* (London, 2005), pp. 127–8.

[179] Edmonds, *History of the Great War*, p. 140.

[180] *Year book*, 1914, p. 104.

[181] Letter book of J. H. Hunt, 20 July 1915. I am grateful to Dr Mary Martin for allowing access to this source.

[182] YMCA, K26 YMCA War Work No. 13. France. O. McCowen to A. K. Yapp, 24 July 1915.

[183] Yapp, *In the service of youth*, p. 158.

[184] YMCA, K26 YMCA War Work No. 13. France. O. McCowen to A. K. Yapp, 19 September 1915.

In entering into this new sphere of operations, the YMCA was making a massive commitment at a time when its resources (and perhaps its human resources especially) were stretched to the limit. Furthermore, this work was bound to grow with the formation of new armies and the lengthening of the British line on the Western Front, which grew from 70 miles in September 1915 to 110 miles by February 1917.[185] Nevertheless, and as Edmonds remarked, the colonization of army areas by the Red Triangle continued apace: 'These centres developed rapidly, so that by the end of 1916 the YMCA was to be found at most of the important towns and villages from Poperinghe in the north to Albert in the south.'[186] Naturally, what they offered was basic in comparison to larger centres in base areas but they still provided refreshments, writing materials and other comforts to the more exposed soldiers of the BEF. As one evocative description of a YMCA centre in an army area ran:

> [T]he conditions are as different from those of the great base camps as those are from home work…Picture a long, dimly lighted hut, with a queue of khaki-clad men, stretching right back to the door, and often beyond…For four hours the queue has continued, constantly renewed, in spite of the strains of a concert from the adjoining marquee, where some 600 men roar ready applause. At the upper end of the hut three figures…toil at the top of their speed without pause save for the all-too-brief space needed to refill the urn. The cups of tea served in an evening seldom fall below a thousand, and often go beyond this, and buns and biscuits by the caseful, and 'smokes' without end, are exchanged for tattered, dirty low-valued French notes and other money.[187]

It was indicative of the general efficiency of YMCA organization amidst the upheavals of war that, to some at least, the Red Triangle seemed capable of working logistical miracles. One veteran recalled of a marquee that had been pitched in Bazentin Wood at the height of the battle of the Somme:

> [It] had a trestle table-counter stacked with everything [that] could be eaten or smoked or mixed for drinking. There were biscuits, slab cake, dates in fancy boxes, figs, chocolates and sweets, oranges, tins of sweetened milk, of cocoa, bottles of camp coffee…Hoe's sauce and Tomato Ketchup.[188]

Nor, indeed, were entertainments neglected, especially given the portability of film projectors. As Oliver McCowen wrote in 1917:

> One feature of this forward work is the use we make of Pathéscopes. Our workers…are deluged with applications for performances. A 'party' is sent to convey the equipment; any old barn is used. The Colonel and officers are generally present, and the other night one of the audience produced a mouth-organ, and led the whole audience in a sing-song, while the Pathéscope pictures were being shown.[189]

[185] *Statistics of the military effort of the British Empire*, p. 639.
[186] Edmonds, *History of the Great War*, p. 140.
[187] J. I. MacNair, 'Sketches from the Front', *Red Triangle Papers*, XIII (n.d.).
[188] R. Holmes, *Tommy: the British soldier on the Western Front 1914–18* (London, 2004), p. 600.
[189] O. McCowen, 'The winter push', *Red Triangle Papers*, XIV (n.d.).

Despite government pressure for economy in food consumption later in the war,[190] it seems that Edmonds rather overstated the frugality of the Red Triangle's provision in forward areas when he wrote, 'In the ruined houses, barns and cellars, and in dug-outs in which the YMCA worked near the front, tea, coffee, cocoa, bovril and oxo, with biscuits, cake and cigarettes, were the principal articles provided; and notepaper and a few books and old newspapers were [also] available.'[191] Whatever their relative quality, by May 1916 the YMCA was running 111 centres in base areas and 47 centres in army areas, the newest of these being located between Arras and the Somme, where Third and Fourth Armies had just taken over part of the Allied line previously held by the French.[192] Furthermore, the ground gained during the battle of the Somme (July–November 1916) demanded more Red Triangle centres. As McCowen notified Yapp that September:

> I have just returned from the 4th Army. I saw the Army Commander yesterday morning, and offered him several Huts for forward positions on territory taken from the Germans...I think we shall be allotted 3 places in the near future – places which recently figured as the scene of very heavy fighting.[193]

While it was deemed prudent that YMCA marquees in forward areas should be 'of a dark brown colour' so as to be 'as inconspicuous as possible to enemy aircraft',[194] this caution reflected a greater concern for the patrons of these centres than for their workers. While we have seen that many of the latter were prepared to court danger, there was also a rather gung-ho tendency for senior YMCA secretaries to put their workers in harm's way. For example, in a revealing letter of November 1915, P. H. S. Sitters, yet another veteran of Territorial camp work before the war,[195] wrote to Yapp reporting that he had been 'busy securing fresh openings' in the vicinity of Ypres, his object being 'to secure a position about a mile in advance of Reninghelst, at a place called Ouderdom'.[196] However, on learning from a staff officer of the 9th (Scottish) Division that Ouderdom was not a particularly busy location, Sitters offered to establish centres at Canada Huts and Dickebusch Huts instead. Understandably, this offer seems to have aroused some misgivings. As Sitters explained:

> As both camps are only about a mile behind the Line, my offer to place tents there was not at first received with a great deal of enthusiasm, because of the great danger attending the positions. However after assuring Col. McHardy that YMCA workers were prepared to share the same dangers as the men, he

[190] YMCA, J7 National Council signed minutes, 2 March 1917.

[191] Edmonds, *History of the Great War*, p. 140.

[192] A. F. Becke, *History of the Great War based on official documents. Order of battle part 4. The Army Council, GHQs, armies, and corps 1914–1918* (Uckfield, 2007), pp. 92, 102; *YM*, 19 May 1916, pp. 452–3.

[193] YMCA, K27 YMCA War Work No. 14. France. O. McCowen to A. K. Yapp, 27 September 1916.

[194] YMCA, K26 YMCA War Work No. 13. France. 'Report on YMCA Work in Third Army area', 12 February 1917.

[195] *Year book*, 1914, p. 106.

heartily agreed to my suggestion, with the result that we visited the Camps and selected two very fine sites.[197]

Having made the journey up to the camps amidst the excitement of a daily German bombardment, Sitters crowned his afternoon's work by making an even bolder suggestion:

> We returned to the Divisional Headquarters for tea and I seized the opportunity to tell Col. McHardy how much we would welcome the chance of doing something for the men in the trenches. He was surprised to learn that our men were willing to take such risks, and promised to take the matter up with the general. I suggested that they should build us a 'Dug-Out' in the trenches and we would run it as far as practicable on lines similar to those of our tent and Hut work.[198]

If permission for these projects was granted the following day,[199] some YMCA secretaries clearly needed strong persuasion not to follow their untutored instincts. On surveying the ravaged landscape around Beaumont Hamel in the winter of 1916–17 with the goal of establishing 'a system of dug-outs for the distribution of free refreshment', Harold Down at first selected a 'dug-out formerly occupied by a German General, which was panelled and decorated'. However, a group of sympathetic officers 'were rather sceptical as to the success of my project, and frankly asked me if I intended starting a suicide club'. In the event, wiser counsel prevailed and a somewhat safer site was selected for a marquee.[200]

Having infiltrated forward areas the previous year, the battle of the Somme presented the opportunity for the Red Triangle to commence work among the wounded during offensive operations. In July 1916, and in the wake of what seems to have been the Australian attack on Pozières, a number of YMCA workers went to assist at a casualty clearing station, their work among the Australian wounded inspiring the first of the Association's *Red Triangle Papers*. As the pamphlet's anonymous author remembered:

> When we arrived the sight which presented itself to us beggars description. Hundreds of men were lying about everywhere with head, leg, and arm wounds [and] were now awaiting the arrival of the train which was to convey them to a hospital outside the range of the guns…We did not need to spend much time discussing what we could do, for the men soon recognized and welcomed the YMCA, and we were immediately invited to write postcards and fill in field cards [while] Mr. McKibbin hastened to the Tynemouth hut for cigarettes, as there was a sad lack of smokes and money in this company of wounded heroes…After the train had departed there were still some 350 officers and men left, and much work still to do…The YMCA entertained this

---

[196] YMCA, K26 YMCA War Work No. 13. France. P. H. S. Sitters to A. K. Yapp, 2 November 1915.
[197] *Ibid.*
[198] *Ibid.*
[199] *Ibid.*
[200] YMCA, K26 YMCA War Work No. 13. France. H. A. Down, 'Pioneering on the Western Front. 3½ years with the YMCA', pp. 14–15.

batch of officers and men to food and refreshments. In some instances the secretaries had even to feed men who were suffering from severe shell-shock and who were unable to hold a cup in their hands. In one such case a secretary fed a man, lifting alternately to his mouth a Dolly cake and a cup bearing the Red Triangle and containing a drink of lemonade.[201]

While this work seems to have been improvised for the occasion, in November 1916 Harold Down approached the 51st (Highland) Division with a request that the Red Triangle be allowed to attach itself to one of the division's advanced dressing stations for its attack on Beaumont Hamel. With permission duly granted, stores were (with some difficulty) transported to the ADS where Down and his colleagues awaited the inevitable stream of wounded from the attack:

> Our work began with the early dawn – a few stragglers struck down in the first advance, wounded but quite cheery, their chief anxiety being whether they would get a 'Blighty' [but] the men who came in later were a pitiable sight indeed. Most of them with just a rough dressing on the battlefield had walked, or rather hobbled down, to the dressing station…ragged, torn, bleeding and exhausted – the salvage of war.[202]

In terms of their work, which was undertaken amidst German shellfire, Down recalled that:

> In common with the [Royal Army Medical Corps] we provided the men with refreshments and a smoke…It was difficult to impress them with the fact that the YMCA were not selling things. One man said, 'It's a good job someone thinks of us, Sir.' And both officers and men were not slow to show their appreciation of the little we were able to do for them. But our work did not end with giving them drinks. We posted letters and field cards, distributed writing paper, gave a helping hand to some of the boys who could only limp along, and rubbed the legs of a good many who had cramp.[203]

This *rôle* was to become commonplace during the BEF's set-piece offensive battles of 1917. At Arras that April the YMCA distributed thousands of pounds worth of goods to the walking wounded of Third Army.[204] Furthermore, and prior to the capture of Messines by Second Army in June 1917, it was arranged that thirty-four temporary Red Triangle centres should be set up near the dressing stations of the attacking divisions. Consequently, and as Edmonds noted, 'every wounded man who, alone or assisted, was able to walk to a dressing station, passed through one of these, where hot cocoa, sandwiches, biscuits, chocolates [and] cigarettes, were given to him, and if he so desired a postcard was filled in and despatched for him'.[205] Similarly, Harold Down wrote of the situation in Fifth Army during the third battle of Ypres (July–November 1917):

---

[201] Anon., 'At a clearing station in France', *Red Triangle Papers*, I (n.d.).
[202] YMCA, K26 YMCA War Work No. 13. France. H. A. Down, 'Pioneering on the Western Front. 3½ years with the YMCA', p. 12.
[203] *Ibid.*
[204] Dunkerley, *The Red Triangle circle*, p. 14.
[205] Edmonds, *History of the Great War*, p. 140 n. 2.

Our plans were highly approved by the military authorities, and we were given every facility to organize [our] work. We were asked to attach ourselves to Corps Walking Wounded Stations, and arrangements were made to commence at a moment's notice our work at Brielen, Vlamertygne, and Dickibusch, and [we] subsequently did similar work with three Casualty Clearing Stations near the village of Remy.[206]

In fact, the efforts of the YMCA around Ypres in 1917 were relayed to the British public by Philip Gibbs, Britain's most celebrated war correspondent, who recounted how

The YMCA is busy in another tent or dug-out. It has a cheery way of producing hot cocoa on the edge of a battlefield and of thrusting little packets of chocolate, biscuits, cigarettes and matches into the hands of lightly wounded men as soon as they have trudged down the long trail for walking wounded.[207]

An inevitable consequence of the Red Triangle's integration into the life and even the operations of the BEF was the militarization of its ethos and structures. Emblematic of this was the adoption of a military-style uniform for its workers. Initially, these were clad in their civilian clothes with only a Red Triangle badge as a distinguishing feature. However, given the level of wartime paranoia over the activities of enemy agents, this proved problematic in an active theatre of war; by 1915, a worker in Le Havre had already been reported to the Military Police as a spy on account of omitting to wear his Red Triangle badge.[208] Consequently, after only two months in France McCowen was urging upon Yapp the necessity of designing a suitable uniform, hinting in January 1915 that 'There is a feeling amongst some of the Officers that we should adopt it. They say we would be regarded by Officers and Men as more belonging to the show where everyone is in Khaki, and that civilians are viewed with suspicion and suffer an initial handicap here.'[209] Furthermore, there were the sensitivities of the civilian population to consider, France having already grown accustomed to the principle of universal military service. As one secretary wrote to Yapp less than a fortnight later:

There seem to be practically no young men left in the towns in this country. I feel quite uncomfortable sometimes when walking through the town in which I reside, as I have to run the gauntlet of women who in many cases have both husband and sons at the front…I am quite certain that they look upon me as a defaulter, for numbers of French folk cannot believe that service is [not] compulsory in England.[210]

Still, the introduction of a YMCA uniform appears to have been delayed until the summer of 1916, with GHQ in France being keen to ensure that it should be

---

[206] YMCA, K26 YMCA War Work No. 13. France. H. A. Down, 'Pioneering on the Western Front. 3½ years with the YMCA', pp. 21–2.

[207] Ibid., p. 22.

[208] Anon., YMCA war work in Britain and Flanders, p. 14.

[209] YMCA, K26 YMCA War Work No. 13. France. O. McCowen to A. K. Yapp, 20 January 1915.

[210] Ibid., S. Hyde-Coleman to A. K. Yapp, 1 February 1915.

cut in such a way 'that our men will not run the danger of being mistaken either for officers or privates'.[211] In the event, the khaki uniform adopted by male workers in France, Egypt, Mesopotamia and Salonika (and, from October 1916, by senior male personnel in Britain) incorporated a service cap adorned with a Red Triangle badge and a tunic with a standing collar and Red Triangle badges on its shoulder straps and right sleeve. Despite the concern of the military authorities to avoid this, the uniform was in fact 'made on lines somewhat similar to that worn by officers' and uniformed YMCA secretaries – especially if wearing trench coats or other telltale marks of officer status – were routinely, if mistakenly, saluted.[212]

While its male workers adopted military uniform (and even sported their old medal ribbons if they were former soldiers)[213] YMCA organization in France gradually conformed to the higher organization of the BEF. Although army secretaries were an original feature of the Association's work in army areas, by late 1916 a lower tier of corps secretaries was also evolving, although these did not become common until 1918.[214] However, while this organization was suitable enough for the relatively static conditions of 1916 and 1917, the more mobile warfare of the war's final year, and in particular the so-called 'Advance to Victory' of late summer and autumn 1918, called for the creation of a subordinate tier of divisional secretaries. As Harry Holmes explained in an article of November 1918 entitled 'Keeping step with the victors':

> For the first time an experiment has been made of attaching men, as the official YMCA representatives, to certain Divisions. This plan has been very successful in the work of the Australian, Canadian, and New Zealand Associations, and our leaders, after experience of working with a mobile army, find that this method brings the quickest and largest measure of efficiency. The YMCA men belong to the Division, move up with the Division, are found sites for their work by the Division, and share, as Mr. MacDonald so well put it, 'the honour and protection of the Division'. There can be no doubt that this official attachment of Association Secretaries to Army Divisions is the best plan of organization for Army work, especially when that Army is constantly moving.[215]

In preparation for occupation duties in the Rhineland, this liaison was devolved down to brigade level. In December 1918 *The Red Triangle Bulletin* announced that 'A comprehensive scheme has been put up for the armies of occupation in Germany, and has been accepted in entirety by the authorities. It includes a staff of a hundred YMCA workers with each army, and a centre with each brigade.'[216]

[211] YMCA, K27 YMCA War Work No. 14. France. O. McCowen to A. K. Yapp, 4 July 1916.
[212] *Times*, 27 September 1916, p. 5; Hornung, *Notes of a camp-follower*, p. 12.
[213] Hornung, *Notes of a camp-follower*, pp. 223, 242.
[214] YMCA, K26 YMCA War Work No. 13. France. H. A. Down, 'Pioneering on the Western Front. 3½ years with the YMCA', pp. 9, 26.
[215] H. N. Holmes, 'Keeping step with the victors', *The Red Triangle*, November 1918, p. 86.
[216] Anon., 'On the Western Front since the Armistice', *The Red Triangle Bulletin*, 6 December 1918, pp. 2–3.

However, an unfortunate corollary of the extent to which YMCA work was shaped by the circumstances of the British army on the Western Front from 1915 to 1917 were the huge material losses it incurred during the massive German offensive – and resulting 'Great Retreat' – of spring 1918. The apotheosis of YMCA work in France was reached in 1917, a year in which the BEF was mainly on the offensive and in which the YMCA was free to refine its work in bases, army areas and in support of limited and, at their best, methodical, set-piece attacks. Although the unexpected German withdrawal to the Hindenburg Line early in 1917 caused some dislocation (with the YMCA being compelled to relocate centres in its aftermath) the dynamic at the end of the year was still one of expansion, with McCowen speaking enthusiastically of 'the rapid growth of the work in France' and the need for another sixty-eight huts.[217] Indeed, there was a renewed burst of activity early in 1918, as Fifth Army moved south in order to take over a large section of the Allied line previously held by the French, a process that saw the British sector of the Western Front reach its maximum length of 123 miles.[218] As Harold Down, then its assistant army secretary, recalled:

My own work at this time [was] in connection with the necessary arrangements with Corps and Divisional staffs, for sites, transport from railheads, erection of huts and the hundred and one details relative to their opening. Our general work in the Army Area was developing rapidly. Never in the history of our work had we made such progress in developing our work on well-organized lines, and from the higher command downwards never had such facilities been given to us, and site after site was carefully chosen for these new huts. We gradually laid aside our maps and arranged our work as if we had come to stay. Occasionally, an officer would tell us that we were building huts for the Boche, but we looked with confidence upon the line of reserve trenches which were being prepared far behind our advanced huts.[219]

The anticipated German onslaught on the Western Front – in effect, a rolling series of offensives against various parts of the Allied line which lasted from March to July 1918 – broke on the front of the British Third and Fifth Armies in the area of the Somme on 21 March 1918; nearly three weeks later, on 9 April, another offensive was launched against the British First and Second Armies in Flanders. Their consequences for YMCA work at the front were catastrophic. The precipitate retreat of Fifth Army in particular led to the loss or destruction of dozens of centres and vast quantities of stores. As Harry Lyne, its army secretary, lamented to Yapp:

Things never looked better and brighter for us than they did before the Push. Our work was developing nicely – stores were beginning to come through and we were pretty well off for men. We little knew then that within two days we should have lost everything...We had actually 33 centres working, 2 in the

[217] *The Red Triangle Bulletin*, 9 November 1917, p. 4.
[218] *Statistics of the military effort of the British Empire*, p. 639.
[219] YMCA, K26 YMCA War Work No. 13. France. H. A. Down, 'Pioneering on the Western Front. 3½ years with the YMCA', p. 28.

course of erection, and 2 military centres which we had taken over and which we were preparing to open, 4 stores and our own Headquarters...Although we have lost everything that we had we have still hope within us and are trusting to get back right into the thick of things in the very near future.[220]

Although a small party of displaced workers held on at Amiens, assisting with the wounded and distributing stores to troops in transit until ordered to leave in early April, there was no disguising the magnitude of the disaster. As Harold Down wrote, 'Our great tragedy of the moment was that we had lost all our huts; all our energies; all our ambitions gone to the four winds, or shall we say gone to the Boche.'[221]

On the same day as this doleful communiqué, R. G. MacDonald of Third Army tried to console Yapp by informing him that his 'few remaining centres' were 'very flourishing' and that seventy-five displaced Red Triangle workers were enjoying the hospitality of a Third Army rest camp.[222] However, more bad news flooded in after the commencement of the German offensive in Flanders the following week. On 13 April McCowen reported to Yapp that

As a result of the recent military operations up North, I regret to say that we have lost a considerable number of huts in addition to those which I wrote you of a few days ago. This means that up to the date of writing over 100 centres have been either taken or destroyed by the enemy, or are so near the present fighting as to be entirely useless for our work.

While McCowen averred that losses had already been 'enormous' and that 'it would take at least £150,000 to cover our losses of these past few weeks',[223] Barclay Baron furnished a clearer picture of the situation in Second Army area four days later. In total, no fewer than thirty-five centres had been evacuated and while in 'many of these cases stuff was given away free in large quantities, in others it was looted immediately by British stragglers. Stores at Bailleul, Romain [and] probably at Wulverghem fell into German hands. Stores and much Australian equipment were burnt by us at Meteren.' Nevertheless, work continued amidst these setbacks; as Baron went on, 'We are running walking wounded work in five or six Casualty Clearing Stations, and "stragglers posts" to round up lost and frightened men and [we] hope to get marquees going as soon as things settle a little.'[224] Apart from such resilience, the only consolation that McCowen could glean for Yapp in mid-April 1918 was that 'on the whole the list of huts which I now send you were not heavily stocked at the time and that in every case the workers are safe and have succeeded in bringing in their money'.[225]

If a fresh appeal to the public for funds to replace '£150,000 worth of the

[220] YMCA, K27 YMCA War Work No. 14. France. H. Lyne to A. K. Yapp, 3 April 1918.
[221] YMCA, K26 YMCA War Work No. 13. France. H. A. Down, 'Pioneering on the Western Front. 3½ years with the YMCA', pp. 34–5.
[222] YMCA, K27 YMCA War Work No. 14. France. R. G. MacDonald to A. K. Yapp, 3 April 1918.
[223] Ibid., O. McCowen to A. K. Yapp, 13 April 1918.
[224] Ibid., B. Baron to A. K. Yapp, 17 April 1918.
[225] Ibid., O. McCowen to A. K. Yapp, 13 April 1918.

YMCA's essential equipment' was quickly underway,[226] the Red Triangle's work in army areas was much attenuated throughout the rest of 1918. Short of transport and, therefore, of resources during the 'Advance to Victory', YMCA leaders were compelled to move forward and to make do as best they could. As Harry Holmes put it:

> At no period during the time the Association has been in France have our Army Secretaries been faced with a larger problem, or one that tested more shrewdly their courage, resourcefulness and adaptability...The rapidity of army movement has made it almost impossible to secure transport, as every available vehicle is needed to carry supplies for the advancing troops. One of our marquees, attached to an advanced dressing station, moved at least seven times in sixteen days.[227]

Nevertheless, their undaunted efforts continued to attract plaudits. For example, William Beach Thomas, one of the BEF's official war correspondents, told in one of his despatches how 'A dashing cavalry officer, very much of the old school, possessing a voice that would carry about two miles, begged me with great earnestness to do him one service. Would I mention the YMCA? It had provided his men with hot coffee before riding out.' Similarly, a brigadier-general wrote to *The Red Triangle Bulletin* declaring that: 'I want to let you know how much I was impressed with the work done by the YMCA. It was simply magnificent. Almost before [our objective] was consolidated your representative had a distributing centre, and was serving biscuits and chocolates to the men. All ranks are enthusiastic.'[228]

Discipline, education and morale

As suggested by the previous testimonial, the Red Triangle usually benefited from the active support of a great many senior officers, and by no means only in France. The military value of its army work was clearly reflected in the tributes it received from some of the British army's most senior generals. In Mesopotamia, for example, where the expansion of YMCA work in 1916 was concurrent with the transformation of a hitherto mismanaged campaign,[229] the commander-in-chief, Sir Frederick Stanley Maude, sent a New Year message to the YMCA acknowledging its 'excellent work' and wishing it well for 1917.[230] Similarly, in October 1918 Sir Edmund Allenby (the conqueror of Jerusalem, who had entered the Holy City on foot the previous year) wrote an enthusiastic preface to a short history of YMCA work among the men of his Egyptian Expeditionary Force, declaring that 'No one has more reason than I to be grateful to the YMCA for its work in connection with the army...Broad-minded Christianity, self-regardless devotion to work, a spirit of daring enterprise, and

---

[226] *Ibid.*, A. K. Yapp, 'The YMCA in the Great Retreat'.
[227] Holmes, 'Keeping step with the victors', p. 85.
[228] Anon., 'In the Great Advance', *The Red Triangle Bulletin*, 30 August 1918, p. 3.
[229] H. J. Blampeid, *With a Highland Regiment in Mesopotamia* (Bombay, 1918), p. 31.
[230] *The Red Triangle*, 16 March 1917, p. 219.

sound business guidance have built an organization which has earned the gratitude of the Empire.'[231]

The commanders of the BEF were no less fulsome in their praise. In November 1915, Field-Marshal Sir John French commended the Association's base work in particular, stating how

> The problem of dealing with the conditions at such a time, and under existing circumstances at the Rest Camps, has always been a most difficult one; but the erection of huts by the YMCA has made this far easier. The extra comfort thereby afforded to the men, and the opportunities for reading and writing have been of incalculable service, and I wish to tender to your Association, and all those who have assisted my most grateful thanks.[232]

As we have noted, Sir Douglas Haig was strongly supportive of YMCA work in First Army in the summer of 1915. However, as commander-in-chief he continued to show his support, a disposition that may have been strengthened by the fact that Lady Haig was 'a constant worker' at a YMCA officers' hostel in London.[233] In April 1917 Haig endorsed the expanding work of the YMCA by visiting two of its centres at the height of the battle of Arras. As *The Red Triangle* reported:

> A most encouraging incident to our workers was the unexpected visit to two of our centres during this period of the Commander-in-Chief himself. Sir Douglas Haig found time to chat with our men for several minutes, complimented them very warmly on the work they were doing, and expressed the hope that it might be continued.[234]

Furthermore, in a meeting with Oliver McCowen that October, Haig once again pledged his support for the work of the Red Triangle, McCowen reporting how 'He was extremely busy, but spoke most sympathetically and gratefully about our work [and] promised to help us in any way he can.'[235] Finally, in April 1919, and on his return to England, Haig paid a warm tribute to the work of the Association:

> The conclusion of my period of command in France provides a fitting occasion on which to renew the warm expression of my gratitude to the YMCA for the splendid work carried out by their organization during more than four years among the troops serving under me. No difficulties or dangers have been too great for the YMCA to overcome in their efforts to provide for the comfort, entertainment and recreation of the men. The value of their work has been inestimable, and I feel confident that it has been deeply appreciated by all ranks.[236]

Such strong sympathy for the YMCA among such senior officers no doubt stemmed from several factors, including the paternalistic ethos of the late

---

[231] J. W. Barrett, *The war work of the YMCA in Egypt* (London, 1919), p. vii.
[232] YMCA, K40 Typescript extracts of letters of appreciation. Field-Marshal Sir John French, 23 November 1915.
[233] Yapp, *In the service of youth*, p. 158.
[234] *The Red Triangle*, 20 April 1917, p. 341.
[235] YMCA, K27 YMCA War Work No. 14. France. O. McCowen to A. K. Yapp, 17 October 1917.
[236] *Times*, 21 April 1919, p. 2; *The Red Triangle Bulletin*, 6 June 1919, pp. 3–4.

Victorian officer corps, personal religious conviction and even conjugal loyalty. However, and in narrowly professional terms, it was also abundantly clear that the work of the YMCA enhanced military discipline. As one commentator remarked in 1915:

> Every man that is kept from the guard room of the British camps in France strengthens the morals of the whole battalion. That is the reason why the officers are giving such a warm welcome to the YMCA. They know that wherever the YMCA hut is established in a camp it makes for good discipline and a contented battalion. The YMCA does much more than this for the men, but at least everyone will recognize that this feature is not the least important of its recommendations.[237]

Indeed, in January 1916 a military report attributed a marked reduction in drunkenness in Second Army area to the growing presence of the Red Triangle.[238] When McCowen brought this to the attention of Second Army headquarters, he received the following reply from Major-General A. A. Chichester:

> I am directed by the Army Commander to inform you that he has read the report with much interest and he wishes me to express to you his high appreciation of the good work being done by your Society [sic]. The entertainments and comforts provided are greatly enjoyed and have had a good effect in decreasing the number of cases of drunkenness especially in Bailleul and consequently improving the efficiency and discipline of the men generally.[239]

In November 1917, the provost marshal of the BEF, General Horwood, was inclined to be more blunt with McCowen, saying that 'he believed in the YMCA, not because it was Christian, but because his special task was to maintain discipline, and he found that wherever the YMCA hut went up, the crime sheet mechanically went down'.[240]

However, the work of the YMCA was also conducive to good morale, its numerous facilities and activities helping to mitigate the austere and even harsh conditions of service life for millions of British soldiers. As one visitor to France noted in 1917:

> One is forced to the conclusion that the YMCA has become an integral part of Army life, as necessary as the baker and the tailor, keeping up the spirits, restoring the mental balance of the man resting after a period in the trench, keeping the minds of the men alert and active, linking their lives with home and all that home means, helping to keep them mentally and physically and morally fit, and generally providing the 'morale' without which the military machine is but a blunt instrument.

[237] YMCA, K26 YMCA War Work No. 13. France. 'The YMCA at the Front. Lure of the drink', 1915.
[238] YMCA, K26 YMCA War Work No. 13. France. O. McCowen to A. K. Yapp, 24 January 1916.
[239] *Ibid.*, A. A. Chichester to O. McCowen, 1 March 1916.
[240] *The Red Triangle Bulletin*, 9 November 1917, p. 4.

Significantly, the same visitor had been struck by the latitude that had been given to the Association by the army, noting of the regime in one rest camp that the 'general impression is that the Rest Camp is run by the YMCA, the Army providing the rations'.[241] It was with some justification, therefore, that John Oxenham could claim in 1918 that

> [W]ithout the YMCA the Army especially could never have done what it has done, nor have done it half so well. And in that I shall be confirmed by every officer in the field or at home who has the welfare of his men at heart...It has not only enabled the men to fight, it has done infinitely more. It has enabled them to carry on through all this novel and distasteful business of war without becoming mere fighting machines.
> It has kept them human in the midst of unnatural and at times inhuman conditions.[242]

While the work of the Red Triangle clearly helped to mitigate the hardships of army life, it also helped to enhance morale through its extensive educational activities. As education was a core element of the Association's work in peacetime, this commitment was naturally extended to the French bases from the outset. During the course of the war the YMCA supplied 'a constant stream of books and magazines to its huts at home and overseas'.[243] Small libraries were even to be found in its centres in the front line and reading matter was freely distributed to soldiers in transit. A great deal of this literature had a 'solid and educational value', particularly after the YMCA took over the work of the Fighting Forces Book Council.[244] Furthermore, from the start of its overseas work it was anticipated that 'lectures and classes' would form part of the programme for 'every hut and centre'.[245] However, while lantern lectures abounded in the early months of the war, these were improvised and uncoordinated affairs. Despite the appeal of French language classes and lantern lectures on such patriotic themes as 'Napoleon and England, Nelson [and] Joan of Arc',[246] given the terrible demands of the war on the Western Front and an army that was overwhelmingly composed of non-professional soldiers, it became increasingly necessary to justify their sacrifices to the comparatively well-educated citizen soldiers of the British army. Conscious of the need 'for more systematic lecturing', in 1916 the Association began to engage workers on standard contracts who would devote themselves solely to lecturing work. While most of these 'were confined in their activities to the Base towns and areas', one of their number, namely F. J. Adkins of Sheffield University, 'had a series of extraordinarily successful tours through all the

---

[241] YMCA, K26 YMCA War Work No. 13. France. 'G.R.C.', *Memoranda of a visit to France*, undated, p. 3.

[242] Dunkerley, *The Red Triangle circle*, p. 3.

[243] Koch, *Books in camp, trench and hospital*, p. 13.

[244] *Ibid.*, p. 14.

[245] Anon., *A short record of the educational work of the YMCA with the British armies in France* (London, 1919), p. 7.

[246] *Ibid.*

Army areas, delivering lectures at most of the Army and Corps Schools, as well as at numerous Divisional Headquarters'.[247]

In the winter of 1916–17 the Association sought to augment this provision by 'getting distinguished men from home to come out to France as lecturers on special passes for brief periods'. With the support of the military authorities, these 'special lecturers' began their work in January 1917, with as many as a dozen of them in France at any one time before the scheme was suspended at the end of March in preparation for the battle of Arras.[248] Held to be an 'unqualified success' and credited with introducing 'an entirely new element into the life of the Bases',[249] all of these 'special lecturers' were carefully vetted, with prospective speakers being approved by a War Office Lectures Committee and by the Educational Committee of the YMCA.[250] As a memorandum from the Educational Committee made clear, the scheme had a strong military rationale and was by no means intended as an academic free-for-all:

> There is reason to believe that the troops behind the line in France, besides their natural desire for entertainment and recreation, would welcome a largely increased provision of Lectures of a more solid and thoughtful character... Consequently the YMCA, at the invitation of the War Office, has undertaken to organize a special service of Lecturers to visit suitable centres in France for periods varying from a fortnight to three months or more...The Lectures should aim not merely at affording amusement to the men in their unoccupied hours, but at giving them some solid understanding of the causes and aims for which they are fighting, and at maintaining and strengthening their morale both as soldiers and as citizens. Some Lectures would deal with subjects directly related to the war, others with military, naval and political history, others with the allied countries, others again with science, literature, travel, or other subjects of general interest...It is obvious that men who are personally out of sympathy with the war and the national policy which it implies are hardly suitable for this work. Nor would any mere profession of orthodoxy in these matters be of much value. The committee hopes that its appeal will meet with a response from men who, whatever their differences on other subjects may be, are inspired by an active patriotism, and undertake this work in a spirit of service to the welfare of the British Empire and the victory of the Allied cause.[251]

Significantly, control over the scheme tightened with its resumption in the winter of 1917–18. Given that the intervening months had witnessed widespread mutinies in the French army, the rout of the dispirited Italian army at Caporetto, the collapse of the Russian army with the Bolshevik Revolution and symptoms of failing morale in the BEF, the authorities were keen to leave nothing to chance. Prof. C. Sanford Terry of the University of Aberdeen remembered an ominous briefing that he and three colleagues received at Boulogne in March 1918:

---

[247] *Ibid.*
[248] *Ibid.*, p. 8.
[249] *Ibid.*
[250] YMCA, K26 YMCA War Work No. 13. France. 'Lectures for the forces in France'.
[251] *Ibid.*

Major – , a young man probably half the age of the youngest among his audience, managed, with great tact, to convey the fact, without stating it, that we must mind our p's and q's, that GHQ had its eye upon us unblinkingly, and would pack us homeward with no compunction if we infringed the rules of conduct imparted to us by our mentor. Then the YMCA advised us from another, and sometimes challenging, angle, but also conveyed the impression that we were to work under the observation of a never-slumbering eye.[252]

It was symptomatic of the importance that was now attached to these 'special lecturers' by the military authorities that their numbers were increased (with twenty at work in the BEF at any one time between early January and late March), that their lecture tours were now extended to army areas and that their work was planned to continue 'throughout the fighting period of the summer'.[253] If the scheme was intended to become 'a constant feature of the recreational side [and] the beginning of the educational side of life in the fighting divisions',[254] the German spring offensive which commenced on 21 March led to its temporary curtailment. However, although its lecturers were reduced to a cadre of one in mid-April, by July 1918 the scheme had been fully revived and it continued 'without interruption' for the remainder of the war.[255] Exclusive of attendance figures in army areas, an estimated 73,000 soldiers attended its lectures in July 1918, a figure that had climbed to 114,000 by November.[256]

Evidently, some of these lecturers possessed plenty of force and charisma. Dr John Kelman, for example, a Presbyterian minister from Edinburgh, appears to have had a major impact on his audiences. In January 1917 he was reported by McCowen as having 'had a magnificent time in the Second Army';[257] that October, and having been released by his presbytery for a four-month stint on the Western Front,[258] Kelman had a tonic effect in Third Army area as well. According to R. G. MacDonald:

[I]n fourteen days he addressed thirty meetings with an audience averaging from five hundred to six hundred officers and men in each, and that in all he spoke to sixty to eighty Generals, some hundred Staff Officers, one thousand five hundred to two thousand Officers and from anything like twelve thousand to fifteen thousand men. In doing so he aroused the greatest enthusiasm and kindled to a flame the old ideas which were beginning to burn very low for many. Very many officers and men alike said how great an inspiration he had been and how great a tragedy it would be if his mission to the Army in the field were interrupted or ended.[259]

Among others, Kelman made a strong impression on Sir Douglas Haig, a fellow

[252] C. Sanford Terry, *Lectures at the Front* (Aberdeen, 1918), p. 2.
[253] Anon., *A short record of the educational work of the YMCA*, p. 8.
[254] *Ibid.*
[255] *Ibid.*
[256] *Ibid.*, p. 43.
[257] YMCA, K27 YMCA War Work No. 14. France. Oliver McCowen to A. K. Yapp, 16 January 1917.
[258] *Ibid.*, Oliver McCowen to A. K. Yapp, 10 January 1917.
[259] YMCA, K26 YMCA War Work No. 13. France. R. G. MacDonald to A. K. Yapp, 19 October 1917.

Scot and Presbyterian, and it was by dint of his efforts that McCowen was able to secure an interview with Haig in October 1917, at the height of the third battle of Ypres.[260]

In view of the clear significance of its educational and other work for the critical issue of morale, the YMCA was involved in top-level initiatives to bolster the flagging spirits of the BEF during and after the dismal autumn of 1917. The early autumn of 1917 saw the nadir of British morale on the Western Front, depths betrayed by the 'mutiny' at Etaples and by a wartime peak in executions for desertion.[261] Hence, Baron served as the YMCA's representative at a conference on morale that was convened by the deputy chaplain-general of the BEF, Bishop L. H. Gwynne, in mid-October. As a result of its deliberations, the Red Triangle was enlisted to help ensure that the soldiers' desire for far-reaching social change after the war was properly instructed, and channelled towards victory rather than revolution, through the concerted action of army chaplains and the Association's special lecturers.[262] Although the implementation of Gwynne's 'Scheme of Reconstruction' was largely frustrated by the German spring offensive of 1918, this collaboration in political education resulted (at the very least) in a publication entitled *Victory and after...?*, a pamphlet written by senior chaplains of the First Army and published by the Red Triangle in 1918.[263]

Besides its own 'special lecturers' programme and Bishop Gwynne's 'Scheme of Reconstruction', the YMCA was involved in other educational initiatives during the last year of the war. For example, such was the acknowledged lack of system in its educational work in the French bases that in the winter of 1917–18 the YMCA began to recruit the services of 'a limited number of professional teachers – one or two for each base – whose duty it was to start what classes they could in the YMCA huts'.[264] While this offered some scope for the structured and extended study of languages, history, maths and the sciences, a much larger project in which the YMCA became involved was the Army Education Scheme. Launched in June 1918, this sought to promote morale and discipline by creating an integrated system of voluntary adult education throughout the BEF, a system represented by new 'Active Service Army Schools'. While the military authorities were to implement the scheme in army areas, the Red Triangle was to be the sole 'agent of the Army in all educational matters' in the French bases. As part of an agreement reached with the War Office that May, the YMCA appointed Sir Henry Hadow ('one of the first educational experts in England') as its director of education in France and later appointed 'a sub-director of Education and a large staff of professional teachers' for each base,

[260] YMCA, K27 YMCA War Work No. 14. France. O. McCowen to A. K. Yapp, 17 October 1917.
[261] D. Englander, 'Discipline and morale in the British army, 1917–1918', in *State, society and mobilization in Europe during the First World War*, ed. J. Horne (Cambridge, 1997), pp. 139–40.
[262] Church Missionary Society Archives, University of Birmingham (hereafter CMS), XCMS ACC 18/F1/50–4, Diaries of L. H. Gwynne, 18–19 October 1917; Snape, *God and the British soldier*, pp. 109–11.
[263] YMCA, K24 YMCA War Work No. 4. Religious. *Victory and after...?*, 1918.
[264] Anon., *A short record of the educational work of the YMCA*, p. 9.

all of whom 'would be engaged in England specially for this work'.[265] While a newly created YMCA Universities Committee oversaw the work from London, the Red Triangle made another huge financial commitment by agreeing to provide 'secretarial and clerical staff', by meeting 'the cost of the maintenance, travelling expenses, and fees of lecturers and teachers' and by supplying 'the buildings, equipment and libraries required'.[266] The coherence of the scheme across base and army areas was enhanced by the use of an agreed reading list of 'about a hundred textbooks' and was assisted by the appointment of army education officers. In the bases of the BEF, their responsibilities included identifying officers and other ranks to act as teachers or lecturers, liaising between base commandants and their sub-directors of education and compiling weekly returns on educational activities.[267] According to Hadow, the objectives of the scheme's broad curriculum were essentially military, vocational and political:

(1) To raise and maintain moral [sic] among the troops.
(2) To develop the study of the privileges and duties of Citizenship of the British Empire.
(3) To prepare for the return to civil life:-
    (a) By learning again what has been forgotten.
    (b) By carrying on studies which have been laid aside.
    (c) By taking up new studies, e.g. languages, or for those who contemplate a change to out-door life, agriculture, carpentry, etc.
    (d) By acquiring a theoretical knowledge of a trade which has been practised.[268]

Despite the terminal impact of the Armistice, the YMCA's participation in the Army Education Scheme continued until the end of April 1919 and it was generally regarded as the crowning achievement of a much greater educational effort. As early as June 1918 over 4,000 soldiers were attending its classes, a number that had more than trebled by November before falling to just over 8,000 the following February.[269] Praised by the Adult Education Committee of the Ministry of Reconstruction in its report on 'Education in the Army' (July 1918),[270] in an encomium of May 1919 the president of the Board of Education, H. A. L. Fisher, underlined the true extent of the Association's wartime achievements in the field of education:

The experiment of organizing educational work upon the Lines of Communication of our Armies in the field was, so far as I know, entirely novel in character, and it was undoubtedly worked in circumstances of peculiar difficulty...[The YMCA] divined and did their best to satisfy a real hunger for

---

[265] *Ibid.*
[266] *Ibid.*, p. 10.
[267] *Ibid.*, pp. 16–18.
[268] *Ibid.*, p. 15.
[269] *Ibid.*, p. 31.
[270] Parliamentary Papers, *Ministry of Reconstruction. Second interim report of the Adult Education Committee, 'Education in the army'* (1918), p. 4.

intellectual improvement among our troops. To them, and to the Army Authorities in France, under whom they worked, belongs the credit of introducing and developing the largest system of adult education which has ever at any one time been launched from this country.[271]

Tensions

Despite the YMCA's close and deepening relationship with the military authorities, theirs was by no means an untroubled partnership, however. Barclay Baron found Brigadier-General (later Major-General) J. J. Asser to be an insufferable tyrant at Le Havre and, as an army secretary, he had very different experiences of Sir Henry Rawlinson and Sir Herbert Plumer as army commanders, especially when Rawlinson turned against Gwynne's 'Scheme of Reconstruction' and its proponents in the winter of 1917–18.[272] Furthermore, the Association's ultimate reliance on the sympathetic patronage of senior officers could not overcome some major practical problems, especially given its unofficial status. As one secretary observed:

> The YMCA has, of course, no official standing in a military area...We have to depend for water, for transport, for rations, for orderlies to help, for indeed everything, except actual supplies, on the indulgence of the Army. The Commanding Officers are generally very appreciative [and] they are helpful as far as they can. But after all, the Army has a war on, and a division's shell and shrapnel are more important in the war than the YMCA buns and biscuits. Hence complications arise that try the patience of a leader. If a division would be content to remain sitting comfortably round, our problems would be simple; we could depend on trained orderlies, and on all that is needed to make things go smoothly. But, sad to say, the divisions have often business elsewhere, and they up and forsake us and leave confusion behind, for they take their orderlies and their water-carts and their lorries, and many other helpful things and people.[273]

In a similar vein, R. H. MacDonald complained from Third Army area in February 1917 that:

> The development of our work in this area has been retarded by many difficulties. The most serious one of late has been common to all the Centres in France, except Havre, the lack of railway transport, causing a famine for stores in practically all our Huts, and delaying the opening of several through lack of equipment. Even after the arrival of trucks our transport troubles are still insistent owing to the anomalous position we are in. On the ground of military necessity and the lack of transport no military transport can be detailed for the conveyance of our goods. On the other hand, to limit the use of petrol and also unofficial transport on the road, we are forbidden the possession of a lorry... No civilian cartage is available. We are therefore forced

---

[271] Anon., *A short record of the educational work of the YMCA*, p. 5.
[272] CMS, Diaries of L. H. Gwynne, 30–1 January 1918, 4 February 1918.
[273] MacNair, 'Sketches from the Front'.

to subsist on the charity of friends, who have never failed us so far, but often find it considerably difficult to help us.[274]

However, if the pressures of war caused logistical headaches they could also create less palatable problems. The sexual misadventures of the British soldier in France meant that a maternity home for French girls had to be established at Le Havre, an institution that was kept secret from the military authorities as it plainly exceeded their understanding of YMCA army work.[275] Furthermore, the army's perennial battle against venereal disease meant that Barclay Baron was approached with a view to installing a disinfecting station in a Red Triangle centre in Amiens.[276] Similar pressure was also exerted for the YMCA to abandon its blanket ban on playing cards and alcohol on its premises. On both accounts, senior YMCA figures in France found themselves caught between the military authorities (who were naturally keen to maximize the appeal of the Association's facilities) and the sensitivities of the WEC at home. In November 1915, for example, L. G. Pilkington received an admonitory letter from A. K. Yapp on the subject of playing cards:

> The question of cards as raised in your letter was discussed at the War Emergency Committee yesterday, and it was then agreed that we must re-affirm the decision previously laid down. We all agree about this. I am so sorry that there should be differences between you and us about this, but it is a matter of firm conviction with us that it would be unwise to introduce them into our YMCA centres.[277]

If the spectre of gambling was thereby kept at bay, the serving of alcohol on premises used by officers and their relatives proved to be a constant bone of contention between the WEC and its more pragmatic representatives in France. As early as January 1915, Pilkington had requested permission for the sale of alcohol in his planned officers' club at Le Havre:

> If the YMCA put up an officers' club, may we sell intoxicants there? It will be a great help if we can because it will help a lot of young officers to stay in camp instead of going into town where [there] is grave danger of their being caught by women…If intoxicants are sold it will be warmly supported by all the best officers and they will take good care that it is not abused. Let me know what you decide as soon as possible as the site has been given and plans must be prepared.[278]

This request met with a curt refusal from Yapp, a staunch teetotaller,[279] who replied: 'Quite frankly I would rather see the place an admitted failure and set apart later on for the use of the troops, than do what I believe would be absolutely

[274] YMCA, K26 YMCA War Work No. 13. France. 'Report on YMCA Work in Third Army area', 12 February 1917.
[275] See Chapter 1, pp. 112–13.
[276] See Chapter 1, p. 112.
[277] *Ibid.*, A. K. Yapp to L. G. Pilkington, 2 November 1915.
[278] *Ibid.*, L. G. Pilkington to A. K. Yapp, 31 January 1915.
[279] *ODNB.*

wrong and indefensible from a National as well as from a moral standpoint.'[280] In a further letter Yapp went on to explain the dire implications of such a concession:

> As [the] YMCA it would be impossible for us to sell intoxicants. The question of principle is involved, and apart from everything else we should alienate the sympathy of many of our best and keenest supporters if we did anything of the kind. I am not convinced in my own mind that it would be impossible for the hut to be made a great success without intoxicants, so that I think we should proceed with the hut at once, and say the other matter is under consideration.[281]

However, the issue could not be set aside indefinitely as the army's sense of propriety and hierarchy was offended by the notion that officers could be treated as were the other ranks in this matter. In September 1916, therefore, the issue was once again broached by Oliver McCowen, who explained to Yapp:

> It is...impossible to render the best service to officers who come [to the Officers' Club] for meals unless we recognize that in this country no one drinks water unless they are quite sure of its origin, and practically everyone drinks the light wine of the country. We are handicapping the success of the Club by our present position in this respect. Two Generals came in to dinner the other night and when they asked for some light wine and were told they could not be supplied, they got up and went out. I should not recommend that these things should be supplied in England where customs are entirely different, but I feel very strongly that we should make a change in France. I am absolutely certain that we are doing ourselves more harm than good, as men are coming in and saying that the stand we are taking in this matter is in line with the reputation which we had before the War.[282]

Caught between conflicting pressures, Yapp's response was to prevaricate:

> [I]t is quite possible that we may be handicapping the success of the Officers' Club in Havre by making it a teetotal show, but I think we should be handicapping the success of our whole work in France and elsewhere if we yielded on this point...Of course, I do not know the conditions as well as you do, and it may be that the type of white wine you suggest would not contain more alcohol than ginger beer for instance. If that is the case I do not see any reason why it should not be supplied, i.e. if it is not intoxicating, even though it might be called wine, but otherwise I think we should remain firm.[283]

However, the crisis deepened with the revelation that wine was already being served, if not sold, on an officers-only basis in France. This news elicited a protest from E. C. Carter, the American-born national secretary of the Indian YMCA and a member of the National Council, who wrote to McCowen objecting that this was a dangerous precedent to set, that it was unfair to ordinary soldiers and that it would compromise the Association's involvement in any attempts 'to

[280] YMCA, K26 YMCA War Work No. 13. France. A. K. Yapp to L. G. Pilkington, undated.
[281] *Ibid.*, A. K. Yapp to L. G. Pilkington, 3 February 1915.
[282] YMCA, K27 YMCA War Work No. 14. France. O. McCowen to A. K. Yapp, 18 September 1916.
[283] *Ibid.*, A. K. Yapp to O. McCowen, 28 September 1916.

suppress the liquor trade in England during the war'. He also urged that more effort should be made 'to supply the very best French and English table and mineral waters'.[284] McCowen, however, was undismayed and unrepentant, retorting that

> The liquor traffic in England has grown into one of the greatest social evils of the present day. The custom in France of drinking light wines at meals has never become a social evil, or a public question. The two stand on a totally different basis, and this must be borne in mind in deciding our policy... We have to set up safeguards for Tommy because he has not got the social safeguard of the General, or the Officer. We should lose in the estimation of Tommy if we did provide liquor for him. This, however, does not apply to the provision of light wines to officers with meals. The attempt to make them teetotal is very much resented, and we lose tremendously in their estimation in attempting to do so.[285]

Significantly, there were no further repercussions for McCowen; in the end, and as if by the tacit consent of those concerned, the issue was allowed to drop, Carter terminating his involvement by stating his position to Yapp: 'I sympathize with McCowen in his predicament in this matter, though I do not agree with him.'[286]

Wider work and broader horizons

Despite the scale and importance of its work at hundreds of centres in the bases and with the armies of the BEF, these labours comprised only part – albeit the major part – of the work of the Red Triangle with and for the soldiers of the British army; significantly, of the 2,000 YMCA centres open for their benefit at the beginning of 1918, only a quarter were located in France or Belgium.[287] In addition to its centres on the Western Front and in Great Britain itself, the Red Triangle was also well represented in the war's so-called 'sideshows', including the Dardanelles, Salonika, Mesopotamia, Italy and East Africa (where it enjoyed a local monopoly of the British army's 'dry' canteens).[288] Beyond the Western Front, its beneficial presence was perhaps most keenly felt in Egypt and Palestine. As F. A. McKenzie wrote:

> The work in Egypt presented some of the most spectacular sides of the YMCA campaign. In Cairo the famous Esbekieh Gardens, skating-rink, and open-air theatre were taken over and made into a great centre of social life. The movement spread to wherever the British Army went around the [Sinai] Peninsula. YMCA men accompanied the Army across the desert to Palestine and a YMCA branch was opened in Jerusalem not many hours after [General

[284] Ibid., E. C. Carter to O. McCowen, 30 October 1916.
[285] Ibid., O. McCowen to E. C. Carter, 3 November 1916.
[286] Ibid., E. C. Carter to A. K. Yapp, 8 November 1916.
[287] McKenzie, 'Welfare work', p. 404.
[288] The Red Triangle Bulletin, 6 June 1919, p. 3; McKenzie, 'Welfare work', p. 404; YMCA, J7 National Council signed minutes, 14 July 1916.

Allenby] moved through. At the Kargeh Oasis, away west of Mersa Matruh towards the [Libyan] frontier, the YMCA planted itself with the British outposts. It had its stations all along the Suez Canal…here were many camps around Alexandria, and at Sidi Bishr there was a very large rest camp for men exhausted by their desert work.[289]

Similarly, while Lena Ashwell's concert parties earned a formidable reputation on the Western Front, their shows represented only a fraction of an estimated 186,000 concerts that were given by 'professional artists' under YMCA auspices across the world and over the course of the war.[290] Finally, while approved lecturers were sent to enlighten the troops in France, the Association sent others as far afield as Egypt, Italy, Salonika and India as part of an educational service that would eventually cost the YMCA at least £120,000.[291]

The ubiquity of the YMCA was only matched by the sheer diversity of its work. While R. G. MacDonald aptly described the typical YMCA secretary on the Western Front as 'the handy man par excellence',[292] in 1917 a Presbyterian army chaplain in Mesopotamia marvelled that: 'There was no limit to their beneficent activities. They were there to promote the physical, moral, social, and spiritual well-being of the soldiers; and as far as the interests of the lads were concerned, it may truly be said that "nothing was alien to them."'[293] In addition to the versatility of its workers (one of whom even facilitated the transfer of a British national from the ranks of the French Foreign Legion to those of the British army)[294] YMCA publications also adjusted to the needs of the time. *YM. The British Empire YMCA Weekly*, an illustrated magazine for soldiers, commenced publication in January 1915, eventually being renamed *The Red Triangle: The British Empire YMCA Weekly*. Priced at a penny a copy, it featured an array of national and Association news, personal commentary, cartoons and biographies. A representative issue of January 1917 included a glossary of terms used by R. W. Service in his popular *Ballads of a Chechaco* and *Rhymes of a sour-dough*, an article on F. C. Selous ('A mighty hunter') and some 'Football reminiscences' of 'An old county player'.[295] Indeed, such was the popularity of the magazine that, in order to cope with the sheer volume of news and information it received, it was superseded in September 1917 by the monthly *Red Triangle* and by a weekly news supplement known as *The Red Triangle Bulletin*.[296]

The comprehensive nature of the Association's army work also embraced soldiers who were absent on leave, the incapacitated, internees and even the female personnel of the Women's Army Auxiliary Corps. Wholesome

---

[289] McKenzie, 'Welfare work', pp. 406–7.
[290] Yapp, *In the service of youth*, p. 85
[291] *Ibid.*, pp. 88–9.
[292] YMCA, K26 YMCA War Work No. 13. France. R. G. MacDonald to A. K. Yapp, undated.
[293] W. Ewing, *From Gallipoli to Baghdad* (London, 1917), p. 254.
[294] YMCA, K26 YMCA War Work No. 13. S. Hyde-Coleman to A. K. Yapp, 1 February 1915.
[295] *Red Triangle*, 12 January 1917, pp. 6–8.
[296] *Red Triangle*, 27 July 1917, p. 675.

accommodation was provided in London and, while a YMCA hotel and information bureau were also opened in Paris, in London teams of vigilant YMCA volunteers were at hand to guide and even transport visitors and those in transit, a notable aspect of this work being the motorized patrols that roved the capital at night in order to snatch the tempted and unwary from harm's way.[297] By 1916, the Association was running an Employment Bureau for discharged servicemen through which 'hundreds of men were brought into touch with employers and saved from the necessity of tramping about in search of work';[298] this facility (which was run by L. G. Pilkington following his move from Le Havre) was extended after the Armistice, when it secured positions for more than 37,000 demobilized servicemen.[299] The Association was also sensitive to the needs of British troops who, whether as escapees or as invalids, found themselves in the custody of neutral powers, the Dutch and Swiss authorities allowing the Red Triangle to open huts in their internment camps.[300] With the formation of the WAAC in 1917, its commander formally requested that the Young Women's Christian Association 'do for the women in khaki what the YMCA had done for the men'. Consequently, twelve centres were opened for the use of WAAC personnel under their joint auspices, 'the two triangles, red and blue, being displayed side by side'.[301]

A great deal of the Association's energy was also lavished upon soldiers' families. Among the facilities offered by the YMCA hut at Waterloo Station was an annexe for women who had come to London to welcome their husbands home on leave or to bid them farewell on their return to France.[302] Furthermore, from its wartime headquarters in Tottenham Court Road the Red Triangle ran an inquiry service for the relatives of soldiers who were reported missing in action. A 'Missing soldiers' column was a regular feature of *YM* and *The Red Triangle* and, until America entered the war in April 1917, its inquiries were assisted by the American YMCA, which had access to details of prisoners of war in Germany.[303] The pangs of separation were also assuaged by the YMCA's 'Snapshots from Home League'. This organization recruited the help of thousands of amateur photographers in taking photographs of the families and friends of British servicemen. By May 1917 '650,000 soldiers had been supplied with photographs as a result of the effort' and, once again:

> This work was performed without charge. Men of HM Forces were supplied with forms upon which they stated that they desired photos of their wife, parents or sweetheart living in the place specified. These were returned to the YMCA Snapshots League [and] forwarded to the nearest voluntary helper.

---

[297] Yapp, *Romance of the Red Triangle*, pp. 177–8, 180–1; Anon., 'The work of the YMCA', pp. 188–91.
[298] Anon., 'The work of the YMCA', p. 191.
[299] YMCA, J7 National Council signed minutes, 11 January 1918; Yapp, *In the service of youth*, p. 132.
[300] McKenzie, 'Welfare work', p. 407.
[301] *Ibid.*, pp. 419–20.
[302] Anon., 'The work of the YMCA', p. 190.
[303] See, for example, *YM*, 24 November 1916, p. 1098; Anon., 'The work of the YMCA', p. 191.

When the photos were prepared the photographer dispatched copies in special weatherproof envelopes to the soldier in France, Salonika, Egypt or elsewhere.[304]

However, the most poignant work on behalf of soldiers and their families was the YMCA's visitation scheme. This commenced in June 1915 with the opening of a YMCA hostel in France for the use of civilians wishing to visit dangerously wounded relatives in base hospitals. By January 1919, the number of these hostels had increased to ten with the number of visitors averaging 150 a week, these being hosted by the Red Triangle entirely free of charge.[305] One sad recipient of this hospitality expressed his thanks to the Association as follows:

> It was a sad home-coming, but we shall never forget the privilege we had in being able to come over and see our loved one before parting from us. We shall never forget also the kindness and never ending sympathy shown to us whilst at [Camiers]. Although my visit was naturally a painful one it was made more bearable by the kindness and sympathy shown by you and all those who are associated with you in your gracious work, and I cannot thank you sufficiently for your goodness to both my wife and myself.[306]

Not surprisingly, alongside its battlefield assistance to the wounded it was this aspect of the Association's wartime work that was most highly esteemed by the British public.[307] As R. J. Campbell (who had served as a YMCA worker in France) explained in 1916:

> Amongst the fine things being done by the YMCA there is none finer than the shepherding of the relatives of the wounded who are officially allowed to visit their boys at the various bases...When a brave lad is giving his life for his country, and is too grievously hurt to be able to go and breathe his last in the home that sent him forth, it is no more than a public duty to bring father or mother, wife or sister to visit him near to the scene of his sacrifice and say farewell if such it is to be. But when these people are poor, as they frequently are, and unaccustomed to going far from their own doors, the very prospect of journeying to a foreign land where war is raging, and finding their way about among people who speak in a strange tongue, is apt to be somewhat alarming...Here is where the YMCA steps in. Its representatives meet these rather bewildered folk on the quays, convey them in motor cars to YMCA hostels provided for the purpose, obtain the necessary permits for them, and pass them on in the same way to whatever centres they are making for. Arrived there they are taken charge of by the YMCA workers as before, comfortably housed and fed, conducted to the hospitals where their wounded lie, and in short looked after from first to last during their brief stay. It is a beautiful mode of service, and one of which it is impossible to speak too highly.[308]

---

[304] YMCA, J7 National Council signed minutes, 4 May 1917; Anon., 'The work of the YMCA', pp. 191–2.
[305] YMCA, K27 YMCA War Work No. 14. France. 'The latest YMCA statistics', 20 January 1919.
[306] YMCA, K40 Typescript extracts of letters of appreciation. Anon., undated.
[307] Yapp, *In the service of youth*, p. 90.
[308] R. J. Campbell, *With our troops in France* (London, 1916), pp. 40–2.

Such was the expansive nature of its work among and for the military that many beneficiaries of the Red Triangle were neither British nor even Christian. The arrival of the Indian Corps in France in autumn 1914 and the temptations that assailed Indian troops in Marseilles quickly prompted the WEC to take remedial action. As Joseph Callan, an Indian secretary on the ground, warned:

> Our party of eleven including four Indians arrived here on the 8th [November]. Permission has been granted for us to remain here and to begin work for the Indian sepoy. This [has] already become so serious that the Officers of Indian regiments are anxious for someone to co-operate with them in helping to keep the troops from immorality…This is the worst that can happen for India and Christian Missions there. If this great army of men goes back to India with such an idea of civilization in the Christian West, then there will scarcely be a village in Northern India where the missionary will not be hindered in his work.[309]

Within a week, however, McCowen was able to report that 'an ideal plant' was now ready for 'the Indian work', this comprising of 'Three cosy double fly marquees end on, and boarded.' Furthermore, the YMCA had also secured 'free permission for visiting and intermingling with the Troops'.[310] Although of a delicate nature due to the volatile religious sensibilities of Indian troops and somewhat curtailed by the withdrawal of most of the Indian Corps from France the following year, work with Indian cavalrymen, gunners and labourers continued on a smaller scale on the Western Front for the remainder of the war.[311]

If long-term missionary concerns led the WEC to take the Indian Corps under its wing in France, the same was also true of the Chinese Labour Corps, which began to arrive in 1917. Despite a difficult start caused by insufficient staff, depleted stores and the German spring offensive, by the end of 1918 it was reported that fourteen centres for the CLC were now in operation and that canteens, English language classes, theatrical performances and cinema shows were in full swing. In common with its work among Indian labour companies, this progress was greatly facilitated by effective leadership provided by a partnership of experienced British missionaries and native YMCA secretaries. However, once again, and in the interests of good order, direct evangelism was eschewed in favour of Christian service, it being noted that among the gangers and 'educated Chinese' were men 'who, by their education are bound to have much influence in China when they get back' and who would be well disposed to Christianity because of their experiences in France. The situation was expressed in the following exchange: 'To what extent has Christianity been brought before the labourers? a Chinese YMCA man was asked. "Through the YMCA at any rate," was the reply, "they will have seen Christianity on *active service*."'[312]

---

[309] YMCA, K26 YMCA War Work No. 13. Joseph Callan to A. K. Yapp, 17 November 1914.
[310] *Ibid.*, O. McCowen to A. K. Yapp, 24 November 1914.
[311] YMCA, K27 YMCA War Work No. 14. France. O. McCowen to A. K. Yapp, 17 October 1917; *Statistics of the military effort of the British Empire*, pp. 160–1.
[312] YMCA, K26 YMCA War Work No. 13. '1918. Chinese work'.

Some similar hopes were also entertained of work with the Portuguese Expeditionary Force. This also arrived on the Western Front in 1917, a force that was trained and largely equipped by Britain and which served in the British sector under British command. Possibly encouraged by anticlerical persecution of the Catholic church in Portugal and by its premier's confident assertion that Catholicism would be extirpated 'in two generations',[313] the YMCA prepared for the arrival of Portuguese troops by allotting them huts, recruiting workers in Portugal and securing the services of a director who had served as a YMCA secretary in Brazil; 'The Portuguese Authorities', it was noted in October 1917, 'are giving all facilities.'[314] However, if there were proselytizing undertones to work with the hapless soldiers of the PEF, a very different approach was adopted towards the Catholic Belgians. Fighting on home soil, operating with a greater degree of independence from their British allies and with the Catholic church in Belgium strongly identified with Belgian patriotism, the religious dimensions of YMCA work among Belgian troops were conspicuous by their absence. Inaugurated in the last year of the war, a telling description of the opening ceremony for the first hut for Belgian soldiers was sent to Yapp in September 1918. Written by P. H. S. Sitters (now identified as 'one of Mr McCowen's right-hand men in France')[315] it was clear from the attendant speeches that the driving force was one of sheer admiration for Belgian resilience. As Sitters explained in his effusive address to General Dubrel:

> [T]he gift of this YMCA hut was an expression of the gratitude which the British people felt toward Belgium for the magnificent stand she had made in the cause of justice and freedom [and] we were out to do all we possibly could by means of canteens, concerts, lectures etc. to promote the welfare of Belgian troops [and] in our huts they would find at all times a most cordial welcome.[316]

Besides these deliberate attempts to embrace other national, and indeed religious, groups, the British YMCA on the Western Front also found itself in close collaboration with its counterparts from the Dominions, the United States and France. While J. J. Virgo, the national field secretary of the YMCA, completed a 60,000 mile global tour in 1917 in order 'to bring about closer cooperation between the home organizations and associations throughout the Empire',[317] the relatively static nature of YMCA work and the shifting nature of its different national constituencies on the Western Front virtually demanded co-operation of this kind. As one visitor to France wrote in 1917:

> At every wayside Camp and halting-place, the sign of the Red Triangle is seen [and the] international character of the work becomes apparent. Where a Canadian Division has recently been camped one finds the huts of the

[313] N. Perry and L. Echeverría, *Under the heel of Mary* (London, 1988), p. 183.
[314] YMCA, K27 YMCA War Work No. 14. France. O. McCowen to A. K. Yapp, 17 October 1917; *The Red Triangle Bulletin*, 8 March 1918, p. 3.
[315] *The Red Triangle Bulletin*, 18 January 1918, p. 4.
[316] YMCA, K26 YMCA War Work No. 13. P. H. S. Sitters to A. K. Yapp, 5 September 1918.
[317] *Times*, 24 July 1917, p. 3.

Canadian YMCA, now working with British brigades, and staffed by British secretaries. Further on, one comes across English huts, with Canadian brigades, staffed and supplied by the Canadian Headquarters. An American tent by the wayside, with the advance guard of the American troops, is side by side with a long-established English centre for the British troops that still predominate in the neighbourhood. The best of good feeling and close co-operation everywhere exists, and councils are frequently held with a view to avoiding overlapping, with its attendant waste of time, energy and supplies.[318]

By 1918, and with the build-up of the American Expeditionary Force, YMCA work among the Anglophone components of the Allied armies in France was being co-ordinated at the highest levels. In March, *The Red Triangle Bulletin* reported that 'An International Conference of YMCA workers was held the other day in Paris, when representatives of the American, Canadian, Australian, New Zealand, and British YMCA's met together for two days to pool their experience and concert measures for the future.'[319]

Significantly, co-operation with the French demonstrated just how well off the British YMCA actually was in terms of its material and human resources. In January 1916, and even before the effects of the battle of Verdun were felt, Yapp received the following briefing from S. Hyde-Coleman, his informant in Paris:

> You will be glad to learn that the French work is really progressing. It goes by the name of the 'Foyer du Soldat' and the French National Council have established 14 places at various points...Some of these little Huts are within two miles of the firing line. The workers are attached to the 'service auxiliare' of the Army, and wear a distinctive uniform with F.S. in monogram on the gorget patches. Some of them are men who have been wounded and incapacitated; in one instance a worker in charge has had an arm amputated and has received the [Croix de Guerre].[320]

Following his move southward with Fifth Army early in 1918, Harold Down noted that Fifth Army YMCA took over several huts previously run by 'the Franco-American Foyer-du-Soldat (The YMCA with the French Army)'. It also opened an additional hut for the use of French troops at Foreste.[321] If the potential of the French YMCA was seriously limited by the small number of Protestants in France, its activities took place under the aegis of the French Red Cross and were bound by its iron rule that, owing to the dismal pay of the French soldier, 'nothing may be charged for'.[322]

[318] YMCA, K26 YMCA War Work No. 13. France. 'G.R.C.', *Memoranda of a visit to France*, undated, p. 6.
[319] *The Red Triangle Bulletin*, 8 March 1918, p. 3.
[320] YMCA, K26 YMCA War Work No. 13. France. S. Hyde-Coleman to A. K. Yapp, 18 January 1916.
[321] YMCA, K26 YMCA War Work No. 13. France. H. A. Down, 'Pioneering on the Western Front. 3½ years with the YMCA', pp. 26–7.
[322] L. Binyon, 'Canteens in France', www.greatwardifferent.com/Great_War/Nurses_6/Canteens. Consulted 10 September 2008.

Matters spiritual

Amidst all of this (largely) disinterested philanthropy, and in keeping with the threefold symbolism of the Red Triangle, the YMCA did not neglect the spiritual dimension of its work with the British army. In YMCA huts the business of the day was normally concluded with 'family prayers', a short, informal service usually consisting of a hymn, a prayer and the national anthem. In addition, and whenever possible, its centres held their own Sunday evening services led by YMCA workers or friendly army chaplains.[323] The Association was also active in publishing and distributing millions of tracts, testaments, hymnbooks, prayer books, prayer cards and abstinence pledge cards.[324] However, while much of this literature was available free of charge, indiscriminate distributions were discouraged and even the Association's wartime edition of the New Testament ('a nicely-printed pocket edition, bearing the Red Triangle on the cover') was to be had only on request.[325] A good deal of caution was also exercised in the distribution of tracts, for as Yapp explained:

> I found it very difficult to obtain tracts which would appeal to the men and at the same time contained anything like a definite spiritual message. Sometimes grants reached us of most unsuitable literature. On one of my visits to France I came across a large supply that had somehow got through, entitled 'Thoughts for the Aged and Invalids'... During the first six months of the War I used to write a new religious booklet every Sunday morning. They were brightly illustrated, and couched in language that plain men could understand; as far as possible, I avoided religious phraseology, but tried to get in a direct and helpful message. More than two millions of these booklets were distributed; we did not deal them out haphazard, but the men had to come and ask for them if they wanted them.[326]

Naturally, Yapp's aim of promoting a more progressive and inclusive image of the Association was a long-term goal and, given its evangelical character and constituency, early in the war a revivalist atmosphere naturally set the tone of many of the services held on YMCA premises. As one Wesleyan chaplain wrote wistfully in 1917:

> In the early days of the war at Aldershot, and later also on Salisbury Plain, one remembers the packed chapels and YMCA huts, the Holy Crusade spirit of the men, the mighty volume of fervent song, the rich, melting after-meetings, the numerous conversions, the many vows of the warriors going forth to fight for the cause of God in a strange land.[327]

Likewise, Laughlan Maclean Watt, a Scottish Presbyterian minister who had been

---

[323] Anon., 'The work of the YMCA', pp. 183–4; Yapp, *Romance of the Red Triangle*, p. 212.
[324] YMCA, K24 YMCA War Work No. 4. Religious. YMCA publications during war time; Yapp, *Romance of the Red Triangle*, p. 212.
[325] Yapp, *Romance of the Red Triangle*, p. 212; Yapp, *In the service of youth*, pp. 110–11.
[326] Yapp, *In the service of youth*, pp. 109–10.
[327] T. L. B. Westerdale, *Messages from Mars: a chaplain's experiences at the Front* (London, 1917), p. 86.

engaged by the YMCA to serve as 'a roving missioner' around the bases of the BEF,[328] recalled that:

> When I was out first, at the beginning of the war, nothing impressed me more than the deep atmosphere of devotion which pervaded the men in the camps. This was, after all, most natural, for the men who were carried oversea on the first wave of the movement were the absolute cream of the country, borne out of the professions and the trades on a great impulse of enthusiasm, stirred to the depth by the noblest ideals...Volunteers in every great cause are always idealists. The tide of religion that swept over them was like a vast contagion of enthusiasm; and one can never forget what it meant in the YMCA huts, and places where prayer was wont to be made.[329]

YMCA leaders in France were at first firmly convinced that a religious revival was taking hold among the men of the BEF. In February 1915, McCowen informed Yapp of a centre at Le Havre where there had been 'quite a movement among the men, between 50 and 60 have definitely entered the Christian life'.[330] The following month he went on to write:

> You will, I know, be glad and thankful to learn of the sound religious work that is going on in our huts. I have already told you of the work at the Remount camp. In our large double hut in Camp 15, scores of men have received very definite blessing; this is also true of Camp No. 10.[331]

A few weeks later, P. H. S. Sitters noted that religious work at Le Havre was booming among YMCA staff and soldiers alike:

> You will be delighted to know that we are building up a strong spiritual work in Havre. Since your visit we have started a weekly prayer meeting. The 'Quiet Room' at Headquarters draws an ever-increasing number of our helpers. All these opportunities for prayer and meditation are being well taken advantage of by our workers and the result is seen in the great number of conversions taking place in the various camps. During the past fortnight I have been able to start work in six hospitals. It is badly needed, the men having nothing to do find the time hangs heavily. Most of them have been at the front and looked into the face of Death, consequently they are ready to listen to the message of Christ.[332]

Indeed, it was in order to maximize and consolidate these apparent gains that the Religious Work Committee of the YMCA launched its War Roll scheme at Easter 1915. Its signatories were required to take the following pledge: 'I hereby pledge my allegiance to the Lord Jesus Christ as my Saviour and King, and by God's help will fight His battles for the Victory of His Kingdom.' Signatories also gave their name and number, their regiment, home address, denomination and the name of their local church or chapel. In time, they received a welcoming letter

---

[328] *YM*, 19 February 1915, p. 128, and 2 April 1915, p. 268.
[329] L. Maclean Watt, *In France and Flanders with the fighting men* (London, 1917), pp. 72–3.
[330] YMCA, K26 YMCA War Work No. 13. France. O. McCowen to A. K. Yapp, 22 February 1915.
[331] *Ibid.*, O. McCowen to A. K. Yapp, 15 March 1915.
[332] *Ibid.*, P. H. S. Sitters to A. K. Yapp, 26 April 1915.

and a membership card. By December 1915, the scheme had produced 30,000 signatures;[333] however, by the end of 1917 this number had risen to more than 300,000, with 10,000 letters of welcome being sent out that October alone.[334] By the end of the war, the total number of signatories may have reached as many as 500,000.[335] While seeking to confirm soldiers in their faith, a secondary goal of the scheme was to lend substance to the Association's claim to be an auxiliary of the churches. If this consideration dictated the loose phraseology of the pledge (which Yapp termed 'a simple declaration of faith and resolve' that was nevertheless 'sufficiently definite to be of use')[336] it also required that the names of signatories were forwarded 'to the headquarters of each denomination', an exercise that triggered, so it was claimed, thousands of pastoral visits to homes across the country.[337] The same logic also meant that by 1918 the YMCA was lending a helping hand to some very unlikely partners; an internal memorandum noted that 'Cards are accepted for, and distributed to all denominations, including Unitarians, Swedenborgians and the smaller sects; while a special arrangement has been made with the Rev. Father Plater, S.J. to keep in touch with Roman Catholic Soldiers who sign the cards, through the Catholic Social Guild.'[338] Eventually, this rationale saw the scheme subsumed into a consolidated War Roll that was inaugurated following a meeting at Lambeth Palace between representatives of the YMCA, the Church Army, the Church of England's Men's Society and the League of the Spiritual War.[339]

Nevertheless, the Red Triangle's War Roll clearly attracted some eminent supporters. Among its signatories was Sir William Robertson, chief of the Imperial General Staff (and thus the Empire's top soldier) from December 1915 to February 1918.[340] Furthermore, its burgeoning appeal seems to indicate that the British army's late war conscripts were no less susceptible to religious influences than were its regulars, volunteers and Territorials in the early war period.[341] Still, while its signatories may have represented almost 10 per cent of the 5,700,000 men who served in the British army during the First World War,[342] judging the success of the scheme is problematic. In 1916, an analysis of 241 War Rolls by the WEC revealed that, of more than 24,000 signatories, a quarter 'gave no indication of any Church relationship, or desire to join any denomination'.[343] Given this and other factors (notably the support of the previously committed, to say nothing of the perennial dangers of backsliding)

[333] *YM*, 10 December 1915, p. 1149.
[334] *The Red Triangle Bulletin*, 5 October 1917, p. 1, and 9 November 1917, p. 5.
[335] Yapp, *Romance of the Red Triangle*, p. 212.
[336] A. K. Yapp, 'Our outlook', *The Red Triangle*, 11 May 1917, p. 423.
[337] *The Red Triangle Bulletin*, 5 October 1917, p. 1.
[338] YMCA, K24 YMCA War Work No. 4. Religious. 'Memorandum of YMCA War Roll work', 1918.
[339] *Ibid.*, *What is the War Roll?*, n.d.
[340] Bourne (ed.), *Who's who in World War One*, pp. 250–1; YMCA, J7 National Council signed minutes, 3 May 1918.
[341] Snape, *God and the British soldier*, p. 160.
[342] Simkins, 'The four armies', p. 241.
[343] YMCA, J7 National Council signed minutes, 3 November 1916.

the Association was inclined to treat its results with caution. In 1918 a YMCA memorandum on the War Roll hedged that

> It is not claimed that all the names of the men who sign these cards are pure conversions. Many are re-affirmations of faith; some are for the encouragement of others, while a small proportion have little meaning at all. Even so, each card is of value, because it enables ministers to get [into] direct touch not only with the man's home, but also with the man himself, and thus, it is felt from every point of view that the work is its own justification.[344]

As one of the *Red Triangle Papers* argued, a further and very powerful justification for the War Roll was the comfort it often provided to the bereaved. As this pamphlet explained:

> The Secretaries of the Religious Work Department have the sacred privilege of dealing with what is undoubtedly the most sorrowful class of correspondence addressed to the YMCA Headquarters. Amidst the unending deliveries of mails at Tottenham Court Road there is no one set of letters which call forth greater sympathy than those received from the relatives of Soldiers who have signed the YMCA War Roll, and subsequently been killed in action.[345]

Illustrative of this correspondence, and of the comfort that could be derived from the gesture of a signatory, was a letter sent by 'The WIFE of PRIVATE J.S.', who wrote:

> Just a few lines to thank you for your kind letter and the cards, but I am sorry to tell you that my husband has been killed in action...I will keep the cards and letter for my children, for I was pleased to know that he signed the YMCA War Roll before he went to the Front, and I trust he kept the Pledge...I am left to fight through the world with three very small children, the youngest being only six months old, but I must put my trust in God, and He will help me, for He has promised to be the husband to the widow and the father to the fatherless.[346]

Whatever the fruits of the War Roll, there remained throughout the war a strong belief that the YMCA was faced with a unique religious opportunity and Yapp himself remained unshaken in that conviction. Writing in May 1916 following a visit to the Western Front, he averred that:

> One comes back from France not only convinced of the great opportunity before the YMCA, but also feeling that this is the supreme opportunity for the Church of Christ to regain its hold on the manhood of the country, and that if it fails now, humanly speaking the opportunity will have gone for ever. There is nothing 'panicky' about the religion of the men at the front, but their thoughts are turned to God as possibly never before...For these men, as well as for the Church, it is a time of crisis. Never were men more ready to listen

---

[344] YMCA, K24 YMCA War Work No. 4. Religious. 'Memorandum of YMCA War Roll work', 1918.
[345] Anon., 'Killed in action', *Red Triangle Papers*, XVII (n.d.).
[346] *Ibid.*

to any man who has a message for men... They crave for reality, and the message that always appeals to their imagination and grips their attention is the message of Jesus Christ and Him crucified.[347]

Significantly, this impression had been confirmed by Prof. D. S. Cairns, the future author of *The army and religion* report, whom Yapp had visited at Rouen, in a YMCA hut where 'between six or seven hundred men [were] taking part in an ordinary week-night service'. As Yapp explained:

A lot of them had just arrived from Egypt and the Dardanelles, and several came to the quiet room after the meeting was over for a heart-to-heart talk with the Professor. Coming forward to greet us, [Cairns] said, in words that could not fail to impress one, 'I knew you had a great opportunity before I came out here. Now I know that the greatest spiritual opportunity in Christian history is with you – rests on your shoulders.' It was a strong expression to use, but no one acquainted with the facts would call it exaggeration.[348]

As this scene illustrates, however much it may have been obscured by other activities, there remained a strong evangelical thread in the rich and varied tapestry of YMCA war work. While Cairns and other workers clearly enjoyed some local success, the most celebrated figure who could 'give a message for men' was 'Gipsy' Smith, 'probably the best-known and most successful international evangelist of his day', who, in Yapp's judgment, 'did wonderful work for the YMCA in France'.[349] Smith's first sojourn among the BEF in this capacity occurred in the early summer of 1916, when by all accounts his preaching made a powerful impact. Writing for the *Methodist Recorder*, a Wesleyan army chaplain noted how the redoubtable Smith had even stolen the show at one of Lena Ashwell's concert parties:

[His] services are not always on conventional lines. I have seen the Gipsy sandwiched into the middle of a 'Lena Ashwell' concert party, and trembled for the result. But he always gets in his message. I have seen the artiste on such an occasion fail to take her place in the programme after the Gipsy, because she had been obliged to leave the platform to go 'and have a good cry'. She came back and sang a sacred song. Many a man has gone to the concert hall and found it 'The house of God and the gate of heaven.'[350]

Buoyed by the stir caused by Smith, Yapp wrote to McCowen in June: 'I am quite convinced myself that he has exactly the Message the men need at the Front, and I think it would be a thousand pities to let him return home.' Indeed, it appears that the impressionable Cairns was also quite a fan, Yapp reporting how 'Professor Cairns was here yesterday and I had a long talk with him on the same subject. He is immensely impressed with the value of the service Gipsy Smith is rendering at the front just now.'[351] For his part, Smith found much that was

[347] *YM*, 19 May 1916, p. 450.
[348] *Ibid*.
[349] *ODNB*; Yapp, *In the service of youth*, p. 176.
[350] *YM*, 23 June 1916, p. 567.
[351] YMCA, K27 YMCA War Work No. 14. France. A. K. Yapp to O. McCowen, 24 June 1916.

encouraging among the men of the BEF. Speaking on his return to England, he observed how receptive they had been and how their very presence in France underlined the fact that the churches had not failed them:

[I]f the Church had failed we shouldn't be fighting. Where does the love of righteousness come from? Whence springs the love of honour, the love of truth? Haven't they their roots in God's eternal throne? Whence do you get noble deeds, self-sacrifice, willingness to die for others? Do you get these things from the heart that is deceitful above all things and desperately wicked? Whatever men say, these things come from above. All unselfishness and noble sacrifice have their roots in the Cross.[352]

Eventually, Smith returned to France the following winter where, in the wake of the battle of the Somme, he found the men to be 'more thoughtful and responsive than during his previous visit'.[353] As McCowen wrote to Yapp in January 1917:

You will be glad to hear that Gipsy Smith is having a great Time with the Troops in France. He is now with us at the Advanced Base [Abbeville] and is having great audiences nightly. The response of the men is wonderful. Only last night, in the Princess Victoria Hut, when he invited men who wished to be prayed for, to stand, the whole audience of four hundred immediately rose to their feet. He tells me it is much the same everywhere.[354]

On this occasion Smith was called upon to help save the life as well as the soul of a penitent sinner, for as McCowen confided:

A rather extraordinary incident occurred only last night, when, at the close of one of his meetings, a deserter came to him and gave himself up. The Gipsy went with him at once to the authorities, and pleaded that this very serious offence might be leniently considered and was given the assurance that, as things had happened, they would consider, as favourably as possible, the request that he had made. This may make all the difference between life and death for the man concerned.[355]

While there was, inevitably, an element of preaching to the converted as many of his hearers had already heard him speak in England, Smith's visit of 1917 was deemed to be a signal success, with R. G. MacDonald writing to Yapp:

Gipsy Smith has just returned to Abbeville after three great weeks at Arras, where he has done wonderful work; and expects to cross to England on Saturday or so. Would it be possible to arrange a great meeting in the Queen's Hall a fortnight hence for him to address? He has a most thrilling and touching story to tell of his work out here; and his testimony to its value and opportunity would be of great worth.[356]

---

[352] *YM*, 25 August 1916, p. 783.
[353] YMCA, K27 YMCA War Work No. 14. France. O. McCowen to A. K. Yapp, 6 January 1917.
[354] *Ibid.*
[355] *Ibid.*
[356] YMCA, K26 YMCA War Work No. 13. France. R. G. MacDonald to A. K. Yapp, 22 February 1917.

Indeed, that spring Smith went on to tour 'a series of towns in England reporting on his experiences at the Front', apparently meeting with 'a most hearty welcome everywhere'.[357]

However, the work of evangelism in Red Triangle centres was not reliant on civilians and nor did it necessarily diminish as the war went on. Arriving in France in the winter of 1917–18, E. W. Hornung observed how a YMCA hut near the front line was frequented by soldier evangelists. He observed, for instance, how on one occasion its 'Quiet Room' was disturbed by two soldiers who 'were engaged in some form of violent prayer or intercession…One, and he much the younger of the two, appeared to be wrestling for the other's soul, to be at all but physical grips with some concrete devil of his inner vision.'[358] A more regular visitor, however, was a bespectacled NCO of the Royal Army Medical Corps, who 'must have been a street preacher before the war' and who was allowed to hold evangelistic services of his own every Tuesday evening. As Hornung remembered, on these occasions his 'uncompromising harangue' was audible throughout the hut as he gave vent to 'an astounding flow of spiritual invective'. Nevertheless, and as Hornung conceded, 'It was impossible not to respect this red-hot gospeller, who knew neither fear nor doubt, nor the base art of mincing words; and he had a strong following among the men, who seemed to enjoy his onslaughts, whether they took them to heart or not.'[359]

Still, neither the efforts of 'Gipsy' Smith, the work of enthusiastic secretaries nor even the old time preaching of an element of zealous soldiers could avert the accusation that the Association as a whole had lost its evangelical identity. To some degree, this was a function of the growing diversity of its workers, who could hardly be expected to further an agenda they did not share. However, it was also an inevitable corollary of attaining a much wider basis of public support as well as a crucial welfare rôle in the army at large. Given these developments, the identification of its centres as venues for evangelical mission work was more problematic than helpful for the YMCA's new and more inclusive wartime image. Significantly, YMCA involvement in revivalist work was even downplayed, with those fervent congregations who worshipped voluntarily at its centres in 1914–16 being blandly portrayed not as seekers but as 'eager listeners' who were 'interested in unconventional religious services with plenty of singing'.[360]

Furthermore, the Association strongly denied that its activities were subversive of denominational attachments. While a handbook for YMCA workers sternly admonished that 'No attempt to detach men from their respective allegiance is sanctioned or authorized',[361] even 'Gipsy' Smith said of his evangelistic work in France:

[357] YMCA, J7 National Council signed minutes, 13 April 1917.
[358] Hornung, Notes of a camp-follower, pp. 25–6.
[359] Ibid., pp. 31–2.
[360] Anon., 'The work of the YMCA', p. 184.
[361] D. S. Cairns, The army and religion: an inquiry and its bearing on the religious life of the nation (London, 1919), Appendix II, p. 451.

I kept to essentials, and kept off everything that would look like or sound like dividing lines...I made it quite clear that though I had nothing to do with denominationalism, a man ought to be all the stronger Churchman of whatever Church he is a member for listening to me.[362]

While the Association kept its workers in check, Yapp went to great lengths to disown any hint of controversy or sheep-stealing, declaring in 1918 that

The YMCA is a Christian Association, the Red Triangle a Christian emblem, and for that very reason the freedom of the Association is given to every enlisted man, Protestant and Catholic, Anglican, Free-Churchman, Jew, Hindoo, Mohammedan – men of any religion, every religion, and no religion at all, are equally welcomed beneath its roof, and no man will ever hear unkind or disrespectful things said from a YMCA platform concerning the faith he holds dear.[363]

In earnest of these sentiments, the Association opened its doors for the services of all of the army's recognized denominations.[364] For this, it even earned the thanks of Cardinal Bourne and the endorsement of the army's senior Jewish chaplain, who wrote to *The Times* in February 1915 'appealing for aid for the YMCA and testifying to its magnificent work'.[365] In fact, British Jews were so enthusiastic about the Association that it even acquired a Jewish affiliate in the form of the Jewish Naval and Military Association; several YMCA huts were financed by subscriptions from synagogues while, in the East End, a YMCA hut was built in the Mile End Road 'with a public notice telling what it was – a gift from Jewry to Christendom in a cause which made both one'.[366]

In 1916, a London newspaper portrayed 'the new religion of the YMCA' as 'a religion of limitless helpfulness', a description that strongly appealed to Yapp, who argued that

[T]he new note struck by the YMCA in its war work has been the note of unity as opposed to controversy, and that of practical service as opposed to mere theory... The YMCA message of the 'cup of coffee' is only another expression of the Master's message of a 'cup of cold water'. The 'serving of tables' in the YMCA hut, if carried out in the proper spirit, is merely following in the steps of Him Who washed His disciples' feet.[367]

Nor, indeed, did the practical service of the YMCA lack its advocates as a subtle means of evangelization. Basil Bourchier, vicar of St Jude-on-the-Hill, Hampstead Garden Suburb, contended that

The British Tommy is a man of few words, but nobody is so quick as he to weigh the situation up. He knows quite well that the Christ spirit of service is

---

[362] *The Red Triangle*, 23 March 1917, p. 248.
[363] Yapp, *Romance of the Red Triangle*, p. 234.
[364] Anon., 'The work of the YMCA', p. 343; *Catholic Federationist*, May 1917, p. 1.
[365] McKenzie, 'Welfare work', p. 406; *Times*, 9 February 1915, p. 9.
[366] M. Adler (ed.), *British Jewry book of honour* (London, 1922), p. 18; McKenzie, 'Welfare work', p. 406.
[367] *YM*, 19 May 1916, p. 450.

responsible for the presence of those behind the counter, and mentally he registers the fact...a man who is not possessed of any deep religious convictions (i.e. the average Englishman) is pretty certain to be susceptible to the religious influences of the person for whom he comes to entertain feelings of friendship and regard...Though a secular and unconsecrated building, the YMCA hut is the church of the soldier in this foreign land [and] here it is that, Sunday and weekday, our men congregate to receive their spiritual as well as their bodily food. Say what you will, the future religion of the nation, represented as it is out here by our very best and bravest, is being largely moulded in the huts of the YMCA[368]

Likewise, Canon James Adderley of Birmingham Cathedral remarked on this strategy of good works:

Theologians may tell the Britisher that this is not the whole of Christianity, but he will always remain convinced that it is the larger part of it, and, after all, he has the 25th Chapter of St Matthew to lend considerable weight to his opinion. The YMCA has undoubtedly given the cup of fresh water to millions and it will not lose its reward.[369]

However, new approaches could not obscure the fact that, as Yapp freely confessed, 'the primary aim of the YMCA always has been, and is, to lead men to a saving knowledge of [Christ]'.[370] Inevitably, this meant that many among the YMCA's traditional evangelical constituency struggled with the direction of its wartime work and with its practical and theological justifications. Among them was Herbert Hayes, a pious NCO of the Army Ordnance Corps, who had experienced YMCA work in the French bases and who confessed that:

There were times when it seemed to some of us who loved the spiritual more than the social side that we could have successfully given more emphasis to the former; but as time went on, and men who had been avowedly antagonistic to the things of God became interested and began to yearn after the privileges of the eternal kingdom, we began to realize that a work was going on through concerts, games, and social fellowship that was as truly of the Holy Spirit as was the winning of souls by the definite preaching of the Gospel. Men were being led to the Christ, who by direct preaching might have been driven away because of the prejudice we were gradually undermining. It was a form of strategy in the eternal conflict.[371]

Others, however, remained unconvinced. Early in 1915, the Soldiers' Christian Association disaffiliated itself from the National Council, hoping thereby 'to keep more exclusively to its original special object of seeking to bind together Christian soldiers in the love of Christ, and help them to evangelize and to witness for Him among their comrades'.[372] Indeed, the many symptoms of the

[368] Anon., 'The Red Triangle from the clerical point of view', *Red Triangle Papers*, unnumbered, pp. 1–2.
[369] J. Adderley, 'The Church of England and the YMCA', *Red Triangle Papers*, XX (n.d.), p. 2.
[370] Yapp, *Romance of the Red Triangle*, p. 235.
[371] *YM*, 5 May 1916, p. 406.
[372] YMCA, J7 National Council signed minutes, 9 April 1915.

Association's departure from its historic identity were strongly criticized by conservative evangelicals in general, who deplored much of its wartime work as entirely secular. Addressing veteran workers at a meeting in London in May 1919, Yapp admitted that 'He had a drawerful of criticisms at home, many of them as yet unread. One recent charge levelled against his organization – by a clergyman – was that it was really a Young Men's "Comfort" Association, and in no true sense Christian.'[373] However, some critics went much further. On 6 March 1916, the WEC was told how a certain Mr Fegan had got hold of an internal circular and had 'written to friends of Christian work throughout the country accusing the Authorities of the YMCA of neglecting spiritual work, of compromising with Rome, and of modernism in method'. The committee's response was to enlist a sympathetic barrister 'to approach Mr. Fegan with a view to [a] suitable explanation'.[374] That same month, *The Christian* magazine published a piece claiming that the YMCA had forgotten 'its own distinctive message and commission' and was in danger of becoming 'the friend and victim of the World'.[375] This fresh accusation again forced the WEC to take action, its members resolving to write to the magazine, to lobby its editor and to pass a unanimous resolution to the effect 'that Mr. Yapp is faithfully and loyally carrying out their policy in the administration of the War Work of the Young Men's Christian Association'.[376]

While its traditional following was deeply divided over the question of its war work, the British YMCA could at least console itself with the fact that its determined efforts to embrace the churches resulted in a closer relationship with the Army Chaplains' Department. Significantly, this was not true of the Canadian or of the American Expeditionary Forces on the Western Front. In the case of the Canadians, their chaplains very much regarded the YMCA as a 'para-church' which sought to subvert denominational loyalties.[377] In the case of the Americans, the privileged position of the 'Y' was such that its secretaries were ranked as officers and it was given a complete monopoly over commercial canteens in France.[378] Because of its ubiquity and the initially low ratio of chaplains to soldiers in the US army,[379] the *rôle* and status of the 'Y' rendered the office of the Protestant army chaplain in the AEF all but redundant. As Bishop Gwynne noted in December 1917:

> Bishop Israel an American Bishop turned up to spend four days with me. He told us that the organization of the Chaplains' Department in the [AEF] was at present in a state of chaos and that practically the spiritual ministration of the troops was in the hands of the YMCA…the American YMCA did not give

[373] *Times*, 19 May 1919, p. 9.
[374] YMCA, J112 War Emergency copy minutes, 6 March 1916.
[375] Reznick, *Healing the nation*, pp. 29–30.
[376] YMCA, J112 War Emergency copy minutes, 21 March 1916.
[377] D. Crerar, *Padres in no man's land: Canadian chaplains and the Great War* (Montreal, 1995), pp. 75–80.
[378] Yapp, *In the service of youth*, 138; T. A. Hoff, *US Doughboy 1916–19* (Oxford, 2005), pp. 53–4.
[379] D. R. Herspring, *Soldiers, commissars and chaplains* (Lanham, MD, 2001), p. 33.

the chaplains a look in. They were in fact on the shelf which they bitterly resent. There are no compulsory [church] parades and voluntary ones are as a rule held in the YMCA huts in which only those...allowed to take the services or preach [are] allowed to do so by the YMCA authorities.[380]

In contrast, Red Triangle centres soon came to be regarded as essential assets by British army chaplains of all stripes. Initially, of course, they were most sought out by evangelical Anglicans and Nonconformists. The evangelical chaplain-general, Bishop John Taylor Smith, was a vice-president of the YMCA in 1914 and he consistently patronized the Association and its members. For example, soon after the outbreak of war he promoted E. J. Kennedy, an elderly Territorial chaplain, to the post of senior chaplain of the 7th Division, partly on the strength of Kennedy's long years of service to the Association (twenty years earlier Kennedy had been honorary secretary to the English National Council and a member of no fewer than three of its committees).[381] Furthermore, when speaking at the opening of the 'Church Family Newspaper Hut' in Gillingham in 1917, the bishop said that 'he hoped the hut would prove not only the birthplace of souls, but also an armoury for saints'. He went on to describe YMCA huts as 'a blessing to the Army [which] provided a common platform for all who worked for the Lord Jesus Christ'.[382]

However, given the fierce party struggles that beset the Anglican branch of the Chaplains' Department in 1914–15, Taylor Smith's support may not have served to reassure Anglo-Catholic chaplains as to the good faith of the Red Triangle or its workers, especially as the ministers among them assumed (or were accorded) the title of 'padre', an appellation that more properly belonged to members of the Army Chaplains' Department.[383] Nevertheless, and despite some signs of friction between them, tensions seem to have eased fairly quickly. For example, when Noel Mellish (an Anglo-Catholic chaplain and future winner of the Victoria Cross) arrived at Rouen in July 1915 he found two YMCA huts serving his depôt; these, he said, were staffed by 'capable men and energetic ladies who by their zeal and sympathy are doing very much to help and brighten the lives of our men...The managers of both these huts have invited me to come in whenever I wish, and our relations are very friendly'.[384] Significantly, the exploits of this 'VC Padre' were later recounted in *Told in the huts: the YMCA gift book*, wherein it was duly noted that Mellish had called upon a local Red Triangle centre to supply chocolate to the wounded whom he was tending as he earned his award.[385] Similarly, another Anglican clergyman was determined to scotch any rumours of discord when he wrote in 1915:

[380] CMS, Diaries of L. H. Gwynne, 10 December 1917 and 13 December 1917.
[381] E. Kennedy and A. Howell, *Some records of the life of Edmund John Kennedy* (London, 1917), 193; *Year book*, 1914, p. 4; *Year book of the English Union of Young Men's Christian Associations*, 1893–4, pp. 8, 10.
[382] *The Red Triangle*, 12 January 1917, p. 19.
[383] An illustration of a YMCA worker leading a service and entitled 'The Padre' featured recurrently in *Told in the huts*, ed. Yapp.
[384] H. Montell (ed.), *A chaplain's war: the story of Noel Mellish VC, MC* (London, 2002), p. 47.
[385] G. Hamlin, 'The VC padre', in *Told in the huts*, ed. Yapp, pp. 56–7.

Another lie to be nailed to the counter is the scandal – hinted at rather than expressed – that the Army Chaplains find it difficult to co-operate with the YMCA. Only in one single case have I found this true, and the facts speak for themselves. Army Chaplains are 'quartered' in many of the huts, and take their share with the other workers in the work of the hut: one of the Mirfield Fathers, who was out here as an Army Chaplain, lived for some time, I believe in a YMCA hut; while, on the other hand, I, as a YMCA worker, have frequently taken Parade Services 'under orders' from the Anglican Chaplains. It is instructive, too, to notice how frequently the YMCA huts are mentioned in the weekly list of Parade Services, and to see in how large a number of cases it is in a YMCA hut that Celebrations of the Holy Communion are held. In fact, one often wonders where the Anglican Chaplains would find facilities for their Celebrations, were it not for the YMCA.[386]

In view of a basic lack of initial training until a very late stage in the war,[387] many of the army's temporary chaplains turned to the YMCA and its centres when settling into military life. Writing of his experiences at a training camp in England early in the war, one Anglican chaplain recalled that: 'For several weeks I haunted the YMCA hut. I said prayers there, and helped to sing hymns there and sometimes o'evenings I preached there. I played the piano there. I joined in concerts there.'[388] Later, the Association threw him another lifeline at Rouen where

> There was a Scotch minister running one of the YMCA huts. I stood behind his counter on two afternoons a week, hoping that my men would come to talk to me. Several of them did. I did the same in another YMCA hut on the other side of the road. I used a quiet room adjoining the hut for the Eucharist and Intercession services whenever I could gather a company of the devout.[389]

Such were the merits of this approach that in 1917 Everard Digby, an Anglo-Catholic chaplain who had already served as a YMCA worker in France,[390] positively urged this course of action upon new chaplains in his *Tips for padres*:

> If there is a YMCA hut in your camp, try to put in an occasional half-hour there, behind the bar, or talking to the men, and take a service for them when they ask you. Do not be afraid of trying to work with Nonconformists. You will be surprised to find how much you have in common.[391]

In addition to this type of individual collaboration, formal co-operation between the YMCA and the Army Chaplains' Department increased as the war went on, being presented to hut leaders as a matter of policy from December 1916.[392] While it had been reported at a conference of senior Anglican chaplains in June 1916 that united services were being held in YMCA centres at Etaples on

---

[386] Anon., *YMCA war work in Britain and Flanders*, pp. 19–20.
[387] M. Snape, *The Royal Army Chaplains' Department 1796–1953: clergy under fire* (Woodbridge, 2008), pp. 204–7.
[388] 'Temporary chaplain', *The padre* (London, 1916), p. 31.
[389] *Ibid.*, p. 50.
[390] *YM*, 7 May 1915, pp. 391–2.
[391] E. Digby, *Tips for padres: a handbook for chaplains* (London, 1917), p. 30.
[392] Yapp, *Romance of the Red Triangle*, p. 196.

weekday evenings,[393] in January 1917 ecumenical co-operation was extended at the base when a local conference resolved that all services should henceforth be arranged between senior Anglican and Free Church chaplains in consultation with the YMCA.[394] By the end of 1917, the pattern of practical co-operation developed at Etaples was being urged by senior Anglican chaplains as an example to be followed throughout the British bases in France.[395] However, within a few months the ecumenical tide was flowing to such an extent that the 'Etaples scheme' had been overtaken by a bolder initiative involving chaplains and the YMCA at Rouen. As Yapp was informed:

> I daresay you have heard of the experiments that are on foot along the lines of United Church Services in our huts…The principle is that of a United Service conducted jointly by the C. of E. and Non-C. of E. [chaplains], the first part Liturgical and the second conducted on non-C. of E. lines. For instance a C. of E. man will take the first part of the Service, a non-C. of E. the second and vice-versa the following Sunday. I have seen the Chaplain General, Bishop Taylor Smith, out here, and he told me it was the finest bit of constructive work towards Church Union that he has yet seen, and that the scheme had his very earnest approval and prayers. I have also seen the Principal Chaplain, Major-General Simms, who is backing up the adoption of it in our centres. I feel sure that this will be the ideal system for our huts after the war.[396]

The ecumenical momentum within the Chaplains' Department and the YMCA continued well after the Armistice. With the coming of peace, Neville Talbot, a senior, liberal and outspoken Anglo-Catholic chaplain, was offered the position of the religious work secretary of the YMCA.[397] Although this offer was declined, in March 1919 the YMCA was also party to a joint chaplains' statement on Christian unity. This called for collaboration in 'all matters affecting the social and moral welfare of the people'; for 'joint Conferences, Conventions and Retreats' as 'a regular and normal part' of church life; for attendance 'as an act of Christian courtesy [at] Induction Services'; for an 'interchange of pulpits' and, ultimately, for inter-communion.[398]

As the *rôle* of the YMCA in France was increasingly seen as assisting rather than competing with 'the great and important work' of the Army Chaplains' Department,[399] the radicalization of the latter tended to carry the Association along in its wake. Hence, the drift of the Association's war work and its professed desire to act as 'the handmaid of the Church'[400] served to align it with a radical ecclesiastical agenda at home. In 1919 this was illustrated by the publication of

---

[393] Museum of Army Chaplaincy, Amport House, Andover (hereafter MAC), 'Proceedings of ACGs' conferences', 6–7 June 1916.
[394] YMCA, K27 YMCA War Work No. 14. France. O. McCowen to A. K. Yapp, 16 January 1917.
[395] MAC, 'Proceedings of ACGs' conferences', 7 November 1917.
[396] YMCA, K26 YMCA War Work No. 13. Unknown correspondent to A. K. Yapp, undated.
[397] F. H. Brabant, *Neville Stuart Talbot: a memoir* (London, 1949), p. 72.
[398] YMCA, K24 YMCA War Work No. 4. Religious. *Resolutions on Christian unity*, March 1919.
[399] Yapp, *Romance of the Red Triangle*, p. 196.
[400] YMCA, K24 YMCA War Work No. 4. Religious. 'Memorandum regarding the interdenominational position of the YMCA', December 1916.

The army and religion: an enquiry and its bearing upon the religious life of the nation, a report that had been sponsored by the Religious Work Sub-Committee of the WEC and which had been compiled and very largely written by the Scottish academic and YMCA volunteer, D. S. Cairns.[401] The inspiration of the report was twofold; first, to provide for the churches 'more information as to the attitude of the men in the Army towards religion' and, second, to examine 'how to make effective the presentation of the Christian Gospel in the period after the War'.[402] Hence, while it purported to be an objective investigation into the religious attitudes and behaviour of the soldiers of the British army (the findings of which were summarized in part one, 'The facts'), the nub of the report was a manifesto for far-reaching change in the post-war church, a manifesto that included the reinterpretation of Christian doctrine, the 'Christianizing' of the social order, the democratization of church government and an emphatic commitment to the cause of international peace.[403]

Although largely based on a collection of nearly three hundred memoranda and guided by a distinguished steering committee that represented a broad cross-section of British Christianity, the report itself was deeply flawed. Roman Catholic input was slight, Irish and Welsh evidence was deliberately excluded[404] and the committee's joint convenors (namely D. S. Cairns and E. S. Talbot, the bishop of Winchester) were clearly hand in glove. While E. C. Carter had been designated to lead the project with Cairns (who had originally been given carte blanche 'to associate with him such Leaders from the Churches as he thinks most fitted to help him in the matter'),[405] after the United States entered the war in April 1917 Carter was packed off to Paris to begin organizing YMCA work for the American Expeditionary Force.[406] When Carter was succeeded by the bishop of Winchester, whom Cairns had admired since the publication of *Lux mundi* in 1889, the objectivity of the report was seriously compromised for Cairns was also a close friend of his son, Neville Talbot, a fellow luminary of the Student Christian Movement whom Cairns had already declared to be 'great in every way'.[407] While Bishop Talbot used his influence to solicit Roman Catholic assistance,[408] it was notable that at a conference of senior Anglican chaplains only Neville Talbot showed much enthusiasm for this latest YMCA venture, Bishop Gwynne wisely thinking 'it best that each organization should act upon its own lines, thus arriving at two independent views'.[409]

However, an independent view was not to be had. While Neville Talbot's aphorism 'The soldier has got Religion; I am not so sure that he has got

---

[401] YMCA, J114 War Emergency Committee copy minutes, 13 March 1917; Cairns, *The army and religion*, p. viii.

[402] *Ibid.*, 12 April 1917.

[403] Cairns, *The army and religion*, pp. 238–418.

[404] *Ibid.*, p. ix.

[405] YMCA, J114 War Emergency Committee copy minutes, 13 March 1917 and 12 April 1917.

[406] *The Red Triangle Bulletin*, 7 December 1917, p. 3.

[407] Brabant, *Neville Stuart Talbot*, pp. 30–4, 42; *YM*, 22 September 1916, p. 877.

[408] RP, 'Bishop of Winchester's enquiry'.

[409] MAC, 'Proceedings of ACGs' conferences', 28–9 November 1916.

Christianity' set the tone for part one of *The army and religion* report,[410] Cairns concluded that only 'about four-fifths' of the men were in a 'vital relationship with any of the Churches'.[411] In reaching this verdict, Cairns shrugged off the evidence of the War Roll (which he dismissed as the product of 'the stress of abnormal conditions')[412] and argued that the work of evangelists such as Gipsy Smith had simply served to illustrate the numbers of men 'outside the communion of the Churches', their 'confusion and ignorance regarding the Christian message and ideal' and 'their readiness to hear a straight and living message'.[413] Indeed, the origins as well as the contents of the report show just how much its conclusions were predetermined. In January 1917 Cairns had declared that

> My feeling is that what the Churches need is to have brought before them the real state of matters, viz. that they have lost, or are in danger of losing the faith of the nation, and that they have got to look deeply into the matter and set their hearts and minds to the problem of how the situation may, by God's grace, be retrieved before it is too late.[414]

That month, E. C. Carter had written to Oliver McCowen from England, stressing how important it was to indulge Cairns, who had now been released for YMCA work for a year by the United Free Church College, Aberdeen. As Carter emphasized, 'Without his assistance it would have been impossible for us to secure the present magnificent response from the Scottish Churches to our YMCA appeal';[415] he then went on to explain what Cairns was planning to do and, indeed, what he went on to accomplish:

> Professor Cairns has had heavily laid upon him the conviction that the YMCA ought to make a very serious and searching enquiry with reference to the attitude of the men in the armies, to Christ and to the Christian Church. He believes that perhaps three-quarters of the youth of the nation, at this time, are out of vital touch with the Church. He desires to mass the evidence from responsible sources, in order to enable the YMCA to issue a masterly book which shall arrest the thought of the nation, and lay the lines for the work and thinking of the Church, for the next twenty years.
>
>   In connection with this enquiry, he would like to go out to France in about a month's time for six weeks, and be free to visit our workers and a few of the chaplains in, say, three different bases, and in, say, two of the armies...He is getting the backing of the very best men in England and Scotland for this investigation. If the YMCA can make a contribution of this sort, it will be one of the biggest services which we can possibly render in the present crisis.[416]

[410] A. Wilkinson, *The Church of England and the First World War* (London, 1978), p. 161; Cairns, *The army and religion*, p. xiv.
[411] Cairns, *The army and religion*, p. 189.
[412] *Ibid.*, p. 399.
[413] *Ibid.*, pp. 398–9.
[414] S. P. Mews, 'Religion and English society in the First World War', Ph.D. dissertation, University of Cambridge, 1973, p. 174.
[415] YMCA, K27 YMCA War Work No. 14. France. E. C. Carter to O. McCowen, 24 January 1917.
[416] *Ibid.*

Post-war entanglements

The months following the Armistice left the YMCA with more on its hands than a beguiling and grandiose manifesto for church reform. In addition to maintaining its services for large numbers of troops in Europe, the Middle East, India and North Russia, the lessons of the conflict needed to be applied to post-war British society. From January 1919, therefore, the YMCA was preparing another public appeal for a further £8,000,000.[417] As Yapp explained to former Association workers that May:

> [T]he greatest discovery [the YMCA] had made was that of the hut as a social centre. In country towns and villages, and especially in the slums of East London, with the right people in charge, there would be in the hut the finest solution of such moral problems as that of intemperance and 'the boy'. The great thing was to provide counter-attractions to temptations, rather than make frontal assaults on them. The association was on the eve of a very big financial effort to help on its post-war schemes of usefulness.[418]

In the meantime, however, there were still soldiers to provide for. On the strength of his experience of Germany and his success as an army secretary, in the wake of the Armistice of 11 November 1918 Barclay Baron was detailed to take charge of YMCA work with Second Army in the British zone of occupation in the Rhineland.[419] The development of this work was a huge task; although demobilization saw its numbers fall to only 40,000 by the end of 1919, the British Army of the Rhine (as it was renamed that April) still numbered more than 220,000 men by the time Baron returned to England in May.[420] Furthermore, the occupying forces were plagued by serious internal problems; grievances over demobilization led to several military strikes early in the year and senior generals and politicians were even fearful of British troops being suborned by local Bolsheviks, it being accepted that they might, at the very least, refuse to suppress food riots given the wretched state of the civilian population.[421] In view of these problems, and their potential to undermine Britain's position in the peace negotiations, when Sir William Robertson took command of British forces on the Rhine in April 1919 he was emphatic that 'high morale, a contented spirit and good discipline were in present circumstances more important than any standard military training'.[422]

As ever, the Red Triangle rose to the challenge; by July nearly ninety YMCA centres were in operation, these being staffed by around 200 male and 120 female workers, the latter being admitted into the zone of occupation in March. Operating largely in commandeered premises, the jewel in the crown was

---

[417] *Ibid.*, 'The latest YMCA statistics', 20 January 1919.
[418] *Times*, 19 May 1919, p. 9.
[419] Anon., 'On the Western Front since the Armistice', *The Red Triangle Bulletin*, 6 December 1918, p. 3.
[420] *Statistics of the military effort of the British Empire*, p. 107.
[421] D. G. Williamson, *The British in Germany, 1918–1930: the reluctant occupiers* (Oxford, 1991), pp. 32–6, 48–9.
[422] *Ibid.*, p. 35.

'Cologne Central', formerly 'a large German music hall and restaurant',[423] which was 'crowded every night for lectures, concerts, cinema or variety performances, while the smaller Loreley Hall [was] used for lectures, discussions and a flourishing German Class'.[424] Naturally enough, the pattern of YMCA work in the Rhineland largely resembled its work in the bases of France: concert parties toured the zone of occupation; a YMCA 'Athletic Director' was attached to each army corps (as were 'two or three experienced lady teachers of folk dancing'); lecturers arrived to co-operate with army education officers; lending libraries were established at each YMCA centre and a 'united service was held in all the huts on Sunday evenings', the Association still seeking 'to co-operate with chaplains of all denominations in every way possible, and to put its huts, whenever practicable, at the disposal of the chaplains on Sunday mornings' for parade services. Once soldiers' wives were permitted to visit their husbands in Germany, the YMCA arranged suitable 'social gatherings' for them. Finally, once demobilization commenced via Holland, a YMCA 'canteen and recreation room' was established on each of the six Rhine steamers that took returning troops to Rotterdam, books and games and 'a concert and whist drive' being provided for each two-day trip.[425]

In addition to buttressing discipline and morale, as in the French bases an important aspect of these activities was to provide a wholesome alternative to insalubrious local attractions. Embracing as it did a hungry and war-weary population, the British zone of occupation in the Rhineland swiftly and inevitably acquired some of the seedier characteristics associated with Britain's imperial garrisons. In May 1920, this issue assumed political dimensions when questions were raised in the House of Commons concerning 'the continual and alarming rise in the incidence of venereal disease' amongst British troops in Germany, this being three times greater than that which obtained among those in Great Britain.[426] More worrying still from a moral point of view was the fact that the demobilization of older men and the survival of conscription until April 1920 meant that the British Army of the Rhine included an abnormally large number of corruptible young soldiers.[427] As 'A VOICE FROM THE RHINE' warned:

> Our Army in Germany is composed largely of…young soldiers. They are to be found en masse in the chief military centres like Cologne, Duren and Bonn, and in small detachments in the country villages. Soon the feeling of novelty wears off. Military duties are light, and our boys, placed amid an alien population whose life they cannot share, are exposed to all the dangers of idleness and boredom. It is a familiar sight to see them drifting about in

---

[423] YMCA, K29 YMCA War Work No. 16. After Armistice. Cologne. Anon., 'With the army of the Rhine', YMCA Campaign Leaflets, XII (n.d.).

[424] Anon., 'With the army on the Rhine', The Red Triangle, March 1919, p. 263.

[425] YMCA, K29 YMCA War Work No. 16. After Armistice. Cologne. Anon., 'With the army of the Rhine', YMCA Campaign Leaflets, XII (n.d.); 'Scotsman', 'Homeward down the Rhine', The Red Triangle, August 1919, pp. 461–4.

[426] Hansard, House of Commons Parliamentary Debates, 11 May 1920, 217, and 20 May 1920, 1608.

[427] K. Jeffery, 'The post-war army', in A nation in arms, ed. Beckett and Simpson, p. 215.

groups in the streets gazing listlessly into shop windows, doing nothing but kill time. When this sort of thing goes on day after day for months, nothing but some strong influence for good can save them from the worst results of demoralization...Is the War over? Who can say that it is until the last of these boys comes back from the Rhine?[428]

As the organizing hand behind this work in the Rhineland, Baron was extremely busy before returning to England in May 1919. In addition to overseeing the opening of dozens of new centres and the transportation of workers and equipment from Roubaix over 'villainous roads' in the depths of winter,[429] he found time to co-write *A guide-book to Cologne for British soldiers*, which came full of architectural detail and with information concerning clubs and church services for all denominations in Cologne and Bonn.[430] Baron also described his work in three articles for *The Red Triangle* in 1919, in which he averred that 'For those of us who had the first share in it...service with the YMCA in Germany cannot but seem the final privilege and the most honourable reward of the Association's four years with the soldier on the Western Front.'[431] Nevertheless, he was fully conscious of the difficulties of the new situation, and especially of trying to influence young soldiers who had not seen active service and who had not learnt to appreciate the YMCA:

> The Army is doing every mortal thing to entertain and teach them...We are working step by step with the authorities in every department of the men's life 'out of school hours' so to speak. Entertainments, sports, education, religion – we co-operate closely with General Headquarters and in the Corps and Divisions in all these things...Nowadays it is often like running a boys' club at home, for lots of these men don't look more than sixteen. One odd thing about them is that, not having come to rely on the YM in bad times like the veterans, they haven't got the 'hut-habit'. But we are teaching them that our centres are not merely grocers' shops but their own club.[432]

Still, it nevertheless seemed to Baron (and especially in view of the chaos that reigned elsewhere in post-war Germany) that the YMC.A was at least contributing to a nascent process of reconciliation in the British zone of occupation:

> War is always born of misunderstanding: perhaps our Army of Occupation is acting, unconsciously, as the best Mission of the World's Peace...We have a vital place, recognized on the Rhine by the Army as perhaps never so clearly before, in helping to maintain that discipline and keenness and good humour and readiness to learn and to serve, which are the glories of the British soldier.[433]

---

[428] YMCA, K29 YMCA War Work No. 16. After Armistice. Cologne. 'A voice from the Rhine', n.d.

[429] B. Baron, 'First days on the Rhine', *The Red Triangle*, April 1919, p. 306.

[430] B. Baron and L. Hunter, *A guide-book to Cologne for British soldiers* (Cologne, 1919).

[431] Baron, 'First days on the Rhine', p. 306.

[432] B. Baron, 'A hectic day', *The Red Triangle*, July 1919, pp. 426–7.

[433] B. Baron, 'An excursion on the Rhine', *The Red Triangle*, June 1919, p. 384.

Conclusion

What, then, was gained through this vast and multifaceted wartime endeavour? This question is perhaps best answered from three different perspectives – that of the army, that of the soldier and that of the Association itself. In the case of the British army, the YMCA was certainly the most important civilian organization in that 'great welfare network' which helped sustain its morale throughout the worst trials in its long history.[434] The vast majority of the men who served in its ranks were, of course, citizen soldiers (Territorials, Kitchener volunteers and, from 1916, conscripts) and their willingness to endure their lot was an essential prerequisite for Allied victory. As the ultimate fate of the Russian, German, Ottoman and Austro-Hungarian empires and the near defeat of France and Italy in 1917 serves to demonstrate, for the great powers in the First World War victory and defeat were determined not so much by territorial conquest as by the willingness (or otherwise) of their non-professional soldiers to see the war through to a victorious conclusion. That the British army persevered, notwithstanding its heavy losses on the Western Front and protracted battles of attrition such as the Somme and Passchendaele, was due to the fact that this collective willingness remained intact. While various reasons have been put forward as to why this was the case (reasons that range from the basic stability of civilian society to the survival of civilian music-hall culture in the British army)[435] the morale of the British Tommy was clearly sustained by the fact that, whether he was aware of it or not, his was a fairly privileged lot in comparison with that of his French, Italian, Russian, Turkish and even German counterparts.[436] As we can see very clearly from the expansive and multifaceted war work of the YMCA, enormous and sustained efforts were made to meet his religious, emotional, material and intellectual needs. However antithetical this idea may be to the popular mythology of Britain and the First World War (a mythology in which bungling chateau generals and their voracious firing squads loom large), the fact is that the British soldier was remarkably well looked after. In part this was a function of the paternalistic ethos of the generals who commanded the British army, an ethos that had taken root in the nineteenth-century officer corps and which led them to be sympathetic and supportive of the Association's work. As Yapp testified, 'In my experience, those on whom rest big responsibilities for military matters are, almost without exception, keenly interested in everything pertaining to the welfare of those under their command. They welcome the YMCA because it brings with it that human touch that cannot be obtained through official channels.'[437] However, the comparatively fortunate

---

[434] I. Beckett, 'The nation in arms, 1914–18', in *A nation in arms*, ed. Beckett and Simpson, p. 25.

[435] A. Watson, 'Culture and combat in the western world, 1900–1945', *Historical Journal*, LI (2008), 529–46 at 541–2.

[436] S. Audoin-Rouzeau, 'The French soldier in the trenches', *passim*; J. Gooch, 'Morale and discipline in the Italian army, 1915–18', *passim*; I. Davidian, 'The Russian soldier's morale from the evidence of tsarist military censorship', *passim*, in *Facing Armageddon: the First World War experienced*, ed. H. Cecil and P.H. Liddle (London, 1996).

[437] Yapp, *In the service of youth*, pp. 160–1.

situation of the British soldier was also a reflection of the fact that his commanders were accountable to the political leaders of a liberal, Christian, socially responsible and increasingly democratic society; in this respect, and as Yapp realized, the beneficent work of the YMCA very much represented 'the embodied goodwill of the British people towards its beloved army'.[438] Hence, the war work of the YMCA was not only indicative of the underlying strengths of the British army but also of the society that produced it.

From the perspective of the individual soldier, the YMCA was usually regarded as a benign provider of religious and pastoral care, practical relief, education, entertainment and sundry creature comforts. While this largely replicated the *rôle* of the churches in civilian life,[439] the context of war seemed to give its work an added lustre. As one American admirer purred in 1917: 'In view of all that this organization is doing at the front, it is no wonder that the grateful soldiers interpret the ever-welcome YMCA sign as meaning "You Make Christianity Attractive."'[440] For his part, 'A soldier in France' enthused in April 1916:

I am at the Base and everywhere you go there is either a Hut or the motor cars with the Red Triangle flying about. I myself say many a time that the YMCA has been the saving of many a life. If the folks at home knew of the good work the Association is doing out here, I am sure every rich or poor person would offer you a contribution to help you in the building of more Huts.[441]

With the development of YMCA work in army areas, another soldier wrote in 1917:

The only chance we have to get any luxuries is when we get back away from the firing line at the YMCA, and I can tell you that the YMCA out here has done a tremendous lot of good – that's the first thing we look for when we are on the line of march, is to find a YMCA and then we know we can get a nice cup of tea and a piece of cake, and without those places out here things would go very hard for the Tommies. We can always get rest and comfort there, and when we come away from the firing line we want it too.[442]

Another infantryman put the matter more starkly to E. W. Hornung in the winter of 1917–18: 'But for the YMCA...I believe I should have gone mad.'[443] Years later, a former guardsman averred that 'It might well be said that wherever there were troops, there was also the YMCA, with its canteen, its cheerfulness and its never-ending effort to bring some at least of the comforts of civilization into our existence.'[444] However, although they served many purposes and had a broad clientele, YMCA centres were probably most prized by those who also valued their religious work. Gilbert Mortimer, in civilian life a United Methodist Sunday school teacher, wrote from Great Yarmouth in April 1916:

[438] Yapp, *Romance of the Red Triangle*, p. 106.
[439] Snape, *God and the British soldier*, p. 226.
[440] Koch, *Books in camp, trench and hospital*, p. 16.
[441] YMCA, K40 Typescript extracts of letters of appreciation. 'A soldier in France', 28 April 1916.
[442] *Ibid.* 'A soldier in France', 1 February 1917.
[443] Hornung, *Notes of a camp-follower*, p. 24.
[444] Messenger, *Call-to-arms*, p. 459.

The YMCA is crowded every night with chaps writing home…it is a grand place and every body feels at home as much as is possible under the circumstances…It is grand to come into a place like this, everybody is welcome & the folks try their best to make one feel homely. There is also a concert & games room and about the middle of the evening a hymn is sung & a prayer offered. It is an excellent institution.[445]

As for the YMCA, the results of the war were decidedly mixed. While there were few clear signs of a significant religious revival in the army by 1918, Yapp was convinced that the work of the YMCA for the British soldier had at least exploded 'The old conception of Christianity – a long face and a regular seat in Church.'[446] Furthermore, he believed that the YMCA had delivered a powerful vindication of practical Christianity to an entire generation:

> The British soldier hates a sham, and instinctively classes the hypocrite with the Hun. He may not understand our Shibboleths; he has no use for our controversies, but he can and does understand the Life of the Master, when he sees the beauty of that Life reflected in some humble follower of His, who day by day is risking his life at the Front, that he may supply a cup of cocoa to a wounded soldier.[447]

Nevertheless, and while there is some anecdotal evidence from later years to suggest that this impression was not unfounded,[448] this was a rather intangible achievement to say the least.

Far less elusive was the fact that the post-war YMCA failed to live up to inflated wartime expectations. Hailed by Yapp as 'one of the greatest social and religious movements of our time',[449] in the midst of the war others were also disposed to predict a great peacetime future for the Association. Donning the mantle of a prophet in the last months of the war, Canon James Adderley warned the Church of England that

> The YMCA knows its power and is about to flood England with huts and recreation rooms directly the war is over. It has the power to start a new Methodist movement in every parish. It does not wish to do this. Sir Arthur Yapp has definitely disclaimed all idea of doing such a thing. But so did John Wesley and we know what happened. The Church drove Methodism outside and it might very well happen again, that in spite of itself, the YMCA might become a sect…The YMCA has made friends with the Army. When the Army becomes once more the People, the villagers and town folk of England, it proposes to continue and enlarge that friendship. Woe be to the vicars and rectors who pass by on the other side![450]

---

[445] Liddle Collection, University of Leeds, Gilbert Mortimer papers.
[446] *Times*, 19 May 1919, p. 9.
[447] Yapp, *Romance of the Red Triangle*, pp. 198–201.
[448] Snape, *God and the British soldier*, pp. 215–16.
[449] A. K. Yapp, 'Introduction', in Told in the huts, ed. Yapp, p. 8.
[450] Adderley, 'The Church of England and the YMCA', pp. 2–4.

Likewise, in 1918 John Oxenham asserted that

> [W]hen the work of armies and navies is ended...the work of the YMCA will be greater then than ever...If it fulfils its clearly-defined mission – and I believe it will – it will become one of the greatest of the many new great forces which will make for the rebuilding of Life on the deeper, wider, nobler foundations to which we all look forward in prayerful hope.[451]

In addition to playing a key *rôle* in the reconstruction of religion and society in post-war Britain, it was even anticipated that the work of the YMCA would serve to replenish and revitalize the depleted ranks of Christian missionaries after the war. As K. J. Saunders explained in *The East and the West* in July 1917:

> [T]he Association is trying to get the best missionary speakers into the huts, and to give them a free hand to describe the work that their societies are doing, that they may enlist recruits for Mission service [and] it seems likely that amongst this great mass of men, all of whom have answered the call to adventure and sacrifice, and many of whom cherish the Crusader's zeal, the missionary appeal should find such a response as it has never found before...In view of the terrible losses sustained in the death on the battlefield of so many who were already missionaries, or who were training for missionary work, this is of special interest.[452]

Such grandiose visions proved quite delusory, although the YMCA did see some 'steady development of new branches at home' in the post-war years and its war work did help to stimulate a diffuse demand for club rooms and village halls in civilian life.[453] The scale and success of YMCA war work were beguiling in so far as they rested on the combined efforts of a broad and varied coalition of interested parties and individuals. Under the pressure of a national emergency of unprecedented scale and intensity, the YMCA was able to attract a large and diverse body of supporters, admirers and fellow travellers, a loose if considerable following that would quickly disperse with the coming of peace. As the case of Barclay Baron serves to illustrate, the YMCA was not the natural home or even the first loyalty of the majority of those who, for personal and patriotic as well as religious reasons, gave their services or their money to the Association. While Baron, like so many ex-servicemen, found his natural home in the Toc H movement, there was no shortage of other schemes and organizations in the post-war churches and in British society to distract and absorb the energies of such temporary supporters of the YMCA.

However, on the credit side the war at least established the Association's position as a national institution. In addition to its unprecedented prominence, its leading figures and key workers received a fair measure of public recognition. In

---

[451] Dunkerley, *The Red Triangle circle*, p. 3.

[452] K. J. Saunders, 'The missionary opportunity of the Young Men's Christian Association in the camps', *The East and the West*, July 1917, 277–82 at 279–80.

[453] *ODNB*, A. K. Yapp; K. Grieves, 'Huts, demobilisation and the quest for an associational life in rural communities in England after the Great War', in *Warfare and belligerence: perspectives in First World War Studies*, ed. P. Purseigle (Leiden, 2005), pp. 243–64.

1917, Arthur Yapp was among the first to be appointed a Knight Commander of the Order of the British Empire and was also called upon by the prime minister, Lloyd George, to help run the government's Food Economy Campaign.[454] Significantly, the inauguration of the Order of the British Empire in June 1917 was largely dictated by the need to recognize the kind of war work that the Association exemplified for, as Peter Duckers has stressed, 'The war effort had drawn in civilians, men and women, of every rank and status throughout the British Empire on a scale never before seen. Nursing, ordnance production, charitable work, transport, industry and recruitment were just some of the many vital civil activities deemed worthy of formal acknowledgement.'[455] Given its rationale, scores of YMCA workers were appointed to the Order of the British Empire; no fewer than forty-nine in January 1918 alone, including twelve as commanders, thirteen as officers and twenty-four as members.[456]

Finally, the war went a long way to divest the YMCA of what was widely seen as its 'namby-pamby' Victorian image. Indeed, the ordeal recast the YMCA as a repository of those virtues long associated with Christian manliness – virtues such as courage, stoicism, determination and self-sacrifice.[457] While twelve of its pre-war members earned the Victoria Cross and more than 1,200 'made the supreme sacrifice while serving in the fighting forces',[458] it was the Association's army work that was generally regarded as marking the decisive shift in its ethos and public image. In 1916, and with the Association already clearly rescued from the realm of Gilbertian caricature, an Anglican army chaplain wrote of the 'wonderful record of the YMCA' in the following terms:

> Before the war, whether fairly or not, men were apt to associate it with milk and water. The Christian young man was one who gave no trouble to his mother, one in whom his aunts rejoiced. The YMCA itself had found its place in comic literature and in popular songs as a symbol of harmlessness, a place where it was 'safe' to be. In most men's minds YMCA stood for something purely negative and rather soft. Since the war, the Association has shown its youth, its manhood, and its Christianity by rising to a great opportunity, and there are literally millions of young soldiers who will be eternally grateful to it, not negatively for what it is not, but positively for what it is and for what it has done for them.[459]

However, all of this took a heavy moral and financial toll on the Association. To its conservative critics it appeared that, in pursuing its army work, the YMCA had lost its soul to gain the world; it had become reliant on the help of women, liberals and agnostics and its centres had swarmed with actors, Ritualists, Roman Catholics and Jews. In addition to its neglect of the Great Commission, while it had resisted the encroachment of gambling it had nevertheless indulged smoking,

---

[454] *Ibid.*; Yapp, *In the service of youth*, pp. 142, 112–14.
[455] P. Duckers, *British orders and decorations* (Princes Risborough, 2004), p. 30.
[456] YMCA, J7 National Council signed minutes, 11 January 1918.
[457] Reznick, *Healing the nation*, p. 11.
[458] Yapp, *Romance of the Red Triangle*, p. 73; *Year book*, 1921, p. 90.
[459] T. W. Pym and G. Gordon, Papers from Picardy (London, 1917), p. 128.

secular entertainments, Sunday trading and even drinking on its premises. While these developments did not go unchallenged at the time, complaints about the Association's methods persisted long after the Armistice. In February 1921, for example, a bitter public attack on its work in the Rhineland was launched by W. Talbot Hindley, an Anglican clergyman and an agent of the Soldiers' Christian Association, who accused the YMCA of 'sending men to hell and ruining England' and vowed 'that it should not get a penny more in subscriptions if he could help it'.[460] Furthermore, its critics were not content with mere words, for a legal challenge to its war work was mounted in the Court of Chancery in 1918, a challenge that claimed it was unconstitutional under the national Memorandum of Association. While Mr Justice Neville proved to be a good patriot and entirely unsympathetic to the claim,[461] it proved impossible for the YMCA to disengage swiftly from its costly wartime commitments once the war had been won. While public subscriptions ceased abruptly with the signing of the Armistice,[462] the cost of victory meant that the YMCA continued to run hundreds of centres in France, Belgium, Germany, Mesopotamia, India, Constantinople, the Caucasus, North Russia, Egypt and Palestine.[463] However, by this time it was burdened with vast quantities of unwanted stores and, with expenditure in France and Belgium alone running at £1,000 a day in 1919, it soon accrued debts of around £1,000,000.[464]

The Association's laurels were also tarnished by questions concerning its financial probity. In March 1919 a court-martial in Coblenz found 'three former secretaries of the Young Men's Christian Association' guilty on charges of embezzlement, among them a clergyman who had stolen £5,600 'entrusted to him by soldiers to be sent to their homes'.[465] A further problem was the odour of profiteering and the strength of public feeling this charge could arouse. In 1917, Anglican chaplains had despaired over the lack of transparency in the Church Army's trading practices and, in 1920, searching questions were asked about the secular Navy and Army Canteen Board by the Central Profiteering Tribunal.[466] However, the turn of the YMCA came in March 1919. Three weeks after the conviction of its secretaries in Coblenz, the suffragan bishop of Swansea, Edward Latham Bevan, posted a list of accusations against the Association in the correspondence columns of *The Times*. These concerned the allegedly competitive, unnecessary and wasteful work of the Red Triangle in relation to its denominational equivalents, the price of goods sold in its centres and its perceived failure to produce 'a full and complete balance-sheet' for a British public that had treated it with 'unstinted confidence and generosity'.[467] In the event, all of these charges were refuted by the auditors of the War Emergency

---

[460] A. K. Yapp, 'The YMCA in Cologne', *The Red Triangle*, April 1921, pp. 247–9.
[461] YMCA, J7 National Council signed minutes, 14 June 1918.
[462] Yapp, *In the service of youth*, p. 134.
[463] *Times*, 19 May 1919, p. 9.
[464] Yapp, *In the service of youth*, pp. 136–7.
[465] *Times*, 3 March 1919, p..10.
[466] MAC, 'Proceedings of ACGs' Conferences', 6–7 November 1917; Hansard, *House of Commons Parliamentary Debates*, 20 May 1920, 1608–9.
[467] *Times*, 29 March 1919, p. 7.

Fund and by the findings of a three-man commission of inquiry appointed by the YMCA itself. This commission consisted of Sir Richard Vassar Smith, the head of Lloyd's Bank, Sir Frederick Gore-Browne, KC, and Lord Askwith, an eminent barrister and the country's leading industrial arbitrator.[468] As the commission established, the relevant accounts had been duly compiled and published, funds raised for war work had been devoted to that end and the Association's profits had not been excessive after its costs had been taken into account. Furthermore, it confirmed that these profits had been used for 'the benefit of the Naval and Military Services' and, for good measure, corroborated Yapp's argument that the prices charged by the YMCA had been fixed by the military authorities in order to prevent the army's own canteens from losing out.[469] Still, and however groundless the bishop's accusations proved to be, the Association's post-war inheritance of scandal, accusation and disappointed hopes was a poor reward for its vast, innovative and even heroic wartime endeavours.

---

[468] *Times*, 4 April 1919, p. 7, and 15 April 1919, p. 8; *ODNB*.
[469] *Times*, 31 March 1919, p. 7, and 20 May 1919, p. 6; Reznick, *Healing the nation*, pp. 20, 34; Messenger, *Call-to-arms*, pp. 458–61.

PART 2

MEMOIRS AND LETTERS

MEMOIRS

Chapter 1

The back parts of war

Early in 1915 I was approached by the Cavendish Association (an extension of the Social Service ideals of the Cavendish Club)[1] concerning a project for an Officers' club in Le Havre. The need for such a place, it was said, was growing more apparent every month that the war went on. A good deal was being done for the welfare of the men, in one way and another, very little for the commissioned ranks who, it was assumed, could look after themselves. Officers were landing every day at this great base for the first time in France, others spending the night there before the leave boat sailed to take them home; others, in a good many cases maimed or unfit men, who were employed at the base had nowhere to go when off duty but gloomy billets and overcrowded messes. Plenty of cynics would, of course, receive the scheme with the old retort, 'Well, after all there's a war on', but the army authorities were ready to back it.

The man to initiate the club was to be selected, if possible, by the Cavendish Association; the club, when founded, was to be managed and financed by the YMCA, by far the largest voluntary body working for the welfare of the troops. I was invited to go over and survey the situation and was provided with a temporary permit. In mid-June (after a stormy crossing by the Southampton route which has only just been discontinued) I landed at Le Havre and reported to the YMCA secretary, Leonard Pilkington.[2]

He was a striking figure, with a fine-drawn ivory face from which a pair of extraordinary dark eyes – the eyes, some said, of a fanatic – bored into yours as you faced him. He was obviously overworked and, as he clenched his hands while talking to you until the knuckles went white, he seemed to be 'living on his nerves'. 'Pilk', as I soon found, drove his team hard and himself much harder; he was on duty, early and late, in his office or round the centres seven days a week without any hour of recreation. His uncompromising Christian code made other people feel shy, his stern rectitude held them at arm's length. One could imagine him in another age an ascetic under hard self-discipline in the desert. In the next

---

[1]   See Introduction, pp. 10–11.
[2]   See Introduction, pp. 38–9, 69.

few days, I came very close to him, for we discussed all manner of things late into the night, and I slept, rolled in blankets, on a table in his office while he worked on before seeking his own camp bed. Then I found not only admiration but genuine affection for this lonely man growing: I longed to help him to escape from himself and find ease.

Accommodation in the Havre base in wartime was, of course, at a premium, but premises for the club had already been sighted, a large merchant's house lying back from a quiet but central street in an unkempt garden. With its mansard roof and tall windows it took after the squire's house, dignified by the name of *chateau*, which you sight so often at the end of a gloomy avenue of trees as you drive through the villages of the Pas de Calais. Though plans were already laid to adapt it for a club and even some of the furniture bought, the family was still in occupation and it would not be in our hands for at least a couple of months. This was a great disappointment, and I was glad when Pilkington suggested that I should use the time to gain some first hand experience of work in a typical YM hut where they were short-handed.

The camps at Havre, as at all the bases, were of many kinds. Up the Harfleur Valley, a few miles outside the town, there were nineteen Infantry Base Depôts[3] accommodating some 70,000 men. From these the reinforcements of various units – the Guards[4] at the lower end, the Canadians[5] at the top – were sent 'up the line with the best of luck' after a so-called 'rest'. Most of these were commanded by elderly colonels, with the stamp of Aldershot or Poona[6] who sighed for a return to 'real soldiering' *après la guerre finie*.[7] In the vast untidy region of the docks there were camps for technicians in the army, workshops or for dock-labourers. On the high ground round about lay the hospital camps and a large base for remount horses. Most of these camps were tented throughout the war and when the dull, camouflaged canvas was white with snow or under the lash of a

---

[3]   The original purpose of these depôts was to ensure a steady flow of fully trained reinforcements to their parent units. Initially, every infantry division established its own IBD on arrival in France, there being forty such depôts by mid-1916. However, heavy losses during the battle of the Somme (July–November 1916) meant that some depôts were unable to keep pace with the demand for replacements. Consequently, the divisional affiliations of these depôts were superseded by regimental ones, each depôt supplying a group of regiments recruited from the same geographical area. In the winter of 1917–18, a further round of reorganization reduced the number of depôts, curtailed their training functions and increased the number of regiments for which they were responsible. C. Messenger, *Call-to-arms: the British army 1914–18* (London, 2005), pp. 265–73; *Statistics of the military effort of the British Empire during the Great War 1914–1920* (London, 1922), p. 640.

[4]   Several battalions of Foot Guards went to France with the original BEF in August 1914. With the raising and arrival of additional Guards battalions a separate Guards Division was formed in France in August 1915. M. Middlebrook, *Your country needs you* (Barnsley, 2000), pp. 34–5.

[5]   Four Canadian infantry divisions saw service on the Western Front. However, only the 1st Canadian Division had arrived in France by the summer of 1915. F. W. Perry, *History of the Great War based on official documents. Order of battle of divisions part 5A. The divisions of Australia, Canada and New Zealand and those in East Africa* (Malpas, 1992), pp. 57–78.

[6]   Aldershot had been the regular army's principal home station since the Crimean War. Poona, situated about a hundred miles south-east of Bombay, had been one of British India's most important military stations since the early nineteenth century.

[7]   Ungrammatical, British army French.

bitter sea wind, men clemmed with cold could be heard blasphemously lamenting the loss of cosy billets in the battered villages near to the line, where you had at least skirting-boards with which to make a blaze on the hearth.

The camp to which I now went, was, I am thankful to say unique. It was most uncleverly sited upon an enormous dump of clinkers, rolled flat, facing their convenient place of origin, a very large munitions factory from which, when the hooter blew, there issued every evening hundreds of French women of all ages but unmistakeably alike, for their hair, hands and faces were stained a dirty orange by picric acid in their work on TNT.[8] It was more than a year after my service in the camp ended that a heavy explosion shook the town and we stood bareheaded in the street as a long column of grey French army wagons went by, each piled several tiers deep with the coffins of these women.[9]

'Cinder City' was in effect a prison camp, surrounded by a ten-foot hedge of barbed wire, leaning inwards at the top. True, this was not as impregnable as it looked, for some 'old lags' knew the point where (it was hinted, with a suitable tip to the sentry) they could make nocturnal sorties. The population, which was housed this time in long barrack huts of the usual pattern, was sharply divided at that period of the war into two very different categories. Nearly half of them were regular soldiers of the original Expeditionary Force, not a few now over military age, whom the newspapers at home had been wont six months earlier to lump together as 'the Heroes of Mons'. These were men who had failed, deserted or committed crimes during the famous retreat of 1914 or soon after it.[10] It would have been easier perhaps and more humane to have sent them home, demobilized or to serve their sentences. As it was they were marched out every morning, in parties under guard, to do sanitary fatigues and other dirty jobs in the town. They presented a sorry spectacle as heroes, for some were sick, others of very low intelligence, others as men without hope, rotting away: more than once during my stay a man ended it all by cutting his throat. The official classification of these men was hideously apt: 'Base Details'.

The other element in the camp was of quite a different character. It was at least a homogeneous body bound together by its trouble – an entire battalion of young Territorial soldiers[11] which had been led by their officers out of the

---

[8] Their counterparts in British munitions factories were dubbed 'canaries'. M. Brown, *The Imperial War Museum book of the First World War* (London, 1991), p. 205.

[9] Similar explosions occurred in British munitions factories, notably at the National Shell Filling Factory at Chilwell, near Nottingham, where 134 people were killed and 250 injured in an accident on 1 July 1918. *Ibid.*, p. 208; www.bbc.co.uk/insideout/eastmidlands/series2/blast_chilwell_somme.shtml. Consulted 7 August 2008.

[10] The battle of Mons was the first encounter between the BEF and the German army and was fought on 23 August 1914. Although the BEF largely held its positions along the Mons-Condé Canal, it was compelled to retreat the following day to avoid being outflanked. Its retreat, punctuated by fierce rearguard actions, continued for two weeks, taking the BEF 200 miles towards Paris. J. Keegan, *The First World War* (London, 1998), pp. 107–22.

[11] The part-time Territorial Force had been created in 1908 by R. B. Haldane, the Liberal secretary of state for war. Largely composed of the former Volunteers, the intended *rôle* of the TF was primarily the defence of mainland Britain. Although more than 90 per cent of its soldiers volunteered for service overseas following the outbreak of war, there were doubts as to their

trenches on their first tour of duty in the line, it was said because their relief failed
to take over at the time advertised. Rather oddly perhaps, these officers were still
in command, doing penance with their men, and I came to have a poor opinion
of the senior ones especially. The NCOs, from the sergeant-major downwards,
were average good soldiers, finding *morale* difficult to maintain in their stagnant
conditions, and the men themselves, many very young, were a fair sample from
an English provincial town. The best of them – and there was a due proportion of
such – felt their humiliation keenly. They longed for an opportunity to redeem
their dishonour and I believe it was eventually given them. Meanwhile they had
the deadening duty of providing the endless guards that were needed in the base.
Their plight was an open secret, and maybe the thumb of scorn was often jerked
over his shoulder by a man no better than himself at the smart young sentry, his
tell-tale regimental badge shining, outside Base Headquarters.

The YMCA personnel were the only civilians or strangers of any kind allowed
to enter the camp and the hut with a red triangle on it the only bright spot. I settled
down at once to share duties with the hut leader, to share with him also the tiny
bedroom, partitioned off from the kitchen, which was well filled with two
wooden bunks and an office table. We had one orderly[12] attached to the hut who
slept in a cubby hole on the premises. He was an old-style bombardier
moustached like Bairnsfather's Old Bill,[13] a lazy, good-tempered Irishman who
was drunk whenever he could smuggle enough beer through the wire. One night
he got out to poach eels in the canal and made the whole hut stink when he fried
them for us. He was never tired (as we soon became) of the story of his battery
in action during the Mons retreat. He caricatured the major adjusting his monocle
to give the wrong range – 'damn it, men, where *are* they? – and brought the scene
to a climax when his own field gun was knocked out – 'up she went', was his
invariable phrase, 'no more bloody use than a bladder on a stick!'

The remaining staff of the hut were billeted in the town, no woman in any
case was allowed to sleep in a camp, and half a dozen cars every night had a busy
round collecting them from various quarters and taking them home. There were
two devoted pairs who arrived in Cinder City each morning in time to get the
place ready for opening up. Mr and Mrs Stedman in a very antique car of their

efficiency. Significantly, as secretary of state for war, Lord Kitchener chose to recruit a new force
of wartime volunteers under the aegis of the regular army (his celebrated 'New Army') rather than
prioritize the expansion of the TF ('a town clerks' army') under its County Associations. I.
Beckett, 'The Territorial Force', in *A nation in arms*, ed. I. Beckett and K. Simpson (Manchester,
1985), pp. 128–31; A. Rawson, *British army handbook 1914–1918* (Stroud, 2006), pp. 7–8, 23;
Middlebrook, *Your country needs you*, pp. 97–101.

12   See Introduction, pp. 31, 37.
13   Bruce Bairnsfather (1888–1959) was the leading British cartoonist of the war. A pre-war regular
officer and trained artist, he was serving with the 1st Royal Warwickshire Regiment when he shot
to fame with the publication of some of his work in *The Bystander* magazine in 1915. Such was
the appeal of his cartoons (which were even reproduced on ceramics) he was eventually sent on
morale-boosting drawing missions to the Italian and American armies. His most famous comic
creation was 'Old Bill', who has been described as 'the archetypal, morose, sour but indomitable
"old contemptible"'. P. Haythornthwaite, *The World War One source book* (London, 1992),
pp. 366–7.

own,[14] and two little maiden sisters, charmingly called Dove.[15] The doors opened at ten, in accordance with camp orders, but long before that every man in the camp not on duty seemed to be in the queue outside them. 'Char and wads'[16] disappeared in quantity and were replenished, Wild Woodbines continued their appointed task of helping to win the war,[17] and, especially on pay-day, there was an onslaught on those appalling 'silk postcards', machine-embroidered with flags and forget-me-nots and legends like 'To my Dear Old Mum'. Steady sales were an essential of a YM hut – the only one, the critics sneered – but we reckoned that our paramount purpose was friendship, and it was nowhere more wanted than in Cinder City. I still have the picture in my memory of a man, upstanding and handsome but plainly ill, sitting down at a trestle table to write a letter home. He had not got beyond the first line when he dropped his head on his arms and began to cry like a child. No one took heed but Mrs Stedman, a most understanding and sensible mother to many a grown-up man here; she left the counter, laid a firm hand on his shoulder and presently had talked him back into the semblance of a soldier. She knew his wretched story and it was nothing out of the common.

The hut closed at mid-day for an interval while the men (and ourselves) had dinner. When it reopened there were a few customers, but a sudden wave when the parties marched in from their work in the late afternoon mounted to a flood as darkness set in. By ten o'clock when we closed down every bench was full and men crowded round the counter, mug in hand, to chat with the helpers. Once a week there might be a talk with lantern slides in the course of the evening and most nights there was a scratch sing song.[18] Very popular were the organized concerts, advertised by a notice on the door, with visiting singers, conjurors or funny men. None had a louder welcome than Sergeant Lovelace, leading with his fine tenor voice the prime sentimental favourites of the day – 'Little grey home in the West', 'When Irish eyes are smiling', 'They'll never believe me',

---

[14] The identification of male YMCA workers is problematic, as only the records of those who worked at home, or who went overseas from late 1917 to 1920, have survived. However, Mrs G. Stedman (and, presumably, her husband) hailed from Bramley, near Guildford, and she served at Le Havre from June 1915 to March 1916. Mrs Stedman was classed as a 'Motor Driver'. YMCA Archives, University of Birmingham (hereafter YMCA), K47 Transcript list of ladies who served in France and overseas.

[15] Agnes and Mary Dove were from London and served at Le Havre from July to September 1915. They were both classed as a 'Voluntary Canteen Worker'. YMCA, K47 Transcript list of ladies who served in France and overseas.

[16] Tea and cakes (or buns). J. Brophy and E. Partridge, *The long trail: soldiers' songs and slang 1914–18* (London, 1969), pp. 82 and 160. Both Brophy and Partridge were veterans of the First World War.

[17] The British soldier consumed tobacco in vast quantities, the war creating 'an image of the "Tommy" as a constant smoker of "fags" which psychological and physical pressures encouraged him to live up to and which efficient distributive systems ensured he could'. Both cigarettes and pipe tobacco were widely and freely distributed as comforts by army chaplains, the most celebrated clerical tobacconist being G. A. Studdert Kennedy (or 'Woodbine Willie'). From 1914 to 1918, the exigencies of war saw a major shift in British smoking habits; the war 'democratized the cigarette' and pipe tobacco was largely eschewed in its favour. M. Hilton, *Smoking in British popular culture 1800–2000* (Manchester, 2000), p. 126; G. Corrigan, *Mud, blood and poppycock* (London, 2004), p. 99.

[18] See Introduction, p. 44.

'The only girl in the world' and 'The broken doll'; his 'Come to me, Thorah' was heart-rending. But perhaps the best of his repertoire, because grotesquely unfitting to the time and place, was 'When you come to the end of a perfect day': there was nothing this audience could do less, or wanted less to do, than to 'sit alone with your thought', but it hypnotized them into a mood when they could forget their troubles.

The peak of entertainment, however, was the rare visit of Lena Ashwell's Concert Party.[19] Lena Ashwell, a distinguished actress,[20] conducted her own company of professionals round the theatres of that war with unflagging spirit and success. She was indeed the unofficial precursor of ENSA in the war to come,[21] but I never heard her efforts under the fire of criticism as her successors' were to be. She certainly gave us a rattling show, applauded wildly by both officers and other ranks, one night in Cinder City.

We had, of course, plenty of minor drawbacks to contend with. In dry windy weather the cinders underfoot, long since trampled into fine black dust by army boots, blew in eddies across the camp and filled the nostrils and the food. When you went to bed at night you found your whole body shaded in all the tones of sepia. If it rained, on the other hand, the camp was soon bogged down in sticky jet-black mud which sucked at your boots and plastered the wooden floors. Try as our small staff would, keeping the place clean passed the wit of man and woman. Our best was not nearly good enough for the camp commandant of the base,[22] who inspected us at irregular intervals. He was a small man, immensely

[19] See Introduction, pp. 32, 44.
[20] Born Lena Margaret Pococke, Lena Ashwell (1872–1957) was the daughter of a deeply religious naval officer who later went on to become a clergyman. She used her father's middle name for professional purposes. Brought up in Canada, she was educated at Bishop Strachan's School for Young Ladies in Toronto and at the University of Toronto before progressing to the Lausanne conservatoire and the Royal Academy of Music. In 1891 she abandoned a musical career in favour of the stage. Although success eluded her initially (a situation that was partly due to her strong Canadian accent and partly the result of an unhappy marriage to a fellow actor) by 1900 Ashwell was one of London's leading actresses and, in 1906, she began a distinguished career in theatre management at the Savoy Theatre. A keen supporter of women's suffrage, Ashwell also aimed to develop the educational and cultural *rôle* of the theatre among all social classes in Britain, an ambition that underpinned much of her work during the First World War. From 1915, she became a tireless organizer of concerts for troops on the Western Front and elsewhere, eventually recruiting more than twenty-five troupes of actors (who were paid expenses only) and raising £100,000 to support their work. Appointed an OBE in 1917, Ashwell's concerts for the troops were comparatively high brow, often featuring excerpts from Shakespeare as well as songs and recitations. Ashwell married Henry Simson, a distinguished surgeon, in 1908 (the year in which she divorced her first husband for drunkenness and violence) and died as Lady Simson in 1957. *ODNB*; *Times*, 15 March 1957, p. 13.
[21] The Entertainments National Service Association was formed in 1939. Working in collaboration with the Navy, Army and Air Force Institute (or 'Naafi') it staged thousands of variety shows for the entertainment of service personnel at home and abroad, the quality of which was variable to say the least. Its critics were wont to translate its acronym as 'Every Night Something Awful'. H. Miller, *Service to the services: the story of Naafi* (London, 1971), pp. 29, 74–6.
[22] Brigadier-General (later Major-General) Joseph John Asser (1867–1949) commanded the base at Le Havre from 18 July 1915 to 2 December 1916. Asser had not, in fact, risen from the ranks but was an outstanding logistician who had distinguished himself in the Sudan. Having been attached to the Egyptian army for sixteen years he was recalled to the army within weeks of his retirement

self-important partly for that reason, who wore his blue-banded staff hat at a jaunty angle.[23] He had risen from the ranks and was now disposed, on a well-known principle, to take it out of the ranks whenever opportunity presented itself; civilians, as we were, offered him a sitting target. I had got along with him well enough (tea and a cigarette are good allies) until an abysmally wet day when he strode into our hut in an ill temper, took one look at the floor and ordered that we were to close at once and not to open again until we had reduced it to an Aldershot barrack-room standard and he had passed it. We had no choice but to close down and spend the afternoon scrubbing; during half that night we were on our knees going over it again. We made some impression, but Aldershot was impossible. Next morning the floor was still not dry and I pinned a notice on the door that the hut was closed by camp commandant's orders. It was a very profane crowd that huddled in the rain outside to read it, and it may have been as well that our common bugbear did not show up for his inspection. After dinner we opened as usual. Some men in brief authority answer Euclid's definition of a point – they have 'position but no magnitude'.

A week after I arrived in Cinder City the hut leader received a wire from home that his father was dying. He got compassionate leave immediately and a permit to cross by that night's boat. He packed hurriedly, tossed the keys of the strong-box to me and said goodbye: I never saw him again. Automatically I took his place and Pilkington confirmed it.

Surprisingly quickly two months went by until I went into the town to undertake at last the opening of the Officers' Club. I had made only hurried visits to 'Soixante-Quinze', our headquarters in an ink-splattered Commercial School in the main avenue, and had seen 'Pilk' for no more than a few minutes at a time. We now spent a morning in the Club premises together with French workmen, surveying furniture and ordering redecorations.

But there was a good deal more to the visit. We were joined that day by Oliver McCowen,[24] who was in charge of all YMCA work in France and subsequently in Flanders and Germany also. I had not met before this genial, strong-minded

---

in July 1914. Such was his success in organizing the unloading of supplies at Le Havre that he was promoted to inspector-general of communications and, in April 1919, he succeeded Haig as commander of British troops in France and Flanders. Asser was created CB in 1915, KCVO in 1917 and KCMG in 1918. Promoted to lieutenant-general in June 1919, he later served as governor of Bermuda and retired from the army as a full general in 1930. *Times*, 5 February 1949, p. 6; A. F. Becke, *History of the Great War based on official documents. Order of battle part 4. The Army Council, GHQs, armies, and corps 1914–1918* (Uckfield, 2007), p. 16.

[23] Staff officers were usually distinguished by their red cap bands and red gorgets (i.e. lapel tabs), hence the nickname 'red tabs'. However, in 1916 blue superseded red for camp commandants and certain other staff officers. D. S. V. Fosten, R. J. Marrion and G. A. Embleton, *The British army 1914–18* (London, 1978), p. 30; Messenger, *Call-to-arms*, pp. 355–6.

[24] Oliver McCowen (?–?) was the son of a wealthy Tralee tradesman and trained as a laywer, building up a practice in Tralee before becoming a full-time YMCA secretary. He then worked in Burma and India and was on holiday in Ireland when war broke out. Following a short spell of camp work with the army in Ireland, McCowen was charged with developing YMCA work in France. By 1917 the YMCA could claim that he had gained 'the confidence equally of the YMCA staff in France, our own Headquarters, and the military authorities'. *The Red Triangle Bulletin*, 26 October 1917, p. 4; See Introduction, pp. 38–9.

Irishman with a queer twitch in one eye, a man with whom I was often to cross swords later but whom I came to admire and reckon my friend. He had been summoned from his headquarters at Abbeville on urgent business, to which the affair of the Club was only secondary. Pilkington, it was plain to both of us, was reaching the end of his tether. It was imperative that he should go home, at least for some time, on leave, a proposal which even now he violently resisted. A difficult council of war later that night decided that I should go home for a week or so at once, for my temporary permit was expiring, and return to take over the YM leadership of the base in Pilkington's absence. I think that neither McCowen nor I really believed that he would recover his balance enough to bear this burden again: in the event we were justified in our surmise. He had given to this work since the earliest days more than anyone had a right to ask, all that he had to give.

I went home to enjoy, with my wife, the delights of our eldest son, now six months old, and to make preparations for a job which was totally unexpected but, I felt, inescapable. For the next two years, as it turned out, I was to direct the work in Havre. It was multifarious and constantly developing as the war dragged on into new phases.

The Officers' Club, my original assignment, duly opened, but now it could be no more than a side issue in the whole plan of operations. It was immediately popular and fulfilled, as evidence showed, some of the purposes for which we designed it. In charge of it I put a pair of workers who proved to be ideal – Miss Royce, a big-hearted, vigorous Australian,[25] and Wilson,[26] the kindly and most humorous Presbyterian minister of Portrush in Northern Ireland, who was eventually killed in an army car crash near Havre. The Club had its ups and downs but I remember only one crisis. I was rung up one morning in the office by Miss Royce who made me come at once – 'something dreadful has happened'. I hurried round, expecting to find an officer hanging from the back of a door, but the trouble was in the kitchen and advertised itself loudly almost before the front-door was opened. The stone flags in the middle of the kitchen had risen an inch or two and through the cracks stinking sewage was seeping until the whole floor was under the foulest liquid. I closed the club and rang up the Town Hall, and in half an hour a pair of horses towed a lumbering contraption up the drive. This was *le vidange*, a big tank on four wheels surmounted by a Heath Robinson[27] pump with a pipe like a boa constrictor. The two men in charge started to pump out the

---

[25] Elizabeth Royce, who was by now living in Essex, was classed as a 'Housekeeper'. She served at Le Havre from October 1915 to August 1919. YMCA, K47 Transcript list of ladies who served in France and overseas.

[26] W. A. Wilson, a Presbyterian minister from Coleraine, was killed on 20 March 1918 and was given a military funeral. He was mourned by the YMCA as 'one of the most successful workers we have ever sent to France'. At the time of his death he was responsible for the Officers' Club at Le Havre. He was the author of a letter sent to Rachel Baron in August 1916 (see Appendix I). *The Red Triangle Bulletin*, 29 March 1918, p. 4.

[27] William Heath Robinson (1872–1944) was a popular illustrator and cartoonist known for caricaturing the excesses of the machine age. The term 'Heath-Robinson contraption' was in popular use before the First World War. www.bbc.co.uk/history/historic_figures/robinson_william_heath.shtml. Consulted 4 December 2008.

sewage and presently the floor subsided. 'This must not happen again', I said severely to the sanitary inspector who had turned up to supervise, 'how often shall we need *le vidange?*' 'When the kitchen floor comes up you'll know', he said and went away. Le Havre, like many French cities had, perhaps still has, no main drainage, but I have often wondered if its architects always put the cesspool under the kitchen.

The YMCA staff in Havre at this time numbered something less than a hundred, of whom more than half were women. As soon as the Conscription Act was passed our men, of course, had to attest and be examined by a medical board.[28] In trying to forecast the possible dislocation of our work we made a list at once. A small handful, we knew, would be taken for military service and would go home to join up. A much larger number, either over age, obviously unfit or exempt as ministers of religion, we should justifiably retain. There remained a few border-line cases. In the event the medical board classified me B.3, which stood for 'home service',[29] but I was advised by the examiners to carry on with the direction of work which the army authorities on the spot had come to regard as essential. One outstanding hut leader, Whitley, a son of the Speaker whose monument is the 'Whitley Councils',[30] refused to attest: I had long known him to be a conscientious objector.[31] We said goodbye to him with sincere regret and he went home to waste, I suppose, much valuable time in prison, alongside many willing Quakers, in ignominy which he did not deserve. Our manpower for the moment was lamed but the breaches could soon be repaired.

Some of our staff were decidedly odd characters, others individualists only suited to special jobs of work and it was not an easy team to manage. We had to build up and maintain a voluntary discipline of our own, based on a strong *esprit*

---

[28] The first Military Service Act was passed in January 1916 and the first conscripts were called up in March. The Act initially applied to all British males resident in mainland Britain who were single, with no dependants and aged between eighteen and forty-one on 15 August 1915. However, in May a second Act was passed that extended conscription to married men as well. Exemptions remained, however; while the male population of Ireland was excluded from these Acts, exemptions applied to the medically unfit and to hundreds of thousands of men in reserved occupations. T. Wilson, *The myriad faces of war: Britain and the Great War* (Cambridge, 1988), pp. 396–401; Rawson, *British army handbook 1914–1918*, p. 34.

[29] The army's medical classification system was refined as the war went on. According to the system introduced in mid-1916, category B.3 denoted men who were fit for sedentary work on lines of communication overseas. Under an earlier definition, Class B men were deemed to be temporarily unfit for overseas service. Rawson, *British army handbook 1914–1918*, pp. 30–3.

[30] These industrial councils of employers and employees were named after John Henry Whitley (1866–1935), the Liberal MP for Halifax who chaired the subcommittee on reconstruction which recommended their creation in 1917. Whitley served as Speaker of the House of Commons from 1921 to 1928 and became president of the National Council of Social Service in 1921, having shared an interest in youth work with Barclay Baron. *ODNB*.

[31] The Military Service Act of January 1916 made provision for exemption from combatant service on the grounds of conscientious objection, without actually defining its nature. The cases of 16,000 or so who sought exemption on these grounds were heard by local tribunals and, in 80 per cent of cases, a form of military or civilian exemption was granted. However, around 1,500 'absolutists' refused to co-operate and were liable to prosecution under military and civilian law. Wilson, *Myriad faces of war*, pp. 398–9; Brown, *Imperial War Museum book of the First World War*, pp. 252–6.

de corps. Our status as civilians attached to the army was anomalous and the final arbiter of it was the assistant provost marshal.[32] I had frequent dealings with the APM, a captain who had been badly wounded and was now on 'light duty', which was by no means always light. Fitzpatrick was a fine character and we became very good friends. Each of our workers carried on his or her person a 'red permit', an indispensable four-fold document, printed in English and French, with a passport photograph attached.[33] It referred vaguely to the only section of the Army Act which would cover us, and I once had to remind a recalcitrant lady who made a fuss about her rights that this referred to 'camp followers', the disreputable women who in earlier days had trailed around with British troops in India.[34] The base controlled a bridgehead of its own, a few miles deep, and any movement of ours beyond it required in theory a 'blue permit', printed entirely in French. There were road blocks at the main points of exit and I remember sailing through one in a YM car when the woman driver waved in the face of the armed French guard a packet of *papier poudiée*, the equivalent of the modern lady's compact.

The great majority of our people were, of course, fully employed in the work of the huts, the routine of which has been sufficiently described in the case of Cinder City. The huts were numerous but not uniform in their atmosphere: that depended both on the team running a hut and on the men using it. There was an obvious difference between the customer of 'Annexe I' or 'Workshops', where engineers[35] or the RAOC[36] were plying their essential skilled trades for 'the duration', and the reinforcements in the Harfleur Valley, fighting men coming and going, and even there a strong distinction between the depôt of the 60th,[37] the North Country regiments in Camp 15 and the Canadians in Camp 19. In each hut

---

[32] The BEF had its own provost marshal who was responsible for policing the army in the field. He was represented at a local level by a hierarchy of deputy and assistant provost marshals who commanded detachments of Military Police. *Statistics of the military effort of the British Empire*, p. 642; Fosten, Marrion and Embleton, *The British army 1914–18*, p. 16.

[33] See Introduction, p. 38.

[34] Although British armies on campaign in nineteenth-century India often had an enormous tail of camp followers (including native prostitutes), the term and the phenomenon were much broader than Baron implies. R. Holmes (ed.), *The Oxford companion to military history* (Oxford, 2001), pp. 170–1.

[35] Royal Engineers. The duties of the Corps of Royal Engineers were many and varied and its units specialized in a wide range of skills including building, tunnelling, signalling, mechanics and meteorology. By November 1918 the corps had reached a strength of nearly 360,000 officers and men and comprised almost 10 per cent of the British army. Rawson, *British army handbook 1914–1918*, pp. 104–9; *Statistics of the military effort of the British Empire*, pp. 165–72, 231.

[36] Royal Army Ordnance Corps. The 'Royal' prefix was not awarded until after the First World War. The Army Ordnance Corps was responsible for the supply of armaments, ammunition and other military stores and also had repair and salvage duties. By November 1918 it numbered nearly 40,000 men. Rawson, *British army handbook 1914–1918*, pp. 150–2; *Statistics of the military effort of the British Empire*, pp. 195–7, 231.

[37] The 60th Rifles was the pre-1881 designation for the King's Royal Rifle Corps, a designation that survived unofficially into the twentieth century. With the reorganization of the Infantry Base Depôts in the summer of 1916 (see above, n. 3), the KRRC was linked to No. 47 IBD which sent drafts to regiments with London connections such as the London Regiment and the Rifle Brigade. A. Makepeace-Warne, *Brassey's companion to the British army* (London, 1998), p. 188; Messenger, *Call-to-arms*, pp. 267–8.

we had, as far as possible, two or more long-term workers who started as friends or grew together on the job; these were reinforced as required by those who came out at frequent intervals from home on a three-month contract – and were not always easy to fit. As the war went on our manpower inevitably tended to decline in quality. A good deal of it consisted of clergy or ministers, a class exempt from military service, others were men rejected when conscription came in. Most of them came with a genuine impulse to serve the troops, a few apparently out of mere curiosity and they were weak links in the chain. On the whole we had, like any battalion or ship's company, our fair share of successes and failures. Of the keenness, commonsense and hard work of the permanent core there was never any doubt.

One or two huts presented special problems and needed carefully chosen staff to deal with them. The most difficult of these was that in No. 9 (later 39) Hospital, the biggest hospital for venereal disease in France.[38] Pilkington had got leave to erect a large wooden building there, the only institution of its kind behind the barbed wire; the gates of the hospital were strictly barred to all other visitors. This hut possessed a well-fitted stage and an exceptional library of books, for we discovered in No. 9 – doctors and psychologists may be able to explain why – a standard of education and intelligence to be matched nowhere else in the base. The atmosphere in the audience was peculiar and uncomfortable; perhaps anyone who has lectured, say, to prisoners in Pentonville has sensed something like it. Some men were weighted by shame and despair at their condition, others were frankly cynical. In no section was this more outspoken than in the officers' lines, where I once spent an hour in company with the very conscientious, hard-bitten commandant. When T. R. Glover of Cambridge,[39] the author of *The Jesus of history*, who was serving in the YMCA as a lecturer, came with me one evening to speak in No. 9 he was very well received and there was an excellent discussion, but he was too overcome by the atmosphere of the place to face it for a second time.

This unpalatable subject, about which in Havre we said little but tried to do at least something, deserves a few more words here. Ever since the returning crusaders (according to one theory) introduced the scourge of VD into Europe the problem of its control has been baffling; there has been some medical, no great moral, solution. In Havre it lay within the province not only of the army doctors but of the APM, and their prime object had to be military efficiency; they were concerned to return the

---

[38] Venereal disease was the greatest and most avoidable cause of illness among British soldiers in France and Flanders, being even more ubiquitous than trench foot. There were more than 150,000 hospital admissions over the course of the war and its incidence peaked at nearly thirty admissions per thousand troops in 1915. Conditions and treatments in VD hospitals were commonly construed as deterrents in themselves and, until 1916, when an officer committed suicide as a result, the army informed the next of kin of VD patients of their ailment as a matter of course. B. Harrison, 'The British army and the problem of venereal disease in France and Egypt during the First World War', *Medical History*, XXXIX (1995), 133–58, *passim*; Rawson, *British army handbook 1914–1918*, p. 133.

[39] Terrott Reavely Glover (1869–1943) published *The Jesus of history* in 1917. With a foreword by Randall Davidson, the archbishop of Canterbury, it was written for the Student Christian Movement. A classicist and the son of a Baptist minister, from 1911 Glover lectured in ancient history at Cambridge and was elected president of the Baptist Union in 1924. T. R. Glover, *The Jesus of history* (London, 1917); http://janus.lib.cam.ac.uk. Consulted 3 September 2008.

sufferers as soon as possible in fit condition to the front line. In Havre a system of licensed houses had been set up;[40] a whole street had been cleared of other inhabitants and filled with French girls, under inspection by RAMC[41] doctors, to whom only British soldiers had access. I remember a dark night when I was returning late to my billet, in uniform passably like an officer's (all YM workers were ordered to assume this in 1916),[42] and a military policeman saluted me with 'Excuse me, sir, are you looking for the Rue de Gallion?' He was trying to be helpful.

A question about the licensing system had been asked in Parliament and its existence was abruptly denied by a minister. This could not escape our notice on the report and I discussed it with the APM. As a good Roman Catholic he found the whole business most distasteful. 'But', he said, 'look at my figures', and he showed me a graph which recorded week by week the decline of the disease in Havre compared with Rouen where there was no such control. At a later stage in the war I was to be asked by another APM, an old friend, to allow him to open a cleansing station[43] on YMCA premises at Amiens, so that men on twelve hours' leave from the line could slip in and out without attracting notice. He was confident that it would save many disasters, but I replied, rightly or wrongly, that the sign of the red triangle could not cover this operation. Later still I was party to a large conference of army chaplains being held at YMCA headquarters in occupied Cologne, where a street of licensed houses was so blatant as to attract the ridicule of German passers-by.[44] There as a result decisive action was taken by the army commander himself.[45] It was all a complicated question, on which upright men differed and found it hard to agree on the right answer.

In Havre there was a minor corollary, with which I had to deal. Pilkington had established a small home for unmarried mothers – the mothers French, some of them little more than children, the fathers British soldiers. For this we rented a pleasant little villa on the edge of the town, beside the road leading to Ste Addresse, the promontory which guards the entrance to the port of Le Havre. Its existence was a secret even from our own workers, for if advertised we were sure it would be closed down by the army authorities as work well outside the

---

[40] These *maisons de tolérance* emulated the French system of licensed brothels and had a highly controversial precedent in the regulation of soldiers' brothels in the army's Indian stations. R. Holmes, *Sahib: the British soldier in India 1750–1914* (London, 2005), pp. 480–1; Harrison, 'The British army and the problem of venereal disease in France and Egypt', pp. 142–3.

[41] Royal Army Medical Corps. The functions of the RAMC were as diverse as those of the RE and the AOC. It was responsible for the army's general hygiene and for a complex system of casualty evacuation and treatment. By November 1918 it numbered nearly 140,000 men. Rawson, *British army handbook 1914–1918*, pp. 133–49; *Statistics of the military effort of the British Empire*, pp. 185–6, 231.

[42] See Introduction, pp. 52–3.

[43] Yet another strategy in the army's fight against VD, disinfecting facilities drew on the army's Indian experience and on the policy of its French allies. In 1916 an Army Order directed that all soldiers who had exposed themselves to VD should seek disinfection within twenty-four hours. As disinfection apparatus was installed in common urinals, the policy proved unpopular with those whom it sought to protect. Holmes, *Sahib*, p. 483; Harrison, 'The British army and the problem of venereal disease in France and Egypt', pp. 146–8.

[44] See Introduction, pp. 90–1.

[45] The details of this 'decisive action' are unclear.

province of the YM, whose sole commission was the welfare of British troops. The place was run, with the help of a trained nurse, by a member of our staff, Miss Fortey.[46] She was the sister, as it happened, of an old school-friend of my own, and a noble character who was to leave an honoured name for her service in a Roman Catholic sisterhood. She came to my office one day in tears, on her way back to the home from an interview with the French *police des moeurs*,[47] who should have been her best allies. With her own ears she had heard them give the address of one of her girls, lately discharged with her baby, to a British officer. Would I come with her at once and have it out with the base commandant? I was not on good terms with him and had to remind her what would infallibly happen: it did not greatly matter that I should be in further trouble, but her home would be closed down and she herself sent home, her work of love and rescue ended. She had to see the point.

Let me turn to another very different venture which was to demand the building of a big new YM hut of its own. I had come to know Canon Hannay (the novelist 'George Birmingham'),[48] a chaplain over age to serve at the front and

[46] Here Baron appears to be in error as no woman named Fortey worked for the YMCA in Le Havre during the war. She may, however, have belonged to another organization such as the Catholic Women's League. YMCA, K47 Transcript list of ladies who served in France and overseas.
[47] Police who dealt with moral and sexual matters, such as the running of licensed brothels.
[48] James Owen Hannay (1865–1950) was rector of Westport, county Mayo, from 1892 to 1913. A talented writer, he adopted the pseudonym 'George A. Birmingham' after his literary output caused some local controversy. An active figure in the Gaelic League, the growing politicization of this cultural organization was reflected in his expulsion in 1914 for his supposedly objectionable portrayals of Irish rural life (his novel and stage play *General John Regan* took as its theme the erection of a local monument to a bogus Irish hero). Having been made a canon of St Patrick's Cathedral, Dublin, in 1912, Hannay left Westport in 1913 and embarked upon a lecture tour of the United States from which he returned two years later. Although fifty years old and married with four children, he then applied for a temporary commission in the Army Chaplains' Department and was interviewed by the chaplain-general, Bishop John Taylor Smith, on 29 December 1915. Duly pronounced 'A.1', he was commissioned on 11 January 1916 and served for a year, the standard length of a temporary chaplain's contract at this time, returning to England in January 1917. He served at Le Havre from January to May 1916 and at Boulogne thereafter. Though no longer with the Department, Hannay contributed to *The church in the furnace* (1917), a controversial collection of essays by seventeen army chaplains that made a trenchant case for reform in the Church of England. Hannay's essay was entitled 'Man to man', in which he appealed for a greater concentration on the essentials of faith and morals. He also published *A padre in France* (1918) in which he described his work as an army chaplain. His portrayal of the YMCA and its work was largely sympathetic and he remarked on how there was 'less aggressive religiosity' in YMCA huts than in the early months of the war. With Baron and his ilk in mind, he claimed that the Association was 'more and more drawing its workers from a class which instinctively shrinks from slapping a strange man heartily on the back and greeting him with the inquiry – "Tommy, how's your soul?"' Hannay was appointed rector of Carnalway, county Kildare, in 1918 but resigned this living and his canonry in 1922 due to failing health and after the violence of the Anglo-Irish War. Having briefly served as chaplain to the British legation in Budapest, in 1924 Hannay was appointed to the rectory of Mells in Somerset. Following a disastrous fire at Mells in 1929 and the death of his wife in 1933, Hannay was appointed vicar of Holy Trinity, Kensington, in 1934. A prolific author until his death, in 1946 Hannay received an honorary D.Lit. from Trinity College Dublin. *ODNB*; *Times*, 3 February 1950, p. 7; Museum of Army Chaplaincy, Amport House, Andover (hereafter MAC), Chaplains card index; *Army List*, July 1916 and July 1917; Church Missionary Society Archives, University of Birmingham (hereafter CMS), XCMS ACC/18/Z/1 Army Book of L. H. Gwynne, p. 151; M. Snape, *The Royal Army Chaplains' Department 1796–1953: clergy under fire* (Woodbridge, 2008), p. 184; F. B. MacNutt (ed.), *The church in the furnace: essays by seventeen temporary chaplains on active service in France and Flanders* (London, 1917), pp. 335–46: J. O. Hannay, *A padre in France* (London, 1918), pp. 123–30.

now attached to the Base Depôt of the 60th in the Harfleur Valley. One morning he called on me with a problem which he thought that the YM, if anybody, could help to solve. Up and down the Valley he had noticed a number of boys in uniform – on careful investigation he reckoned there were as many as three hundred of them, one at least barely fourteen years of age. They had been accepted by the recruiting officers at home, most, though perhaps not all, by giving a false date of birth. They had been sent up to the fighting areas eventually and, not surprisingly, returned to the base again as unsuitable soldiers for the front line. Meanwhile they were not shipped to England for demobilization, which would appear the commonsense course, but kept at the base on fatigues and rather desultory training.[49] Herded with older men, who were toughened and usually disgruntled, they were well on the road to demoralization. Hannay and I went at once to ask an interview with the base commandant with a proposition for a 'Boys' Club' in our minds. The great man flared up at once – 'Boys!' he burst out, 'there are no *boys* in the army.' 'Young soldiers, sir', we corrected ourselves hastily and his hackles went down. After a rather ticklish half hour he agreed to an experiment, on certain conditions. The YMCA was to produce, furnish and maintain the premises and all its activities at its own charges, the young soldiers should be under strict supervision, also provided by us, and we were to arrange an educational programme for them to be approved by himself.

These three conditions we set to work, with Hannay's enthusiastic help, to satisfy as soon as might be. A site for another large hut in the overcrowded Valley was not easy to find, and when found was very awkward, for it had to be on a steep slope and that meant building the front elevation on six-foot stilts. Behind these – for it's an ill wind that doesn't blow somebody good – the 'old sweats' were later discovered at night playing the forbidden game of Crown and Anchor.[50] It was a large hut, divided into several good rooms, and at that time in the war it was very expensive, as well as maddeningly slow, to erect. At last it was done, and we were proud of a beautiful job.

As for supervision, my mind's eye had leapt in the first moment of the project to Miss Nettleton,[51] one of the most original of our workers. She was an elderly

---

49   Until May 1915, when the age requirement for enlistment in the Territorials was raised to nineteen in line with that of the New Army, the minimum age for enlistment in the Territorial Force was only seventeen. However, the problem of under-age volunteers was endemic and large numbers saw active service. In June 1916 an Army Council Instruction decreed that parents could reclaim their sons if they were under eighteen; however, those already serving in France and aged between eighteen and nineteen were retained for training at base. In 1917 a special holding unit was established at Etaples and, from April of that year, its soldiers were returned to their units once they reached eighteen. Messenger, *Call-to-arms*, pp. 75–6, 271.

50   Crown and Anchor. Although the army tolerated certain forms of gambling, Crown and Anchor (of which there were several variants) was illegal. It was played with special dice (marked with crowns, anchors, spades, diamonds, clubs and hearts) and with a board marked with the same symbols. It was, as Denis Winter noted, a game for 'the gambling hard core'. D. Winter, *Death's men: soldiers of the Great War* (London, 1978), pp. 153–5.

51   Irene Nettleton, from Battersea, was classed as a 'Canteen Worker' and served at Le Havre from August 1915 to October 1919. YMC.A, K47 Transcript list of ladies who served in France and overseas.

maiden lady, who loved to tell stories of her wild and wonderful *ménage* in a cottage at home. Stout and untidy in her ill-fitting khaki tunic, she looked the part of an unpredictable loveable aunt on the stage. She drove her own rattletrap 'Tin Lizzie', always in trouble which any army workshop enjoyed putting right for the sake of her company. She kept a monkey in her billet, which constantly raided other people's rooms and left her own hairbrush out of reach on the roof. Her favourite exclamation, which became a byword, was 'Its a dog's life – and not a lap dog's either.' She was full of laughter and left a trail of it everywhere in her wake, but she was full also of sterling good sense and generous affection. I offered her the Young Soldiers' Club and she took it, lock stock and barrel, without hesitation.

The third condition, the grandiloquent 'educational programme', we were able to satisfy sufficiently. A number of the 'boys' were barely literate and Miss Nettleton could deal with the three R's. Some of them were not at all too old to sit round her on the floor like children while she read them *Treasure island* or *The wind in the willows*: this could be counted as an hour of 'English'. We enlisted a small corps of lecturers from among the chaplains and the elderly colonels who commanded IBDs – the Infantry Base Depôts in the Valley. (I only hope that these speakers kept clear of Henry V, for, Harfleur itself being almost within shouting distance of the camps, the standard peroration to talks in the Valley was 'Once more into the breach, dear friends!'[52] – a climax which set old soldiers cursing under their breath: this old so-and-so wasn't *their* dear friend and they had been once too often in the breach already.) A course rather vaguely called 'History', and talks about 'Life on a Farm' or 'How to become an Engineer' or even 'How I shot my first Tiger' didn't look so bad on paper. When submitted to the base commandant he passed it, through with how much scrutiny I do not know. Actually all this was not mere camouflage. We could reckon it, within limits, as 'liberal education', for it drew out of some young soldiers interests and capacities they had never suspected in themselves.

The Club opened unobtrusively, a set-up of which any boys' club at home might have been proud. Its membership, well defined, were required to parade there punctually for their schooling and were free to come in at will for their recreation; all other entrants were barred. We equipped it well with table tennis (in those days still 'ping pong'), boxing gloves and a punch-ball; the piano, dominoes, draughts and even 'snakes and ladders' had a non-stop run every evening. But Miss Nettleton herself was the centre of attraction. She groomed their minds; she mothered them – and some missed this bitterly, while others had never known it before; she unravelled their loneliness and their disillusionment into laughter. I have never consciously met one of her pupils in the years since then, but I think there must still be men, now beyond middle age, who recognize their lasting debt to her.

In the last weeks of June, 1916, rumours were rife of preparations for the biggest offensive ever; this was 'top secret', in the modern phrase, but was

---

[52] The opening words of Act III Scene I of Shakespeare's *Henry V*, spoken before the walls of Harfleur.

confirmed – in strict confidence of course – by everyone you met at the base. One afternoon I went, with a couple of others, up to the headland of Ste Addresse, where, putting our ears to the turf, we heard distinctly – as, indeed, friends in Kent were doing – the continuous thudding of the massed lines of our guns upon the Somme, a hundred and twenty miles away.[53] The attack opened on the first of July, ever to be remembered as the bloodiest day of British arms. By that evening the Fourth Army had advanced several miles on most of its front at a cost of over 60,000 casualties.[54]

The visible repercussions of the attack took several days to reach Havre base. As far as we ourselves were concerned they took the form of a call for immediate improvisation, of which Miss Inskip[55] was the herald. She came from a family well known in Bristol and was built on a large-boned family pattern shared by her brother who commanded the Guards depôt in the Harfleur Valley. She, too, was an individualist, an untiring worker on a difficult, single-handed YM job. Her work, carried out with her own shabby Ford, made very difficult demands and knew no hours. It was to meet, look after and see off again the next-of-kin of dangerously wounded, usually dying, men in the hospitals of Havre, whom the War Office was sending out from home.[56] For many months now a little stream of these bewildered, grief-stricken men and women, many of whom had never crossed the Channel before, had been arriving and departing every day, and Miss Hoare[57] was always there to receive them calmly and kindly, to drive them to tragic bedsides and take them back to billets, to comfort them and buy a few flowers for the funeral and to see them settled on the boat for home. She never lost her presence of mind, her patience or her gift of sympathy in the pressure and the daily emergencies of this task which we had undertaken to fulfil.

I was sitting at my desk as usual on a July morning, engaged in the wearisome routine of censoring workers' letters or making up returns in triplicate, when Miss Hoare burst in, more roused than I had ever seen her. She took me by the arm: 'Come with me at once', she said, 'to the Quai d'Escale.' This was a quay in the docks used by civilians landing in peacetime but long since a berth for Red Cross

[53] More than 1,500 guns and howitzers were assembled to support the Somme offensive in what was the heaviest British bombardment of the war up to that point. The gunners of Fourth Army, which bore the main brunt of the attack, fired more than 1.7 million shells in the course of an eight-day barrage from 24 June to 1 July. P. Liddle, *The 1916 battle of the Somme* (Ware, 2001), p. 23.
[54] Baron greatly overstates the degree of success encountered on 1 July. At a cost of more than 19,000 killed, only on the southern sector were significant gains made; even then, the total area of ground won amounted to only three square miles. R. Prior and T. Wilson, *The Somme* (New Haven, 2005), pp. 104–12.
[55] Grace and Hilda Inskip, both of Clifton Park House, Bristol, and both classed as 'Canteen Worker. Voluntary', were serving in Le Havre in July 1916. The former served at the base from July 1915 to August 1919 while the latter was present from July 1915 to November 1916. YMCA, K47 Transcript list of ladies who served in France and overseas.
[56] See Introduction, p. 70.
[57] Here Baron may still be referring to one of the Inskip sisters, although his evident confusion may arise from the fact that the Inskips were not the only unmarried sisters working with the YMCA at Le Havre at this time; Helen, Joan and Sybil Hoare, all of Charlwood Farm, East Grinstead, were also present throughout 1915 and 1916. YMCA, K47 Transcript list of ladies who served in France and overseas.

ships; the large railway terminus alongside was now a military hospital into which trains from any part of France could deliver patients at the door.[58] Trains had been doing this all night, for the casualties in the opening days of the Somme battle exceeded all estimates and caught the doctors unprepared. Some of these trains had been passed on from one overcrowded hospital to another, to Rouen some hours ago and then to Havre. Here they could no longer draw into the station itself but came to a halt several hundred yards up the line, for the platform and the very track itself were spread thick with stretchers with men lying upon them for whom there was not a bed empty in the wards. Doctors and nurses, working all they knew, were almost too exhausted, certainly far too few to give attention to these men. Some were whimpering or raving with pain, others calling out faintly, monotonously for water, a few were already dead. A hospital train which drew up as we arrived on the scene began to unload its pitiful freight of wounded who had been rolling across France for more hours than they could count. The stretcher-bearers who went forward to take them out were grey-haired dock-labourers from Tees and Tyne, some nearly seventy years of age, in rough blue uniforms, who had been sent in for this emergency duty.[59] They told me that no rations had reached them since yesterday, and they were now so tired that, for all their lifelong skill with heavy weights, I saw a stretcher slip from the fingers of one pair and a wounded man roll out upon the ground. The Quai d'Escale that morning was a battlefield in miniature.

Was there *anything* we could do to help? I made my way along the platform between the stretchers and saw the commandant, the senior doctor of the hospital, coming towards me, with his sergeant-major a pace in rear. I knew that words must be the fewest possible and to some clear point. I saluted him and said 'May I feed the stretcher-bearers, sir? They're done.' He paused and looked at my cap-badge with haggard eyes. 'Do what you damn well like – so long as you don't get in the way', he replied and passed on. I took this for a graceful answer, giving far more than I had dared to ask.

Miss Hoare took me back in her car to headquarters for a busy morning. As we drove a picture came suddenly into my mind. It was of a battered little coffee-stall standing derelict on another quayside a mile away. (I had guessed rightly the first time I had noticed it that it was a relic of those society ladies who had opened unauthorized canteens when the BEF first landed and whom, it was said, Lord Kitchener himself, when he came over, ordered peremptorily home.)[60] I sent a

---

[58] The wounded were evacuated in several stages that led, via dressing stations and casualty clearing stations, from regimental aid posts in or near the front line to hospitals at base or in Great Britain. Although sometimes transported by barge, the wounded were usually conveyed by an ambulance train from casualty clearing stations to base areas. J. Keegan, *The face of battle* (London, 1996), pp. 266–8; Rawson, *British army handbook 1914–1918*, pp. 141–7.

[59] Here Baron may be referring to men of the 16th ('Transport Workers) Battalion of the York and Lancaster Regiment, which was formed in March 1916 at Colsterdale. This unit was largely run on civilian lines and its function was to ensure the smooth operation of dock facilities. Messenger, *Call-to-arms*, pp. 227–8; E. A. James, *British regiments 1914–1918* (Heathfield, 1998), p. 100.

[60] Ever averse to the interference of enterprising civilians, Kitchener even ordered the arrest of William Beach Thomas of the *Daily Mail* after an unsanctioned visit to the front in 1914. J. M. Bourne (ed.), *Who's who in World War One* (London, 2001), p. 286.

couple of workers to spot this and stand by. They found that someone had been keeping chickens in it, but they borrowed scrubbing materials from a French workman's house and cleaned it out before we arrived to move it. But *how* to move it? The thing stood on four small iron wheels but they would never reach the Quai d'Escale over a mile of cobbles before it fell to pieces. Then I called to mind a friend, an officer in MT (Mechanical Transport as opposed to HT – horses) and rang him up. Could he scrounge a Foden steam wagon, the heaviest army transport of that war, for an hour's job? Stout planks and long ropes would also be needed, and what about a couple of men? He demurred but he complied. Before noon the coffee-stall stood beside the railway track at the hospital.

There was a good deal more to be done – to track down our 15cwt van, already on its round of the camps, and send it back to our stores to load up with a big tea-urn, bread, cases of biscuits and all manner of oddments; it was quite as important and more complex to collect a good team from among workers already scattered on their normal duties, to do the new job. I decided to take the first shift, with two very reliable friends, myself. In addition I picked three women to go with us; they were armed as a start with haversacks full of cigarettes and post-cards – for two prime ways in which a wounded man finds relief are in lighting a fag and sending a message home.

We got down to it. Our first shift lasted unbroken for thirty-six hours, though reliefs came and stayed on to reinforce our strength. Tea and food for the stretcher-bearers and the orderlies who could snatch a few minutes from the wards were thankfully consumed and replenished; they went back to work making macabre jokes among themselves. The pressure was a little relieved when the first hospital ship, fully loaded, drew away and steamed out for England. But another train came in to fill a gap scarcely noticeable. I now had time to scramble aboard, before the engine came to a halt, with a welcome among the bunks and a Woodbine all round.

Meanwhile our team of women were doing good service. They snatched pillows and brown blankets from some limited dump they discovered for the men in the worst pain, they moved about continually with big enamel jugs of water, they knelt beside one stretcher after another, bending low to catch a weak voice among the hubbub as it dictated a message for a postcard – sometimes even now the time-honoured one, 'I am in the pink.'(How many letters and postcards, incidentally, how many million, carried our trade-mark of the red triangle, our best spokesman, into homes all over the world in the four years of war?) They needed all their self-control to confront so much agony, the smashed and blinded faces, the cries trailing into delirium, or the man with both legs blown away whom I saw drag himself up with a crazy laugh and call out 'My God, both of 'em!' before he fainted away. Proper medical attention could not reach them for a long time. Seen at close range, this was like a little corner of the field of Magenta which drove a Swiss observer to found the Red Cross.[61]

---

[61]   The battle of Magenta was fought between the French and the Austrians on 4 June 1859. However, it was actually the carnage at the later battle of Solferino, fought three weeks after, which led Henri Dunant to found the Red Cross. Holmes (ed.), *The Oxford companion to military history*, pp. 453–4.

The pressure of the first terrible days and nights was gradually eased; it fluctuated now with the ebb and flow of the great, unseen battle along the front. Our own small work was soon perfectly organized, with a rota of reliable women to keep it running round the clock; it was already taken for granted by all concerned as a side line in the routine of the hospital. Still the trains came in, but not now treading on each other's heels, still the loaded hospital ships went out and returned for more – not even now was the platform clear of the stretchers of men waiting for beds. So the little we amateurs could do was still in their day's work.

One early afternoon, however, when I had gone down to the Quai d'Escale to see how things were, I found myself landed with a new assignment. The sergeant major, now a firm ally of ours, asked me if I had anybody who could talk German: the German-speaking French interpreter had gone off to lunch and had not shown up again.[62] I had only myself and I undertook the business which seemed unlikely to last long. It was to take the deposition of a prisoner who was dying in one of the wards. I was taken to his bedside and sat down to catch the answers he gasped out to the routine questions on a form put into my hand. His name and regimental number and his age, his division, how long in the line, at what point, with how many casualties and so on. Before I had got any distance down the list I saw that there would not be time to finish it. He had spoken in a strong Bavarian accent and had given his birthplace as Mittenwald. I knew that lovely village in the shadow of the Karwendel and broke off to tell him so. All the fear went out of his ashen face and tears came into his eyes. I laid my hand on his and told him he would very soon be comfortable. It was so: he smiled, closed his eyes and was dead.

I left the ward and was preparing to depart altogether when the sergeant major came up with another message. An interpreter was urgently needed on board the hospital ship now lying at the quay: she was full of the first batch of German prisoners[63] and due to sail tonight. The colonel in charge, a doctor of course, met me at the top of the gangway. One only of his nurses, he explained, had a few words of German, the rest of his staff none at all. Would I come with him first to one or two puzzling cases? There was a nauseating smell, which many people know, in the large ward – in peacetime, I suppose, the ship's first-class lounge – we first entered. Some of the patients, who lay in the cots all round the walls and in a line down the middle, were still wearing the field dressings they had put on themselves days before as they lay on the battlefield or the bandages, now caked with blood, applied in our own overworked first-aid posts when they were picked up as prisoners. There had been no time to renew these and that was the first task now.

---

[62]   Despite strong cultural links between Britain and Germany in the pre-war years, German speakers were rare in the British army in 1916, even among its intelligence officers. C. Duffy, *Through German eyes: the British and the Somme 1916* (London, 2006), pp. 30–4.

[63]   The BEF took around 40,000 German prisoners in the course of the battle of the Somme, or three times the total taken up until June 1916. As numbers grew, many were retained in France for employment in labour companies. *Statistics of the military effort of the British Empire*, p. 632; Messenger, *Call-to-arms*, p. 228.

My first 'case' was a man whose cot stood in a dim alcove in a corner of the ward once occupied, I fancied, by a writing table in the ship's lounge. There was an electric lamp over it but it was not lit. The colonel told me that at every attempt to switch on this light in order to attend to the patient he became violent and started to scream. They thought he was seriously wounded but had had no chance to find out. I walked slowly towards him, speaking to him quietly in his own language, until I reached his bedside. I turned on the light and he began on the instant to struggle and scream, his face distorted with terror; I turned it off again. Then I began to ask him questions about his home, his wife and children and his work and he calmed down until I finally got at his trouble. 'They' always told us, he said, that the English killed their prisoners – as soon as you were asleep in hospital they cut your throat, and that was why the doctor wanted to switch on the light. I beckoned to a nurse and she came forward. Meanwhile I promised the man to stand by to see fair play. She gave him a hypodermic shot in the arm and was able to take him in hand. This was just an instance, not rare as we found, of propaganda in the German army designed to deter its men from surrender.[64]

My next 'case' proved more recalcitrant. In a cot a little apart in the middle of the ward lay an officer prisoner. The colonel already knew that he was suffering from a dangerous internal wound and feared that at any time a fresh haemorrhage might kill him. The awkward thing was that the prisoner, if this began, had no means of telling the medical staff about it. Would I arrange with him some sign, by a word or gesture, to be used in emergency? So, far, I was warned, he had been most uncooperative. I went up to his bed and – on the principle of saying 'officer' to a policeman instead of 'constable' when trouble is brewing – addressed him politely by what I guessed to be a rank above his. I was met by a torrent of abuse. The idea of putting an officer to bed among the common soldiers, *gemeine soldaten*! The English, all the world knew, were barbarians – they had no code of military decency. There was nothing to be done: I left him to die if that was the answer. This was a very simple example, which did not take me by surprise, of Prussian army manners.[65]

I was then taken by the colonel to the wards on the decks below and tried to help him with a number of other cases. At last we reached the lowest deck of all, in which the most seriously wounded men, carried first on board, had been laid. Many of these, it was plain, would not live to see Southampton Water in the

---

[64] Despite Baron's indignation, the summary killing of German prisoners by British troops was by no means unusual in the heat of battle, especially if these prisoners were snipers, machine-gunners or other lethal specialists. Duffy, *Through German eyes*, pp. 34–6; R. Holmes, *Tommy: the British soldier on the Western Front 1914–18* (London, 2004), pp. 547–54.

[65] The imperial German army reflected the federal nature of the German empire and its opponents were conscious of (and sought to exploit) its internal diversity and tensions. Largely for historic reasons, Prussian units were regarded as the solid core of the German army while Saxons and Holsteiners were regarded as comparatively lacking in martial spirit. In rear areas, Germany's historic divisions even meant that it was sometimes necessary to keep Prussian and Bavarian troops apart. Duffy, *Through German eyes*, pp. 24–6; H. Strachan, 'The morale of the German army, 1917–18', in *Facing Armageddon: the First World War experienced*, ed. H. Cecil and P. Liddle (London, 1996), pp. 387–8, 390; Winter, *Death's men*, pp. 218–19.

morning. That was a prospect with which I had tried to cheer other patients in this shipload of suffering but several times they had been alarmed and blankly incredulous – no shipping had crossed the Channel for months, they had been told, because of the complete mastery of German submarines.[66] Meanwhile the foetid atmosphere of this lowest deck was hard to breathe, the sights and sounds were beyond description here. I know nothing of the regulations for loading a hospital ship but to select the patients on the danger list to be carried the longest distance, down flights of steep companion-stairs to face the longest wait in the worst atmosphere seemed to a layman unreasonable.

I had much other work on hand and asked the colonel's leave to go to it. His reply was to beg me to stay on board and cross with the ship to England; he would see that I got a passage back. 'If you can't', he said, 'we shall have a whole lot of chaps dying on our hands before they can tell us.' I had to remind him that I too was a man under authority, bound very closely by the red-tape of the base; it would take about a week, I said, to get a movement order. I shook hands with him and turned to go.

At the head of the gangway I was confronted by the sergeant major with the third request that afternoon. A well-known Personage had unexpectedly arrived and insisted on inspecting this interesting ship: he hadn't had any truck with enemy prisoners before. He was certain to ask questions and would need an interpreter. I was put about but felt bound to comply. The Personage came aboard, accompanied by two immaculate aides, one a very handsome Guards officer. He himself, I couldn't help thinking at once, would look perfect on the stage in the *rôle* of the genial general of a musical comedy – generous white moustachios, scarlet tabs and gleaming brasswork and several rows of medal ribbons, dazzling field-boots and spurs that had never been across a horse's back and actually yellow gloves and an ivory knob to his walking stick. I would not thus present what looks, but is not, a caricature, if his conduct had not outraged all of us who witnessed it in the next hour or so. He seemed to regard this tragic ship as an entertainment, out of which he could get some good sport. He pointed with his stick at the specimen of a Prussian officer – and I for one didn't resent that at all. On the deck below he addressed a string of questions to prisoners and some of these I felt bound to mistranslate grossly. In this ward there were a number of 'walking wounded'; though most of them found walking difficult or impossible. Those seated struggled to their feet and propped themselves, standing as *stramm*[67] as they knew how, against the wall when this representative of martial glory came into view. Among these was a pathetic, weedy creature of about seventeen, quite six foot six tall, the only soldier present from a Prussian Guard regiment. He was

---

[66] While unable to prevent the deployment of the BEF to the continent in August 1914 or to seriously challenge British naval supremacy in the English Channel, the submarine nevertheless transpired to be the most potent weapon in Germany's naval arsenal. In the North Atlantic, unrestricted submarine warfare against Allied (and neutral) shipping brought Britain to the verge of defeat in 1917. P. G. Halpern, 'The war at sea', in *The Oxford illustrated history of the First World War*, ed. H. Strachan (Oxford, 1998), pp. 104–18.

[67] Straight, to attention.

forcibly held up at attention by the arms of the men each side of him. The Personage pounced upon him with delight. 'Now I want to talk to this blighter', he said in his booming voice and, turning to me, he said, 'Tell him I hope his wound is giving him hell.' I duly translated this as 'The general hopes your wound isn't too bad now.' I caught the handsome Guardsman's eye as I said it: he registered astonishment, then he winked at me – he knew German as well as I did! From that moment we were partners in the game. There were plenty more chances to play it as the 'Old Man' wandered slowly down the rank of this wretched guard of honour until one or two men collapsed and fell out. 'Got tired of the smell of our HE[68] and packed up, what?'...'I hope you lost plenty of your own dirty pals up there.'

The crowning effort of grossness, as it seemed to all of us, was yet to come. We went down into the shambles of the lowest deck and the sister in charge of the ward came forward with a regulation curtsey to the Personage; she was nearly dropping with fatigue. 'Don't you do too much for these brutes, sister, not too much, mind you', he boomed. Her face went white with anger and she bit her lip to stop an unregulation reply: 'I am trying to do my proper work, sir', was all she said and turned away to go back to it.

We were all very glad when we got our distinguished guest into the clear, open air again and had saluted him down the gangway. I was to come to close quarters with plenty of battlefield casualties later, our own and the enemy's, apart or in company with each other, but I never saw another round played of the sport of kicking a man when he is down. You will look for it in vain in the long catalogue of games at which the British excel.

The Battle of the Somme kept all the bases in a ferment of work – the provision and the transport of reinforcements of men, horses and materials to supply its insatiable needs, the repair of its human and mechanical damage in wounded men and worn-out guns. Havre bore its full share in this. Besides, it was here that the great surprise of July the First,[69] the British secret weapon, was first landed. It lay in mounting quantity for days in the docks under tarpaulins and a strong armed guard and was sent up to the front in long trainloads before our curious eyes could get the least glimpse of it. We were soon to have almost hourly news of this potent mystery. The *Daily Mail* man, for instance, described on the opening day of the attack how he had seen 'a *Tank* lolloping into Flers'. We could not know that a British invention had revolutionized our war and was to be the instrument of incredible disasters and of crowning victory in a second World War still in the womb of time.

Every department in the base was preoccupied with its duties day and night; our own hands, however insignificant in the giant scheme of things, were very

---

[68] 'HE high explosive. Shells used more for destroying fortifications and trenches than for murder and maiming', in Brophy and Partridge, *The long trail*, p. 107.

[69] The first operational use of the British Mark I tank did not occur on the Somme until 15 September 1916 when they were used in an attack on German positions between Courcelette and Flers. P. Hart, *The Somme* (London, 2005), pp. 370–407.

busy too. And so it came about that the finale of the little episode of the Quai d'Escale was anti-climax, for which I had to blame my own lack of foresight. Under every stress the cast-iron procedure of the base must be upheld, not a yard of red-tape missing which would not have to be accounted for. A fortnight or more had gone by before I remembered that I had omitted to use a few inches of it. Whether wisely or not, I decided to take the case straight to the base commandant. Anyway it would come round to him in the end and it seemed best to get it over now, full blast. I went, therefore, like a delinquent boy, certain of at least a wigging, to the headmaster's study.

My offence was a heinous one. I had moved the rickety canteen to the Quai without written, or indeed any, sanction and in dumping it there I had 'erected an unauthorized structure on military property'. To aggravate this YMCA personnel were being employed in a place which they had no permit to enter. All of us must now take the consequences of having acted on the spur of an emergency.

The whole business was not as simple as it sounds. To put up anything in the base, almost down to a dog-kennel, required [an] initial request to Base Headquarters in writing, followed, if this was successful, by submission of architect's plans in triplicate to the commandant, Royal Engineers. There would be delay before the plans came back from the CRE, usually with modifications which might require another set to be drawn. An army surveyor would inspect the site and a lot more paper was usually consumed before Base Headquarters initialled the scheme and a civilian contractor got his licence to proceed with the work. I had, of course, been through all this in the building of the Young Soldiers' Club and the enlargement of several of our huts. Quai d'Escale canteen would have had to submit to the same routine – though probably, if allowed, we should have been told to build one *de novo*: the whole affair, under present pressures, might well have occupied a month or, like enough, would never have happened at all.

I was granted an interview by the great man and, standing strictly at attention, received an almighty ticking off. I think a more imaginative person would, in the circumstances, have left it at that, with 'Well, carry on now but don't ever do this again.' He ordered me to close the canteen within the hour, to clear the ground next day and to withdraw all YMCA staff forthwith from the hospital. I went straight from Base Headquarters to the commandant of the hospital, with whom I had hardly exchanged a word since our first half-minute interview and told him we were pulling out. 'But you can't do that', he said irritably, 'we *want* you people here'. Base commandant's orders, I said laconically. He used language which is nobody's business now. Then he thanked us handsomely and we departed with lively regret.

There is one criticism, common even before the first war,[70] about which I feel bound to say something. It is that the YMCA has allowed the 'C' in its title to go by default, that, for all effective purposes, it is no longer a Christian force. 'YMCA religion' in some quarters is a convenient phrase for a non-committal,

---

[70] This seems unlikely. See Introduction, pp. 19–22.

humanitarian ideal of decent living, the highest common factor of all vague deistic beliefs. Certainly today there is not the fervent evangelical missionary urge about it which led a young London draper's assistant, afterwards Sir George Williams,[71] to found it nearly a century ago. Prophets like him or John Buchman[72] or Billy Graham arise to fire men's faith in every generation, each after his kind. The flame they kindle burns brightly for some time, fed alike by the critics and the worshippers; then it dies down, either into a steady warmth or into a heap of ashes. This has been the universal pattern of religious revival since the beginning.

I can claim no right to say anything about this aspect of the YMCA in peacetime or even at home during those four years of war. I only know what we saw and took part in during our service in it overseas.

The original rule was that every hut should close at night with a hymn and short evening prayers, but in many cases this was soon honoured more in the breach than in the observance.[73] On Sunday afternoon an hour was normally devoted to an 'act of worship', with the singing of old favourites and a short talk by the leader, a chaplain or a visitor. This was in effect the pattern of a 'Pleasant Sunday Afternoon' at home: I have spoken at PSAs and sometimes wondered whether they were much more than a genial preparation for Sunday tea.

There were, however, outstanding examples which drew a packed congregation, some of them hungry sheep indeed who were fed.[74] In Camp 19, for example, among the tough Canadian reinforcements, Padre D. J. Hiley[75] was a real power. He lived in our hut, almost the prophetic figure of a Moses, and one day I caught him there reading one of the books of Moses in Hebrew: it was his invariable morning exercise. He was a Baptist minister built like a dray-horse but was now over-age for the front line, who had gone into the pits in South Wales as a boy and become a renowned prize-fighter in his mining village; men said that this was how he had lost an eye. Early in our friendship I attended a Sunday service which he was conducting in our hut. The wet canteen in the Camp had just closed after its midday session and, as this was normally a day of rest, several members of the congregation appeared to be 'one-over-the-eight'. One of these

71 George Williams (1821–1905) inaugurated the YMCA on 6 June 1844 with a small band of like-minded shop workers. The national (and international) growth of the movement over the next fifty years was matched by the success of Williams's business affairs. He was knighted in 1894 and eventually interred in St Paul's Cathedral. *ODNB*.

72 Actually Frank Buchman (1878–1961), the controversial American evangelist and founder of Moral Re-Armament. *Times*, 9 August 1961, p. 10.

73 See Introduction, p. 74.

74 An allusion to a chapter in C. E. Montague's *Disenchantment* entitled 'The sheep that were not fed', wherein Montague claimed that Anglican army chaplains had failed to provide soldiers with the spiritual and theological sustenance they craved. C. E. Montague, *Disenchantment* (London, 1924), pp. 69–83.

75 David John Hiley (1860–1948) was the pastor of a church in West Norwood and was commissioned on 26 July 1915 as a chaplain of the United Navy and Army Board, a body that represented Baptists, Congregationalists and United and Primitive Methodists in chaplaincy matters. Very much a show-man, he gained some celebrity by giving a public blessing to a Roman Catholic soldier 'about to entrain for the Front', an incident that was depicted in a number of wartime publications. Hiley went on to become President of the London Baptist Association and of the Baptist Union of Great Britain and Ireland. *Army List*, July 1916; F.C. Spurr, *Some Chaplains in Khaki*, second edition (London, 1916), Preface; *Baptist Handbook* (1949), p. 302.

kept interrupting Hiley's vigorous sermon from the back. He finished and then roared out 'That man – come up here!' The culprit staggered up the room and was given a leg up on to the platform. Hiley, in the same tremendous tones, turned to the hut-leader beside him with 'Bring out the gloves!' Two pairs of boxing gloves were produced and Hiley and the man, now astonished and much sobered, put them on. The preacher with one scientific blow knocked his indifferent listener backwards off the platform on to the floor, whence two of his friends carried him out. Hiley announced the next hymn and the service proceeded as if nothing had happened. Is it surprising that fighting men respected him? What's more, they loved him.

This brings me to say a little more about the chaplains who ought to have been, in many cases were, our best allies. I have to confess that on the whole we did not see the best of the Chaplains' Department at the base. Some who came out were not judged fit enough to go up to the trenches, others had been up and were sent down again because their physique or their moral courage had broken down under the strain. One of these, an old friend of mine, was a very delicate man but a fine scholar. He had made a plucky attempt in vain and now sat in his tent in one of the camps among two thousand potential parishioners lamenting that the College library at Oxford would not send him out the books he needed for his theological studies. There was a sprinkling of chaplains, whom I respected least of all, who spent a deal of time at the bar in the officers' mess and traded in bawdy stories which the other ranks, at any rate, sincerely resented from such a source, who were very fussy about salutes to their officers' uniform and liked to write below their signatures 'Chaplain Captain', a rank not to be found in the Army List.[76] And in contrast to these unattractive and idle stewards of the Gospel there were among the chaplains some magnificent characters, mostly elderly men working beyond their strength until one fine day this was noticed by the authorities, apt to be slow in these personal issues, and they were sent home.[77] We missed

---

[76] These tendencies were also discerned and criticized by the travel writer Stephen Graham, who served in the 2nd Scots Guards in 1917–18. S. Graham, *A private in the guards* (London, 1919), pp. 256–7.

[77] Among such figures were Canon Hannay (see above, n. 48), who was branded 'Permanent Base' after his medical examination for the Chaplains' Department, and Edmund John Kennedy, an Anglican chaplain and leading figure in the YMCA (see Introduction, p. 84). Although a Territorial chaplain, Kennedy was appointed senior chaplain of the regular 7th Division prior to its departure for Belgium in October 1914. He was injured at Ypres later that month and returned to France the following March where, at the age of fifty-nine, he distinguished himself as a base chaplain at Boulogne. Working closely with the local YMCA, Kennedy encouraged sporting activities of all kinds and enlisted the support of the base commandant for a grand tug-of-war tournament. He returned to England that August and died of meningitis in October. Significantly, it was not unknown for tried and tested YMCA workers to volunteer for the Chaplains' Department, a case in point being the Congregationalist minister George Smissen, who served with the YMCA in France from June to September 1916 and who was commissioned as a United Board chaplain on 9 January 1917. He was wounded on 19 August 1917 while serving as a chaplain with the 15th Sherwood Foresters. He was awarded the Military Cross for his *rôle* in the same action and won a further MC in September 1918. He was demobilized in April 1919. Hannay, *A padre in France*, pp. 21–2; E. Kennedy and A. Howell, *Some records of the life of Edmund John Kennedy* (London, 1917), pp. 194–254; *Army List*, July 1917; www.1914–1918.net/heroes/smissen.htm. Consulted 18 June 2008.

them sorely in a field where there was such a harvest waiting and so few reapers.

Some of the chaplains would never set foot on YMCA premises.[78] But I at least believed – and some other chaplains proved me right – that this was neutral ground where they might talk with anyone over a mug of tea, so to speak off the record. These opportunities did not seem to come easily in the constrained atmosphere of the base. Once Canon Hannay said to me 'What do you suppose a man in my depôt has to do if he wants to talk to me about his wife or his soul?'

'Buttonhole you as you go out or in, I imagine.'

'Not a bit of it. First he has to clean his buttons, shine his boots, blanco his belt, and then report to the sergeant of the guard who marches him across the parade ground to the door of my tent, salutes with a click and says "Rifleman Tomkinson, A., wishes to speak to you, sir". The sergeant then does a smart "about turn" and marches off, leaving us face to face like a pair of dumb fools, with anyone who is about watching the whole caper.'

One afternoon I came upon a meeting of teacher and pupil of a less official nature. In a corner of our 'Centre' (that is, in a large room, not a hut) in the town I found two men sitting over books together at a table, with tea cups upon it. One was a young corporal, the other a grey-headed private in the Red Cross,[79] wearing a uniform much stained with oil, obviously an ambulance driver or mechanic. I noted with curiosity that their books were a Greek Testament and a small Liddell and Scott dictionary.[80] The ambulance driver looked up with a smile and said to me, 'Let me introduce myself. I am the ex-rural Dean of Southwell, and I am coaching this corporal for an exam in his theological college.' He went on to tell me that he had applied for a chaplaincy early in the war but had been refused leave of absence: 'they were picking all the duds for chaplains then', he said wryly, 'the parsons they were glad to see the backs of for a while'.[81] However that may be, he had cut loose, joined the ranks of the

---

[78] See Introduction, pp. 84–5. J. O. Hannay noted the initial antipathy felt towards the YMCA by many Anglican chaplains, rightly seeing it as an extension of civilian feuds between Anglicans and Free Churchmen. While Noel Mellish maintained in a letter to his Deptford parishioners that YMCA huts at Rouen in 1915 were 'staffed by capable men and energetic ladies', in his memoirs he wrote of how they were in fact 'mainly run by men who quite clearly had a bias against the Church of England and regarded me as poaching on their preserves'. Nevertheless, the evidence indicates that mutual suspicion had largely dissipated by the end of the war. Hannay, *A padre in* France, pp. 127–9, and H. Montell (ed.), *A chaplain's war: the story of Noel Mellish VC, MC* (London, 2002), pp. 44–8.

[79] Here Baron seems to be referring to the RAMC. Partly due to the initial difficulties involved in securing a temporary commission in the Army Chaplains' Department (see below, n. 81), many Anglican clergy instead volunteered for the RAMC while others enlisted in combatant units. Though the latter course of action posed problems under canon law, similar choices were made by the clergy of other Protestant denominations. M. Snape, *God and the British soldier: religion and the British army in the First and Second World Wars* (London, 2005), p. 150.

[80] Henry George Liddell, dean of Christ Church, and Robert Scott, dean of Rochester, published their *Greek–English Lexicon* in 1843. A standard reference work, it had passed through eight editions by 1901.

[81] The selection of Anglican chaplains by the chaplain-general and former CMS missionary, Bishop

Red Cross and got out to France. I asked him if he found much of a field for pastoral work in his present duty. 'Good lord, yes', he replied, 'my usual run is to take men to hospital at Étretat' (20 miles from Havre) 'and I always have a few books in my ambulance I can lend and a bit of time for talk. Men are in the mood usually: it's one of the best chances in the world for evangelism.' Later on I met his sergeant and asked about him. 'We're always looking out', he answered, 'for a chance to get the old boy on the mat – it would be fun. But he's too good a man for us, one of the best we've got.'

Besides the chaplains there were a number of members of our own staff, laymen as well as ordained ministers, the prime motive of whose service was the precept and practice of religion. Among these for a spell was Sir Victor Buxton,[82] of whom a story was told with so little malice that he laughed over it himself. He worked in Camp 18 in a hut very well run. His practice was to keep a little supply of old-fashioned tracts under the counter when he was serving there and to hand one to a customer with 'a word' as he came along for a cup of tea: it was a practice about which there may well be two opinions. One night when there was an enormous rush of reinforcements he had no time for his usual routine, but as he turned the tap of the tea-urn in rapid succession and handed the cup over the counter he passed across with it one of his tracts. At last the supply of them ran out – but no! there was a fresh batch of leaflets further up the counter. He snatched them and began to distribute them with his charming smile and a hasty 'Read that, my lad.' He came finally to the last copy of the leaflet and had time to glance at its heading: it said 'Twelve reasons why you should drink Horlick's Malted Milk.'

Besides those wearing the cap-badge of the Maltese Cross[83] or of the Red Triangle there were the professional evangelists who came out for a tour from home. Their expenses (and I suppose some sort of fee) were paid from London, we were responsible for feeding and billeting them and arranging their programme. We received a number of famous figures in this field – Gipsy

---

John Taylor Smith, was a source of great controversy in the Church of England during the early months of the war. Despite the needs of an expanding army and a surge of volunteers for the Army Chaplains' Department, Anglo-Catholics believed that their own candidates were being discriminated against in favour of evangelicals, a suspicion that was by no means ill founded, although sheer administrative inefficiency no doubt played its part. J. O. Hannay wrote of how one candidate's repeated applications to the chaplain-general had been answered after 'many months' by an evangelical tract on conversion. Snape, *Royal Army Chaplains' Department*, pp. 185–7; Hannay, *A padre in France*, pp. 24–5.

[82] Sir Thomas Fowell Victor Buxton (1865–1919) was onetime president of the Anti-Slavery and Aborigines Protection Society, treasurer of the CMS and chairman of the Missions to Seamen. In addition to his religious interests, he was a big-game hunter and had served as high sheriff of Essex. Buxton had been commander of the 1/2nd Essex Volunteer Regiment and five of his sons went on to serve in the First World War, one of them being killed in France in 1916. He died in England as a result of a road accident. *Times*, 2 June 1919, p. 9.

[83] A blackened Maltese cross surmounted by a crown was the contemporary badge of the Army Chaplains' Department. Rawson, *British army handbook 1914–1918*, p. 126.

Smith,[84] John McNeill[85] and Madame X,[86] for example – who went the round of the bases, staying several weeks at a time in each. They differed not very much in their technique and were, in my recollection, all alike in their stout figures. I must confess that I found the machinery of their profession unattractive – its advertising methods, its tricks of voice and gesture designed to find the weak spots in an audience. All of them were self-centred (as actors, including the greatest, usually are), some were frankly greedy at table and entirely idle outside their scheduled hours of oratory. It is not rare for religion to display, like the drama, two diverse faces, one for the lighted stage seen from the auditorium and one behind the untidy scenes when the curtain is down.

Of them all we, who had to live with them and not only attend some of their meetings, liked Gipsy Smith best. He paid recurring visits to Havre, where each appearance of his big, swarthy face was genuinely welcome. He was the only one of them, as far as I can recall, who ever volunteered to lend us a hand in emergency. He had his reward, for as soon as he began to serve behind the counter word went round and men flocked in to get a talk with him.

I had to take the chair at his biggest meeting which filled the great army cinema in the Valley. In the front row sat most of the elderly IBD commanders, behind them officers, senior and junior; two thousand other ranks filled the body of this enormous wooden box up to the high back benches. Gipsy was billed to

[84] Rodney ('Gipsy') Smith (1860–1947) was born of gipsy parents and, while born in a tent in Epping Forest, grew up travelling around East Anglia. Following the death of his mother from smallpox in 1865, Smith's father and uncles experienced a religious conversion and, as the Three Gipsy Brothers, became well-known evangelists in their own right. Converted at the age of sixteen in a Primitive Methodist chapel in Cambridge, Smith began preaching the following year and eventually fell in with the Christian Mission of William Booth, which soon became the Salvation Army, preaching in London and the north of England. While his membership of the Salvation Army helped him to overcome his lack of formal education, he was expelled in 1882 after courting, then marrying, one of his converts and for accepting gifts from admirers. After working as an independent evangelist in Staffordshire, in 1888 he was employed by the Manchester and Salford Methodist Mission and went to America in 1889, where he was befriended by the renowned evangelists Dwight L. Moody and Ira D. Sankey. He embarked upon an evangelistic tour of the world five years later and, on his return to Britain, was engaged as a missioner by the National Free Church Council, a post he held until 1912. In recognition of his stalwart work for the YMCA during the war, Smith was appointed an MBE in 1918 but his career as a travelling evangelist lasted for another thirty years, until his death on board the *Queen Mary* while en route to New York. A commanding, intriguing and attractive preacher, it was claimed that he had preached to more than 40 million people in the course of his public career. *ODNB*; *Times*, 14 August 1947, p. 7.

[85] John McNeill (1854–1933) was the son of a Renfrewshire quarryman who began his working life as a railway porter at Inverkip and ended his secular career at the head office of the North British Railway in Edinburgh. After studying at Edinburgh and Glasgow universities, McNeill trained as a minister in the Free Church of Scotland and was ordained in 1886. In 1892, and after serving as a minister in Edinburgh and London, he joined Dwight L. Moody and embarked on an international career as 'a travelling evangelistic preacher', visiting (among other destinations) America, Canada, Australia and South Africa. His career, however, was punctuated by brief periods of settled ministry in England and Canada and, in the inter-war years, he went on to gain further celebrity as a religious broadcaster. *Times*, 20 April 1933, p. 15.

[86] A reference to Madame Strathearn, a singer who toured Le Havre, Etaples and Calais in 1916 and who never completed a performance 'without some definite message of helpfulness to the men'. *YM. The British Empire YMCA Weekly*, 17 March 1916, p. 241.

put on an abridged version of his most famous record, 'The Story of my Life', which normally took two sessions to complete. It was, of course, the history of his bringing up in a gypsy caravan and the climax of his conversion, and it was a real work of art. Every paragraph, every intonation from grave to gay, every *tremolo* and *crescendo* had long ago been worked out in detail; here two verses of a hymn in his beautiful tenor voice and then the thunders of hell or the trumpets of salvation. It was a symphony played by the composer, fascinating to listen to. I watched the changes that passed over the ranks of faces riveted upon him, I saw (this is not embroidery but fact) tough old colonels reach in their sleeves for their handkerchiefs. And then the inevitable, expected moment of 'witness' arrived. 'Is there not a man here who would like me to pray for him?' pleaded Gypsy. Silence as a few overwrought men rose to their feet. 'I know there are more, don't be afraid!' – the hall was now sprinkled with standing figures. 'More!', he urged, 'there are many more' – and indeed there were, perhaps half the audience, taking courage from each other. Then his prayer, every phrase a work of art, for he was a genuine poet. A rousing hymn broke the tension and then we all streamed out into the darkness and the smell of the incinerators burning ordure beside the stream. At supper afterwards somebody asked him how he had got on. 'Wonderful, wonderful!', he said, 'we were greatly blessed: I had only to say the word and they stood up to a man'. Had he hypnotized himself as well as his audience, or was this only the sort of *façon de parler*[87] upon which a revivalist can keep himself going? I could not tell, and no one could assess the permanent results, if any, of the evening's experience.

In what state of health was the Christian cause as we saw it at a French base, let alone in our whole nation? Again I cannot tell and I do not believe that anyone could have infallibly assessed it. The war had not touched off the landslide from institutional religion – that was well down the hill already and was to go much further before there were signs – as some of us believe there are now – that the churches could recover ground again.[88] But this is not the place for speculation.

Too many callow observers at work among the troops snatched at signs and wonders. To them a crowd of men singing hymns was the signal of a revival of true religion.[89] But all soldiers, because they are ordinary men up against extraordinarily unfriendly conditions, love singing, whether the hymns of their childhood or the obscene versions of their marching songs.

---

[87] Patter.

[88] This statement reflects the relative buoyancy of British Christianity in the 1950s, whose outlook was brightened by the apparent success of Billy Graham's 'crusades'. C. G. Brown, *Religion and society in twentieth-century Britain* (Harlow, 2006), pp. 177–223.

[89] The question of how far the war served to trigger a revival of religion among the millions of soldiers of the British army was a matter of keen interest and debate among the churches and perceptions differed among contemporaries as they do among historians. While there are problems of definition, it is nevertheless clear that old-style revivalism could have a powerful appeal on occasion. N. E. Allison, 'Baptist chaplains' revivalism at the front (1914–1918)', *Baptist Quarterly*, XLII (2007), 303–13; R. Schweitzer, *The cross and the trenches: religious faith and doubt among British and American Great War soldiers* (Westport, CT, 2003), pp. 185–93; Snape, *God and the British soldier*, pp. 164–8.

Wherefore, men marching
On the road to death, sing!
Pour your gladness on earth's head,
So be merry, so be dead.[90]

That young poet was marching to die: another took up the story-

'O, but. Everyone was a bird: and the song was wordless; the singing will never be done.'[91]

I remember a young chaplain at Havre who saw the Kingdom of God coming when there was a sudden demand at the counter of a hut for pocket Testaments which were given away for the asking. He was sadly dashed when after a few days the demand as abruptly ceased. It had been caused by a temporary shortage of the French 'A.G. papers', in which men rolled tobacco, and the thin paper pages on which the Good News was printed were almost ideal for an outsize cigarette. I tried to comfort him. 'I have known worse uses for the Bible', I said, 'if only a man reads the page before he smokes it…'.

There was a very different observer who lived at our headquarters for a good many months. This was John [sic],[92] the grand old Scots Professor from Aberdeen, whom the YMCA had brought out to France to help him to collect more evidence for a survey he was making; it was published in [blank] under the title of *Religion in war-time*.[93] This was sober, painstaking work by a very wise man and his general conclusions were, I think, too sombre for the vague optimists. We greatly enjoyed his company at our headquarters as he sat talking gravely, humbly, humorously at the supper table; he was a man to be revered, listened to and loved.

---

[90] From Charles Hamilton Sorley's poem 'All the hills and vales along'. Sorley (1895–1915) had an ironic and self-deprecatory style and was held in high esteem by Siegfried Sassoon and Robert Graves. He was killed in October 1915 while serving as a captain in the 7th Suffolk Regiment. Sorley's collection *Marlborough and other poems* was published posthumously in 1916. Bourne (ed.), *Who's who in World War One*, p. 272; M. Drabble (ed.), *The Oxford companion to English literature* (Oxford, 1995), p. 932.

[91] From Siegfried Sassoon's poem 'Everyone sang'. Siegfried Sassoon (1886–1967) is one of the most celebrated of the British war poets. Although an aggressive soldier (he was known as 'Mad Jack' in the 2nd Royal Welch Fusiliers) he made a public statement condemning the war in 1917, a gesture that almost resulted in his court martial, and famously threw the medal ribbon of his Military Cross into the River Mersey. After treatment for shell shock at Craiglockhart Military Hospital, Sassoon returned to active service but was discharged from the army in July 1918 after a shooting accident. Bourne (ed.), *Who's who in World War One*, pp. 258–9.

[92] David Smith Cairns (1862–1946) was the son of a Presbyterian minister and was educated at Edinburgh University. He then trained for the Presbyterian ministry, during which time he studied at Marburg University, and was ordained in 1895. In 1907 he became professor of systematic theology at the United Free Church College, Aberdeen, and played a significant part in the World Missionary Conference held at Edinburgh in 1910, producing a report entitled *The missionary message in relation to nonchristian religions*. A key figure in the Student Christian Movement, by the outbreak of the First World War Cairns was an experienced and well-travelled lecturer. Appointed an OBE in 1918 in recognition of his wartime work, his academic career continued to flourish after the war and in 1923 he was elected moderator of the General Assembly of the United Free Church. *ODNB*.

[93] Actually *The army and religion* (1919). See Introduction pp. 86–8.

What then was the contribution of the YMCA with its unrivalled opportunities among so many thousands of men oblivious of religion or brought face to face with it by their circumstances for the first time, others – and these were many – unsettled and sincerely perplexed, and others again, faithful church members, who felt themselves starved of the practices which they had enjoyed at home? Of the last category I had had a melancholy experience at Cinder City where we discovered gradually a number of men – not, I will say at once, all Anglicans – who had been deprived for a long time of the opportunity of Holy Communion. There seemed to be no chaplain responsible for ministering to the camp, at least none of us had ever seen one until I pointed it out and were promised a visit. Meanwhile the women workers and I rigged up a small, simple chapel, an unusual feature of a YMCA hut, in a disused store room near by; we were pleased with it when it was done. The padre came, fresh I guessed from his theological college, and was glad to be called in. What would be the best hour for a celebration? I had already canvassed this difficult question with the prospective communicants. The only hour of the week which would be possible for them all was Sunday evening after a day's work. It couldn't be done, he said, because it was contrary to the tradition of the Church or, better said, his own churchmanship.[94] I am afraid I exploded at this but he was adamant. After a heated argument he went away, and no one took his place.

If we were sometimes let down thus by our proper partners we more often, I suppose, let our cause down ourselves. In the continual serving of tables religious observance very easily goes to the wall. We could claim to have used pretty widely some of the conventional 'means of Grace' – evening prayers, a Sunday service, preachments by the best talent available, missions conducted by visiting evangelists. But our organization was too widespread, with each hut a law unto itself in these matters, too dependent on volunteer workers of various quality who constantly came and went, to make a coherent system of religious practice possible. Even Pilkington, with his intense religious conviction, could not have welded the YMCA into a strong missionary force.

I believe that our best Christian work was personal and private and therefore imponderable. With the thousands of reinforcements in the Valley this was bound to be fleeting and a matter of chance: you might meet a man for a couple of days and never see him again – he went up the line and might be dead a week later for all you could tell. With the often thousands of 'permanent base' men, whether technicians, clerks or labourers, it was different. Many of them came into the same hut every night, perhaps for several years. Real friendships often sprang up between them and our workers, all kinds of questions were discussed, personal problems were unravelled and joys or sorrows shared. The hand of God could make itself visible in these relationships: I am sure it often did. I am sure also that the influence of many of our women, precious to men long separated from their homes, was a gift beyond price.

---

[94] Anglo-Catholics maintained that Holy Communion should only be received fasting, hence it was usually administered at early morning mass. D. Gray, 'Earth and altar: the evolution of the parish communion in the Church of England to 1945', *Alcuin Club Collections*, LXVIII (1986), 16.

In general it can be said with certainty that the YMCA stood in men's minds for righteousness, however undefined. At the heart of the work, as we knew, there was a direction which never doubted for an instant that, whatever the vicissitudes of war, 'the City of God remaineth'.[95]

This is little more than a record of some of the activities of our workers in one only of the bases in France occupied by the British army: Calais and Boulogne, Etaples and Dieppe and Rouen would all have the same tale to tell, each with many variations. Every base had its own character, quickly sensed but hard to trap or define, and all of them shared much in common – the ships coming and going on the open sea (or, in the case of Rouen, up the river) with their freight, apparently inexhaustible, of men and materials, training grounds (like the hated Bull Ring at Etaples)[96] for fighting men out on what was euphemistically called a rest, offices and workshops and repair hangars where thousands of men did much the same work, year in, year out, as they would have done in peacetime but under military discipline and for a soldier's pay, great hospitals, railway marshalling yards, stores and bakeries, dépôts for horses and mules and clothing and ammunition, all the requisites without number to meet the stupendous wastage of war.

They also acquired very soon an atmosphere of their own, as difficult to counter as to define. The shortest term that fits it is 'fed-up', or in the modern service man's vocabulary, 'browned-off'.[97] Our war was once summed up as 'moments of boredom punctuated by moments of terror'.[98] At the base the boredom went on for years, very little relieved by terror – though I chanced to be in Etaples through the terrible night in 1918 when the hospitals were bombed to blazes.[99] The area under the command of a base was limited to a mile or two in any direction and there were no chances for most men of stepping over the boundary. Beyond lay a different world, the broad lands of 'L. of C.' – Lines of Communication – with its villages in the fresh countryside where troops were billeted, and beyond that again the five 'Army Areas',[100] a broad fringe of them

95 An allusion to St Augustine's *City of God.*
96 'BULL-RING: Training grounds at the Base, where up-the-line soldiers, just out of Base hospitals and convalescent camps, were put through arduous "courses" by P.T. and other instructors who had rarely, if at all, been under fire. From Spanish bull-fights because of the cruelty involved and the fact that the training ground was often sited on sand. The most notorious was at *Etaples.*' Brophy and Partridge, *The long trail,* p. 77.
97 'Fed up, disgruntled, disheartened. The slang phrase became popular in the Second World War. The reference is probably to a dish that has been overcooked.' A. Room (ed.), *Brewer's dictionary of phrase and fable: millennium edition* (London, 2001), p. 172.
98 The origins of this cliché are now obscure.
99 Etaples was subject to sustained air raids during the German spring offensives of 1918. On 19 May, an attack on a local railway bridge issued in the bombing of British hospitals and in 300 casualties, including several nurses. M. Brown, *1918 year of victory* (London, 1998), pp. 109–10; *Times,* 1 June 1918, p. 4; M. Gilbert, *First World War* (London, 1994), p. 424.
100 The BEF was divided into armies as it grew from around 166,000 men in August 1914 to nearly 1,350,000 in May 1916. First and Second Armies were formed in December 1914; a Third Army was created in July 1915 and a Fourth in February 1916. The Reserve Army (renamed Fifth Army five months later) was created in May 1916. Middlebrook, *Your country needs you,* pp. 25–6; *Statistics of the military effort of the British Empire,* p. 64 (iii); Becke, *Order of battle part 4,* pp. 71–120.

hideously devastated, where the fighting went on. But as far as the 'permanent base' man was concerned – the clerk or the craftsman, the storekeeper and labourer – all that might as well have been in America. Too often he felt himself to be imprisoned, with an indeterminate sentence.

This was as true of the staff of the base, the commissioned officers who commanded the camps or controlled the many departments, as of the men. Some of these were 'dug-outs'[101] who had come back to the army in any capacity in which it could use them. Many more had borne their share of fighting in the front line but, through age or sickness or disablement or sheer incapacity, were unlikely to renew the experience for a long time or ever again. As the spirit of a big school depends very much on the headmaster, so did that of each base on its base commandant – and we, by general consent, were not very lucky.

Regulations in an army or a government office – complex, meticulous and constantly multiplied or changed – are inevitable, but the game of red tape is too easy to play for those who have unlimited opportunity. A copy of Base Orders was put on my table every afternoon. It was irreverently called 'Comic Cuts' by some people but there was a very small ration of humour in it and a large ingredient of irritation. One day we all noticed the terse statement, to be read as a command, 'Officers and men will not in future shave the upper lip.' The military moustache, of course, has an honourable history going back into primitive obscurity: the Vikings and the hordes of Genghis Khan had worn it to enhance the terror struck wherever they showed their faces. And now we enjoyed watching the struggling hairs sprout along the grinning lips of our friends: it was terrible, but not in a literal sense. After a few weeks Base Orders repeated this command with formidable emphasis – 'Any officer or man found shaving the upper lip will be severely dealt with.' Backsliders now took notice; I myself, though not bound by the order, grew a small moustache (which I have never removed in the forty years since then) in a vain race with a Presbyterian chaplain, a wager which cost me five shillings. Charlie Chaplin's early films were then at their zenith, and his famous moustache provided the pattern for most subalterns; some, with patient art, reduced their versions to two circular spots, the size of a pea, under their noses.

The irritation due to niggling, nagging restrictions at the base was more serious. It led to endless grousing, but that after all is the soldier's privilege, his time-honoured safety valve. In the later stages of the war it flared up into 'incidents' which were not allowed to reach the home newspapers. At Etaples in 1917 there was a so-called 'Mutiny', a model of good behaviour as mutinies go.[102] The men in the reinforcement camp were forbidden, unlike their officers,

---

[101] In addition to denoting shelters within a trench system, this term was also 'a facetious name among officers for an oldish officer returning from retirement to active service and displaying little efficiency'. Brophy and Partridge, *The long trail*, p. 94.

[102] The Etaples mutiny was the most serious outbreak of its kind among British troops during the course of the war. However, Richard Holmes has argued that, as with lesser incidents, it demonstrated 'that it was generally resentment at what was seen as unfair treatment, rather than class tension or anti-war spirit, that drove men to disobey'. The system of local leave was open to much

to bathe in the sea which was out of bounds to them, and now they marched, properly under their own NCOs to Paris Plage to break the rule, while 'loyal troops' (a provocative term that was used) stepped back on the road to let them pass; the officers for a day or two sensibly confined themselves to barracks. When I revisited Havre soon after the armistice in 1918 I was invited by my successor to visit 'our devastated area' and was astonished, when we drove the length of the Harfleur Valley, to see the ruins of officers' messes and Expeditionary Force Canteens blackened by fire. A mass of small restrictions, added to the inevitable snail's pace of demobilization, had breached the discipline of good men who wanted above all to get home and leave soldiering behind.[103] These things were regrettable and could not be passed over, but it was a lack of imagination, a failure of simple human understanding in too many of those who controlled the bases that was at the root of trouble. They had a very difficult duty to do, but I believe that those they commanded would have backed them with better will if they had chosen some different ways of doing it.

The atmosphere of the base, then, could be compared with a trap in which all ranks felt themselves caught. The further one got away from it (as I was to find) the more one's spirit was liberated. The nearer a man came to the ultimate business of fighting the firmer comradeship held, the more real regimental loyalties, the tougher the humour, the more heartfelt the cursing and the singing and, I have no doubt, a man's religion. By the spirit in such things he was upheld even in the immeasurable miseries and agonies of trench warfare; he was genuinely alive, with death just round the corner, in a sense that the base hardly knew. I was to discover, sooner than I yet suspected, that the atmosphere of an Army Area was as different from that at the base as chalk from cheese – the one a clean, solid, close-grained substance, with a firm outline, capable even of being hewn into shapes of beauty, the other a lump, easily becoming amorphous, always tending towards malodorous decay.

---

abuse in base areas and it was not unknown for venal non-commissioned officers to sell local passes and other privileges. The mutiny at Etaples began on 9 September 1917 with the arrest of a New Zealander who had overstayed his pass into the town; when a crowd gathered to secure his release, shots were fired by a military policeman which resulted in the death of an innocent bystander, namely Corporal W. B. Wood of the 4th Gordon Highlanders. This fatality resulted in several days of rioting and acts of collective defiance such as the bathing incident mentioned by Baron; red flags were also in evidence on occasion. However, through the intervention of scores of officers and a battalion of the Honourable Artillery Company (a prestigious Territorial regiment) order had been largely restored by 13 September. Although a host of lesser charges were also pressed, only four men were actually tried for mutiny and only one execution ensued – that of Corporal Jesse Short of the 24th Royal Northumberland Fusiliers, who had abused an officer in charge of a patrol and had urged (unsuccessfully) that he be thrown from a bridge. Given the modest nature of the unrest, a storm of controversy followed the depiction of the Etaples mutiny in the BBC drama *The monocled mutineer* (1986), which featured hordes of mutineers entering the town, raping and murdering French civilians. Holmes, *Tommy*, pp. 347–8; Messenger, *Call-to-arms*, pp. 402–4; D. Todman, *The Great War: myth and memory* (London, 2005), pp. 36–8.

[103] Ironically, acts of collective indiscipline among the soldiers of the BEF were a much greater problem *after* the Armistice than before it. A strike at Calais in January 1919 was particularly serious. Holmes, *Tommy*, p. 347.

Our job, as I have said, was not merely buns but friendship, in whatever theatre of war it was done. We were expected to provide not only the elementary luxuries to supplement army rations but a touch of the amenities of home. We were ready, beyond our contracts, to undertake any legitimate service we could compass. I do not believe that, taking it all round, the YMCA or any of the other voluntary bodies privileged thus to work for the welfare of the troops betrayed their trust.

Chapter 2

Fresh fields

The spring of 1917 opened with very hard weather. For a short spell I was sick in a hospital on the Hill at Ste Addresse, where all the water was frozen up – though we washed comfortably enough in tepid water from the rubber bottles in our beds which had been filled with melted snow the night before. As soon as I was back at our headquarters McCowen, my chief, came over from Abbeville with fresh orders. I was to take over and develop the YMCA work in an Army Area; that of the Fourth Army on the Somme.

Looking back, it seems remarkable and most regrettable that only at this late stage of the war was such an assignment possible. Hitherto our work had been strictly confined by the authorities to the bases and the scattered territory of 'L of C'. It was only after protracted negotiations at Sir Douglas Haig's GHQ at Montreuil that McCowen had won us the liberty, much better late than never, to serve where the need was most.[1]

So far all we had in Fourth Army was a small outpost at Amiens, with an elderly secretary marking time until some proper plan could be made. He ran a small hut at the entrance to Amiens station, a busy railway junction for troops, and he had one man, without transport and almost without any supplies, wandering about the old battlefield miles away.[2] It wasn't a set-up that counted, and I was charged with trying to make it so.

Arthur Reade,[3] in peacetime the warden of a Settlement in East London, took my place in Havre and McCowen drove me to Amiens. We spent the night with the secretary, who was packing up to go home, and next morning took the long straight road due eastwards towards St Quentin, which was still in enemy hands. The signs of war increased until we turned off, left-handed, into a devastation such as I had never seen or imagined up till then. A close view of destruction

---

[1] This work had in fact begun as early as 1915. See Introduction, pp. 46–7.

[2] A reference to the Somme battlefield of 1916. Amiens, the capital of the department of the Somme, lies some twenty miles to the south-west. M. Middlebrook and M. Middlebrook, *The Somme battlefields* (London, 1994), p. 316.

[3] Arthur Reade, later a medical doctor, had served as one of Stansfeld's medical assistants at the OMM. B. Baron, *The doctor: the story of John Stansfeld of Oxford and Bermondsey* (London, 1952), pp. 18–19.

actually in the process (I was to have my fill of it later) can be uncomfortably exhilarating, but the ruins of the Somme, dead, silent, stinking months after the battle had moved beyond them, were melancholy beyond words. At this first view they were thinly blanketed with snow which served not so much to soften their outlines as to throw the black skeletons of churches and tumbled heaps of houses into higher relief. They might have been there a thousand years, they seemed to hold no prospect of resurrection.

Before long we got news of our man, for he seemed already to have made his number with some of the troops we met, and tracked him down to his billet in what remained of the village of Meaulte, one of the points upon the starting line from which the Fourth Army had sprung out to the attack on the fateful first of July. He was not there when we arrived but we were warmly welcomed by an apple-cheeked old Frenchwoman who had lately returned to remake her home in this battered cottage. She stoked up a blaze upon the hearth with rafter-logs from the ruins next door and we thawed ourselves out, for we had travelled – as always in those days – in an open car. After dark our man stumbled in, wearing a fleece-lined leather jacket over his shabby tunic and heavy artillery driver's boots. He was thoroughly exhausted and his first act was to reach in the cupboard and pour himself a stiff whisky before coming to grips with two strangers. Since first daylight he had been out and about, tramping round the small detachments which covered the miles of this country and prospecting for our work to come. He was Walter Ashley, son of Sir William Ashley the Cambridge economist.[4] We were destined (though neither of us that night could have had an inkling of it) to work together until long after the Armistice. I could not have had a better friend nor a more resourceful and efficient second-in-command.

The old lady cooked us a capital meal out of army rations and we sat long over smokes and a map. Next morning – it was Good Friday, fittingly commemorated by this Golgotha of a landscape – the three of us made for Péronne, which had seemed on the map a likely point to set up our headquarters. Soon we had left behind us the lofty tapering spear of one angle of Becordel church-tower, a monument of the opening hours of the battle, which was precariously to defy the winter storms of several winters to come. And now we were encountering names that were already historic, names I had heard on the lips of our own men or of German prisoners in Havre – Mametz Wood, Maricourt, Givenchy and Flers.[5]

---

[4]   William Ashley (1860–1927) was in fact a leading economic historian who, while at Harvard in the 1890s, had held the first chair in economic history in the English-speaking world. He was later the first Professor of Commerce at the University of Birmingham, a post that he held from 1901 to his retirement in 1925. Knighted for his wartime services to government in 1917, in addition to his economic expertise Ashley was also a leading Anglican layman whose sympathies lay with the liberal wing of the Church of England. He was buried in Canterbury Cathedral in 1927, Walter being his only son. *ODNB*; *Times*, 25 July 1927, p. 8.

[5]   Of these, Mametz Wood and Flers were behind German lines at the commencement of the Somme offensive. Baron seems to be confusing Givenchy for Ginchy, which was also behind German lines on 1 July. The German defences on the Somme in 1916 incorporated a number of heavily fortified villages and Winston Churchill later described them as 'undoubtedly the strongest and most perfectly defended positions in the world'. R. Prior and T. Wilson, *The Somme* (New Haven, 2005), pp. 37–9.

Often they were no more than names painted on a board beside the road. Half a dinner-plate crowning a low heap of rubble on the arms of a cast-iron cemetery cross sticking drunkenly out of it were the only signs of centuries of a lost civilization. The tokens of our own enlightened age were more persistent. Mile after mile the discarded ironmongery of battle – the frayed tin-hats, the ruined tank with its torn track withered like a dragon's tail against the sky, the rusty rifle thrust upright upon its bayonet into the ground, with the name of its dead owner on a scrap of paper in a bottle at its foot,[6] showed that our men had passed that way. The sour-sweet smell of death hung heavy in the air, and in the ditch at one point, a more recent casualty, the carcass of a horse, hideously inflated with the gases of decay, stuck its four legs grotesquely up and brought this foulness to a momentary climax. Of animal life there was no heartening sign, only the host of questing flies, the rats that sneaked everywhere among the rubble and those rougher-coated, savage village cats, gone wild, that had lived upon the bodies of the dead. It was relief, almost an excitement, when we came upon a single heron standing motionless among the reeds of a marsh by the roadside.

For background to this monotonous destruction the rolling ridges of the Somme country, lightly powdered with snow, stretched away to the horizon. They offered a cold prospect that Good Friday as we drove towards them, but within a week or two we were to see them in their beauty, blue hills scored with the gleaming white scars of trenches dug in the chalk and splashed with the brilliant red fields of poppies which betokened the interruption of man's husbandry. 'Though poppies grow in Flanders' fields' was the refrain of moving verses written by an invalid lady at home,[7] but surely even more they belonged to the stricken fields of the Somme. They were far more significant to us all than those 'roses of Picardy' about which soldiers loved to sing.[8] They were very soon to become, and to remain even now, the universal symbol, or remembrance of the dead in two wars. Sighted in the distance, they were like splashes of fresh arterial blood staining the ground. Not for nothing had this Somme country borne the name of '*Santerre*' in earlier times. '*Sang-Terre*', or '*Sainte Terre*' – the derivation is disputed, but either way the name is significant. This for the British had become both the 'Field of Blood' and, in a grim sense, a 'Holy Land'.

---

6   This precarious means of identifying graves prior to marking was preferred by the Graves Registration Commission, a body formed from the British Red Cross Society in February 1915 and militarized that autumn. The GRC divided the British sector of the Western Front into different areas for the purpose of recording and marking graves. In relation to their occupants, chaplains were advised 'to write all details on a sheet of paper, then, having placed it in a bottle carefully stoppered, to bury the bottle neck downwards in the filled-in soil, so that only the bottom can be seen'. A. Rawson, *British army handbook 1914–1918* (Stroud, 2006), pp. 346–7; E. Digby, *Tips for padres* (London, 1917), pp. 85–6.

7   The words are those of John McCrae and are taken from his celebrated poem 'In Flanders Fields', which first appeared in *Punch* in 1915. McCrea (1872–1918) was a distinguished physician and a senior Canadian army medical officer. He died of pneumonia at Boulogne in January 1918. *Dictionary of Canadian Biography Online*. Consulted 4 December 2008.

8   The song 'Roses of Picardy', by Frederick E. Weatherley and Haydn Wood, appeared in 1916. Deeply romantic and full of bathos, it was inspired by Weatherely's affection for a French widow. www.firstworldwar.com/audio/rosesofpicardy.htm. Consulted 4 December 2008.

Of human life – and that after all was our only real concern – there was plenty of evidence as we drove along this rutted, shell-pocked road, We crept up along the flank of a long convoy of lorries, with men hanging out through the flaps at the back to grin and call out a greeting. We met a string of loaded limbers coming down, mule drawn, the drivers glumly hunched in their leather jackets. We drew into the verge to allow a jingling horse battery, with all its transport behind, to pass back towards the warm billets they had not known for many weeks; these men laughed and flung jolly obscenities to us when they saw the sign upon our windscreen. Now and again we pulled up to chat for a few minutes with little parties which were still clearing the road and using the rubble of a village for first aid to its torn surface. At one halt (on this day or another like it) I found my eyes resting on a rough cross planted in the ditch, no rare site for a grave. The name scrawled in paint upon it was Raymond Asquith,[9] a true symbol of that 'lost generation' which we were to lament in the years to come and which we have never recovered.[10]

Péronne is an old town, once beautiful, which still lies partly within its medieval walls beside the River Somme. It was not new to men of our race when we occupied it in 1917, for five hundred years earlier Henry V had lain there, the turning point before his march north to Agincourt to join what Winston Churchill has called 'the most heroic of all the land battles England has ever fought'.[11] As our car rolled gently down the slope towards one of its gates I was cheered to see 'Bristol Bridge' boldly displayed on a signboard on the edge of the moat; it was like a greeting from home. The temporary wooden causeway (Bailey bridges were to wait more than twenty years for invention)[12] had been built by the Gloucesters[13] when they came in. It was now guarded by a sentry with fixed bayonet who stepped out and demanded our pass to enter the town. Of course we had not got one, but the sentry solved it with a laugh as he looked at our windscreen – 'Why, it's only the bloody YM!' This was a cordial password for

[9] The eldest son of Britain's Liberal prime minister, Raymond Asquith (1878–1916) was a gifted writer and classicist who became a fellow of All Souls in 1902. Called to the bar in 1904, Asquith was in the early stages of a political career when war broke out in 1914. He joined the Queen's Westminster Rifles in January 1915 but transferred to the 3rd Grenadier Guards as a lieutenant six months later and arrived in France that October. Due to the intervention of his father, he served briefly as an intelligence officer at GHQ but he returned to his battalion prior to the battle of the Somme. He was mortally wounded during the British attack on the Flers-Courcelette sector on 15 September 1916 and died en route to a dressing station. *ODNB*.

[10] The 'lost generation' is one of the most emotive and enduring myths of the British experience of the First World War. However, one third of British males of military age never served in the armed forces and, of those who did, nearly 90 per cent survived. M. Middlebrook, *Your country needs you* (Barnsley, 2000), p. 134; D. Todman, *The Great War: myth and memory* (London, 2005), p. 45.

[11] W. S. Churchill, *A history of the English-speaking peoples*, I: *The birth of Britain* (London, 1956), p. 318.

[12] The steel, prefabricated Bailey pontoon bridge was widely used by the British army in the Second World War. G. Forty, *The British army handbook 1939–1945* (Stroud, 2002), pp. 282–7.

[13] No fewer than twenty-four battalions of the Gloucestershire Regiment saw service in the First World War. The regiment's regular reserve battalion and two of its pre-war Territorial battalions were based in Bristol; a further two Territorial and six New Army battalions had been formed or raised in the city by April 1915. E. A. James, *British regiments 1914–1918* (Heathfield, 1998), pp. 72–3.

which I was often to be grateful later when I came to forbidden places. We exchanged news with him and drove on into the town.

The broad main street of Péronne was already very well known to folks at home through a much-reproduced official photograph. The centre of interest in this was the ruined town hall which bore on its façade an enormous notice-board (now in the Imperial War Museum) with the words *Nicht ärgern, mer wundern* – 'Don't be angry, only astonished.' This motto was obviously intended to apply to all the tangled destruction we saw round us. Péronne had not been battered to pieces by our shell-fire or taken by assault. It had been blown up with solemn Teuton thoroughness before the enemy showed a clean pair of heels in front of our advance.[14] The ruins of the cathedral, the theatre and the public buildings had clearly fallen to heavy charges, but every single dwelling-house had been systematically wrecked by small grenades, some scarcely larger than a pigeon's egg (we picked them up quite often, unexploded),[15] tossed in through the open windows or under the stairs. We were neither angry nor astounded by this, but made the best use of what remained.

What did draw blasphemy from the countrymen especially among us was that, with the same thoroughness, the Germans had rooted up every garden, neatly sawn off every fruit tree in the whole fruitful countryside and smashed or burnt every agricultural machine. What is more, the place bristled with booby-traps of their devising. These showed much misplaced ingenuity, even a schoolboy sense of humour. The commonest was a fountain pen or any other desirable trifle lying on the floor of a room or a dug-out with a wire, concealed by shavings or scraps of plaster, attached; the first man to pick it up was blown to pieces or seriously hurt and in the early days not a few were. When I took over a badly damaged schoolroom and patched it up for our work I imported a piano from the debris of a drawing room along the street, forbidding any of the eager furniture-removers to strike a note until we had examined it. When a sapper gingerly did so he found the hammer of one note wired to a sizeable bomb fixed inside the frame: it would have fatally cut short the first item of a sing-song. More diabolical still was a large explosive charge in the bottom of the bathing place which German troops had made elaborately in the river. It was unobtrusively wired to the underside of a springboard

---

[14]   The German evacuation of Péronne was not as precipitate as Baron implied. In order to shorten their line, rest and refit after their ordeal on the Somme, from 14 March to 5 April 1917 the Germans conducted a strategic withdrawal to the massive defences of the Hindenburg (or Siegfried) Line. This line was actually a series of new positions that had been constructed in secret by 370,000 German troops and Russian prisoners of war. In the wake of the German retreat, the British occupied Péronne on 18 March. Roughly 1,000 square miles was ceded, all of it thoroughly devastated and thickly strewn with booby traps. P. Hart, *The Somme* (London, 2005), p. 529; *Statistics of the military effort of the British Empire during the Great War 1914–1920* (London, 1922), p. 806; H. Herwig, *The First World War: Germany and Austria–Hungary 1914–1918* (London, 1997), pp. 229–30, 248–52.

[15]   By this stage in the war, the German army was making extensive use of small, egg-shaped grenades. These were less powerful than the more famous German 'stick-grenade' and were primed by being tapped against a hard object. P. Haythornthwaite, *The World War One source book* (London, 1992), pp. 71–2; J. Brophy and E. Partridge, *The long trail: soldiers' songs and slang 1914–18* (London, 1969), p. 95.

and the first diver would have blown up his fellow-bathers on the rebound. Most elaborate of all were the time-bombs, constructed on the principle of a weight hung on a copper wire, which passing through a jar filled with acid, suspended it over a charge of nitroglycerine. The thickness of the wire and the strength of the acid determined the timing of the explosion, which might be weeks later. It was so in two cases I remember, one at Villers Faucon, a ruined village a few miles away, which killed the colonel and most of the officers of a battalion of the Gloucesters seated in their mess, and another which blew up the Hôtel de Ville of Bapaume, our neighbour town, with many casualties among the party of French deputies who were celebrating its deliverance. For the first week or two in our own billet it was odd to wake up at night and wonder if one was fated to go sky high at any moment. When I met the town major[16] in the morning his usual greeting was 'Glad to see you again – but your billet's too good to last.'

The town major, who (in the manner of the Army Areas) had 'strafed'[17] us severely in the first moment of meeting for breaking the rules about passes and welcomed us warmly the next, became at once our best friend. He agreed that Péronne was a good centre from which to work and he set us on our way at once by requisitioning the schoolroom for our use and a house suitable for the billeting of our small staff, an assembly point for our prospective workers in the area, a store and an office. The staircase had been blown up but we climbed to bed on a pile of full cases of biscuits. Later I took over the ruined theatre, with a large squad of sappers to shore it up and rebuild the stage, but the floor never proved trustworthy enough for a large audience. The Germans had done their demolition work well and we rather enjoyed defeating it when we could.

McCowen drove away, leaving Walter and me with plenty to do in preparation. We were for the moment, so to speak, dismounted and unable to scour the country which was to be our province. But in a day or two a car arrived for us from the base with the first pair of workers, the forerunners of a steady reinforcement. The chauffeur was Dickie,[18] a Plymouth man with one blind eye and a delicious Devon accent. He was a steady driver and an ingenious mechanic; he soon became a very good companion and went with me through all the worst times to come in places less quiet than this. We fell with a will to fitting up our premises for the use of the troops and ourselves. There was plenty of material lying about the town, but it was aggravating to have to put the deep dug-out in our own garden out of bounds for fear of booby-traps, for it was chock-a-block with the necessities and even the luxuries of furniture. Meanwhile the three-ton lorry from our Base Depôt rolled up, amid cheers, and delivered a first instalment of essential stores. We could make a start.

---

[16] 'TOWN MAJOR: An officer, usually of a rank considerably below that of Major, permanently stationed in a town or large village, with the task to find billeting accommodation as requested by the Area Commandant...for large or small parties of troops passing through.' Brophy and Partridge, *The long trail*, pp. 155–6.

[17] 'STRAFE: Noun and verb: a punishment or admonition...Also used for a bombardment of shells.' *Ibid.*, p. 150.

[18] Unidentifiable.

The work now had a face very different from the one I was accustomed to. There was no question of building huts any more, no negotiations with the CRE, no correspondence save chits or slips of buff paper to say 'please' or 'thank you' (it didn't seem to matter much which you used, so long as one was there) for mutual services between the army and the YMCA. We went where we would and did what we could. The red triangle sign began to fan out over the rolling country in front of Péronne. There was nothing of ours behind us save the little hut at Amiens station, now a 'back area' which I seldom had time to visit. It was mainly a question of manpower; we opened up something when we had the man for it. Walter or I would catch the CO in a fresh corner of the field, offer him a small 'centre' which could surely be housed somewhere, share his bully-beef in the mess and go back to Péronne to make arrangements. At one place the YMCA might be a couple of bell-tents loaned to us or a camouflaged marquee sent up from the base; in the forest of [blank] it was a shack among the trees; at Nesle, where the British right touched the left of a French Army, it was the village schoolhouse. At Roisel which was 'railhead' to which trucks of stores bearing our label now came in at exasperatingly irregular intervals, our work was done at first under cover of a few corrugated iron sheets against a shattered wall. It was there (very late in the war as anyone can see) that I had my first taste of shellfire. As I stood in the opening discussing the details of our arrival with the major in charge, there was the sharp boom of an enemy gun firing directly at the railway, a sudden fountain of earth which pelted me all over and when I opened my eyes the major had vanished. In the next moment I realized that he was lying at my feet, the moment after I was down beside him; in the one after we were both on our feet again pretending that nothing had happened. The next time the gun fired we went down neatly side by side. One lesson was enough to teach me that taking cover might be ungraceful but was not reckoned disgrace.

Fifteen miles, as the crow flies from Péronne lies Albert, a sizeable town, making with Péronne and Bapaume, a perfect equilateral triangle on the map. It lay all in ruins, the most conspicuous of which was the great mass of Notre Dame de Brebières, a hideous pilgrimage church like an erection of a child's red and yellow bricks.[19] What had been the miracle of Albert's 'sheepfolds' which caused it to be built I have never enquired, but here was a sight which was reckoned by the pious a miracle in itself. The tall tower, now battered and holed, was surmounted by an immense bronze statue of the Blessed Virgin holding the Child high above her head with his arms out, stretched in benediction over the town. By a freak of gunfire the whole statue, undamaged, had been blown forwards until it hung at an angle of fifty degrees; the child now leaned out, still blessing, above the tin-hats of Australian soldiers passing by among the rubble. The 'leaning Madonna of Albert' was not only a constant wonder to the troops but was now

---

[19] Its large basilica was the most notable feature of this town of about 12,000 inhabitants. Completed in 1897, it had sought to rival Lourdes as a centre for Marian pilgrimage, a local shepherd having discovered a miraculous statue of the Virgin Mary in a field many generations earlier. Middlebrook and Middlebrook, *The Somme battlefields*, pp. 216–17; M. Middlebrook, *The first day on the Somme* (London, 1984), p. 53.

well known to their relations from the little French coloured etchings of it which they bought in Amiens and sent home.[20]

We were driving towards Albert one day when we were stopped by a MMP – a mounted Military Policeman – and ordered to withdraw down a farm track off the main road. Here we reversed our car and waited to see the reason. In a few minutes quite a long procession of cars began to go by. On the second one we caught a glimpse of the Royal Standard fluttering: King George and Queen Mary, on a visit to the troops, were passing by. The policeman and his horse had moved, and we moved too. With consummate impertinence we fell in at the rear of the procession and nobody stopped us as we drove into Albert. Great preparations had gone forward in a wide open space, which might in better days have been the park of the town. To one side a tin-hatted guard of honour slapped their rifles in a royal present-arms, their bayonets flashing in the sun. All round the ground, behind ropes and military police a dense crowd of soldiers looked on, and under an awning on the far side stood our king and queen, surrounded by notables, among whom we recognized Sir Douglas Haig,[21] in British khaki or French blue. A long line, in single file, of officers and men in one uniform or the other, began to move past the king, to salute, pause a moment and salute again: it was an investiture in the field. One whom we recognized by his face and white moustache, familiar in the illustrated papers, bowed low while the king hung a high decoration round his neck. It was Marshal Petain, one day to betray our cause at Vichy.[22]

We were in clear country now, with very little fresh damage except where a

[20] Variously known as the 'Golden', 'Leaning' or 'Hanging' Virgin of Albert, this gilded statue of the Virgin and Child was dislodged from its original position by German shellfire in January 1915. Secured by French engineers, the statue was visible to British, French and German soldiers alike throughout the 1916 battle of the Somme. Given its sacred nature and dramatic situation, various stories circulated as to its significance, the most popular being that the war would end when the statue fell to the ground, a prophecy that was not fulfilled when it was finally toppled by British shellfire in April 1918. G. Gliddon, *When the barrage lifts* (London, 1987), p. 2; M. Snape, *God and the British soldier: religion and the British army in the First and Second World Wars* (London, 2005), pp. 44–5.

[21] Douglas Haig (1861–1928) is probably the most controversial figure in British military history. Haig succeeded to the command of the BEF in December 1915 and his subsequent direction of British operations on the Western Front (and especially his handling of the battle of the Somme and the third battle of Ypres) has been the subject of fierce (and sometimes hysterical) debate between his detractors and defenders since his death. Whatever his strengths and weaknesses as a strategist (and a growing body of evidence suggests that the latter have been overstated by his critics, who have been reluctant to recognize the technological and political constraints that bound him, let alone the record of allied and enemy commanders of comparable seniority) Haig was plainly a devout and paternalistic officer who was deeply concerned for the welfare of his soldiers, a fact that belies his popular reputation as a callous butcher. While this concern was manifested in his work for veterans in the post-war years, during the war itself it was very much reflected in his support for army chaplains and for welfare organizations such as the YMCA. *ODNB*; J. M. Bourne (ed.), *Who's who in World War One* (London, 2001), pp. 117–19; G. Sheffield and J. Bourne (eds.), *Douglas Haig: war diaries and letters 1914–1918* (London, 2005), pp. 1–43; Snape, *God and the British soldier*, pp. 61–7.

[22] Henri-Philippe Benoni Omer Joseph Pétain (1856–1951) won fame in 1916 as the 'hero of Verdun', leading the defence of the fortress city against a massive German offensive in what would prove to be the most protracted battle of the war. In 1917, he played the leading *rôle* in quelling the mutinies that briefly paralysed the French army on the Western Front. However, during the Second World War his *rôle* as the head of the collaborationist Vichy regime brought an ignominious end to a hitherto distinguished military career. Bourne (ed.), *Who's who in World War One*, p. 232.

railway or an important road junction came under long range shell-fire. The
German army had withdrawn in [blank],[23] secretly, skilfully and very
successfully to the Hindenburg Line. Only along the edge of the Fourth Army
front the guns rumbled, almost lazily, through the blazing summer afternoons
that now followed on a harsh spring. At our backs the foul no-man's land left
by last year's great battles festered in the heat. There was no one alive there
now save road menders and the columns of marching men and trains of lorries,
horse-wagons and guns which used it as a highway to and from the back areas.
The burial parties which would have to dig up the tens of thousands of British
dead and assemble them in orderly war cemeteries had not yet begun their
grisly work.

I remember an afternoon when Walter and Dickie and I drove out into this
lifeless land to fulfil, if we could, a commission that was long overdue. Among
its multifarious odd jobs the YMCA had undertaken, where possible, to trace
the resting places of fallen men and send a photograph to their relatives on
request. A letter from South Africa had been forwarded to me; it was a pitiful
cri de cœur from the mother of an only son, not out of his teens, who had been
killed in Delville Wood, the grave of the first South African contingent.[24] We
drove to the place, which was new to all of us, and began our search. From the
outset we saw it was hopeless. The old trees of the wood were reduced to gaunt
skeletons, every one splintered and half shot away – the picture of which
painters like Paul Nash and Nevinson have left posterity an authentic record.[25]
And under the trees an inextricable jungle of new growth strangled all our
attempts to move about. Death was everywhere underfoot and most palpably in
the air, but here it must remain anonymous until identity disks and regimental
badges could some day be disinterred. We turned away and decided to make a
round on the way home. At Mametz we left the car beside the ruined wood[26]
and walked a few hundred yards on to the open ground, broken by our tanks a

[23]   March–April 1917.
[24]   During the 1916 battle of the Somme, the South African Brigade formed one of the three brigades
       of the 9th Scottish Division. It was committed to an attack on Delville Wood (or 'Devil's Wood'),
       just west of Longueval, on 15 July. The South Africans quickly captured the greater part of the
       wood, which they held for four days against fierce German counter-attacks. At the end of this
       period, three quarters of its 3,153 men were either killed, wounded or missing. Hart, *The Somme*,
       pp. 284–91.
[25]   Paul Nash (1889–1946) was a pre-war artist who served with the Hampshire Regiment on the
       Western Front until he returned to England injured in May 1917. As a result of an exhibition of
       his paintings, based on sketches he had made in France, he was invited by Charles Masterman,
       head of the War Propaganda Bureau, to become an official war artist, in which capacity Nash
       returned to the Western Front. Christopher Richard Wynne Nevinson (1889–1946) was a well-
       known *avant garde* artist before the war and, as a pacifist, he at first served with the Red Cross
       and with the RAMC. After being invalided out of the army in January 1916, he also came to the
       attention of Masterman and subsequently returned to France as an official war artist. His paintings
       (most notably 'Paths of glory', a depiction of British corpses in no-man's-land) were noted for
       their candour. Bourne (ed.), *Who's who in World War One*, pp. 217–19.
[26]   The village of Mametz was captured by the 7th Division on the afternoon of 1 July 1916, one of
       the few tangible successes of that day. In contrast, Mametz Wood was captured by the 38th
       (Welsh) Division at a cost of more than 4,000 casualties after a five day struggle that lasted from
       7 to 11 July. Prior and Wilson, *The Somme*, pp. 104–5, 125–6.

year before. One or two hulks of them still gaped with wide wounds to the sky. And the ground was rough with the aftermath of the fighting; in one place the bones of a man's leg, hastily buried, stuck grotesquely into the air, crowned by a mouldered boot.

We began to walk back to our car and came by chance into a depression in the ground, which might have been a large shell-hole. The lip of it all round was tufted with high grasses in flower, golden silk in the sunshine, and starred thickly with scarlet poppies. The bottom had silted up in the winter rains into a silver beach of chalk surrounding a shallow pool of the clearest water. Beside the water stood the cross of a soldier's grave, two strips of wood held together with a rusty nail which had wept an iron tear down its face. This was partly shadowed by a tall wild mallow, its pink flowers like a rose planted by some friend. It was a composition ready made, a chance vignette from Nature's capricious hand and it held all three of us in the moment motionless. Before we stirred again a Red Admiral butterfly soared over the lip of the crater in his typical lovely flight and alighted on the top of the mallow, to open and close his wings in the sun. Here was the final touch, the symbol of beauty that passes but delights in its short day. It was a small scene consummated, which has never gone out of my mind.

We drove home while the sun was getting low and dark clouds, big with rain, came up from the west at our backs. As we passed through Combles they obscured the last streaks of an angry sunset over the village, the most extensive rubbish heap in this part of the Somme.[27] A reek of putrefaction poisoned the air. Nothing moved in the main street but the scuttling rats and a starving hare which for a moment sat frozen with terror in the glare of our headlights as we turned them on; one of those wild cats bristled in a doorway and spat through its bared teeth as we went by. In the gathering darkness Combles was the theatre for a witches' sabbath to begin. No producer has ever mounted a set so obscene.

There was one striking feature in our area which will never be seen in warfare again – the cavalry. It is strange and sad to us who still lived in their last epoch to realize that the long centuries of the armed horseman are ended, ended as irrevocably as the career of the splendid sailing ship and, in the nearest future, of the majestic steam locomotive. We miss the sight and sound and smell of horses. It is against all reason to lament the change but we must be pardoned for a sentimental regret. For us the 'armoured fighting vehicle', the stream-lined motor vessel and the diesel engine, admirable in their efficiency, will never quicken the heart-beat as their precursors did at every sight of them. The Norman melee at Hastings, the onset, front and flank, of our chivalry at Poitiers, the French breastplates going down before the squares of scarlet at Waterloo, the forlorn hope, not even a hope, that rode up the valley at Balaclava

---

[27] Combles lay on the boundary between the French and British armies on the Somme and was captured by French troops and by the 56th (London) Division on 25 September 1916. Even by the standards of the wider campaign, this small town was the scene of terrible devastation; hit by 3,000 heavy shells on the night of 24–5 June alone, the next day an ammunition train exploded in its railway station. Middlebrook and Middlebrook, *The Somme battlefields*, p. 188; C. Duffy, *Through German eyes: the British and the Somme 1916* (London, 2006), p. 124.

as if on parade[28] are in the history books but already joisted from the boys'
stories by space-ships. All that remains is a bit of play-acting – cowboy outfits
for young children and westerns on the screen for older ones, the Sovereign's
escort of Household Cavalry, leaving their spanners behind for an hour or two,
the musical ride of the Queen's Troop of horse gunners at a military tournament.
The tourist takes snapshots of his girl-friend patting the nose of the mounted
Sentry's horse in Whitehall, but he could no longer harness it, let alone ride it.
The horse will never return to the battlefield: 'the knights are dust, their swords
are rust'.[29] Gone with the glory of horses, too, thank heaven, is their untold
suffering in all the wars of the past. The horse henceforward is no more than a
picturesque anachronism.

On the Somme in 1917 the cavalry was in truth an anachronism already,
though we did not know it. Its prestige was still very high, though it had never
fought a major decisive action. The commander-in-chief and all the army
commanders save one (but he the greatest, Lord Plumer) were cavalrymen.[30]
Many cavalry officers, maybe, still half-believed the remark of one of them that
an important function of their branch of the service was 'to lend tone to a mob'.

Meanwhile the horses on the Somme were a fine sight. The tents and horse-
lines of the 5th Cavalry Division[31] stretched right across a shallow valley in which
there was continual movement going on of men drilling, exercising horses or
taking them to water in the stream which ran along one side. As they waited
month after month for the great 'break-through' for which they were being held
ready it became necessary to draw upon them for the front line, too thinly manned
in places. So night after night parties of 'dismounted cavalry' – a counterpart of
the 'mounted infantry' of the South African War – left their sabres in camp and
shouldered rifles for the trenches. It was unpopular service, not least among those
left behind – one man in five who was now very heavily worked feeding,
grooming and watering four horses beside his own.

We had our own work among these men, especially among the magnificent,
turbaned soldiers of the Indian cavalry brigades in the division. This clearly
called for a knowledge of language, religion, customs and food which none of us

---

[28]   References, respectively, to the hard triumph of William the Conqueror's cavalry at Hastings (14
October 1066); the decisive attack of a small band of Anglo-Gascon cavalry at Poitiers (19
September 1356); the failure of the massed French cavalry attacks against British (and Allied)
infantry squares at Waterloo (18 June 1815) and to the charge of the Light Brigade at Balaclava
(25 October 1854). D. Chandler (ed.), *A guide to the battlefields of Europe* (Ware, 1998), *passim*.

[29]   S. T. Coleridge (1772–1834). This poetic fragment first appeared in Walter Scott's *Ivanhoe* (1819).

[30]   Despite the implication that the BEF's high command was dominated by cavalrymen who were
incapable of fighting a modern war, this was far from being the case. Although Sir Douglas Haig
had been commissioned into the 7th Hussars, by April 1917 only two of Haig's five army
commanders had a cavalry background. Sir Henry Sinclair Horne (First Army) was commissioned
into the Royal Artillery; Sir Herbert Charles Onslow Plumer (Second Army) was commissioned
into the 65th Foot and Sir Henry Seymour Rawlinson (Fourth Army) was a product of the King's
Royal Rifle Corps and the Coldstream Guards. A. F. Becke, *History of the Great War based on
official documents. Order of battle part 4. The Army Council, GHQs, armies, and corps 1914–1918*
(Uckfield, 2007), pp. 71–120; Sheffield and Bourne (eds.), *Douglas Haig*, pp. 495–511; *ODNB*.

[31]   The 2nd Indian Cavalry Division, which had arrived in France in November 1914, was renamed
the 5th Cavalry Division in November 1916. Rawson, *British army handbook 1914–1918*, pp. 234–5.

Illustration 1. Barclay Baron (centre), Oliver McCowen (left) and Harry Holmes (right) outside 'Cologne Central', 1919. YMCA Archives, University of Birmingham.

Illustration 2. Barclay Josiah Baron (standing) at the opening of Bristol's YMCA 'Dug-Out' centre. Jane Baron is seated to his left. YMCA Archives, University of Birmingham.

Illustration 3. The Iron Jelloids Hut, Le Havre. The photograph captures the bleakness and squalor of many of the BEF's base areas. YMCA Archives, University of Birmingham.

Illustration 4. One of Lena Ashwell's ubiquitous concert parties performs for a mixed audience of British and French troops. YMCA Archives, University of Birmingham.

Illustration 5. A YMCA hut for the Chinese Labour Corps at Calais. YMCA Archives, University of Birmingham.

Illustration 8. ''Ere's your lemonade a-coming, 'Erbert!' Published in *YM. The British Empire YMCA Weekly* on 29 September 1916, this cartoon serves as an apt commentary on the dangers of the YMCA's developing work in forward areas.

Illustration 5. A YMCA hut for the Chinese Labour Corps at Calais. YMCA Archives, University of Birmingham.

Illustration 6. The first YMCA staff at the front, 1915. J. H. Hunt (seated) with three army orderlies. YMCA Archives, University of Birmingham.

Illustration 7. YMCA headquarters staff, Fifth Army, 1917. Harry Lyne (seated, centre) with a mixed group of YMCA workers and army orderlies. YMCA Archives, University of Birmingham.

Illustration 8. ''Ere's your lemonade a-coming, 'Erbert!' Published in *YM. The British Empire YMCA Weekly* on 29 September 1916, this cartoon serves as an apt commentary on the dangers of the YMCA's developing work in forward areas.

Illustration 9. A YMCA dug-out in the trenches. Centres such as this proliferated from the winter of 1915–16. A. K. Yapp, *The romance of the Red Triangle* (London, n.d.).

Illustration 10. An artist's impression of an improvised YMCA centre in Ypres, where Dr Magrath distinguished himself in 1917–18. A. K. Yapp. *The romance of the Red Triangle* (London, n.d.).

Illustration 11. A YMCA centre for the walking wounded. The free distribution of comforts to the wounded on or near the battlefield was pioneered during the closing stages of the 1916 battle of the Somme. A. K. Yapp, *The romance of the Red Triangle* (London, n.d.).

Illustration 12. Arthur Yapp (centre), the driving force behind the YMCA's war work, with a motorized field kitchen. YMCA Archives, University of Birmingham.

Illustration 13. A motorized kitchen in the field. Mobility became a pressing problem for the YMCA during the inexorable Allied advance of August–November 1918. A. K. Yapp, *The romance of the Red Triangle* (London, n.d.).

Illustration 14. Army work at home. A throng of servicemen seek accommodation at London Central YMCA. YMCA Archives, University of Birmingham.

Illustration 15. Signatories of the War Roll, an initiative launched by the Religious Work Committee of the YMCA in 1915. The majority appear to be men of the Queen's (Royal West Surrey Regiment). YMCA Archives, University of Birmingham.

Illustration 16. The famous chapel in the 'Upper Room' at Talbot House, Poperinghe.

could command,[32] and an Anglo-Indian worker was sent up to me by Dr Datta, the very fine elderly scholar who controlled all our work among Indian troops in France. One day when I went over to visit the camp I was delighted to encounter a very old friend, Henry Gibbon,[33] chaplain of Balliol College. He had started his career as an officer in the Bengal Cavalry, had been invalided out after an accident and had taken orders. He was over-age for active service now but was in his element as padre of one of the Indian brigades – Mhow or Sialkot, I forget which. We sat talking in his tent and he told me of some of his problems. One was that the division had lain here so long that its men had many friends in the village within reach and not a few of them wanted to marry French girls. The regulations laid down that this could not be done without the CO's consent, and Henry's colonel had delegated the vetting of all such cases to him. He described to me one that had come to him that very morning. He had begun by urging the man to think over very seriously the possible snags before committing himself. The conversation had gone like this:-

'Do you talk French?'

'No sir.'

'Does she know any English?'

'One or two words, sir'.

'Well, that's a bit awkward, isn't it? Another thing – she's a Roman Catholic and I expect you're a Protestant.'

'O, yes sir. But we've settled all that.'

'How upon earth did you manage it [?]'

'Well, sir, you see I takes 'er into the church and I points to the 'eathen images all round and I ses to 'er "No bon", I ses. And she ses to me "Napoo."'[34]

---

[32]   Conscious of the lessons of the Indian Mutiny, of German religious propaganda and of a global, Ottoman-inspired *jihad*, the military authorities in France remained acutely conscious of the cultural and religious sensitivities of their Indian soldiers. While the latter had long been forbidden to change their religion, the involvement of Christian welfare organizations with Indian soldiers was carefully monitored and controlled. In October 1914 an independent Indian Soldiers' Comforts Fund was established in London that supplied clothes, cigarettes, sweets and religious literature to Muslims and Sikhs. The latter were also eligible to receive bracelets, combs, daggers and underpants at the Fund's expense. In the early months of the war the YMCA fell foul of military censors because of its incautious distribution of YMCA stationery to Indian soldiers in military hospitals. Fearful of the alarm that YMCA letterheads stood to provoke in India, censors had to cut them out of personal correspondence. G. Corrigan, *Sepoys in the trenches: the Indian Corps on the Western Front 1914–15* (Stroud, 2006), pp. 198–201.

[33]   Henry Hensman Gibbon (?–1928) was ordained priest in 1892 after training at Wycliffe Hall, Oxford, and was chaplain of Balliol College from 1902. He was a member of the Oxford Pastorate and played a leading *rôle* in the founding of the OMM, also acting as its first chaplain. A former officer in the Bengal Lancers, his decision to take orders was prompted by 'a deep spiritual experience during a severe illness after a polo accident in India'. Although over age, he appears to have been commissioned as a temporary chaplain in October 1915 (being listed as 'R. H. Gibbon') and subsequently served as chaplain to the Indian cavalry in France. Despite the caution that usually prevented such activities, such was his zeal to win souls that in July 1916 he was allowed to attend an Indian cavalryman who had been sentenced to death for shooting an Indian officer. However, this example of evangelical zeal was widely resented by Gibbon's fellow officers as being 'a great piece of impertinence' on his part. *Crockford's*, 1913, p. 569, and 1920, p. 565; Baron, *The doctor*, pp. 5–6; *Army List*, July 1916, 1791e; M. Brown, *The Imperial War Museum book of the Western Front* (London, 1993), pp. 97–8.

[34]   'NAPOO: Finished; empty; gone; non-existent.' Brophy and Partridge, *The long trail*, p. 123.

The cavalry had not much longer to wait. There were already whispers – very secret as always but widely discussed – of an action in which the cavalry were to break through and roll up the enemy: optimists said it would be the end of the war, as optimists had done on earlier occasions. 'The Battle of Cambrai' in due course began, the cavalry drew their swords and rode, but, as so often, heavy rain bogged down the operation on the second day.[35] The cavalry was destined to play its valiant part in some of the hard-fought skirmishes of the heroic final advance which ended on the Rhine more than a year later; its men were the first to occupy Cologne. And then the jingling bridles, the clanking sabres, the bandoliers and spurs and trumpets were hung up for ever.[36] After all it was the tanks not the horses which made victory possible in two World Wars.[37]

As the hot summer wore on into autumn something began to stir on the Somme. Units here and there disappeared overnight, rumours increased that the whole Fourth Army was to move. I went to see the APM, usually my best confidant anywhere. I caught him in the act of gazing at the top of the large-scale map which went up to the ceiling of one wall in his office. His eyes came down instantly to greet me.

'Is it true that we're moving, sir?'

'I've nothing to tell you. You'd better go and ask that carrotty girl in the estaminet – she always knows more about us than I do.'

Then he added an afterthought with a grin: 'All I can say is that the Boche is going to need bathing drawers pretty soon. Good morning to you.'

The APM's sergeant stepped outside with me and dropped one or two practical hints – there was no need to visit the estaminet, though that was often an uncanny source of information. I knew now what I chiefly wanted to know.

Some of the units of Fourth Army were already being transferred to other commands, others were visibly packing up and marching out, usually at night. Some of our own work was melting away. Military transport, on which we relied – and the army helped us wherever it could – grew difficult to come by, then impossible; our own move must bide its time. Leaving two members of our staff in charge at Péronne, Walter and I, with Dickie driving, started northwards to

---

[35] Here Baron seems to be confusing the events of the battle of Arras (9 April–16 May 1917) with those of the battle of Cambrai (20 November–7 December 1917). Although the British deployed cavalry on both occasions with the aim of exploiting apparent breakthroughs, the main cavalry attack at Arras went in around Monchy-le-Preux on 11 April, its tactical success – and strategic failure – occurring amidst unseasonal falls of snow. Marquess of Anglesey, *A history of the British cavalry 1816 to 1919*, VIII: *The Western Front, 1915–1918; epilogue, 1919–1939* (London, 1997), pp. 74–96; T. Wilson, *The myriad faces of war: Britain and the Great War* (Cambridge, 1988), p. 454; *Statistics of the military effort of the British Empire*, p. 640.

[36] Not quite. The British army used cavalry operationally in the early stages of the Second World War, the 1st Cavalry Division serving in Palestine, Transjordan, Iraq and Syria until it was converted to an armoured division in August 1941. Forty, *British army handbook 1939–1945*, p. 330.

[37] However this may be argued for the Second World War, the war-winning significance of the tank has been greatly exaggerated for the First. The British Second Army, for example, had no tank support throughout its advance in Flanders in the autumn of 1918. Becke, *Order of battle part 4*, pp. 279–83.

reconnoitre. It was the morning at last of the long-awaited battle of Cambrai[38] [blank] and as we drove along roads which ran parallel with the front we picked up exciting scraps of news, not all accurate. At one point we came upon a dressing station busy with casualties and watched a lorry load of wounded drive away, with the elated British soldiers standing up in order that their German prisoners might sit down. At Souchez, famous for its sugar refinery battered by fierce earlier fighting,[39] the road ran steeply up hill, with a big notice at the bottom 'Dangerous to pass in daylight', and from the crest we could see the smoke of the barrage that roared ceaselessly all along the ridge to eastward. At Lens we passed the even more notorious landmark of the 'Tower Bridge',[40] a tall pithead structure in this gloomy mining town, now a heap of ruins. We made a detour over the Belgian border in order to have a cup of tea (we had been moving fast since early morning) with Tubby Clayton,[41] an old friend of mine, at Talbot House in Poperinghe.[42] I could not guess that afternoon that I was to serve at home on the staff of Toc H, its aftermath, for the next forty years!

---

[38] Once again, Baron shows some confusion regarding the chronology of the war. Fourth Army's move to the Flanders coast roughly coincided with Second Army's offensive at Messines in June 1917. *Ibid.*, pp. 84, 104.

[39] Prior to 1914, northern France was home to a highly productive sugar industry. The sugar refinery at Souchez was fiercely contested during the Second Battle of Artois, a major French offensive that took place in May–June 1915. S. Audoin-Rouzeau and A. Becker, *1914–1918: understanding the Great War* (London, 2002), p. 57; N. Cave, *Battleground Europe. Arras: Vimy Ridge* (London, 1996), p. 25.

[40] This was actually at Loos. 'Tower Bridge' was a prominent landmark throughout the battle of Loos in autumn 1915. Consisting of 'high twin pylons each topped with an ironwork turret and linked by a long iron walkway', it proved to be an ideal platform for artillery spotters amidst the relatively flat landscape of the surrounding area. L. MacDonald, *1915: the death of innocence* (London, 1997), p. 487; N. Lloyd, *Loos 1915* (Stroud, 2006), pp. 75–6.

[41] P. T. B. Clayton (1885–1972) was ordained priest in 1911 by Bishop E. S. Talbot and had served as a curate at St Mary's, Portsea, prior to the outbreak of war. He was commissioned into the Army Chaplains' Department on 26 May 1915, joined the BEF and was initially posted to No. 16 General Hospital at Le Treport. He was then sent to the 16th Infantry Brigade in November 1915, a brigade which was then part of 6th Division, whose senior Anglican chaplain was Neville Talbot, the second son of E. S. Talbot, Clayton's diocesan bishop. Briefly posted to Boulogne in June 1916 and to the 29th Division that August, Clayton was based in Poperinghe as a garrison chaplain from September 1916, where much of his ministry was devoted to a brigade of heavy artillery. In October 1917, Sir Ivor Maxse, the commander of XVIII Corps and one of the few professed atheists in the higher reaches of the British army, recommended Clayton for a Military Cross 'For most valuable services in "The Salient" and at Talbot House, Poperinghe, for [the] past two years. In addition to daily church services at Talbot House he has held services at Ypres every week for artillery units during [a] period when Ypres was heavily shelled. His zeal and devotion to duty [is] beyond all praise.' When his MC was announced in January 1918 it was noted in the press that he was the third curate from St Mary's Portsea to receive this award. *Army List*, July 1915; *ODNB*; B. Baron (ed.), *Letters from Flanders* (London, 1932), pp. 10–13; P. B. Clayton, *Tales of Talbot House* (London, 1929), pp. 147–9; Snape, *God and the British soldier*, p. 60; Church Missionary Society Archives, University of Birmingham (hereafter CMS), XCMS ACC/18/Z/1 Army Book of L. H. Gwynne, p. 44.

[42] Inspired by Neville Talbot and originally leased from a local brewer, 'Talbot House' (or 'Toc H' in the signaller's phonetic alphabet) was opened in December 1915. It is unclear whether it was named after Neville himself or after his younger brother, Gilbert, who had been killed outside Ypres in July while serving with the 7th Rifle Brigade. Home to a soldiers' club known as 'Everyman's Club', the building also housed an impressive attic chapel known as 'The Upper Room'. Despite its striking egalitarianism (proclaimed by a famous placard that read 'ALL RANK

That night we slept at Malo-les-Bains, the seaside suburb of Dunkirk, in a house that was to become our own headquarters for a new, brief chapter. We began at once to meet officers and men we had known on the Somme and were able to piece together the position. The bulk of the Fourth Army had been left behind among the 'Byng Boys',[43] Lord Byng's Third Army.[44] Only one Corps, the XV, was on the coast under our old army commander, Lord Rawlinson.[45] It was he who had been ordered to throw such masses of men into the Somme Battle between July and October of the previous year, with the staggering loss of over 400,000 casualties. Now he had taken a bull-headed run with the 1st Division at Nieuwpoort on the mouth of the Yser river, which was here the boundary between the Allies and the enemy. It had failed and the division had retired to lick its wounds and re-form.[46]

Our new area was only a narrow strip of coast between Dunkirk and the Yser. It had hitherto been held, on very easy terms of mutual disregard, by the Belgians who grew vegetables out in front of their trenches (so one of our intelligence men told me) and whose front a few miles inland was completely covered by miles of flood let in from the sea in 1914.[47] The arrival of the British was therefore most unwelcome to the French population – and they made no bones about it – for it stirred up a sleeping wasps' nest. All the same, our army commander's headquarters was planted in a big upstanding hotel on the sand dunes,[48] from which on a clear

ABANDON YE WHO ENTER HERE'), the model for Talbot House seems to have been that of the pre–war Church of England soldiers' institute. These institutes had originated in Aldershot in 1880 and had spread to the larger garrisons of the British Empire in subsequent decades. Often linked to individual dioceses, these institutes sought to provide wholesome recreation for ordinary soldiers and were intended to bring them into contact with their chaplains in surroundings where the trappings of rank were at a discount. Given the ban on Protestant chaplains using Catholic churches in France and Belgium for public worship, the famous chapel in 'The Upper Room' was one of many improvised during the course of the war. YMCA Archives, University of Birmingham (hereafter YMCA), K24 YMCA War Work No. 4 Religious. Letter of E. S. Talbot, Easter 1919; F. H. Brabant, *Neville Stuart Talbot* (London, 1949), p. 61; Snape, *God and the British soldier*, pp. 216–18; M. Snape, *The Royal Army Chaplains' Department 1796–1953: clergy under fire* (Woodbridge, 2008), pp. 142–3.

[43] So called after *The Bing Boys*, a popular contemporary revue. Brophy and Partridge, *The long trail*, p. 78.

[44] General Sir Julian Byng (1862–1935). He was raised to the peerage after the war, in 1919, when he was created Baron Byng of Vimy and Thorpe-le-Soken. *ODNB*; N. Gardner, 'Julian Byng', in *Haig's Generals*, ed. I. F. W. Beckett and S. J. Corvi (Barnsley, 2006), p. 55.

[45] General Sir Henry Rawlinson (1864–1925) was, like Byng, raised to the peerage in 1919, when he was created Baron Rawlinson of Trent. *ODNB*; I. F. W. Beckett, 'Henry Rawlinson', in *Haig's Generals*, ed. Beckett and Corvi, p. 165.

[46] This is an unfounded charge against Rawlinson. There had been no attack by 1st Division against Nieuport (or Nieuwpoort), which was in any event behind Allied lines. In July 1917, however, the Germans mounted a spoiling attack on the British bridgehead at Lombartzyde, pushing Rawlinson's troops back across the Yser. R. Prior and T. Wilson, *Passchendaele: the untold story* (New Haven, 1996), pp. 69–70.

[47] In order to prevent further German advances in this low-lying area of Belgium, at the end of October 1914 Albert I, king of the Belgians, ordered the opening of the sluices at the mouth of the Yser, the ensuing inundation creating 'an impassable zone ten miles long between Nieuport and Dixmude'. The Belgian army held much of this quiet sector until the autumn of 1918. J. Keegan, *The First World War* (London, 1998), p. 140.

[48] At Malo-les-Bains. Becke, *Order of battle part 4*, p. 101.

day, the German HQ at Ostend could plainly be picked out, and Rawlinson's staff could play a few chukkas of polo in the afternoon on the sandy beach at their door without fear of interruption. Throughout the war there seemed to be a universal unwritten convention that neither contestant's headquarters were fair game: had they been – who knows? – the war might have come to an end sooner![49]

We decided to stay at Malo, the railhead for new arrivals and stores. Dunkirk was a dull town, destined to write its name in English history books only when the second war began in earnest. It had already grown shabby with bombing and, thanks to the presence of British troops, this now increased night by night. It was also exposed to long-range shelling down the coast by German guns of very heavy calibre, and the Casino at Malo, now the main army offices, which faced our windows, had received a direct hit, with a number of clerks killed. The Royal Navy used the harbour and from it two ungainly monsters, 'monitors' called HMS *Erebus* and *Terror*, which were virtually floating platforms for long naval guns, steamed slowly up the coast after dark to bombard German installations.[50]

We often sat up at night when bombardment from sky or earth was on, playing cards with our elderly landlady in the cellar and I shall always remember a noisy night when more than everything happened at once. We were expecting a new worker, a sixty-year-old clergyman from home, and he arrived amid the warmest welcome possible. For it was pitch dark with a tremendous thunder-storm crashing over the town. In the intervals of this we could hear the duller thuds of bombs falling and then, to cap them, six very heavy explosions at long intervals which rocked the house – the German guns firing. But that was not enough, there came several bursts – pop, pop! – of very much sharper, smaller detonation. In the morning the *Erebus* – or was it the *Terror*? – was lying stranded on the beach within sight of our windows. She had been holed by a shower of small shells (we handled the brass cases in the course of the day) fired by a German submarine. The craft which played this audacious practical joke had bobbed up in the middle of the harbour under the noses of three British destroyers lying there. Our ships were helpless, their guns could not get a bearing on a target so close and so low in the water, and they received some slight damage before the monitor was hit.[51]

---

[49] This is a somewhat misleading quip as to the safety of general officers. As Gordon Corrigan has pointed out: 'Altogether four British lieutenant-generals, twelve major-generals and eighty-one brigadier generals died or were killed between 1914 and 1918. A further 146 were wounded or taken prisoner. Whatever else the generals were doing, they were certainly not sitting in comfortable chateaux.' G. Corrigan, *Mud, blood and poppycock* (London, 2004), p. 194.

[50] These shallow-draught warships were intended to support an outflanking amphibious operation on the Flanders coast in the area of Middelkerke, an operation that was to assist an attack up the coast by Rawlinson's Fourth Army in support of an anticipated breakthrough around Ypres by Gough's Fifth. The ultimate objectives of both armies were the ports of Ostende and Zeebrugge, which were major submarine bases. Prior and Wilson, *Passchendaele*, pp. 69–70.

[51] This incident is typical of the naval war in these waters, as the Germans mounted numerous raids against British shipping from occupied ports on the Flanders coast. However, it did not prevent either *Erebus* or *Terror* from participating in British raids on Zeebrugge and Ostend in April and May 1918. G. Till, 'Passchendaele: the maritime dimension', in *Passchendaele in perspective: the third battle of Ypres*, ed. P. Liddle (London, 1997), pp. 77–8; H. Newbolt, *History of the Great War based on official documents. Naval operations*, V (London, 1931), pp. 240–77.

Our new worker (who later was to face an even more daunting experience and to
be sent home without dishonour but with a breakdown) often laughed about the
warmth of his first hours in France.

The whole British force on the coast was very limited and ours had to be
small to match. There was no question of building huts and requisitioned
buildings were at a premium; marquees did well enough. When I went to
Coxyde,[52] nowadays a holiday resort of fashionable villas, and called on a rather
gruff CO he said, 'Do you chaps *have* to set up in places like this?' I told him
no, we wanted to work anywhere we could be of use. 'Well', was his comment,
'anybody who comes here without being ordered is a damned fool.' And indeed
Coxyde sometimes got its ration of heavy shells which did very little damage,
for they plunged into the dunes, sending up immense fountains of sand. I saw
one nearby distribute a haystack all over the landscape, and a splinter of it,
weighing some pounds, sliced a main pole of our marquee like butter so that it
collapsed, with no one hurt.

For a month or two there was an extremely 'top secret' in our area. The First
Division, badly mauled at Nieuwpoort, was undergoing a refit and very special
training in an old fortification along the coast. This was Fort Mardyck, near
Gravelines, the little port of for the fleet of [?] Pierre Loti's *Pêcheur d'Islande*,[53]
nearly half-way from Dunkirk to Calais. The Division, rumour ran, was
practising for a surprise landing on the far side of Ostend which was to take the
Germans in rear. The whole project was so confidential that the men closely
confined for it were not even allowed to write letters home, and a question was
asked in Parliament – to receive the abrupt answer 'No, sir' – whether it was true
that a whole division in France was in strict quarantine for some mysterious
disease![54] I applied, by word of mouth, for leave to supply Fort Mardyck with
footballs and cricket gear, books and magazines and indoor games of any kind,
and this was granted, without anything on paper, on condition that we did not set
foot inside or try to communicate with anyone expect the guard at the gate. So we
drove a load of stuff that far, saw it unloaded and drove away. In the end, to the
infinite relief of the men concerned, we were told, the attack was called off:
actually the Germans had crack troops of their Marine Corps waiting at the point
fixed for the landing with a red-hot welcome.

Very good friends of ours were the members of the Friends' Ambulance Unit,
who operated from a well-equipped centre in the docks called 'The Cat and

---

[52] Koksijde.
[53] The pseudonym of the novelist Louis-Marie-Julien Viaud (1850–1923). *Pêcheur d'Islande* (1886)
    was one of his most famous works. It was published in English as *An Iceland fisherman* in 1887.
    A. Levi (ed.), *Guide to French literature 1789 to the present* (Chicago, 1992), pp. 383–6.
[54] The 1st Division was selected and trained for the projected amphibious assault on the Flanders
    coast. Supported by a number of specially equipped tanks, it was to be landed in three waves by
    large, wooden landing craft that would be driven aground by accompanying monitors. Trained for
    its task in great secrecy at Le Clipon near Gravelines, its isolation was officially attributed to an
    outbreak of disease. Ultimately dependent on progress around Ypres, the amphibious attack was
    called off in mid-October 1917 and 1st Division left Le Clipon soon after. A. Wiest, 'The planned
    amphibious assault', in *Passchendaele in perspective*, ed. Liddle pp. 205–10.

Fiddle'. I had never come across the FAU before, with their dark grey uniform and the badge of the black, white and red star, the colours (regrettably, if you like) of the old German Imperial flag, granted to them by Bismarck himself for good service to the wounded of 1870.[55] (It is a character of Quaker compassion that it is offered to anyone in need, regardless of creed or nationality; it was to be exercised towards Germans again at the earliest possible moment after the Armistice of our own war.) In Dunkirk they were not merely running an excellent canteen for the British and French working in the docks but doing invaluable service, for which there was no other provision, among civilians wounded or rendered homeless in the raids night after night.

One night when an unusually heavy raid was in progress we were battling through the blacked-out streets in our little car to seek our cellar. As we scooted across the chief square splinters of British anti-aircraft shells were tinkling down and striking sparks on the cobbles round the statue of the pirate-hero Jean Bart.[56] And there I caught a glimpse of a Friends' ambulance stationary, with a casualty being quietly loaded into it. Next morning an acquaintance, a captain in the ASC[57] (the corps was not yet Royal) dropped in to see me; his company worked in the docks, not far from the 'Cat and Fiddle'. He started inveighing against the Quakers –

'Those blasted conchies! If I had my way the lot of 'em would be put up against a wall and shot.'[58]

I changed the subject – 'How did you get on last night?' (several bombs, I knew, had hit the docks).

'OK', he replied, 'we've got the poshest dug-out in the docks, two storeys down.'

I told him what I had caught 'those blasted conchies' doing while he and I were safely under cover, but he would have none of it. Fair-mindedness is a difficult art, especially in wartime.

[55] The Friends Ambulance Unit resumed its humanitarian activities in 1914. In serving the needs of the BEF, the FAU assisted in the evacuation of the wounded, provided help at dressing stations and ran a military hospital at Dunkirk. After conscription was introduced in 1916, members of the FAU were exempted from military service as long as they remained with the organization. F. Goodall, *A question of conscience: conscientious objection in the Two World Wars* (Stroud, 1997), pp. 62–8; C. Messenger, *Call-to-arms: the British army 1914–18* (London, 2005), p. 141.

[56] Jean Bart, or Jan Bart (1650–1702), was a native of Dunkirk who distinguished himself as a French privateer – and as a scourge of the English and Dutch – during the Nine Years War of 1688–97. *Dictionnaire de biographie française* (20 vols., Paris, 1933–2001), VI, 638–41; N. A. M. Rodger, *The command of the ocean: a naval history of Britain, 1649–1815* (London, 2004), p. 158.

[57] The Army Service Corps was essentially concerned with the handling and distribution of supplies and equipment, though it also furnished drivers for ambulance vehicles and artillery tractors. At the outbreak of war it numbered nearly 6,500 officers and men; four years later its strength stood at over 325,000. By November 1918 the ASC was supplying over 5,500,000 men, nearly 900,000 animals and over 100,000 motor vehicles. Divided into six sections, its personnel included drivers, clerks, farriers, bakers, butchers, packers and loaders. Rawson, *British army handbook 1914–1918*, pp. 125–9; *Statistics of the military effort of the British Empire*, pp. 181–4.

[58] Though the FAU were closely engaged in war work, this tirade against conscientious objectors in general illustrates Trevor Wilson's point that, as a group, they remained a 'deeply unpopular minority' in British society until the end of the war. Wilson, *Myriad faces of war*, p. 399.

Now and again I had occasion to visit the hotel on the sand dunes on YMCA business but I had never, in the nature of things, met Rawlinson, until one day he asked me to lunch. I got out of our shabby 'Tin Lizzie' at the main entrance and was peremptorily ordered by the sergeant on duty to go round to the back door reserved for 'other ranks'; this was fair enough. At the top of the back stairs I was challenged again and was quite sorry at the consternation of the NCO on duty when I gave my destination as the army commander's mess. The great man received me very cordially and asked many questions about our work. It was a useful introduction which opened the way to several interviews I was to have with him later. Direct access to the 'head guns' is worth a great deal in the Services, where the steep steps of rank so often bar your passage, but it is not easy to come by.

My next visit to army headquarters, a few weeks later, had quite a dramatic sequel. I had to get sanction from the AQMG[59] for something we wanted to do, and got it easily. The quartermaster's department and every other, so far as I could see, was working normally; clerks were buzzing in and out with papers, telephones were busy, file and trays and maps were on everyone's table as usual. On the following morning I had to call about something else – and found a complete transformation scene. The whole hotel was swept and garnished – or, better said, a few old men of the Labour Corps[60] were leisurely sweeping the floors and all garnishment, every stick of furniture, seemed to have vanished into thin air. The management of Fourth Army had flitted in one night.[61]

Nobody on the spot consented to know anything; they shrugged their shoulders and referred me to someone else who wasn't there; we were left suspended in mid-air. Outside I met an elderly major and consulted him.

'Don't ask me', he said, 'Do you know Cassel – pretty place up on the hill? Why not have a drive round, if you've nothing better to do?'

We took the hint and drove the twenty miles at once, for this could not be sheer inconsequence on his part.

Cassel is a beautiful ancient town, still contained by some of its massive medieval walls and at least one gate. It crowns conspicuously a conical hill, round which the train rambles between Calais and Hazebrouck – the last hill at the

---

[59] Assistant quartermaster-general. The quartermaster-general of the BEF had ultimate responsibility for communications, the transportation of troops (including the evacuation of the wounded) and the movement of supplies. He was represented by deputy and assistant quartermaster-generals at the lower levels of army, corps and division. Rawson, *British army handbook 1914–1918*, pp. 49–52.

[60] The Labour Corps was formed in February 1917 to maximize the efforts of a range of units then employed in a variety of labouring duties. At that time these units included companies of the Royal Engineers, whole battalions of infantry and companies of the ASC and Non-Combatant Corps, the latter being composed of conscientious objectors. Given the needs of front-line units, many of the Labour Corps's personnel were men of low medical category and their involuntary transfer into a new and unglamorous corps was seen as demeaning by some former infantrymen. Still, by November 1918 the Labour Corps numbered nearly 390,000 men. Messenger, *Call-to-arms*, pp. 214–42; *Statistics of the military effort of the British Empire*, p. 220.

[61] On 9 November 1917 Second Army headquarters moved to Italy and Second Army was taken over by the commander and staff of Fourth Army, whose headquarters were transferred to Cassel. However, Second Army was not re-designated Fourth Army until 20 December. Becke, *Order of battle part 4*, p. 101.

western end of a chain grandiloquently marked on the map as the Monts de Flandres; the most easterly one is Kemmel Hill of tragic reputation.[62] The topmost buildings that break the skyline of Cassel from a distance are the church tower and the square block of the casino.

We drove up the tree-covered slope of the hill, under the archway of the gate and parked our car in the picturesque Grand Place, where at a critical moment of the war, still to come, I was to see Sir Douglas Haig, for the second time in company with M. Poincaré, the premier of France.[63] I climbed the steep path to the casino and walked in. A sergeant, whose face I recognized, asked my business and, recognizing me in turn, let me pass. I walked into a big room marked 'Q' and saluted a colonel sitting at one of the tables: he was the AQMG with whom I had done business yesterday. He looked up at me and frowned.

'What the devil are *you* doing here? This is Second Army Headquarters.'
Indeed I had heard tell of it as the headquarters of Lord Plumer, commanding the army which had fought the famous battles of Ypres.[64]

'Excuse me, sir', I said, 'but I seem to know the faces of everybody here.'

'All right' (he burst out laughing), 'as you've rumbled us, tell me what you want.'

Then he spread a map of the Ypres Salient on the table and said, 'I don't know what you people have got here – perhaps you don't – but we shall certainly want you here and here and here. Go and work it out and let me know.' I went in a glad mood.

What was behind this sudden, secret move from the hotel on the dunes to the Casino at Cassel? With greater secrecy still, Lord Plumer with much of his force from Flanders had just moved, not twenty miles but more nearly a thousand, to Italy to restore the Italian army's disastrous retreat at Caporetto,[65] to hold the line of the Piave River and save Venice. For the time – but not for the hardest time yet to come – Rawlinson would hold Ypres which covered the vital Channel ports.

---

[62] See Chapter 3, n. 69.
[63] Raymond Nicolas Landry Poincaré (1860–1934) was president of France from 1913 to 1920. A native of the 'lost province' of Lorraine, Poincaré was an ardent patriot who intervened in French politics, diplomacy and military strategy although his office was essentially a ceremonial one. Bourne (ed.), *Who's who in World War One*, pp. 235–6.
[64] Second Army was originally commanded by General Sir Horace Smith-Dorrien, who was superseded by Plumer at the height of the second battle of Ypres (22 April–24 May 1915). Besides conducting this successful defence of the city against a major German offensive (in which poison gas was used for the first time on the Western Front) Second Army played a major offensive *rôle* at Messines (7 June–14 June 1917) and in the third battle of Ypres (31 July–6 November 1917). Becke, *Order of battle part 4*, pp. 82–4; *Statistics of the military effort of the British Empire*, p. 640.
[65] On 24 October 1917 a joint German and Austro-Hungarian offensive smashed through Italian positions on the Isonzo river, overrunning a substantial swathe of north-east Italy and threatening Venice. The Italian army, exhausted and demoralized by eleven successive offensives on the Isonzo since May 1915, lost more than 275,000 prisoners during its precipitate retreat to the line of the Piave river; in addition, as many as 300,000 Italian soldiers deserted. The catastrophe led to the despatch of six British and five French divisions to Italy from the Western Front and also to the creation of a Supreme War Council which sat at Versailles to direct Allied strategy and facilitate inter-Allied co-operation. M. Thompson, *The White War: life and death on the Italian Front 1915–1919* (London, 2008), pp. 294–327; D. Stevenson, *1914–1918: the history of the First World War* (London, 2005), pp. 377–81; Keegan, *First World War*, pp. 370–6; Haythornthwaite, *World War One source book*, pp. 39–40.

The ubiquitous Fourth Army sign, the boar's head on a red and black ground (it had hung outside our own headquarters in Péronne and Malo) was put away now. I was proud to find myself, through no choice of my own, in charge of YMCA work in the Second Army, the only one of five now fighting, as events would prove, which was to see this business through to the banks of the Rhine itself.

Thoughts of this nature, not formulated as was only possible when we had more leisure to look back or perhaps dismissed when they arose as sentimentalities unsuited to the moment, were in the minds of many of us, I believe, as we witnessed British troops touch their goal, the crossing of the Rhine. The game was over (though our team would not retire to change into 'civvies' for several years to come) and there was time to count the cost. No one could deny that the game had lasted too long, so long that the mood of players and spectators had radically changed. On that distant fourth of August, 1914, Sir Edward Grey[66] had spoken oracularly of 'the lights going out all over Europe' and we had not understood; it might refer literally to the black-out in the streets, the rest was rhetoric. We were confident that victory would be ours in six months and cheerfully chalked 'Next stop Berlin' on the sides of army lorries; we were downright angry with Lord Kitchener when he began recruiting for 'three years or the duration'.[67] The best and the bravest – and they, of course, would be the first to fall – entered the war in the *rôle* of crusaders for a cause greater than themselves; thousands of the volunteers who followed them went to partake in a new sport, not listed among British games since they could remember. There was everything to recommend it; there was von Bethmann Hollweg's unsporting wise-crack about the 'scrap of paper',[68] the caddish invasion of 'gallant little Belgium', the benefit of clergy which gave the game a vague touch of sanctity rather like 'Abide with me' sung at a Cup Tie.[69] Even the highly trained professionals, the little 'Striking Force' at Aldershot,[70] went out to meet the

---

[66] Edward Grey (1862–1933) was foreign secretary in the Liberal government from 1905 to 1916 and sought to preserve European peace in the diplomatic crisis of July 1914. At the end of the month, and hoping that the great powers would 'recoil from the abyss', he even proposed a European peace conference. However, Germany's invasion of Belgium widened the war and precipitated Britain's entry on 4 August. Grey's words 'The lamps are going out all over Europe; we shall not see them lit again in our life-time' were spoken to a friend on the evening of 3 August. *ODNB*; Bourne (ed.), *Who's who in World War One*, pp. 112–13.

[67] The term of enlistment under which Kitchener began to raise his New Army in August 1914. In contrast with the prevailing mood of optimism, Kitchener was convinced that a protracted war was inevitable. Middlebrook, *Your country needs you*, p. 40.

[68] Theobald von Bethmann-Hollweg (1856–1921) was Germany's chancellor from June 1909 until July 1917. In his desire to promote the political and constitutional evolution of Germany, and in order to guarantee its future security, he gambled on a short and victorious war against Russia and France. In defending Germany's consequent invasion of Belgium on 4 August 1914 he dismissed the 1839 Treaty of London (which Prussia had signed and which guaranteed Belgian neutrality in perpetuity) as 'a scrap of paper'. Bourne (ed.), *Who's who in World War One*, pp. 25–6; M. Gilbert, *First World War* (London, 1994), p. 32.

[69] This custom commenced as late as 1927. Snape, *God and the British soldier*, pp. 53–4.

[70] A reference to the original BEF, whose component divisions were based mainly in southern England and Ireland. In an era of peacetime conscription, Britain was alone among the great powers of Europe in maintaining a small professional army. Middlebrook, *Your country needs you*, pp. 23–7.

enemy with that 'joyalty of mind' which an English commander had noted in his troops in Flanders four hundred years before.[71]

It was not long before the crusading and the sporting mood began to change, as inevitably as darkness treads on the heels of light. However cleanly you try to play it – and countless men tried their utmost to do so – war is an unspeakably dirty game, for man, as someone said, is 'the most savage of the beasts of prey'.[72] War is murder, by whatever code you try to legalize it and dress it in gay colours and heroic veneer – and only a few men are by nature murderers. Christmas succeeded Christmas, four times over, and there was no visible sign, except in the unshaken hearts of the most faithful, of the Prince of Peace. 'Blood and sweat and tears', in the words of an old warrior,[73] there were in plenty, utter boredom, filth of body and mind, bitter bereavements, suffering beyond words, death in its most terrifying and disgusting forms. In this dark night of war, to redeem but not to excuse it, there were lights that shone all the brighter because of the darkness. There was the steady light of comradeship among men sharing everything, whether discomfort, danger, anxiety or ease, comradeship of a quality more real than they had ever known before or, one is tempted to believe, have ever quite recaptured since. It rose to their lips in irrepressible songs, it rose highest to meet the worst contingency, it issued in daily acts of decency towards others and gave its final token in acts of self-sacrifice which held nothing back.

There must have been a great many people during the First World War who never thought of the YMCA except as a ubiquitous agency for distributing tea, buns and tobacco to service men at a reasonable (some said at an improper) commercial profit. In the premises where this business was carried on a man could obviously shelter from the rain, sing a song and write a letter – there was evidence on so many breakfast-tables that a son or husband in uniform had access to a free ration of writing-paper.[74] From what has been said in the preceding pages it is, I hope, plain that this is not the whole, nor even half, of the story – even within the narrow limits of a base in France. When it comes to areas where men were actually fighting – and it took an unreasonable time before the YMCA was granted permission to come to them – the picture widens out very considerably, as I hope to show.

I hold no brief for the YMCA as a permanent institution, but I take up no stupid attitude of superiority towards it. I discount the quite amusing sneer of the forgotten music-hall song about 'sitting alone in the YMCA because I'm afraid to go home in the dark'.[75] I believe it to be one of the clubs – there may be even better ones – which a normal young man of small means is wise to join if he

---

[71] The phrase is that of Sir John Smyth, who used it of English troops in Flanders in 1589–90. Clayton, *Tales of Talbot House*, pp. 104–5.

[72] This is possibly an allusion to Nietzsche. *The Columbia world of quotations*, 41636. www.bartleby.com. Consulted 8 December 2008.

[73] A reference to Winston Churchill's speech in the House of Commons on 13 May 1940, three days after he had become prime minister. *The Columbia World of Quotations*, 12378. www.bartleby.com. Consulted 8 December 2008.

[74] See Introduction, p. 24.

[75] Unidentifiable.

wants a comfortable lodging, food reasonable in price and quality, sport and recreation and the fellowship of his own kind. Does that sound rather 'up-stage'? I hope not. You see, I do not know the YMCA in peacetime. I have seldom even entered its doors, and then never without a welcome.

I only knew it in wartime, when like many thousands of others not serving in the 'fighting forces' (and one has to remember that a large proportion of those were never called upon to do any actual fighting)[76] I saw in it the best opportunity of active service. We never joined it, we did not hold its membership card. Some of us enjoyed the experience of working with it on a three-months' ticket, a good many others for a much longer period; some of us, like myself, found ourselves enlisted in it, by our own free will, for 'duration' but seldom beyond. This is not said in a detached or dispassionate mood. We guarded jealously the traditions we helped to shape, we relied upon the *esprit-de-corps* manifest among us, we are still proud of the record of our service. We had our own share in the fortunes of the armies and our own modest honours in the victory.

---

[76] A salutary fact that is generally overlooked in the context of the First World War. Contrary to popular impressions, hundreds of thousands of British soldiers never went near the trenches of the Western Front; as late as November 1918, only 44 per cent of the British army was serving in France and Belgium and, of this percentage, only a third were infantry while a quarter were serving either in the ASC or in the Labour Corps. Figures such as these have led Gordon Corrigan to comment: 'The perception of soldiering in the Great War is of a young patriot enlisting in 1914 to do his bit, and then being shipped off to France... Reaching the firing line, he is put into a filthy hole in the ground and stays there until 1918... Most days, if he is not being shelled or bombed, he goes "over the top" and attacks a German in a similar position a few yards away across no man's land. He never sees a general and rarely changes his lice-infested clothes, while rats gnaw the dead bodies of his comrades. Real life was very different.' *Statistics of the Military Effort of the British Empire*, pp. 37, 62, 76; Corrigan, *Mud, Blood and Poppycock*, p. 77.

Chapter 3

Odd job men

I have heard it said, with what accuracy I do not know, that if you stand beside the Round Pond on Hampstead Heath and face due eastwards there is no land in front of you as high as you are until a man comes to the Urals, well over two thousand miles away. The first point in this vast plain of continental Europe that you would touch is Ostend, and that is in Flanders. Flanders may be said, geographically speaking, to begin at Calais (where a very Flemish French can still be heard) and geography has made this western corner of the great plain an inevitable battlefield. French and Spanish, Germans and English have all fought there in centuries past. It was no accident that Waterloo was won on its boundaries or that the British army entered the First World War, in its first month, at Mons, only ten miles from Malplaquet, the scene of Marlborough's battle two hundred years earlier.[1] Both for ourselves and for the enemy the tip of the modern province of West Flanders was the most dreaded theatre of the First War. The pivot of the fighting was, of course, Ypres – 'Wipers' to the British soldier, Yperer to the German – the only city in King Albert's Belgium which the Kaiser's men, after a hasty reconnaissance before our arrival, were never to tread except as prisoners of war.

In our atomic age the name of Ypres, like Crécy or Trafalgar or Alamein,[2] is still remembered, an old-fashioned sound, but the circumstances which gave it this immortality are already buried in the limbo of history books. The briefest reminder may help to set the scene.

When the German army was cheated of the supreme prize of Paris by the French victory on the Marne in the opening days of September, 1914, it turned aside to make a dash for the coast. The British Expeditionary Force, so puny in comparison, accepted the challenge and joined in a 'race for the sea'. It was brought to a halt by a vastly superior enemy force in a small semicircle of wet

[1] Fought on 11 September 1709 during the War of the Spanish Succession, this was a costly – and, indeed, disputed – victory for the duke of Marlborough and Prince Eugene of Savoy over Marshals Villars and Boufflers. D. Chandler (ed.), *A guide to the battlefields of Europe* (Ware, 1998), pp. 21–2.
[2] Fought on 26 August 1346 and won by Edward III, Crécy was the most significant English victory of the early stages of the Hundred Years War. Trafalgar, fought on 21 October 1805, saw Nelson all but annihilate a Franco-Spanish fleet while the second battle of Alamein, fought between 23 October and 4 November 1942, saw the near destruction of Rommel's *Panzerarmee Afrika* by Montgomery's Eighth Army. R. Holmes (ed.), *The Oxford companion to military history* (Oxford, 2001), *passim*.

Flemish ground: there it dug itself in – the 'Ypres Salient' was born. This little patch of earth was to be held, with the most dogged fortitude and many feats of desperate gallantry until the end, for it covered access to the Channel ports, the gateway of England itself. All the might of the greatest military power in Europe could not dislodge the 'contemptible little army'[3] it had begun by despising as mere 'mercenaries' –

> Their shoulders held the sky suspended;
> They stood, and earth's foundations stay;
> What God abandoned, these defended,
> And saved the sum of things for pay.[4]

In defending Ypres troops from the whole British Commonwealth left close upon a quarter of a million dead – almost a quarter, that is, of our total death-roll by land and sea and air, in that war – in Flanders fields.

By the spring of 1915 'First' and 'Second Ypres', two full-scale battles, had been successfully fought by Sir John French[5] and more were to follow. Some points, like Hill 60,[6] changed hands again and again in the most ferocious fighting of the war. And all the time, by day and by night, the guns of both armies pounded the watery Flanders plain until it was reduced to such mud as survivors can scarcely describe or anyone who never experienced it imagine.[7] Men stood over their boots, up to their knees, at times to their waists in liquid mud in the trenches, a great many were 'sunk without trace' in it as they were hit or slipped in the dark off the duck-board tracks which crossed it; ninety thousand names of the missing, carved upon the Menin Gate[8] and the walls of

---

[3]   A view attributed to Kaiser Wilhelm II and a judgment of the size rather than the quality of Britain's pre-war regular army. J. Brophy and E. Partridge, *The long trail: soldiers' songs and slang 1914–18* (London, 1969), p. 87.

[4]   From A. E. Housman's poem 'Epitaph on an army of mercenaries'. Throughout his career as a poet, Housman (1859–1936) was fascinated by the character of the regular soldier, his interest being expressed in *A Shropshire lad* (1896) and in his *Last poems* (1922). *ODNB*; A. E. Housman, *Collected poems and selected prose* (London, 1988), *passim*.

[5]   Popular with leading Liberal politicians, Sir John French (1852–1925) commanded the BEF from its arrival in France in August 1914 to his dismissal in December 1915. Under his command, the BEF succeeded in holding its positions around Ypres but suffered a string of setbacks in the course of 1915, notably in its failed offensives at Neuve Chapelle (March), Aubers Ridge (May), Festubert (May) and Loos. J. M. Bourne (ed.), *Who's who in World War One* (London, 2001), pp. 98–9.

[6]   Lying two miles to the south-east of Ypres, this was an artificial hill thrown up during the building of the railway line between Ypres and Comines. At sixty metres above sea level it was an important vantage point in the low-lying Flanders plain. It was captured by the British on 7 April 1915, retaken by the Germans that May and recaptured by the British in the Messines offensive of June 1917. M. Brown, *The Imperial War Museum book of the Western Front* (London, 1993), pp. 71–2, 169–71.

[7]   The appalling ground conditions for which the third battle of Ypres was notorious were due to the region's high water table, the destruction of the local drainage system and to unusually heavy rainfall in August and October 1917. J. Hussey, 'The Flanders background and the weather in 1917', in *Passchendaele in perspective: the third battle of Ypres*, ed. P. Liddle (London, 1997), pp. 140–58.

[8]   Designed by Sir Reginald Blomfield and unveiled by Lord Plumer in June 1927, the Menin Gate memorial, situated on the eastern side of Ypres, is the principal Commonwealth memorial to the missing of the Ypres Salient. Among the 54,000 names on its panels are those British officers and men who died before 16 August 1917. www.cwgc.org/search/cemetery_details. Consulted 24 December 2008.

Tynecot Cemetery[9] attest this loss. Flanders fighting was summed up in a hackneyed newspaper phrase of the time as 'mud and blood'.

It may well seem anti-climax to turn from this agony to the small affairs of the YMCA. In this vital area our work had been started with great energy by a stout, hearty Canadian, Harry Holmes,[10] and carried on by Harry Lyne,[11] a well-known member of permanent YMCA staff in peacetime, from whom I took over a few days after our arrival. Our headquarters were in Poperinghe, a market-town seven miles due west of Ypres. It was then the first habitable place, with civilians at work, children at school and estaminets open, that a soldier came to when he marched away from Ypres with his face towards home. When he sighted a notice pinned up in a window on the outskirts of 'Pop' which said 'Eggs and Chips – Socks washed' – two things he was most in need of – he knew he had reached civilization again.[12]

We occupied a large building, the premises of the Katholiek Kring (Catholic Club) in the wide Rue de Boescepe, where we ran a canteen and slept ourselves; we had a wooden hut for troops and our main stores for the area beside the railway station,[13] a vulnerable position, for the station was shelled at intervals with uncanny punctuality as the leave train came in.

Round the corner from our HQ was Talbot House, which had been opened by Tubby Clayton in December, 1915. I saw him there most days and by signing my name on the Sunday after our arrival in 1917 on the roll of communicants in the 'Upper Room', the most beautiful chapel on the Western Front,[14] I became – though no one could yet know it – a foundation member of Toc H-to-be. Poperinghe was a bright spot in a region in which, as Tubby wrote, 'everything was vile but man was perfectly glorious'.

[9]   Named by men of the Northumberland Fusiliers, the original 'Tyne Cot' (or 'Tyne Cottage') was a barn located near the level crossing on the Passchendaele–Broodseinde road and was the site of a cluster of German pill-boxes that were captured in October 1917, marking almost the furthest extent of the British advance during the third battle of Ypres. The cemetery contains 12,000 graves, three-quarters of which are unidentified, and the Tyne Cot memorial whose panels chiefly commemorate 35,000 Commonwealth troops who went missing in the Ypres Salient after 16 August 1917. www.cwgc.org/search/cemetery_details. Consulted 24 December 2008.
[10] Harry N. Holmes had worked as a YMCA secretary in New Zealand (1904–11) and in South Africa (1912–15) and was the organizing secretary for Second Army from 1915 to 1918. In 1919, he served as chief secretary in France. *Year book of the National Council of Young Men's Christian Associations of England, Ireland and Wales*, 1914, p. 150.
[11] Harry Lyne had worked as an assistant YMCA secretary at Derby since 1913. *Ibid.*, p. 99.
[12] Although not ravaged to the extent of Ypres further to the east, Poperinghe was an important railhead and was often under fire from German heavy artillery. B. Baron (ed.), *Letters from Flanders: some war-time letters of the Rev. P. B. Clayton (Tubby) to his mother* (London, 1932), pp. 42–3; L. MacDonald, *They called it Passchendaele* (London, 1993), pp. 15 and 78.
[13] See Introduction, pp. 12, 44.
[14] The ornate interior of the chapel was captured in picture postcards of the time and was featured in a Christmas card sent by Baron to his family in 1917 (Illustration 16). Located in a large loft, its hangings (which had formerly adorned the bishop's chapel at Southwark) were donated by Bishop Talbot, a renovated carpenter's bench constituted its altar (which, in keeping with the ethos of Talbot House, was unrailed) and numerous units and individuals donated fixtures, fittings and memorials. The existence of the 'Upper Room' reflected necessity as well as devotion for Anglican chaplains were barred by local bishops from using Catholic churches in France and Belgium. M. Snape, *God and the British soldier: religion and the British army in the First and Second World Wars* (London, 2005), pp. 216–18; M. Snape, *The Royal Army Chaplains' Department 1796–1953: clergy under fire* (Woodbridge, 2008), p. 233.

In the area of Second Army at its fullest extent (it was destined before long to be drastically reduced) we worked at nearly eighty points. They extended from Proven in the north to the old town of Bailleul on the south, as far back as Hazebrouck station, a busy junction for troops, and as far forward as the dug-outs at St Jean and Hussar Farm in front of Ypres. Perhaps the most interesting in point of its situation and the man in charge was at the Lille Gate of Ypres. Vauban's[15] great eighteenth-century ramparts which still defended the city on its eastern boundary – a broad bastion of earth faced with many thicknesses of brick which the heaviest artillery of the First War chipped but never breached – were tunnelled with galleries where a divisional staff, with gas blankets over the entrances, could carry on office work in perfect safety.[16] This great underground system ended beside the Lille Gate in a sort of cave, deep down. Here Dr C. J. Magrath, a schoolmaster from Sheffield, ran an unusual YMCA.[17] It was cool in summer and could be kept cosy even in the hardest days of a Flemish winter; heavy bombardment could do no more than make its electric lights blink. You entered, stooping, from the cobbled street at the limit of the town and went down by narrow steps to the tiny canteen where men chatted and smoked and drank tea elbow to elbow. There was also a low outlet on the outer side to the moat, where dud shells and rusty coils of barbed wire fouled the muddy water in which today water-lilies open again, stout citizens fish and swans float by.

Magrath was apt to welcome a visitor like myself with a 'Wipers Cocktail', his own recipe which he said consisted one part of canteen lemonade, one of SRD (Service Rum Diluted) and one – its most potent ingredient – of moat water. On a still, sunny afternoon when I dropped in he suggested that we should take our tea on top and we carried a teapot, a couple of enamel mugs, condensed milk and packets of biscuits up to the small cemetery – today, with its roses and evergreen trees, perhaps the most beautiful in the Ypres area – which covered his dug-out. We lay on the grass among the wooden crosses, surveying on one hand the southern curve of the Salient and on the other the ruins of the city, much of it by this time no more than breast-high. Presently a heavy shell exploded at the further end, sending up a spout of brick dust somewhere beyond the famous ruin of the Cloth Hall.[18] A few minutes later there was another, this time nearer, and I looked at Magrath.

---

[15] Sébastian le Prestre de Vauban (1633–1707) was the leading military engineer of his day and the first non-noble to become a marshal of France. J. Childs, *Warfare in the seventeenth century* (London, 2003), p. 225.

[16] The French had refortified Ypres along Vauban lines in the late seventeenth century. Between 1914 and 1918 its venerable ramparts proved surprisingly resistant to German shelling. R. Holmes, *Tommy: the British soldier on the Western Front 1914–18* (London, 2004), pp. 21–2.

[17] See Introduction, p. 35.

[18] Together with those of St Martin's cathedral, the ruins of the thirteenth-century Cloth Hall became the 'twin architectural icons' of the city's 'epic ruination'. Favoured by some Britons as a permanent memorial to the war, the rebuilding of the Cloth Hall was a sensitive issue and was not completed until 1967. P. Gough, '"An epic of mud": artistic interpretations of Third Ypres', in *Passchendaele in perspective*, ed. Liddle, pp. 412–13; M. Derez, 'A Belgian salient for reconstruction: people and *patrie*, landscape and memory', in *Passchendaele in perspective*, ed. Liddle, pp. 448–50.

'All right', he said, 'this is the afternoon *strafe*. It'll take them at least six to get round here – there's time for another cup.'

Every four minutes the punctual, painstaking German gunners lobbed a shell in a neat line across the city. At the fifth explosion we picked up our tea-things and went down below. We were scarcely settled there when a tremendous 'crump!' made the lights stagger and the glasses rattle on the shelf. 'All over for the day', Magrath commented. This was one of the quiet periods there occasionally fell, a lull between battles.

Magrath was no mere troglodyte. He was out and about in the city or tramping over the torn ground in front of it where St Jean and other points lay in his 'parish'; loaded with a haversack of cigarettes, a newspaper or two and other small luxuries, he was a welcome visitor among fighting men. In Ypres itself he became one of the most familiar characters, and before our troops left it behind, easily its oldest inhabitant. Army units took their turn and moved out to go up or back, town majors, medical officers and chaplains came and went, wounded, exhausted or transferred: 'Mac' was still there to greet newcomers with his high-pitched laugh. Several times, filling a gap, he was recognized as unofficial acting town major of Ypres, which he now knew like the back of his hand. He was decorated with the Belgian Croix de Guerre before he came home.

The little staff which came with me from the coast contained, beside Walter, Dickie the driver and myself, John Marsh,[19] a Baptist minister and a solid man of all work, and Harry Barlow,[20] a small, very delicate Yorkshire lad, with the heart of a lion, who looked after our accounts. We five had first met on the Somme, had lived together at Malo and had grown into a team of close friends. The work in Second Army required, of course, more staff and workers. Harry Lyne, who now went south to be secretary of the YMCA in the Fifth Army, then newly formed, naturally took some essential men with him, but some of the old hands remained and the gaps were filled with newcomers from bases or from home. There was a stores manager with one or two hands of his own; hitherto we had managed that job among ourselves, including manhandling the cases at railhead in emergency. There were at least two more drivers, for our establishment – on paper – was sixteen cars, of which several ran through thick and thin and several were never fit for the road in my time but had to be duly recorded in the triplicate monthly return required by the army. One of the drivers was a fox-hunting parson from Devon, another a fox-hunting squire from Yorkshire. The rector (Walter, undergraduate-fashion, Christened him 'Ruggins') was rather an indolent fellow, doing his stint but under humorous protest. The other had been out for a long time, a remarkable, much loved character nicknamed 'Dad'. He was older than the rest of us, a stocky figure in a much-stained uniform; he was very deaf and spoke in a quiet, toneless voice. He was a relentless driver, refusing to be baulked by friend or foe; huntin', shootin', fishin' in the tough climate of the East Riding

---

[19] No John Marsh was listed as a minister in the *Baptist Handbook* for the years 1914–1918. However, there was a Frederick Edward Marsh who was listed as a minister in Weston-super-Mare.
[20] Unidentifiable.

had been his life, and he took the minor adventures of his wartime calling in his stride. His deafness silenced the sound of missiles on their way and dimmed their explosion close at hand, and there were many comic stories, near enough to truth, of Dad under fire changing a wheel or strewing the road with tools as he tinkered patiently with his much-worked engine.

We came on the scene in a lull before the dreadful fighting for the Passchendaele Ridge began. In the Flanders plain every foot of height counted in attack or defence, but it is difficult for anyone standing on the top of this low ridge today and looking down its gentle slope to the spires of Ypres in the middle distance to imagine what it meant to our troops attacking in the winter of 1917. All the summer and autumn the rain had been soaking the ground, long since churned into mud by shellfire, and men clawed their way desperately forward yard by yard and week by week. Before Christmas Passchendaele had cost us no less than three hundred thousand men dead, wounded and missing.[21]

> There was laughter and loving in the lanes at evening;
> Handsome were the boys then, and girls were gay.
> But lost in Flanders by medalled commanders
> The lads of the village are vanished away.[22]

Lloyd George, the prime minister, had strongly resisted the plan but his judgment was overborne by the generals.[23] To the officers and men who had to carry it out the long drawn agony was sheer mounting madness. For they could not be told that their task was to divert the enemy's attention at any cost from the mutinies in the French Army which followed on Nivelle's failure in October to advance upon the Aisne and deliver France finally from the invader.[24]

Incessant traffic now poured through the bottleneck of Poperinghe and sometimes blocked its narrow main street – battalions marching up, whistling or singing to keep the step lively on the rough *pavé*, batteries of tanks, artillery, convoys of lorries, loaded limbers drawn by mules, and, coming down from the battle, two

[21] Although casualty figures are disputed, combined British casualties for Third Ypres and for the preliminary offensive at Messines have been placed at around 275,000, including 70,000 killed. R. Prior and T. Wilson, *Passchendaele: the untold story* (New Haven, 1996), p. 195; N. Steel and P. Hart, *Passchendaele: the sacrificial ground* (London, 2001), p. 303.

[22] From Cecil Day Lewis's poem 'Two songs'. In his early life, Lewis (1904–72) was a poet of strong left-wing sympathies and his animus against the British establishment is evident in these lines. He published this poem in 1935, a year before he joined the Communist party. M. Drabble (ed.), *The Oxford companion to English literature* (Oxford, 1995), p. 262; C. Day Lewis, *Collected poems* (London, 1954), pp. 139–40.

[23] This is a reference to Lloyd George's self-serving *War memoirs*, first published between 1933 and 1936. These sought to distance their author from the more questionable strategic decisions of the war on the Western Front, and especially from the Passchendaele offensive of 1917. Bourne (ed.), *Who's who in World War One*, pp. 176–7.

[24] Yet again, Baron shows confusion over the chronology of Allied offensives on the Western Front. Nivelle's offensive was launched on the Chemin des Dames on 16 April 1917 and resulted in 130,000 casualties (including 29,000 killed) in a period of only five days. In the wake of the failed offensive the French army experienced numerous acts of collective indiscipline, protests that are probably better described as military strikes rather than mutinies. The predicament of the French army helped to ensure that the BEF bore the burden of the remaining Allied offensives of 1917. J. Keegan, *The First World War* (London, 1998), pp. 352–8.

companies out of a whole battalion we had seen go up a week ago, the long train of horsed ambulances, the little parties of wounded men able to walk, grey-faced, hoarse with the gas in their throats. Continuously the guns thundered along the whole front, piling up in a *crescendo* and dying down to rise again. After nightfall the church towers of Pop and its tall town hall were a black silhouette against the flashes of the guns, a flickering curtain like the Northern Lights low down the sky.

One anxious result of Passchendaele was a change in the demeanour of the men we met and served all over the area every day. The grousing which is a cherished privilege of the British soldier, the half-humorous cursing, the simple uproarious jokes began to give place to a sullen silence. The authorities who sit behind the battle took note of this and were plainly worried as the weeks went on. We came a good deal closer to it than they, for a man in his ease in the YMCA talks 'off the record', knowing that, in his own words, there will be 'no names, no pack-drill'. Intelligence men, we heard, were now sitting in the cinema at Pop to catch chance scraps of conversation in the dark. But it was the army commander himself who said to me, 'Mind, if you come upon a man talking subversively your duty is to report him immediately to the APM.' I said nothing at all to this, for the thing was not only impracticable but it would have been a preposterous betrayal of trust.

How this interview came to take place requires a little explanation. It had been a practice of the YMCA since early days to bring 'lecturers' out of France on a tour of the bases and this had now spread, with careful selection, to the Army Areas.[25] Such a visitor's success depended less on his lantern-screen or blackboard than on his ability to sit in a circle of men and conduct a free-and-easy discussion after his talk. They were not 'pep-talks' in the accepted sense – we left that to military commanders – but mainly on the origins of the war, its strategy, geography and progress in other places. There were plenty of intelligent men around us to provide a good audience, often a real crowd; they welcomed this diversion as eagerly as they did the books we tried to bring them. The most successful visitors of this kind in our area that winter were, I think, bluff Professor Sanford Terry,[26] giant Sir William [blank] of Edinburgh University and especially the quiet but forceful Professor Medley of Glasgow.[27] There was also an extraordinary character, Professor Adkins,[28]

[25] See Introduction, pp. 59–62.
[26] Professor Charles Sanford Terry (1864–1936) was the Burnett-Fletcher Professor of History at the University of Aberdeen. He lectured in France in March 1918 and subsequently published a short account of his work entitled *Lectures at the front* (Aberdeen, 1918). *Dictionary of national biography*.
[27] Professor D. J. Medley (1861–1953) came from a military family, being the son of Lieutenant-General J. G. Medley of the Royal Engineers. He was the first Professor of History at the University of Glasgow and held this appointment from 1899 to 1931. A celebrated teacher, he also did much to encourage the development of the university's Officers' Training Corps. *Times*, 16 October 1953, p. 11.
[28] F. J. Adkins (?–?) of Sheffield University published several accounts of his work for the YMCA in *YM. The British Empire YMCA Weekly*. In Le Havre in 1915 his lectures (which lasted between an hour and an hour and a half) took as their subject 'European history leading up to the war from the point of view of each of the combatants.' The questions which these provoked from his audience included 'Which is the most Christian nation at present engaged in the war?' and 'Have we any right to assume that God will give victory to the Allies?' Having given the same lectures in England, Adkins maintained that 'as regards both intelligence and interest the soldier audience is superior to the civilian'. F. Adkins, 'Tommy in his hours of ease: lecturing to the troops in

who tramped about in a scandalously untidy YM uniform, his tin hat on the back of his head and a roll of maps under his arm, who found himself laying down the law not only to other ranks but to the assembled staff of XXII Corps; he was very popular.

On Medley's second visit to us Rawlinson invited me to bring him to lunch at Cassel and talked to him about his work. I sat next to General X, a grey-haired soldier of the old style who attacked at once.

'I can't think what you chaps want to bring professors up here for. What on earth do they talk about?'

'Well, sir, how we got into the war and – '

'Bless my soul! All you need to tell the men is – beat the Boche, he's a dirty dog.'

'Some of the men are keen to know exactly *why* they've got to beat him.'

'Because we tell 'em to. Beat the Boche, he's a dirty dog: that's all there is to it.' I was glad of a chance to counter-attack with a different subject. 'Theirs not to reason why' had had a long enough history. The men who had 'to do or die' now in such numbers belonged to a new kind of army in which General X had not been brought up.[29]

Another interview with Lord Rawlinson, my last, came a little later to provide a sequel to the conversation at the lunch table. The iron Flemish winter by then was well set, with snow masking the mud, treacherous ice on the shell craters and freezing fog making even the straight road from Poperinghe to Ypres a nightmare to travel. Passchendaele, thank God, was 'quiet', as things went, by Christmas. But morale in some quarters had still further deteriorated and, (I forget how) Walter and I got wind that all the army commanders had been summoned to GHQ for a conference about it in two days' time. We sat up most of the night writing and typing a memorandum. We guessed, rightly or wrongly, that the result of the conference might be not only an overhaul of discipline and training and leave but probably also a bigger issue of footballs and boxing gloves as a diversion. We could help to provide some of these last at once but we were certain that thinking men – we knew plenty of them – needed more. Talbot House, our neighbour, had a good library, never so much used as in these unhopeful days, and Tubby had been making an experiment with a few sensible officers who discussed affairs quietly with disgruntled men.[30] The YMCA had something to contribute in the same direction. For by this time it had a really large depôt of books at Dieppe which we could draw upon,[31] and its approved 'lecturers', whom we could reinforce by others. On these lines, in some detail, our memorandum offered the help, for whatever it was worth, of the YMCA.

France', *YM*, 23 July 1915, p. 666. See also 'Lecturing at the front: "The people perish for lack of knowledge"', *YM*, 24 March 1916, pp. 257–8.

[29] Some 87 per cent of the 5.7 million men who served in the British army of 1914–18 were wartime volunteers or conscripts. Pre-war regulars, reservists and Territorials made up the remaining 13 per cent. *Statistics of the military effort of the British Empire during the Great War 1914–1920* (London, 1922), pp. 30 and 364.

[30] These informal discussion groups were known as 'grousing circles' and led, so Clayton claimed, to the resolution of a number of local grievances. P. B. Clayton, *Tales of Talbot House: Everyman's Club in Poperinghe and Ypres 1915–1918* (London, 1920), p. 96.

[31] See Introduction, p. 59.

Next afternoon I drove to Cassel to deliver the brief document, if possible in person. I asked for the army commander's ADC[32] and was lucky to find him a nephew of my wife's. 'He's free at the moment – why not go in?': Charlie knocked at the door, gave my name and departed. I handed the envelope to Rawlinson and asked if he could spare a few minutes to look at its contents. Without reply he read it through, with a trace of irritation on his face, while I stood at his table. He handed it back to me – 'Sorry, it won't do', was all his comment. It was then that he added, in a harsher tone, his injunction to report subversive men to the police. I saluted my way out and never set eyes on him again.

It was very natural that the anxious minds of the high command should turn to the Chaplains' Department for information and advice; the padre should know better than anybody the inmost thoughts of the common soldier. One day I received an invitation from the deputy chaplain general to represent the YMCA at a conference to be held at his headquarters at St Omer;[33] I was asked to stay the night. The DCG in France and Flanders throughout the war was Gwynne, a grand old Welsh missionary who had been bishop in Khartoum, a man of faith, zeal and humour, who still lives at a great age.[34] I knew some of the members of the conference when we came together at the table – Neville Talbot, who with Clayton had founded Talbot House in Poperinghe and was to become bishop of Pretoria;[35] Tom Pym, who was to die, all too soon, as a canon of

---

[32] 'AIDE-DE-CAMP. A junior officer employed as a general's "handy man".' Brophy and Partridge, *The long trail*, p. 64.

[33] See Introduction, p. 62.

[34] Llewellyn Henry Gwynne (1863–1957) went to the Sudan as a CMS missionary in 1899, in the wake of its reconquest by an Anglo-Egyptian army under Kitchener, who was then Sirdar (or commander-in-chief) of the Egyptian army, and was consecrated suffragan bishop of Khartoum nine years later. He was home on leave when war broke out and immediately volunteered as an army chaplain, reaching France at the end of August 1914. After several months serving as a base and as a brigade chaplain, he was appointed deputy chaplain-general in July 1915. Despite his distinguished service as the head of the Anglican branch of the Chaplains' Department on the Western Front, promotion in the English church was denied to him after the Armistice (possibly as a result of the hostility of the prime minister, Lloyd George, for whom Gwynne had the deepest contempt) and he returned to the Sudan in 1919. Remarkably, his active ministry continued into his eighties; Gwynne resigned as bishop in Egypt in 1946 and died in England eleven years later. *Times*, 4 December 1957, p. 13; Snape, *The Royal Army Chaplains' Department*, pp. 187–9, 256–7.

[35] Neville Stuart Talbot (1879–1943) was the second son of E. S. Talbot, a distinguished theologian and bishop of Winchester from 1911 to 1923. Commissioned into the Rifle Brigade in 1899, Neville saw active service in the Boer War of 1899–1902. However, in 1903, and by now a staff officer in South Africa, he chose to resign his commission in order to study at Oxford. He was ordained priest in 1909, when he was also elected chaplain of Balliol College, Oxford, where he ministered alongside Henry Gibbon, a former officer of the Indian army (see Chapter 2, n. 33). Along with his brother, Edward Keble Talbot of the Community of the Resurrection, Neville was commissioned into the Army Chaplains' Department on 30 August 1914 and (perhaps unsurprisingly, given his background) he enjoyed rapid promotion while serving on the Western Front. He became senior chaplain of the 6th Division in 1915 (in which capacity he was the driving force behind the establishment of Talbot House), senior Anglican chaplain of XIV Corps in April 1916 and assistant chaplain-general of 5th (or Reserve) Army in September 1916. In January 1916 he was also awarded the MC. On the eve of war, Talbot was preparing to honour a longstanding pledge to become a foreign missionary. However, his wartime experiences increasingly turned his thoughts away from India to the reform of the Church of England; he contributed an essay on 'The training of the clergy' to F. B. MacNutt's *The church in the furnace*

Bristol;[36] Alec Paterson, my oldest friend at Oxford and in Bermondsey, who had been called in as a 'typical infantry officer' – a description as bizarre as anything I had ever heard.[37] There were a number of other senior chaplains there and an

(1917) and he published his *Thoughts on religion at the front* in the same year, a volume that raised eyebrows even among fellow chaplains who shared his enthusiasm for reform. A keen supporter of the Life and Liberty movement after its inauguration in 1917, he was particularly insistent about the need for the reform of public worship. However, his long-term missionary ambitions ultimately outweighed his concern for the home church after he left the army in 1919. The following year he was elected bishop of Pretoria and he embarked for South Africa after his consecration in St Paul's Cathedral on 24 June 1920. *ODNB*; F. H. Brabant, *Neville Stuart Talbot: a memoir* (London, 1949), *passim*; *Army List*, July 1915, 1793a; Church Missionary Society Archives, University of Birmingham (hereafter CMS), XCMS ACC/18/Z/1 Army Book of L. H. Gwynne, p. 227; F. B. MacNutt (ed.), *The church in the furnace: essays by seventeen temporary chaplains on active service in France and Flanders* (London, 1917), pp. 267–87; N .S. Talbot, *Thoughts on religion at the front* (London, 1917), *passim*; Snape, *The Royal Army Chaplains' Department*, pp. 188, 237–9; *The National Mission of Repentance and Hope: reports of the archbishops' committees of inquiry. The worship of the Church, being the report of the archbishops' second committee of inquiry* (London, 1919), p. 39; *Crockford's*, 1937, p. 1297.

[36] Chaplain of Trinity College, Cambridge, Thomas Wentworth Pym (1885–1945) was commissioned into the Army Chaplains' Department on 24 September 1914, arriving in France three months later. In collaboration with Geoffrey Gordon, he published *Papers from Picardy* in 1917, candid essays on religion in the army that were written at the height of the battle of the Somme. Pym also wrote an essay on 'Religious education and the training of the clergy' for MacNutt's volume *The church in the furnace*, a piece that William Temple described as especially 'hard hitting' in a volume that was sufficiently radical to be nicknamed 'The fat in the fire'. In June 1917, and after serving as senior chaplain of the 5th Division, Pym was awarded the DSO and promoted to deputy assistant chaplain-general of XIII Corps. Early the following year, he was moved to Calais (where he met his future wife, who was then engaged in YMCA educational work) and was appointed assistant chaplain general of Third Army in June 1918. Judged by Neville Talbot to be 'about the best Chaplain out', Pym was an outspoken figure even among his contemporaries on the Western Front. A zealous supporter of Life and Liberty, he was among its original council members and in 1918, in a scheme dubbed 'Plus and Minus', Pym even urged his fellow chaplains to 'pool their resources, refuse to go back to the old conditions at home, and form an independent body of priests' until 'the Church of England was either disestablished or free to put her own house in order'; much to his chagrin, his senior colleagues were unmoved by his pleas. In February 1919 Pym was demobilized and he was appointed head of Cambridge House, Camberwell, the following June, where he spent the next six years. After acting as canon missioner of Southwark Cathedral from 1925 to 1929, for three years he served as a canon of Bristol Cathedral until he was appointed chaplain of Balliol College, Oxford, where he served until 1938. He was diagnosed with 'disseminated sclerosis' in May 1931 and, in view of his worsening health, he resigned from his last post as diocesan missioner of Bristol in 1941. *Crockford's*, 1937, p. 1088; *Army List*, July 1915, 1793a; T. W. Pym and G. Gordon, *Papers from Picardy* (London, 1917); MacNutt (ed.), *The church in the furnace*, pp. 291–316; Museum of Army Chaplaincy, Amport House, Andover. Blackburne Papers. 'Souvenir. Conference of Chaplains, FIRST ARMY BEF Aire-September 26–27 1917'; Brabant, *Neville Stuart Talbot*, p. 71; A. Wilkinson, *The Church of England and the First World War* (London, 1978), p. 342; D. Pym, *Tom Pym: a portrait* (Cambridge, 1952), *passim*.

[37] Alexander Henry Paterson (1884–1947) conceived a life-long interest in social questions as an undergraduate at University College, Oxford. A disciple of Dr John Stansfeld (for whom he was a trusted lieutenant) and a prominent figure at the OMM, after forsaking a career as a civil servant Paterson worked for a time as an unpaid teacher in a Bermondsey elementary school. In 1911 he published *Across the bridges or life by the south London river-side*, which made a significant impact on the relatively privileged readership at which it was aimed. On the strength of his work with wayward youth, in 1908 he was appointed assistant director of the Borstal Association and advised Herbert Samuel on the drafting of the Children Act. In 1909 he was appointed to lead a pioneering scheme that provided guidance to discharged convicts and, two years later, he became assistant director of the Central Association for the Aid of Discharged Prisoners, a body formed

observer from Sir Douglas Haig's staff.[38] We were each called upon in turn to say our little piece about the weighty subject of morale; the observer took careful notes. I told them very much what I had tried to say to Rawlinson, and they took it quite seriously. When it came to Alec the DCG said, 'What about you, Paterson? Do you find signs of revolution in your battalion?' 'I'm afraid not, sir', answered Alec, 'I've tried my best but the beggars just won't revolute.'

A few of us laughed, the rest looked puzzled. I think most of us stole a glance at the observer whose face registered dismay and anger; he wrote more busily than ever in his note book. Alec was never cashiered, but I wondered if some intelligence man would be told to keep an eye on him too.

We dined together and the DCG went to bed early, it was his habit. Half a dozen of us sat up late talking. Neville and Tom Pym were in tremendous form and I can still hear the former thundering away at us from the hearthrug about revolution – the lines it must take within the Church, still half-asleep, when the war was over. In the event his plans never seriously disturbed our peace. It is said that you cannot take the Kingdom of Heaven by storm.

The fourth winter of the war seemed interminable. Men's spirits drooped, under comparative inaction, into a kind of gloomy suspension, their hearts turned with an even intenser longing towards home. Slowly the depression began to lift, as spring put its first tentative but unmistakable touches upon the marred face of this melancholy countryside. Moreover Plumer was back from Italy, again in command of his beloved Second Army. Soldiers, busy with their own few yards of a trench or the road that they are marching on, seldom give a thought to the high command except perhaps to curse 'them' for the latest attack which had lost them pals; corps and army 'brasshats'[39] are right out of their ken, they don't always know the name of their own divisional commander – after all, why should they? They have enough to do. But 'Plum' was different from most; he was not a mere Olympian on the remote height of Cassel, they often saw his red face and white moustache about the places where they were doing their work.[40] Sometimes they got a rather courtly smile and a gruff word from

by the home secretary, Winston Churchill. A leading figure in the creation of *The Challenge* newspaper, Paterson enlisted in the 22nd London Regiment (Bermondsey's pre-war Territorial battalion) on the outbreak of war in 1914. He served on the Western Front and rose through the ranks to a commission; he was also badly wounded, mentioned in dispatches and awarded the Military Cross. He was also recommended (twice) for the VC. An Anglican convert from Unitarianism, from 1922 to 1924 he served as the first chairman of Toc H. He also became a prison commissioner in 1922, in which capacity he served with great distinction until his death in 1947. B. Baron, *The doctor: the story of John Stansfeld of Oxford and Bermondsey* (London, 1952), pp. 162–6; *Times*, 10 November 1947, p. 7; Alexander Paterson, www.infed.org/thinkers/paterson. Consulted 20 August 2008.

38 Gwynne's account of this meeting suggests that this was George Duncan, a Presbyterian chaplain who was effectively Haig's personal chaplain at GHQ. CMS, XCMS ACC 18/F1/50–4, Diaries of L. H. Gwynne, 18–19 October 1917; Snape, *God and the British soldier*, pp. 62–3.

39 'BRASS HATS: Generals and Senior Staff officers. So called because of the lavish display of gold lace on their caps.' Brophy and Partridge, *The long trail*, p. 76.

40 Plumer's distinctive build and appearance (white hair, bushy moustache and monocle) reputedly formed the basis of David Low's later cartoon character, Colonel Blimp. *ODNB*.

him and they knew he bothered about them more than he felt free to show. Lord Plumer was a 'soldier's general'.

And with the spring of 1918 the war visibly warmed up.[41] Enemy shelling of the 'back areas' west of Ypres increased with greater purpose. Poperinghe had always had its ration of shells, up to 8-inch, and now they became more frequent; the town grew shabbier day by day, civilians began to pack up and cross the French border a few miles down the road. The rule was made that once out of Belgium they were not to return without further orders. Humorists said that selected British officers were on duty at Abeele, the frontier village, enticing Poperinghe children through the barrier with bags of sweets; their parents would go after them, leaving better billets vacant for the troops in the town.

And then the picture of the whole British front, never a still-life but for long enough more or less stable, dramatically changed. On 21 March 1918, a date long to be remembered, four thousand massed German guns opened fire on the short front held by Gough's Fifth Army, which held our extreme right, far to the south of Ypres, in a final effort to break the junction of the British and the French. The Fifth Army had to give way but the gap was somehow closed. The blows of this gigantic hammer crashed down on our other armies northward in succession – on Rawlinson's Fourth upon the Somme where it drove right across the old battlefield nearly to the gates of Amiens, on Byng's Third round Arras, on Horne's First (which had been Allenby's until he went to Palestine) about Bethune and Lens.[42] Plainly the turn of Plumer's Second, the northernmost of our armies, was now to come. March was over: the all-out onslaught on Ypres, its crowning ordeal, opened on 9 April and continued without pause for just three weeks.

We could not complain that we had not had notice of impending events, though no one could have prophesied their tremendous scale. Long before 21 March the shelling of our area had increased. At Poperinghe, well back from the front, there came a point when I sent all our workers out of the town at night to get a little rest in the hut at St Jan ter Biezen, a mile or two behind us. A pair in rotation, one of them a driver, from our small staff remained with me at headquarters. We kept a car at the back door in case of emergency, for I had already witnessed from a short distance away the complete blotting out of the village of Westoutre, hitherto scarcely touched, in an hour of the enemy's

---

[41] By 21 March 1918, the defeat of Russia, confirmed by the Treaty of Brest-Litovsk earlier that month, had released forty-four German divisions for service on the Western Front. These reinforcements, the ominous American build-up in France and Germany's precarious political and economic situation demanded a final, decisive German offensive on the Western Front in the spring of 1918. In view of the tenacity of the French at Verdun in 1916, this was to be primarily aimed at the British sector of the Western Front between Ypres in the north and La Fére in the south. H. Strachan, *The First World War: a new illustrated history* (London, 2003), pp. 282–6.

[42] Baron is mistaken in some of these particulars. Sir Julian Byng took command of Sir Edmund Allenby's Third Army in June 1917. Furthermore, when the German spring offensives commenced on 21 March 1918, there was no Fourth Army in the BEF's order of battle and Rawlinson was acting as the British representative on the Supreme War Council. A. F. Becke, *History of the Great War based on official documents. Order of battle part 4. The Army Council, GHQs, armies, and corps 1914–1918* (Uckfield, 2007), pp. 89, 105; A. Rawson, *British army handbook 1914–1918* (Stroud, 2006), pp. 45–6.

concentrated fire. There was, I remember, a succession of nights when the methodical German gunners put some 'big stuff' into Pop at precisely forty-five minute intervals, and it was queer to find how soon one can learn to wake up every three-quarters of an hour to listen for the scream of a big shell coming, to mark it fall short or pass over to burst and the next minute to be asleep again.

The tempo quickened steadily until there was hardly a civilian to be seen in the streets of Pop and no military traffic, for it was by-passing us by the 'switch-road' on the northern outskirts. Then Poperinghe was put out of bounds altogether and we moved our headquarters to the top of the nearest hill in the chain of the 'Mountains of Flanders'. Mont des Cats is the most conspicuous and interesting in outline of this little range of hills, a pyramid crowned by a large Trappist monastery. When we arrived the monastic building was already badly damaged, the twin spires mostly down, the library strewn all over the cloister and the last of the monks were just moving out. In their rough white woollen habits, deeply stained with work in the fields, leading their haltered cows or driving the slow Percherons[43] harnessed to great farm wagons piled with their gear, they reminded me, for some reason, of an exodus in the Hundred Years War. (I was entertained, by the way, to see how comfortably they circumvented their vows of silence by an eloquent language of signs.)

We took over the village school, by amicable arrangement and no military authority. It lay in a slight fold of the hill, among scanty trees, a few hundred yards from the summit. The schoolchildren had gone weeks before, but we were quite unable to budge the two placid old nuns who had taught them. They reserved the back room for themselves, we pinned up our maps and ate our meals and slept on the floor of the front one. The bare adjoining schoolroom served for stores and was to have other use sooner than we knew.

And then the deluge! It must have been first daylight on 8 April[44] when we were awakened by a tornado of gunfire a few miles to the south of Mont des Cats which relapsed into a steady drumming. Walter and I drove down that side of the hill into the plain and before long came upon a divisional headquarters in a farm house. We went in for news but they could give us none that was reassuring. The telephone lines to the south, they said, were now cut. All they knew was that the First Army had been heavily attacked at dawn and that the Portuguese, who happened to be holding a section of its front at the time, had broken from their trenches and were streaming in disorder towards the coast.[45] (They eventually

---

[43] A breed of draught horse.

[44] 9 April.

[45] Given Portugal's historic alliance with Great Britain, an undeclared state of war had existed since August 1914 between Portuguese and German forces in south-east and south-west Africa. However, Germany did not formally declare war until March 1916, after the seizure of German shipping in Portuguese ports. While reinforcing its African colonies, Portugal also sent two infantry divisions to France in 1917. Largely supplied with British equipment and trained in England en route, units of the Portuguese Expeditionary Force were holding the British line around Laventie when 'Operation Georgette' broke upon them on 9 April 1918. Inexperienced, politically unsettled and poorly led, the Portuguese 2nd Division disintegrated in the face of the German offensive. Haig's verdict was simply that 'the Portuguese troops with their Portuguese

fetched up at Calais – a crowd of fine peasant types, badly officered – and set up headquarters there for the rest of the story.)

Walter and I hurried back to our eyrie to make plans with the others, for plainly everybody connected with Second Army would soon be heavily involved – how very soon we could not guess. We divided the map of the Salient into three segments, radiating from Mont des Cats. We had at the time three cars with us in running order. John Marsh was to go off in one to cover the most northerly segment, Walter in another for the central one (which included Ypres itself), I in the third to the most southerly where trouble was likely to start earliest. We were to visit in the day every YMCA (as I have said, there were close upon eighty) and issue certain simple instructions in case (we were to tell workers optimistically) there was trouble coming. If they could, they should seek military advice on the spot and, if they had to move, take their time from the troops. Anyone who moved was responsible for bringing away his orderlies (a couple of unfit soldiers were normally attached to each YM) as well as the cash-box and account book. Leaders of wooden huts (which implied almost all our larger centres) should draw a can of petrol at once from the nearest dump and – *only* if the place was very seriously threatened and after getting military sanction – should set fire to the hut and its stores. The rendez-vous for all who might have to move would be Mont des Cats. Above all, everyone must act as best he could: there was to be no panic.

We set out on our rather complicated mission to places widely scattered and some of them only to be reached in the final stage on foot. In the late afternoon I was at Neuve Eglise on my way home, a village little damaged up till then and full of troops, with lorries parked in a long line under cover of trees. Our hut there was in the charge of a queer character, a legacy I would gladly have replaced if men had been less short. He was, in plain slang, a bit 'pansy', being fussy about his personal appearance (some people whispered that he used cosmetics) and his hut had touches of the *boudoir* in its patterned curtains and fancy lamp-shades. He offered us tea and we were by that time heartily glad of it – hot-buttered toast, I remember, and a cake of his own baking! I gave him his orders and he received them with an over-confidence which inspired none in me.

It was well towards nightfall when our three cars reached Mont des Cats

officers are useless for this class of fighting'. For its part, the YMCA was fully aware of the wretched plight of the ordinary Portuguese soldier. As one YMCA worker reported: 'Perhaps there are no soldiers in France who feel more lonely than the Portuguese. No provision has been made by their fellow-countrymen for their comfort and entertainment during leisure hours…during these past winter months there has been little for them but to wander about the frozen or muddy streets and roads, or shiver in their comfortless billets – and curse the war…Kindly feelings towards the British have been engendered because the huts and privileges provided for our own men are opened for and extended to them. "You British are doing much more for us than our own people", has been repeatedly said by grateful Portuguese soldiers.' P. Haythornthwaite, *The World War One source book* (London, 1992), pp. 275–7; M. Brown, *The Imperial War Museum book of 1918: year of victory* (London, 1998), pp. 84–6; G. Sheffield and J. Bourne (eds.), *Douglas Haig: war diaries and letters 1914–1918* (London, 2005), pp. 399–400; YMCA Archives, University of Birmingham (hereafter YMCA), K28 France. Magazine Articles for 1918–19. R. F. Elder, 'With the Portuguese in France', pp. 1–2.

again, but the whole eastern sky, as we looked down from our vantage, was alight with the flames of a barrage which heralds an attack. We supped, compared notes and rolled ourselves in our blankets on the floor to get a little sleep: tomorrow would be a very busy day. Early next morning, 10 April, the onslaught started in earnest. Our three old cars got on the road again to repeat yesterday's round – so far as it would now be possible. Harry Barlow remained at HQ to receive any refugees there might be; he had the use of a field telephone – for I had long since been issued with a set by Signals[46] and had luckily omitted to return it when requested. Before we reached the bottom of the steep, winding hill we met our first man, with his two orderlies and his heavy cash-box all correct, preparing to struggle up it. They were extremely weary but cheerful as they gave us the first fragments of news. The enemy was thought to have broken through on the south of Ypres (before the end he was to penetrate twelve miles into that flank) and everyone was on the move, up or down. The German barrage had lifted forward to let their troops advance and by now these men's little YM would certainly have been shot to blazes or over-run. We speeded them on towards food and rest and continued our journey. One of the first places I went to was Neuve Eglise and the changed picture it presented was astonishing. It was as if an earthquake had passed over it. The fresh damage to bricks and mortar was not so striking as the signs of what had happened to its inhabitants. All along the road where the neat lorry park had been the evening before there was confusion. Several lorries were lying on their side in the ditch, gear of every kind was strewn about, some of it personal like packs and steel helmets. Our hut was gaping at the seams and the leader's lovely curtains were flapping in the wind through broken glass; inside it was an absurd junk shop, with no sign of a shopkeeper. The isolated soldiers to be seen about seemed to be lost, they couldn't tell where the rest had gone. There was nothing for us to do and we drove on.

There was a serio-comic sequel to this episode. The leader from Neuve Eglise failed to report at Mont des Cats, even by telephone or written message. A week or so later a story reached me that he had been seen on that first fateful day breaking into our garage at Bailleul, where an old car stood abandoned as past active service, and eventually driving it away. It was weeks after that, when the tide had turned, that I had to go to our headquarters at Calais base on some business and at the tea table found myself confronted with the hero of Neuve Eglise; he was eating hot-buttered toast again and still trying to register complete confidence. He began to regale us with the epic story of his fearful experiences that night and his gallant efforts to rally the panic-stricken. I interrupted to mention that garage at Bailleul and the fact (it *was* a fact, though the offer, I knew, had been only half-serious) that the APM had offered to bring him before a court-martial if I asked for it – 'and you know', I added

---

[46] At divisional level and above, telephone communications were the responsibility of the Signal Service companies of the Royal Engineers. Rawson, *British army handbook 1914–1918*, pp. 106–7, 109–11.

maliciously, 'the penalty for deserting on active service'. His face turned dead white under any cosmetics there may have been; he left the room and I never set eyes on him afterwards. This was the only serious defection, I am rather proud to say, among our workers in Second Army during the weeks of ordeal which were now to follow.

Survivors of the 'Big Push', as we all called it in 1918, would find it very hard to give a coherent account of what happened. Our troops fought back against impossible odds, the final desperate thrust of a German army which knew that the spirit of the Fatherland was crumbling behind it. They fought inevitably a long-drawn rearguard action – and the British temperament has often proved itself better in a fighting retreat than most others. The retreat lasted day and night for three weeks, and the official communiques at home – once or twice we got sight of a newspaper, days late – always said that it was 'proceeding according to plan'. That may have been plain to the Olympians who direct these things but to any of us mixed up in it no plan was visible at all. It seemed to be, not to speak too flippantly, tip and run on the grandest scale. As a true symbol of this, I have a vivid picture still in my mind of a battery of field guns thrusting and cursing its way up against the stream of retreating infantry on the Armentières road. They halted at the word and deployed across a field on the flank to open fire with one round of each gun in rapid succession, only to limber up and retire a quarter of a mile before repeating the process. They seemed to be firing over open sights, into the unknown brown, hoping to sow delay and disorder, if only for a minute or two, in the ranks of an enemy inexorably advancing. It was like an exercise well carried out under every disadvantage but it looked futile.

On the same road that day our shabby Ford, blocked in the tide of the retreat which flooded towards it, was hailed by a frantic captain wearing the dark red and black brassard of army staff. He jumped on to our running-board shouting at us, 'Have you seen the Somethingth Division? We can't find it!' How were *we* to know the division of the men from all sorts of units who were streaming past us?

It may have been a night or two later that a colonel with a subaltern behind him walked into our room on Mont des Cats. He wanted a telephone: someone had told him we still had one. He must ring up Cassel urgently: we had to tell him that the line, nearly every line, was now blocked. He must find the HQ of his division – did we know where it was? By a strange fluke we knew where it had been the night before – at the Coq de Paille, a farm at the bottom of the western slope of our hill. That previous night Walter Ashley and I had arrived there on foot after midnight, so exhausted that we decided to snatch an hour's rest before climbing the steep hill. The painted heraldic device of the division hung on the fence; we walked into the farm kitchen where an officer was asleep on a camp bed. There were two other beds, recently occupied but empty, and we dropped without more ado on these and were almost instantly asleep ourselves – no one questioned stolen hospitality now. The colonel and the subaltern thankfully drank a cup of stewed tea and consulted our map as we talked and then we drove them down to the Coq de Paille. There was no one in occupation any more – division had moved its headquarters again, destination unknown.

Much more moving to me was the early morning when a motor bicycle drew up at our door and a haggard dispatch rider stumbled in to put a scrap of paper into my hand. It was a page torn out of an army notebook with a scribbled message in pencil from a lieutenant addressed to his commanding officer; the time and date upon it belonged to the afternoon before. The writer was holding on with a handful of men at a point (he gave a rough map reference) but they were nearly surrounded – could help be sent, very soon or it would come too late? The messenger had been trying ever since to find the CO and had failed; the message *must* be delivered to someone – and now to me of all people! The message, I pointed out, was twelve hours old, but the dispatch rider seemed stupefied with his utter failure and weariness. He went dumbly away with his scrap of paper. And I tried to dismiss from my mind a tiny detail in a disastrous landscape – a huddle of brown down there at the map reference, where, in all likelihood, a young officer and a dozen men would be lying together dead.

Such was the plan of the great retreat as we who were too close up saw it in a hundred details hour by hour. Of course we were wrong in our judgment; we could not hope in the heat and urgency of our small duties, to see the plan in true perspective. It was only when the crisis was passing that we thought of Plumer's orderly mind and unshakeable faith in continual action at Cassel or heard the story of how he had opened a conference of senior officers there with the words we had so much distrusted. 'Gentlemen, the retirement is going according to plan.'

Every day was different from the last, its experiences unpredictable, though in truth the calendar did not divide time any more into the hours of dark and daylight. It was, more than ever a 'Book of Days' – and nights. Let me revive the memory of a very few of these.

When the retreat had been in progress – or regress – for perhaps a week McCowen, our chief, arrived from Abbeville in his old-fashioned Studebaker to see for himself how we fared. He drank tea, for tea is the sovereign stay in almost any distress, the solvent of many a problem. Then, having plenty of problems on his mind as well as ours, he curled himself on the floor and slept for an hour. By now the dusk was down and we led him to the monastery gates at the top of our hill, whence he could survey all the lost kingdom of our world. At our feet, below the slope, the village of Meteren was in flames. As we looked down into it we could still distinguish the blaze in our own hut, fired according to orders by its leader before he came away. McCowen was visibly taken aback to have this sight at such close range. He reminded us that a hill-top, whatever its advantage as an observation post, is a bad place to be when there is a chance (as seemed likely enough that night) of its being surrounded by an enemy.

By this time we had not only our small staff to cater for on Mont des Cats. The workers and their orderlies from the Salient, where the cord was being drawn steadily tighter, had been coming in, mostly in good order, to headquarters day after day until the village schoolroom and other buildings we took over, where they had to eat and sleep, were getting very overcrowded: we faced the problems of 'displaced persons' in miniature.[47] Except for a sprinkling of clergy and ministers, they were all unfit or too old for active service, and they had been forced to over-much activity so that some were badly shaken; a few were by nature grousers and that got on the nerves of better men. We had no obvious place to send them elsewhere, no transport we could spare. Soldiers were straggling across Mont des Cats, an awkward route to safety, officers and men in twos and threes or mixed groups of twenty or fifty which had lost their units, and we employed our displaced workers as best we could in serving them. There was always now an army boiler alight by the side of our road for brewing tea, cases of biscuits and cartons of cigarettes, which we distributed – free, of course – to passers by who had not received pay or regular rations for a long time. This work put some heart both into very tired troops and into our own very bored men, but it was little enough for either. Besides, the business of keeping up supplies was getting every day more precarious.

Over the supper table that night with McCowen we ticked off the list of those we could do without. I told them to pack their small belongings, a haversack full, and drew them up on the road in front of the school; I put one of the orderlies, Corporal Rossiter, a capital youngish Cockney, at the head of the column of fours as guide; McCowen himself in his car brought up the rear to rally stragglers. The open car was loaded, mountain-high, with the two old nuns, whom we were forcibly abducting at last, almost buried in their feather beds which, like so many peasants, they insisted on taking with them. It was a comic but pathetic little procession which disappeared down the hill into the darkness as we shouted 'goodbye'. Destination Calais, if possible, we had said; we never knew precisely how many got there. Most of them were good men, who had done all they could, but when the handful of 'indispensables' reassembled in the schoolhouse I have to admit that we all assented, in our hearts, to someone who said 'Thank God, they're gone!'

What of the few who, by the end of the first week, were still clinging on in the field? It was becoming plain that one by one they would have to give way. Meanwhile Walter and I made it routine to visit them every day. This became each time more difficult and I know that we would gladly have been relieved of the duty. But it is a truism, proved up to the hilt in war, that the fact of feeling responsible for the lives of others is the best tonic for courage when one needs it most. Normally we headed first for Ypres, in front of which the line had been drawn closer than ever in its history, until, one Sunday midday, we received the expected message from Magrath that he had been ordered to pull out of a place now only held by machine-gunners. We set out immediately but met him already at Brandhoek on the Poperinghe road, cheerful as usual although his eyes were

---

[47] This is a term coined during the Second World War, when tens of millions of people were displaced in Europe alone. Such was the enormity of the refugee problem that 'DP camps' were a ubiquitous feature of western and central Europe in the immediate aftermath of the war. I. C. B. Dear and M. R. D. Foot (eds.), *The Oxford companion to the Second World War* (Oxford, 1995), pp. 935–6.

bleared with gas. His two faithful orderlies were wheeling the kits of all three in a civilian handcart they had commandeered. This we tipped into the ditch after loading men and kit into our car.

At the Lille Gate a day or two before that we had been halted by a military policeman who tried to dissuade us from going out that way; the so-called York Road, he said, was now under full observation by the enemy. We were bound for a point on it nicknamed Confusion Corner and it would have meant miles of detour to reach it any other way. We decided to try our luck. At one point the car had to dash across a lot of splintered matchboarding, painted green, which had been blown across the road. 'What's that?', said Dickie. 'Our Dickebusch hut', I replied, after looking back. It wasn't a very good joke, though true, but we were glad of something to laugh at.

At Confusion Corner, beside a little copse now badly damaged, was a YM hut and Gallimore,[48] day after day, unexpectedly, still Gallimore. He was an Anglican priest who had been a missionary in Sierra Leone, a man with a clerical face and collar and gold-rimmed glasses, but no 'pale young curate then',[49] as we discovered. His fellow-worker was a Herefordshire farmer in his fifties; he was, I could see, excusably very frightened by the situation round him but when I offered to relieve him had stoutly rejoined 'As long as Gallimore's here I'm with him.' That morning things at Confusion Corner had taken a turn for the worse. A field battery, using the hut and the copse as their only available cover, was firing from a hundred yards behind them. Every time the guns opened fire, especially the one immediately under the lea of the hut, the flimsy wooden walls visibly concertinaed in and out with a grotesque spasm and more crockery and enamel-ware crashed to the floor; the impact on the ear-drums was stunning. It seemed a question perhaps of minutes before the battery would be spotted and put out of action by German guns. I offered to take Gallimore and his companion away then and there, but he refused between bouts of fire in his unperturbed scholarly voice. Trade was slack, he admitted, but the gunners still needed him: theirs was hard work and no rations had come up for them all day yesterday. Reluctantly we left him, after I had ordered that customers must not congregate in the hut, even if they had the chance; his life was his own but he had no right to risk other people's.

We drove away, making now for Dranoutre and Bailleul where we still had men, we hoped, at work. Then we ourselves were spotted. I imagine that our little car speeding along the road parallel to the front line looked much like one of those painted metal silhouettes on a moving board at which you crack off four shots a penny at the shooting booth of a village fair: knock one over and you get your penny back. A German battery may have found some light relief in 'bracketing' us upon the road – a shell a couple of hundred yards in front of us, another as far behind, then a shell much nearer to us and its fellow a similar

---

[48] Herbert Stanley Gallimore, ordained priest in 1912 and who had served as a civilian chaplain in Seville, can be located in *Crockford's*. However, there is no mention of an African missionary background. *Crockford's*, 1920, p. 550.

[49] Gilbert and Sullivan, *The sorcerer* (1877). The lines are those of Dr Daly, 'Vicar of Ploverleigh'.

distance at our backs. Dickie set himself to erratic driving, a pause and then a sprint at reckless speed on this pock-marked road, which we had to ourselves that morning. We were very glad at last to get clear of the jaws of this trap.

We were secretly thankful next morning to be relieved of our daily call at Confusion Corner. Gallimore, with his farmer friend, walked into head-quarters at an early hour. I had never known him angry before or using unclerical language. 'Getting on nicely', he said, 'until some damned brasshat came and ordered us out.' I have seldom come upon a man so dashed or inconsolable. It was several weeks before I received a typed note from the general commanding the 9th (Highland) Division, which was as famous in those days for feats of arms as its sister Highland Division, the 21st, was to be in the Second War.[50] He referred to 'your man at Confusion Corner' whom he had had occasion, personally, to order back. 'If', he went on, 'he is eligible for a military decoration I should like to recommend him for conduct worthy of the best traditions of the British Army.' That is the formal phrase, I know, but I like to believe that it was thoroughly earned by Gallimore. I replied in a letter of thanks, adding that as a civilian he was not eligible.

Some reader may have wondered why we added our car as yet another obstacle to the retreating traffic down the Armentières road. Had the YMCA any business there or was it just 'joy-riding' in such a joyless place? When our well-established static work nearly all over the area was forcibly brought to an end we decided to be as mobile as possible (as everybody else indeed had to be), though the scale of our work could only be very small. Our tiny fleet of cars, therefore, went off every day into the ever-changing blue, generally with a team of three in each and loaded with a portable boiler (its crusted black sides made a bad mess of our uniforms but that was of no consequence now) and as much as we could carry of biscuits, tea, chocolate, cigarettes and matches. Beside the road there would usually be wounded or exhausted men, upon it always hungry men, dying for a smoke. We never met with a rebuff from any rank, however exalted, too often with gratitude far warmer than we deserved.

The first motive which led to one episode was ridiculous. I had received instructions from McCowen that I should pay, at my discretion, compensation in cash to workers for essential kit which they had lost in the retreat to enable them to replace it at the first opportunity. The refugees in the schoolroom, therefore, made out their short lists and handed them to me; I ticked them off item by item and Harry Barlow, as our accountant, paid the cash and filed a receipt; it was a simple operation. The lists were mostly moderate to a fault, some men refused to make one altogether. An exception was handed in by a most meticulous middle-

50 Again, there is some confusion here. Major-General H. H. Tudor commanded the 9th (Scottish) Division at this stage of the war. This was not a Highland division and nor was a 21st Division formed in the Second World War. The later division to which Baron refers was the 51st (Highland) Division which, though captured in France in June 1940, was reconstituted and fought in North Africa, Sicily and north-west Europe. A. F. Becke, *History of the Great War based on official documents. Order of battle of divisions part 3A. New Army divisions (9–26)* (Uckfield, 2007), p. 3; G. Forty, *The British army handbook 1939–1945* (Stroud, 2002), pp. 330–4.

aged Presbyterian minister, who belonged, I fear, among the grousers. His list was a long one and I found myself striking out one item after another. Half way down I came to '1 Bible, India paper...10/6', and called him in; we argued about the items and came to the Bible. I reminded him that Bibles were not kit within the military meaning and that anyway a cheaper one than that was better suited to active service. He persisted: this one went everywhere with him, it had great sentimental value for it had been a present from his mother. My temper was growing short, for I was busy and very tired – 'You may value your affection at half a guinea', I said inexcusably, 'but I'm not going to pay.' He went on arguing in maddening Scots until I exclaimed, 'All right then, I'll fetch your blinking Bible in the morning if I can.'

The hut where the Bible lay, probably by now in ashes, was at Rossignol, up a narrow lane from the Armentières road and my own car started out that way. With me were Harry Barlow, old Dad driving and Nat Berry,[51] one of those rather rare bullet-headed men who seem to have no conception of what fear means. I suppose some men like this have won the Victoria Cross without realizing what they were doing; more winners, I fancy, are heroes just because they were afraid and acted all the same.

We edged our way slowly against the traffic, past the field battery which unlimbered to fire its round, the staff officer who had lost a division, past also the astonishing encounter of two great farm wagons with an aged woman in her bed upon the first and a pathetic little girl dragging an unwilling cow by a halter behind the second, past an old peasant man, who had worked among his beet to the last moment and was now dying alone in the ditch. And all the while the ceaseless procession of weary, unshaven, grey-faced infantrymen slogged past us, their faces blank, with eyes that stared straight in front: they had done all they could except die, now they had one objective – to get the hell out of it.

Our first opportunity came quite soon. On the grass-verge in front of a roofless cottage lay half a dozen wounded men, several others could be seen through the open doorway. We stopped and spoke to a distracted R.A.M.C. corporal who seemed to be in charge. His officer, he said, had gone down the road an hour ago, leaving orders that if things got much worse the corporal was to abandon the wounded and follow him. Berry was out of the car by this time, with the boiler in his arms. 'My job', he said, 'you go on.' I had a little trouble with Harry who was obstinately bent on staying with Berry. At last I said roundly 'We may have to lose one man, we can't afford two' and pushed him into the car. We drove on.

The sequel asks for a few words at this point. For two days we had no news of Berry. Then in the middle of the night he staggered into our room on Mont des Cats, collapsed on the floor without a word and was asleep like a log. He told us his story in the most matter of fact way in the morning. The corporal had got more restive until Berry, with no authority, told him to follow his officer. He himself brewed tea for the wounded and sorted them up as well as he could. Then

---

[51] Berry had worked from 1909 to 1914 as a full-time YMCA secretary in Lancashire, Surrey and Kent. *Year book*, 1914, p. 95.

he carried them one by one to the road and tried to stop any army wagon which would take another man on board. Some refused point-blank to halt even for a moment, for they got cursed for a traffic-jam. At last he got them away to the last man. Things went steadily worse with the enemy advancing – as one man said, 'eight-hundred yards away at a steady walking pace.' Berry had to abandon his precious boiler at last and go himself. On the way back (it had taken the best part of two days) he had found, he said, 'one or two other little jobs'. That was all.

Meanwhile, with 'the best of luck' to Berry, Dad and Harry and I pushed our way on until we came to the little lane to Rossignol, and I remembered the Bible. We turned into it, for there might be work for us there as much as anywhere else; already a first-aid post had been set up at the corner. We drove slowly and I had time to watch a half company of infantry stringing out from the road across the field to our left; they lay down in open order, the muzzles of their rifles in the direction we were going. We drove past them, but an officer got up on one knee and called to us. 'Hi! Where d'you think you're off to?' I told him we had business in Rossignol. 'Well, I wouldn't if I were you', he said, 'the Boche has been there for a couple of hours. Our job's to turn him out – if we can.' The first trees of the village began at the next corner, not more than two hundred yards ahead.

I explained all this into Dad's deaf ear and he set to work edging the car backwards and forwards across the narrow lane until we were facing the way we had come. We were saying goodbye, with laughing apologies for having trespassed through the front line, when a sergeant came stooping down the ditch with a private at his heels. They had gone out with an officer to reconnoitre and the officer had been badly hit; he was lying now on a cottage door they had retrieved, close beside those trees but they couldn't get him any further. Harry looked at me and I explained to Dad who nodded. 'May we have a shot at it?', I called to the officer in the field. 'That's up to you', he replied.

We reversed the car again by patient inches and crept forward as quietly as its old engine would allow. We sighted the white door under the trees ahead, reached it and reversed again. That engine sounded in our ears now like a thunderstorm and we expected at each moment for a bullet to come singing through the trees. We lifted the makeshift stretcher between us and laid it with some difficulty across the folded hood and the back of the driver's seat; its heavy burden looked far gone. Then Dad drove as gently as he could while Harry and I pushed behind. As we passed slowly back through the line of waiting men they raised their heads from the grass with a grin and a suppressed cheer. At the corner of the lane we handed our casualty over to the dressers. He could not speak but he blinked at us with eyes full of pain. We never knew his name, and I have often wondered if he is still alive. Then we sat for a few minutes in the stationary car, the sweat trickling down our faces, wondering what we had done.

It was fully expected that the enemy would attempt to capture the whole small series of the 'Mountains of Flanders' and then try to drive us into the sea at Boulogne. That would have been our Dunkirk, in terms of the World War to come – though who knows whether the same marvellous feat would have rescued the remnant? Kemmel Hill, the first and largest of the range, which we had always thought of as an impregnable keep guarding the Salient, had already fallen. A continuous camouflage screen – tall hop-poles with innumerable tatters of green canvas, threaded on chicken-wire, strung between them – now shielded the road from Pop to Ypres; we were all conscious that a hostile Kemmel, like 'Big Brother', was watching us. At the other end of the chain, in the lower ground between Cassel and the coast, labour companies were hastily scratching line after line of shallow trenches across the fields in the hope that they could be held, if the moment came, long enough to let the bulk of the army reach Boulogne.

It is the labour companies, an indispensable but despised element in an army at war, that brings me to another picture, a small side-show of the 'Big Push'. In the sullen winter, lately over, I had been asked to put up a YM hut at Vlamertinghe, the village at the only kink in the seven miles of road between Poperinghe and Ypres. The site unwisely allotted to us by the army lay far too close to the railway as it crossed the road, a junction to which the enemy was wont to pay attention. But the hut was built and I got a famous, flamboyant local character, General Hunter-Weston, commanding XXII Corps,[52] to open it. That night it was crowded, largely with men of the Labour Corps who were repairing this vital road for the spring offensives which were sure to come. He ended an eloquent speech with, 'Go out now into the highways and hedges and tell your comrades that their Corps Commander greets them.' I wondered at the time what form that message would take in the mouth of any old Labour man, who didn't belong to XXII Corps anyway! The hut had a short life, for in the preliminary bombardment which heralded the 'Big Push' it was blown endways, with fatal casualties, by a direct hit. The leader, a sixty-five-year-old parson, escaped as if by miracle and came into Poperinghe half mad but determined to try again; a week later he was invalided home with what we then called 'shell-shock'.[53]

For the building of this hut no local Labour was to be had – the road repairs were too urgent – and I was advised to try the Chinese. These were volunteers,

---

[52] Widely known as 'Hunter-Bunter', Lieutenant-General Sir Aylmer Gould Hunter-Weston (1864–1940) was a flamboyant and controversial figure. He had performed poorly as a corps commander at Gallipoli in 1915 and also on the Somme the following year. He was effectively sidelined thereafter, not being entrusted with the direction of any major attack until the closing stages of the war. Fond of making grandiloquent speeches to his troops, his election as a Unionist MP for North Ayrshire in October 1916 (his opponent was a clergyman standing as a peace candidate) gave him another platform for his oratorical talents. Baron is mistaken, however, in stating that Hunter-Weston commanded XXII Corps; in fact, he commanded VIII Corps, which held rear areas in Belgium for much of 1917 and 1918. *ODNB*; Bourne (ed.), *Who's who in World War One*, p. 137; M. Moynihan, *Greater love* (London, 1980), pp. 100–1; Becke, *Order of battle part 4*, pp. 181–3.

[53] The term 'shell-shock' was coined in the early months of the war in the belief that psychiatric casualties were caused by the concussion of high explosive shells. Its causes were, of course, far more complex than this and poor understanding of the condition greatly complicated the work of medical officers while calling into question the justice of the army's own disciplinary proceedings. Various forms of treatment for shell-shock were developed during the war (most notably by Dr W. H. R. Rivers at Craiglockhart Military Hospital) and the condition was the subject of a comprehensive War Office inquiry in 1922 which helped to ensure more effective treatment of psychiatric casualties in the Second World War. C. Messenger, *Call-to-arms: the British army 1914–18* (London, 2005), pp. 423–30.

many thousands of them, who came from China on a contract for 'duration', civilians, in a uniform like blue overalls, under military discipline.[54] They were not attached to a particular army, and I had to make my application to Advanced GHQ at Arques, outside St Omer. I had gone in person and asked for the director of labour (Chinese). In a hut under big trees I had found myself saluting 'Sandy' Lindsay,[55] the master of Balliol, seated at the usual trestle table covered with the usual brown army blanket. We had a delightful talk. He had become deeply interested in the Chinese and gave me a chit to the officer commanding a camp of them not far from Poperinghe, which authorized me to draw as many labourers as I needed. They worked wonderfully well, far better than any British workmen I could have had.

The immediate upshot was a request by the Chinese themselves for a YMCA of their own. In their tented camps they were suffering much in the frost and snow, with no facilities of any kind when off duty, for the shops of Poperinghe were some miles off and the estaminets closed to them. I got sanction from McCowen,[56] and the large wooden hut, in sections, duly arrived from the base and was dumped on the frozen ground. I was there to witness the start, and I have never seen workmen fall upon a job as these men did; the building rose before our eyes. When it was finished I was bidden to come again and inspect it and found a marvellously decorated Chinese stage, covered with warriors and dragons in brilliant colours, inside. The whole company stood on parade while the Chinese

---

[54] Although in a state of political turmoil, China formally entered the war on the Allied side in August 1917. However, such was the need for labourers in France that, with the sanction of the Chinese government, the British had already raised a Chinese Labour Corps. Largely recruited from Shantung province, its members were engaged for three years and received some military training prior to leaving China through the British concession at Wei-hai-Wei. The first elements of the CLC left China in January 1917 and, by the end of the war, there were more than 90,000 Chinese labourers serving with the BEF in France. While its backbone was a system of Chinese interpreters and gangers, the CLC was commanded by British officers and non-commissioned officers. Haythornthwaite, *World War One source book*, pp. 163–5; Messenger, *Call-to-arms*, p. 229; *Statistics of the military effort of the British Empire*, p. 160.

[55] Alexander Dunlop Lindsay (1879–1952) was the son of T. M. Lindsay, a Scottish Presbyterian clergyman and the principal of the United Free Church College at Glasgow, to whom he owed his religious and philosophical outlook on life. Following an impressive career as a student at Glasgow University, Lindsay went as a scholar to University College, Oxford, in 1898 and became president of the Oxford Union Society in 1902. Although he eschewed a clerical career, by 1914 Lindsay was a leading moral philosopher and the Jowett Lecturer in Philosophy at Oxford, having also taught at the Universities of Glasgow, Edinburgh and Manchester. Convinced of the justice of Britain's cause, after the outbreak of war Lindsay volunteered for the army and contributed to a series of pamphlets entitled *Why we are at war*, arguing that it was imperative that international law be upheld. Lindsay displayed immense tact and impressive organizational talents in his work with labour units on the Western Front, rising to the rank of lieutenant-colonel, being mentioned in dispatches on several occasions and being appointed a CBE in 1919. His eventual appointment as deputy controller of labour for the BEF was testament to his efficiency in dealing with a large body of troops of many nationalities. He remained, however, a prominent and influential academic throughout his life and his wartime experience greatly influenced his post-war work for the reform of the philosophy curriculum at Oxford (which he sought to make more accessible for returning soldiers) and, more especially, in his celebrated work for the adult education movement. Among his many other achievements, Lindsay became master of Balliol College in 1924, a post which he held for twenty-five years. *ODNB*; *Times*, 19 March 1952, p. 6.

[56] See Introduction, p. 71.

'clerk of the works', with an interpreter, delivered to me not only a highly Oriental speech of thanks but four long panels of oiled canvas (issued to the troops to serve instead of glass in windows) on which one of the workmen had painted delicious flowers and birds and insects to represent the four seasons of the year. He had even added a short poem of his own to each. I asked for a translation of one: it ran 'This little bird likes sitting on this little tree.'

All this sounds, undoubtedly is, a digression. One result of this friendly contact with the Chinese was that I applied for a special YM worker among them – for hardly any of their British officers and NCOs (some of them of the poorest quality) could speak their language. The man sent to me had been a missionary in the China Inland Mission. He spoke Chinese fluently, knew their customs and way of thinking and was able to smooth out some of the troubles in the Chinese camps within reach.

Then the big trouble, the German offensive, burst upon us all. A clause in the contract the Chinese labourers had signed before leaving home guaranteed that they should never come under fire. But now everyone was liable to be under fire, even in the remote back areas. The Chinese panicked wildly, broke from their camps and scattered all over the countryside, making for the coast. Unrationed, unpaid and undisciplined, they lived by marauding civilian houses, pig-sties and chicken-lofts; the population in some villages was terrified at the advent of these yellow strangers, themselves terrified. It was of course a very minor problem in our world which seemed to be altogether falling to pieces. Second Army headquarters certainly had not time to deal with it, indeed it was hardly their business. I went to Cassel, however, and offered to lend them our Chinese worker, provided they could supply him with a car and rations of food and petrol. This they thankfully did, and he was able in the weeks that followed to round up large numbers of wandering Chinese, to pacify them and concentrate them in some of the camps further back. We had no time to supervise his operations. He was simply a free-lance, wearing our name and uniform.

On 28 April (I have evidence for the date), when the retreat was very far gone and the enemy actually west of Poperinghe and level with Mont des Cats on the south side, I was on a round of the very few outposts of the YMCA left on that flank. In the afternoon I came to our hut at Reninghelst, a village about three miles out of Poperinghe and rather less from Kemmel Hill. The hut was badly damaged, empty and forlorn. The leader of it, a charming undergraduate, tall, handsome but consumptive-looking, had been killed in the hut a week before by a jagged shell-splinter that gashed him open as he sat at night totting up his accounts.[57]

The next call was at Ouderdom, where the man in charge was now alone. Stragglers were still retreating past his hut intermittently but in fair numbers. And

---

[57] This may be a reference to a T. Trueman, who died at Dranoutre on 22 March 1918. Alfred Wilcox had been killed at Reninghelst some months earlier, on 18 August 1917. *Year book of the National Council of Young Men's Christian Associations of England, Ireland and Wales (incorporated) for the year 1921, containing a report of the war emergency work of the Association from 1914 to 1920* (London, 1921), p. 90.

under the screen afforded by the edge of a little wood not far away a battery of
our 9.2 guns, hump-backed monsters the size of an elephant, were firing at
regular intervals. The concussion was shattering, and as you stood immediately
behind one of these guns at the moment of firing you could see the great
projectile leave the muzzle and soar out of sight with a noise as if the whole sky
were a giant sheet of calico being ripped across. Comic relief to this nerve-
racking business was afforded by a row of deserted cottages near at hand. Every
time a round was fired another complete row of pink tiles, from ridge to eaves,
rose up and glissaded down the roof into a heap of sherds on the ground.

The leader here was a grizzled business man from Bradford, who had only
reached us from home on the eve of the 'Big Push'. His experience, then, had
been a disordered one, but he seemed to be master of his situation, which
seemed unlikely to hold together much longer. He had his hut in apple-pie order;
he had even dug a neat little dug-out at its back door, and I told him firmly that
he must sleep in it when he had a chance. I told him to give tea and eatables free
of charge to any retreating soldier in need, and he winced a little. When I said
that he might have to move quickly and leave his stores behind, he flared up,
'What! Leave all this stock open to the first scallywag who comes along! Never
done such a thing in my life – I'm a business man. Not me!' The very next day
I had a message that he was in a Casualty Clearing Station[58] with a leg badly
smashed by shell-fire. He was evacuated to England before I had a chance to ask
him any more about Ouderdom.

My next call that day – though now it was dusk running quickly into dark –
took longer. We were passing through the silent, deserted streets of Poperinghe;
all civilians had been evacuated some weeks ago, the town was strictly forbidden
to troops. Talbot House, like everything else, had received peremptory orders to
close,[59] but, knowing Tubby's unmilitary manners, I guessed he might still be
there. As we drove across the big, blank Grand Place, I felt suddenly near the end
of my tether. Dickie and I had been out all day without a bite save a packet of
biscuits and a bar or two of chocolate: tea in such a pass, as every housewife
knows, is the grand restorative – we *must* have tea, for there would be none
otherwise nearer than Mont des Cats. We drew up at the tall white *portes cocher*[60]
of Talbot House, nearly hidden now under a wall of sandbags to ward off blast.
There was a faint bar of light up the crack of the double doors: Tubby was at
home. We forced our way in and found him standing at the foot of the stairs,
improperly dressed in breeches and puttees, a faded blue blazer and no collar. We
murmured 'Tea!', almost melodramatically, and his old batman, Pettifer of the

[58] Casualty Clearing Station. These were field hospitals and important links in the chain of casualty
evacuation. Allocated in the ratio of one per division (or equivalent) their *rôle* was to receive and
treat the lightly wounded and also more serious casualties prior to their evacuation to base
hospitals. Rawson, *British army handbook 1914–1918*, pp. 139–41.

[59] These orders were received on Saturday 6 April 1918. However, and with the support of the senior
provost marshal of Second Army (who deemed it 'Essential to the morale of the Ypres Salient that
Talbot House remain open') Clayton defied these instructions. T. Lever, *Clayton of Toc H*
(London, 1971), pp. 69–70.

[60] Carriage entrance.

Buffs,[61] went off to make it. Then Tubby, looking graver than I have often seen him, began – 'You've heard the news?'

'Lots of it all day, Tubby, but it's not all true.'

'Then you know where our front line is now? In Reninghelst churchyard.'

'We can believe that. We were there early this afternoon.'

'Nothing can stop them now – they'll be in Poperinghe by the morning.'

'What are *you* going to do, Tubby?'

The old familiar spark returned to him: 'O me? I'm stopping here to give the Kaiser his breakfast.'

'And me, Tubby', I said '-is there anything I can do for you?'

He pondered a moment: 'Yes, there is. You can save some of the stuff. It would be a pity if it all went west.'

I knew at once what 'the stuff' would be – some of the precious furniture from the Upper Room at the top of the House. I knew also that it was ready to hand, for they had moved it down some weeks ago to the shelter of a small room on the ground floor. We drank our tea, – or was it the authentic elixir of life? – talked for a time, maybe for the last time our hearts tacitly said, and set to work to pack an incongruous cargo into our open 'Tin Lizzie' at the door. Only the smaller furniture and fitments, of course, could be taken; on the top of them, to hold the load down over the shell-cratered roads we laid 'the big black and gold carpet', which had covered the chapel floor before the altar since the beginning (and does so again at the moment when I write). As an afterthought someone added, to crown the load, the peal of tubular bells, suspended in a six-foot oak frame, which had so often summoned the household to evening prayers. The time had come for good-night. Tubby and I shook hands, which we had not had occasion to do when we met every day, for we felt this was likely to be 'Good-bye', 'God be with 'ee' indeed. Then he told me to hold on a moment, dashed upstairs and returned with a small green-covered book in which he wrote a few words before he put it into my hand. It was Weymouth's *New testament in modern speech*.[62] Upon the fly-

---

[61]   As an officer, a chaplain was entitled to a batman, whose services often proved indispensable. As Everard Digby counselled in his *Tips for padres*, 'A good servant is worth his weight in gold. The wise padre does not look out for a good young man of an ecclesiastical turn of mind. They are all right for assisting in services, but choose an old soldier for your servant…the old sweat will never let you down, and you will not want for many things as long as you can keep him, even if his place is vacant on your Parade Service.' Clayton certainly benefited from having a batman of this ilk. Private Arthur Pettifer of the 1st Buffs (in civilian life a carter from South Hackney) was a recalled reservist with vast experience of the army whom Clayton acquired while chaplain to the 16th Infantry Brigade. Nicknamed 'the General', Clayton affectionately likened Pettifer to Don Quixote's Sancho Panza and to Mr Pickwick's Sam Weller. Undoubtedly, Pettifer made an enormous practical contribution to the running of Talbot House, being awarded the Military Medal in the process and going on to play a prominent *rôle* in the early Toc H movement. He became one of its vice-presidents and was the dedicatee of Clayton's *Plain tales from Flanders*. E. Digby, *Tips for padres: a handbook for chaplains* (London, 1917), pp. 10–11; Baron (ed.), *Letters from Flanders*, pp. 22–4. Lever, *Clayton of Toc H*, pp. 45–6; Clayton, *Tales of Talbot House*, pp. 53–65; P. B. Clayton, *Plain tales from Flanders* (London, 1929), n.p.

[62]   Richard Francis Weymouth's *The New Testament in modern speech: an idiomatic translation into everyday English from the text of 'The Resultant Greek Testament'* was first published in 1903 and a third edition had appeared by 1909. Clayton's possession of this book says much about his pastoral style.

leaf I read: *Barkis from Tubby. T.H.* (The initials of Talbot House, pronounced, in the signaller's alphabet of that war, 'Toc H'.) *28 April 1918.* That, then, is my authority for the date of this episode.

We drove away in pitch darkness. On the camouflaged, cratered road to the frontier and beyond; the car, low on its springs, lurched and rolled; we could not, of course, allow ourselves lights of any kind. And in this rough sea I could fancy that the tubular bells, which incessantly jangled, were playing *Rule, Britannia* and *God save the king*.

It was long after midnight when we climbed the winding ascent of Cassel and at one of the first houses, an estaminet called the *Lion Noir*, we halted: this had been the accessible place in my mind's eye for our cargo to be parked. In the bar the landlord still stood at his counter, on the near side of which two old cronies leaned, discussing, I was certain, the unfailing civilian questions, 'How near are they now? Is it time for us to go?' The landlord, who recognized me, was a little surprised at his pub being taken for a furniture repository, but stowed our precious load under his counter readily enough. We said 'Good morning' this time and drove back the short distance to Mont des Cats. The frowning silhouette of its monastery ruins stood up against the luminous grey of dawn.

There was no sound of battle that we could single out as coming from Poperinghe, but who could pinpoint one place in the universal destruction? I now had brief time to think of Tubby, who had elected, if need be, to go down with his ship, and of Talbot House, the ship itself, a very ark of salvation to many a man near drowning in a sea of troubles, a little cabin lighted with faith and hope and humour in the midst of this welter. It had been – maybe it still remained that morning and might even continue to be on mornings in a future unforeseen, the home of a family unique along the fighting Front. We had not in the YMCA at its best, now I came to think of it, anything that could quite match its character or command such affection.[63] It had done a good work and, if this were the end, regret would not restore it to life. In those past weeks and months all of us had received tidings of the loss of so many friends, with little time to spend on idle regret. Meanwhile here was Mont des Cats and another day's work to begin.

Our front line was never in the cemetery of Reninghelst, if the Kaiser's breakfast was laid in Talbot House it grew cold and was cleared away. This had been a rumour, like the thousand others that fly about when the familiar world seems to be tumbling around one's ears. In this case, as in many others, people said it had been spread by a German agent, disguised as a British gunner officer – had they not noticed his faint accent as he told them? When we had been on the coast how often had soldiers pointed to the position of the windmill's sails at Coxyde, altered since yesterday, sending semaphore messages to the German HQ

---

[63] This was a point made by Clayton himself when he wrote: 'The Englishman, mainly town-bred, loves light, noise, warmth, overcrowding, and wall-paper, however faded…[Talbot House] was a house proper – not one large bare hall with a counter at one end and a curtain at the other, but a house, like home, with doors and windows and carpets and stairs and many small rooms, none of them locked'. Clayton, *Tales of Talbot House*, p. 3.

at Ostend?[64] Several times we met men who had actually heard the volley of the firing party which executed Queen Elisabeth of the Belgians against the wall of her own villa at La Panne – for was she not a distant cousin of the Kaiser's?[65] The loyal royal lady lived, of course, to tell the tale, as did, I suppose, the stationmaster of Poperinghe who was shot once a week for notifying the enemy by some occult means that the leave train was in his station. Rumour in the field was primitive, the cold war of our advanced time lies more scientifically nowadays.

Actually this new day, 29 April, was to be crowned by near-miracle, the turning of the tide. On arrival that morning at our HQ we got the news that the 9th Division, now miles back from Confusion Corner, had gone in during the night at the Scherpenberg, the low hill topped by a ruined windmill, which was the next link to Kemmel in the chain of the Monts de Flandres. Long since there had grown a confidence among us that the 9th Division, like the Guards, was invincible. When the Guards came up other men looked for trouble, which might turn out to be the beginning or the peak of crisis. It made them unpopular but everywhere respected – as I suppose it had done in the Peninsula or the Crimea. Their arrival was like the slogan of thrice-heroic Verdun – *Ils ne passeront pas.*[66] This morning the 9th Division held the Scherpenberg; the enemy would push us no further. This was unreasonable confidence, the fruit of a legend, but it turned out to be true.

The fact, which does not detract from the fortitude of either, was that the German soldier was as utterly exhausted by his headlong advance as his British opposite number by his fighting retreat. This does not mean that there was any moment of pause or a sign of stalemate. The spirit of Second Army, so hardly sustained through the long winter past, now leapt to its height as it began yard by yard to push the enemy back over all his hard-won gains of ground. It was a long, gruelling struggle which found our troops fighting upon the Scheldt when the Armistice was signed eight months later. But now at last it was really a war of movement, an advance which would know no limit but the Rhine.

In all this, too, we had our small part. The eighty points at which the YMCA had operated a fortnight before were now reduced to two. A great many had been over-run by the enemy, utterly destroyed by gunfire or burnt with their stores to avoid capture, a few were still reparable and could be reoccupied. We set to work to start up once more in makeshift premises and moveable marquees; there was no question of ever building huts again in an area soon, we hoped, to be left behind by the battle. We brought workers up from the base as fast as we could use them and reorganized our supplies and transport.

In these ways we had our hands full. Each of our little headquarters staff had

---

[64] Here Baron is referring to a local manifestation of the spy mania that was a marked characteristic of wartime British society, especially in the early months of the war. T. Wilson, *The myriad faces of war: Britain and the Great War* (Cambridge, 1988), pp. 160, 170–1, 176–7, 198, 402–3.

[65] Queen Elisabeth (1876–1965), who married the future King Albert I in Munich in 1900, was a German duchess and a minor member of the Bavarian royal family. *Times*, 24 November 1965, p. 14.

[66] This celebrated slogan was coined by Pétain himself. In realizing its sentiments, the French suffered more than 300,000 casualties in the defence of Verdun. Holmes (ed.), *The Oxford companion to military history*, pp. 948–50.

his own job by day, but after supper we made it a practice for some weeks to go down together to Godewaersvelde ('Gertie-wears-velvet' to the British soldier), the village at the bottom of our hill on the north side. There stood during that time the big marquees of a Casualty Clearing Station. None of us were medicos, but we were allowed to do odd jobs, one of which was cutting the blood-stained clothes off wounded men so that the doctors need waste no time when they came to them. At night the great tents were caverns where grotesque shadows shifted and leapt as the storm lanterns were moved from one case to another. The place was full of the terrible sights and sounds and smells of a hospital in the field; it was a concentrated enclave of suffering in which many died.

For a good many months one of our best men had been attached to a division, the 36th (Ulster),[67] instead of being left in charge of a YMCA centre. This meant that he was temporarily seconded to another command than mine and I saw him only when he came in to draw supplies from our stores. He wore on his sleeve the divisional flash of the Red Hand of Ulster, had his regular place in an officers' mess and moved, with an army lorry allotted to him, wherever the division went. It was an experiment which had worked well, for 'Toc Emma' (a nickname from his initials in the signalese alphabet of the time) was popular with all ranks. He was in peacetime a Methodist Missionary, with his young wife, at Morlaix in Brittany, and I often twitted him over his hopeless task as a heretic to pervert the most devout Catholic population in Europe.

As the Second Army now began to move forward into new country this mobile experiment was repeated – this time with a Cavalry division.[68] Four years of trench warfare in the Flanders mud had offered no chances to any fast-moving formation. The tanks which had gone into action in the Salient had been a disastrous failure, and at Gheluvelt on the Menin Road 'Tank Cemetery' remained a landmark for years afterwards, acres of sodden ground in which the rusty corpses of tanks, twisted and torn, showed how they had been bogged down and shot to pieces as sitting targets. Now the cavalry was brought up at last, not so much to break through as in pursuit when the tempo of the enemy's retirement increased. This was a heartening sight, grown unfamiliar to us since the Somme. For the only cavalry we had seen for a year had been magnificent squadrons of young Frenchmen, mounted on fresh horses, who had passed through Poperinghe to their first – and last – action on Kemmel Hill. They had left their horses at the foot and died to a man on the top when the hill fell. A British airman, flying over during the action, had described to us the sight of their 'horizon-blue' uniforms, up there – 'like a big patch of bluebells', he said – ringed with smoke and flame.[69]

[67] A New Army division that was initially recruited from the ranks of the Ulster Volunteer Force. The privileges enjoyed by this YMCA worker were emblematic of the militantly Protestant ethos of the original division. Snape, *God and the British soldier*, pp. 145–6, 156–7.

[68] See Introduction, p. 53.

[69] Kemmel Hill was stormed by the Germans on 25 April after 'a bombardment of colossal proportions'. However, Haig was less impressed than Baron by the defence of this 'almost impregnable' position, maintaining that French cavalry had been deployed in order 'to collect the French fugitives from Kemmel, and prevent a rout'. Brown, *Imperial War Museum book of 1918*, p. 101; Sheffield and Bourne (eds.), *Douglas Haig*, p. 407.

Now one of our cavalry divisions asked me for a man of their own. They would provide him with a lorry, which we should keep supplied with stores, and we were to find the driver. For this job I picked Hayhurst,[70] an old Lancashire man, a delightful character with lots of initiative. Cockney Corporal Rossiter, who had guided the little marching column of refugees from Mont des Cats, had rejoined us and was eager to go as lorry driver, his trade at home.

We might not see them much for a long time and the night before they set off to join the division we threw a little party for them in a half-built house at Godewaersvelde, where we now had our stores. I have the scene still in my mind's eye – our scratch supper by the light of a leaping log-fire upon the open hearth, Rossiter 'obliging' with *The old Bull and Bush* and *My old Dutch* on his mouth organ. And then little Hayhurst standing up to sing, in a true sweet tenor voice, *Where my caravan has rested*.[71]

Early next morning they drove off in fine spirits, and we never saw them again. Up on the ridges, somewhere beyond Passchendaele where the cavalry was now in action, their caravan rested, not with 'flowers upon the grass' but with Rossiter instantly killed and Hayhurst with multiple wounds from which he died next day.[72]

We still sent out one or two cars each morning with a small crew and a load of supplies. There were many wounded to whom we could give lifts or first-aid, and rations did not always reach men in action or on a rapid move. I remember a day near La Clytte where we sighted a battery on the slopes off the road, which was firing over the ridge of Kemmel at the retiring enemy. We bumped across the rough ground until we came alongside it. The major in command gave us a warm welcome when he found we had Woodbines and biscuits on board and sent his men off duty, two at a time, for five minutes to our mobile canteen. Then an enemy plane came over and in a few minutes the first enemy shell; the battery had been spotted. It stopped firing and the gunners took shelter in a shallow trench they had dug. We scarcely needed the major's advice to clear out. As we turned to go all the men waved a hand to us and one shouted 'Damned good show!' Another time we were doing our best for tired infantry resting on the roadside when a staff Vauxhall, flying the red and black Army flag, drove slowly past. The officer alone in the back – very red face, white moustache – smiled broadly and raised his hand to the brim of his steel helmet: anybody was proud to be thanked by Plumer.

That fortnight of the retreat and some weeks that followed it I count as the

[70] John Hayhurst, a middle-aged, Nonconformist commercial traveller from Blackburn, served with the YMCA in Fourth and Second Army areas in 1918. YMCA, K46 Typescript list of male workers overseas.

[71] A popular ballad, 'Where my caravan has rested' was written by Hermann Löhr (1872–1943) and published in 1909. M. Kennedy (ed.), *The Oxford dictionary of music* (Oxford, 1986), p. 418.

[72] The fate of Rossiter and Hayhurst is open to doubt. According to the Commonwealth War Graves Commission, no Corporal Rossiter died in France or Belgium in 1918. Furthermore, YMCA records show that Hayhurst died in December 1918, some weeks after the Armistice. www.cwgc.org. Consulted 15 December 2008. YMCA, K46 Typescript list of male workers overseas.

most arduous of my life but also, if I may dare to use the word in the face of such grave momentousness, the most exhilarating. It goes without saying that we never had our clothes off, seldom our boots, in that time; we snatched at sleep, when the hour came, as a supreme boon, we ate as and how we could. But we really *lived*, all the more because death was continually at hand and might at almost any moment be our own. There was not time for idleness of body or mind, scarcely for reflection. Even we camp-followers were fully committed to share the fortunes of the men around us. We had always been proud to call ourselves, and to be called, 'YMCA, Second Army'; now we were more than ever before a part of that splendid entity, integrated with it, welcomed, wanted wherever we could be of service. There were no bounds any more, no hampering regulations, no returns punctually to be rendered. We had but to turn up in an awkward spot to receive that hearty and familiar greeting, 'Why, it's the bloody YM!'

Chapter 4

The watch on the Rhine

Mont des Cats had served us well as a headquarters and a rallying point while the German advance was on. The great retreat had flowed over it and round it during that critical fortnight in the history of Europe. The enemy tide had lapped its southern foot at Meteren and had actually been stayed in the next village, [blank], on the road to Cassel and the sea; a trench dug across the road there might literally have been named the Last Ditch. We felt that we had almost acquired a proprietary right to this unrivalled observation post during the great battle. But now that the struggle was out of sight, though not of sound, the disadvantages of our eyrie became more obvious. Up there we were off the main road, out of immediate touch with any military unit, wasting much time and energy in climbing this steep slope. It was time to move HQ again.

For a little while we occupied a damaged house in Godewaersvelde at the northern foot of the hill, for this dull village was at least on the railway line and we could bring up supplies by rail or lorry to our own doors. The small event which put us in occupation of it was unusual. On a dismally wet night, after a long day's drive, I called on the town major of Godewaersvelde to fix up the new billet we had our eyes upon. In a cosy little room I found a benevolent old major in Highland uniform and made my request. 'All right', he said, 'but before we come to that here's something very interesting I have just noticed. Do you know Caesar's *De bello gallico*?' I had to admit that I had read it at school; I fear I betrayed some impatience for we were longing to get something to eat. 'Well', he went on imperturbably, 'have a look at this map', and he spread a couple of maps, 100,000 scale, on the table. 'Where were Caesar's winter-quarters?' 'Why, here and here and here' – and he pointed, I think, to Cambrai and Arras and Bethune. 'The British line all these years!' he said triumphantly, 'We got it dead right – for Caesar was no fool when it came to picking ground.' This lesson in the continuity of history was coming, I then found, from a professor of the subject in a Canadian university, now disguised in a Scottish bonnet. After more talk he gave me a chit requisitioning the house we wanted. On parting he gave me something else I still treasure, the large photograph of a charming French drawing of Cassel in the eighteenth century.

Our perch in Godewaersvelde served us well enough during the reorganization

of YM work in the next few weeks. The least satisfactory of its amenities was a
dead horse, imperfectly buried in our back garden, but the Somme had inured us
to all the loathsome phases of decay. Then I decided to transfer to Cassel itself,
to be in the closest touch with army, the fountain-head of all new movement and
of much of our vital transport. We were allotted most of a dignified old house,
with a superb view over the low ground at the back, though we didn't have much
leisure to enjoy it. The proprietor, a very irascible man with constant grievances,
packed himself into a couple of rooms upstairs. His family were long since
refugees in the south of France and the only member of it left with him was a
mongrel Alsatian dog who preferred us openly to his master. When we came to
leave several months later our landlord presented me with a preposterous account
for damages, nearly all caused by the dissolute soldiery before we arrived: I left
this with the Reparations Department at army HQ to settle.[1] One item was '*Chien
de rasse*[2] ... Frs 2,000'. His dog had indeed disappeared, but I found it later,
happily installed as the mascot of the Army Post Office, which by then had
moved forty miles further forward.

Cassel had already taken on almost the peacetime aspect of a garrison town.
At this stage army musicians from home made their first welcome appearance in
France and every evening at sunset the band of the Yorkshire Light Infantry beat
Retreat up and down the cobbled Grand Place before an admiring crowd of
soldiers and civilians. I never hear the lovely tune of *The ash grove*[3] now without
seeing their drum-major strutting with his silver-headed mace. Here too the mind
was to be officially cared for in its leisure. I was visited by the education officer,[4]
Second Army: there was only one, for an Army Education Corps had to wait for
a second World War to come into its own.[5] S. H. Wood of the old Board of

---

[1] Relations between British soldiers on the one hand and French and Belgian civilians on the other
     could be strained, especially given the need to billet large numbers of troops on the civilian
     population and the damage and pilfering this entailed. In turn, British soldiers resented displays
     of apparent ingratitude and the extortionate prices they could be charged by local vendors of food
     and cigarettes. It was the task of military officialdom to lubricate the situation through the
     payment of billeting rates and compensation. P. Simkins, 'Soldiers and civilians: billeting in
     Britain and France' in I. Beckett and K. Simpson (eds), *A Nation in Arms* (Manchester, 1985),
     pp. 178–87.
[2] Pedigree dog.
[3] Originally a Welsh folk song known as 'Llwyn onn'.
[4] With the blessing of Sir Douglas Haig, from the autumn of 1917 parallel educational initiatives
     were mounted by the chaplain-general, Bishop Gwynne, and the BEF's director of training,
     Major-General Sir Charles Bonham-Carter, with the aim of educating the soldiers of the BEF in
     the cause for which they were fighting. To forward this end, in March 1918 full-time education
     officers were appointed to each army, divisional and base headquarters and part-time education
     officers were appointed for each brigade. Intended to boost discipline and morale, the impact of
     these efforts (which largely translated into talks and lectures on current affairs) were yet to be fully
     felt by the time of the Armistice. S. P. Mackenzie, 'Morale and the cause: the campaign to shape
     the outlook of soldiers in the British Expeditionary Force, 1914–1918', *Canadian Journal of
     History*, XXV (1990), 215–32.
[5] It is unlikely that there was only one education officer in Second Army (see above, n. 4). The
     Army Education Corps was formed in 1920 and mounted a huge educational programme during
     the Second World War. G. Forty, *The British army handbook 1939–1945* (Stroud, 2002), p. 135.

Education[6] was in later years to become a distinguished figure in the Ministry and a friend of mine. At Cassel in 1918 he was sorely at a loss for the tools of his trade. He had been provided by the authorities with a reading room and carpenters to line it with bookshelves but with the merest embryo of reading-matter. He appealed to the YMCA, maid of all work, for help and we filled his shelves with books from our library dépôt at Dieppe. I don't know what Rawlinson's old 'Beat-the-Boche' general would have thought of our operations!

Now and again our small staff treated themselves to modest French cooking in the Hotel de Sauvage, a few doors down the street. Its large, low dining room, with smoke-mellowed Empire decorations and the aura of a century of sauces, had the charm of so many French provincial hotels, though it could not vie with the famous *cuisine* of the Hotel de Cygne at Tôtes or the Ecu de France at Gisors, with its traditional *pied de porc*, which came my way by rare accidents in those war years. The Sauvage dining room was full of red tabs,[7] for many of the great ones from the Casino up the hill took meals there. I was much amused one night to see a waiter behind the service-screen lick his thumb to pick out a tiny label from a box and dab it on each bottle before he served it to an officer: the label bore the date 1916, the best wartime vintage year for French wine. And I was interested to watch a party of subalterns from the Staff lacing with brandy their glasses of *'ving rouge'* or *'ving blong'* to give it some pep: they were too evidently not connoisseurs in civilian life.[8]

As autumn came in, all golden on the woods below our back-windows, Cassel was obviously off the map, and Second Army headquarters moved forward forty miles; our own were advised to move with them. Now we found ourselves at Roubaix, which with Tourcoing and their much greater neighbour, Lille, make up the cotton centre, the Manchester, of France. If Lille is the hub of the industry, Roubaix, besides its mills, contains the residences of some of its merchant princes; I dare say it has the same sort of superior feeling that Hove holds over Brighton. We were allotted a magnificent house, finer than any we had seen since war began and far too fine for our present needs. There was a lodge at the great iron gates, still presided over by a family butler, rather like old Heathers in the barley-water advertisements; who let us in and out. We did not actually eat off gold plates but the cutlery was massive silver and the dinner service fine Luneville. In our dining room the ornament, out of many, which I fell in love with

[6] Sydney Herbert Wood (1884–1958) was appointed a junior inspector of schools under the Board of Education in 1910. After the First World War (in which he won the MC) he went on to have a distinguished career as a civil servant, playing a leading *rôle* in improving teacher training and in planning the 1944 Education Act. He very much shared Baron's 'undogmatic Christianity' and his interest in youth work. *ODNB*; *Times*, 5 March 1958, p. 13, 6 March 1958, p. 12, and 11 March 1958, p. 13.

[7] See above, Chapter 1, n. 23.

[8] 'VIN BLANC: White vin ordinaire. Rarely good in Northern France, but in great demand because the beer was even worse, and spirits – except expensive cognac – not available. *Vin rouge* was not so popular, perhaps because its name was not so amusing to English ears unaccustomed to French.' J. Brophy and E. Partridge, *The long trail: soldiers' songs and slang 1914–18* (London, 1969), p. 160.

was a beautiful small portrait, under its own electric light, of a boy by Daniel Mytens.[9] It was small enough to loot but we looted nothing in a house which gave us, under protest, its generous hospitality. In one bedroom there was a tremendous gilded Louis Seize bed,[10] with brocade curtains, in which, we were assured, the Kaiser had slept on a visit to the back of his front. I assigned this to Harry Barlow as the youngest member of our staff.

The tide of battle had rolled forward but was still breaking upon formidable obstacles. Day after day we could hear the booming of our guns fire miles away along the banks of the Scheldt. We got busy at Roubaix, but the task of moving our men and supplies forward, at a time when everyone else was on the move, entailed exasperating delays. We were indeed hardly set when the unbelievable news, hoped for until hope was nearly dead, went round that an armistice had been arranged; zero hour for signing was to be 11.00 hours on November 11.

On the morning of that day, still remembered on the nearest Sunday in ceremonies all over the British Commonwealth, several of us made our way with a stream of Roubaix citizens to the square of which the town hall occupies one side. A squadron of French cavalry in horizon-blue, with swords drawn, were lined up on one flank, a company of khaki British infantry, with bayonets fixed, on the other, and there was a band. On the first stroke of 11 o'clock a British general came out of the town hall, accompanied by the mayor wearing his tricolour sash; they stood upon the steps side by side. The general read aloud the proclamation of the Armistice, the mayor made a short speech in French; both their voices were blown away by the wind. Then, with the troops presenting arms, the band played the *Marseillaise* and *God save the king,* and the British infantry lifted their tin-hats with three cheers. That was all. The French population, cowed by four and a half years of enemy occupation, seemed too stunned to raise any sort of demonstration; the people, almost silent, though many were in tears, simply melted away to their homes to begin hum-drum life again. That night we saw distant rockets in the sky across the Belgian frontier, which was quite near. At home (we heard later) Piccadilly Circus was louder than on Mafeking Night,[11] but the streets of Roubaix were silent, dark and deserted.

Then another rumour ran like wildfire and was quickly confirmed. The Second Army had been chosen out of the five British armies in the field to occupy German soil. Our cherished name was to give place to another one of honour – the Army of the Rhine. I think I heard all this, so to speak officially, from a colonel on the staff in the street. He was very excited as he rubbed his hands and said, 'You wait and see, my lad: *now* we're going to put old Fritz properly

---

[9]   Daniel Mytens (*c.* 1590–1647) was a Dutch portrait painter who worked for much of his life in England and who achieved some celebrity at the early Stuart court before being supplanted by Van Dyck. I. Chilvers and H. Osborne (eds.), *The Oxford dictionary of art* (Oxford, 1988), p. 348.

[10] Louis XVI.

[11] This refers to the celebrations that took place in Great Britain during the Boer War of 1899–1902 upon news of the relief of the town of Mafeking, in north-east Cape Province, in May 1900 after a siege of seven months. The extreme manifestations of popular jingoism to which the news gave rise led to the coining of a new phrase – 'mafficking'. J. Cannon (ed.), *The Oxford companion to British history* (Oxford, 1997), p. 608.

through the hoop.' How this worked out in his case I was to see the next time I met him, and that was in the streets of Cologne. But I shall come to that later.

Now there was a new business in the air and a good deal of the elaborate nonchalance with which the British hide inner excitement. The army began to pack for its complicated furniture-move: the men could not yet foresee the long, bitter winter march in front of them. Again our own move must wait, no one knew how long. Every lorry was ear-marked for strictly military transport; railway trucks, on which we must ultimately rely, were in shorter supply than ever. We must be content for the moment to be relegated to the category of unconsidered trifles.

All the same not quite so passive as that. McCowen from his base came up again to take counsel with us, and he and Walter and I decided to attempt a little 'recce' on strictly unofficial lines. One of the terms of the Armistice laid down that both the British and the German armies were to move eastward so many miles a day. The Germans were given a start, putting a distance between them and the British which was to be strictly maintained in order to avoid any meeting and possible 'incident'. Liaison officers of both sides in cars were in the intervening no-man's-land to see the conditions kept. We planned to get into this no-man's-land ourselves, not for the empty vanity of showing the flag of the red triangle but to prospect for chances to be of some small service to our own troops when they came up. The first part was easy: when we drove past marching columns or convoys of transport we were, as usual, 'only the bloody YM', an affectionate joke.

We set out in McCowen's car, bigger, faster, more reliable than our own; on board we carried a few supplies and a good stock of tins of petrol. Very soon we were over the Belgian border and on the outskirts of Courtrai. There I sighted, painted in enormous letters along a wall, the cumbrous German word *Kadaververwertungsanstalt*, which Lord Northcliffe's propaganda and Raemaker's savage cartoons had turned to such deadly purpose in the early days of the war.[12] I was eager to see a 'Corpse factory' for myself, and we followed the arrow down a side-road until we stopped at the gates of a big building (it may have been a sugar-beet refinery) and went in. There was no one there but the watchman, an elderly Belgian who was glad to talk to us.

---

[12] A lurid wartime rumour held that, due to a chronic shortage of fats in Germany, the Germans were rendering human corpses into tallow at special installations. While its origins are unclear, it probably stemmed from a misreading (deliberate or otherwise) of German policy in dealing with animal remains. Alfred Harmsworth (1865–1922), Viscount Northcliffe, was the founder of the populist *Daily Mail* and *Daily Mirror* newspapers and was the owner of *The Times*. During the war, the Northcliffe press was marked by its strident advocacy of an all-out struggle against Germany and the *Daily Mail* by the pitch of its jingoism and xenophobia. A powerful political figure in his own right, Northcliffe was appointed director of British propaganda against enemy countries in February 1918. The Dutch cartoonist Louis Raemakers (1869–1956) was also a rich source of anti-German propaganda. Although a neutral by nationality, Raemakers was profoundly shocked by German conduct towards Belgium. His famous wartime work, which was widely reproduced in Britain, typically depicted German atrocities against helpless civilians. P. Fussell, *The Great War and modern memory* (Oxford, 1975), pp. 116–17; J. M. Bourne (ed.), *Who's who in World War One* (London, 2001), pp. 124 and 242.

'How many German soldiers did you boil down every day here?', I began.

He was completely puzzled: 'German *soldiers*?', he said.

'Yes, dead German soldiers – for fat.'

'German soldiers! We boiled down God knows how many horses, mules, cattle. But German soldiers – *mon Dieu*!'

I knew, of course, what his answer would be. We shook hands with this astonished man and drove on.

In a back-street of Courtrai we sought out a cobbler, whose address had been given to me by his son, a Belgian-French interpreter at Second Army HQ.[13] He was overjoyed to see us and tears ran down his cheeks as he read and re-read the few lines from his son I had in my pocket. He offered us bread and cheese and *ersatz* coffee made of acorns, the little enough he had in the house. Then he showed us with great elation a row of brass candlesticks on the mantelpiece which he had hidden, one standing upon another, behind the clumsy joints of his kitchen door for four years while the Germans were incessantly searching houses for every vestige of brass for their shell-cases. And he told us how all that time a German *Eisenbahner*, an engine-driver in the Railway Regiment, had been billeted in the best of his two bedrooms. For two years his lodger had eaten his meals alone and not an unnecessary word has passed between them, until one morning as they came face to face on the narrow stairs the German had said 'Guten Tag, Herr.' The spell was broken; before many days his guest had his feet under the family table. And when the Armistice came and it was time to say goodbye, the German had invited him to spend a holiday with him and his wife and children on the North Sea coast: he hoped to go and to invite them back. It may take more than a World War to hold two honest men apart.

From Courtrai we took the road to Bruges, meeting no khaki or field-grey on the way. The Germans had left the day before and the lovely city, unscarred, was recovering from its first paroxysm of joy and soberly setting its houses in order. The Allied troops were not expected; there was nothing for us to do, we would go on. To Ghent? The Brugeois advised strongly against it: the Germans, they said, were still there. We pressed on until we saw the towers of Ghent, the cathedral and the Castle of the Knights,[14] in front of us along the flat road. When we reached the canal on the boundary we found the bridge blown up and had to make a detour to get into the city.

The last German had gone out only two hours before. Ghent was in a wild ferment, like an ants' nest disturbed. Men, women and children, shouting and

---

[13]   Throughout the Allied counter-offensive in Flanders of late summer and autumn 1918 the Belgian army operated to the north of Plumer's Second Army and, from late September, the latter was part of the multinational Flanders Army Group, which was under the nominal command of the king of the Belgians. A. F. Becke, *History of the Great War based on official documents. Order of battle part 4. The Army Council, GHQs, armies, and corps 1914–1918* (Uckfield, 2007), p. 86; Bourne (ed.), *Who's who in World War One*, p. 2.

[14]   A reference to the Gravensteen ('Castle of the Count') in Ghent. Originally built in the late twelfth century, it was substantially renovated at the end of the nineteenth. www.trabel.com/gent/gravensteen.htm. Consulted 15 December 2008.

singing, mobbed about the streets, feverishly busy with their first task, which was a witch hunt. They were smashing into the shops and houses of the 'collaborators' (a word which did not come into fashion until the second war) and dragging out wrecked furniture into the street; I saw a piano lifted through a second floor window to disintegrate on the cobbles below. Down the vista of almost every street we could see smoke rising and people dancing round the crackling flames of a bonfire. Most macabre of all was the relentless hunting of women who had served the German troops as prostitutes – some of them, we afterwards heard, as the only means of saving their children from near-starvation.[15] When caught these women had their hair cut off, an age-old stigma of degradation; many, they said, were kicked and beaten to death, others rescued with difficulty and hidden in hospital. The enemy, knowing well what was in store for them, had offered the offenders asylum in Germany, and a trainload of them was said to have left Ghent station that morning. To become white slaves in a foreign land or to face the fury of their fellow countrymen, disgrace or likely death? It was as cruel a choice as anyone can imagine.

In a city square we came face to face with the sport of retribution. A crowd of several hundred men were mobbing around something at first unseen. Then a young girl, nearly naked and moaning for mercy, was lifted up waist high above the crowd; her fair hair was jaggedly shaven away and there was blood upon her face. Men howled round her and struck at her with walking sticks. We three started to fight our way into the crowd shouting out *'Laissez la fille, messieurs, laissez!'* in our execrable French, but the elbows of laughing men forced us back. We never reached her and any rescue, I think, would have come too late. The blood-lust of those terrible odds was the saddest and most bestial sight I have ever seen.

We ourselves very quickly became a centre of attention. For we were the first Englishmen and ours the first khaki uniforms they had seen – except for some British prisoners of war – since 1914, when their own men in the old-fashioned blue of the Belgian army had marched away. Wherever we went we were surrounded by an increasing retinue, which sometimes held us up altogether. At one point we were bidden to wait until they brought to us a fellow countryman. This was a British private, still partly dressed in his tattered uniform, who had been hidden, they said, in a wardrobe, with a false back admitting him into some

[15] The plight of the Belgian population under German occupation was severe in the extreme. As many as 1.5 million people – one fifth of the population – fled the country as a result of the invasion and, while occupied Belgium was systematically plundered of its resources, between October 1916 and June 1917 more than 170,000 Belgian workers were deported for work in Germany. Food shortages were endemic and grew worse as the war continued, with the Belgian population becoming heavily reliant on food supplied by the Commission for Relief in Belgium, a private body established in October 1914 by Herbert Hoover and sponsored by neutral powers, principally the United States. Despite this aid, which was distributed by the Belgian Comité Central de Secours et d'Alimentation, starvation took its toll; mortality rates doubled while the birth rate fell by three-quarters. In short, 'The war, for Belgians, was a total disaster.' M. Derez, 'The experience of occupation: Belgium', in *The Great World War 1914–45*, I: *Lightning strikes twice*, ed. J. Bourne, P. Liddle and I. Whitehead (London, 2000), pp. 511–32; J. M. Winter (ed.), *The experience of World War I* (London, 2006), p. 167; P. Haythornthwaite, *The World War One source book* (London, 1992), pp. 148–9.

dark recess, for over two years.[16] He was a bewildered scarecrow of a man now, he seemed to us more than half-mad as he asked in a toneless voice what he was to do next. 'Walk down that road', we said, 'keep on walking until you meet British comrades – they will look after you.' I wonder if he ever got home.

Our escort thrust us into a cafe, which they now filled to overflowing. Someone banged out *Tipperary*[17] on a piano in the corner: as so often, it seemed to be taken as the British national anthem. We were forced in turn to stand on tables and say something, if only 'Vive la Belgique!' amid storms of applause. We were carried along to two more cafés to repeat the process, until our oratory and our French grammar, sustained on German beer, grew more and more reckless. At last we were rescued by a fine-looking old Belgian lady, silver-haired, dressed in neat black, who invited us to her home to spend the night.

There we were grandly welcomed by her courteous old husband and two daughters in their twenties. They brought out all the food they seemed to have in the larder and a bottle of wine, long buried in the garden; by now we were very hungry. Then we turned into comfortable beds, for tomorrow was to start with a great occasion – the march into the city of the Ghent infantry battalion. Tomorrow started very early, while it was still dark, with the son of the house bursting in. He was a captain in the Belgian army, of whom no news had reached the family since the outbreak of war. Somehow he had now dodged the column and got in ahead of his regiment. He brought the crowning news that the king and queen of the Belgians would lead the troops in person.

There was no more sleep for any of us. We breakfasted early and hastily. The old man appeared dressed in a frock coat, with three medals pinned on his breast. McCowen, whose history seemed as faulty as his French, tapped them and said 'For the Franco-Prussian War, monsieur?' With great dignity the proud old man answered, 'O no, monsieur – this one for first prize for tomatoes in 1896, that for my carnations, the bronze one a third prize for chrysanthemums.' The Ghent flower show is one of the most famous in the world.[18]

Then we squeezed ourselves, with our hosts, into the very old-fashioned family *coupé* and drove to the roadside where the crowd had waited since daylight. We hoisted the three ladies on the roof of the car, the rest of us anchored ourselves to it as best we might. After an hour of waiting there was the distant music of drums and bugles, played after the *staccato* mode of the French army, which is always exciting. The head of the column appeared, amid a breaking wave of cheers. The band, and then King Albert, sitting gravely on a tall chestnut and by his side Queen Elisabeth on a white horse, smiling. Both of them carried in their right hands a large bouquet of flowers; into the barrel of every marching soldier's

[16] This was a very risky undertaking on the part of his Belgian rescuers. In October 1915, the Germans had executed Nurse Edith Cavell for similar activities. T. Wilson, *The myriad faces of war: Britain and the Great War* (Cambridge, 1988), pp. 744–5.

[17] Written in 1912 by Jack Judge and Harry Williams, 'It's a long way to Tipperary' became hugely popular in the war years. www.firstworldwar.com/audio/itsalongwaytotipperary.htm. Consulted 5 January 2009.

[18] The 'Gentse Floraliën', now held every five years. www.trabel.com/gent.htm. Consulted 15 December 2008.

sloped rifle was stuck a flower of some kind. I could not conceive how they could have come by them in winter in a country so long occupied by the enemy. This was pure joy to offset the ugly excess of the day before, liberation at last.

Our little venture, then, had no result except the memories of an unforgettable scene. We packed up as best we could at Roubaix and waited impatiently while the army round us melted away into an unfamiliar map. Then Walter and I decided to try again, this time to reach Germany if we could and lay plans there for the work to come. It was a raw, foggy morning, with a smothering of snow, as we set out with Dickie driving; this time we took with us Percy Back,[19] a very competent recent addition to our staff. We headed for Brussels, some seventy miles away, which none of us had ever seen. We did not pause to look at the impressive Cathedral of Tournai, with its five Romanesque spires, but we were bought to a halt for a few minutes at Waterloo by the surprising skirl of pipes. The Black Watch, the first troops we had encountered anywhere, came marching up a sunken road on to the historic field. They looked sombre enough, with their dripping gas-capes round their shoulders and swinging dark green kilts, and I wonder if any man among them realized where he was and was greeted by the ghosts of the Scots Greys, with the Gay Gordons clinging to their stirrups, who had charged here a hundred and three years before.[20]

Wet and cold ourselves by now, we were tempted by the rare sight of a very smart pastry-cook's shop window in Brussels. There we drank imitation coffee (which is always better than imitation tea) at some fabulous price and stopped short at one cake each – beautifully simulated cream on a foundation apparently of wet plaster – when we found that they cost the equivalent of five shillings a piece. They tried to give us change in German marks, foisted upon the city in quantity when the occupying army retired, but we refused them. (During the next few months, when we had to make this journey several times again, we found that by accepting marks in Brussels at the exchange value the Germans had forced upon the Belgians and exchanging them at a German bank in Cologne at the value the British had enforced there we could nearly double our money – a currency racket of which we had no scruple of availing ourselves while it lasted!)

At Louvain we stopped a moment to admire the magnificent Gothic town hall and did not forget to be angry outside the blackened ruins of the famous library.[21]

---

19   Unidentifiable.

20   This is a reference to an incident during the battle of Waterloo (18 June 1815), when men of the 92nd (Highland) Regiment, or the Gordon Highlanders, seized the stirrups of troopers of the 2nd (Royal North British) Dragoons, or the Scots Greys, during their ill-fated charge against the French. I. Fletcher, *Wellington's Regiments* (Staplehurst, 2005), p. 182.

21   The university town of Louvain, 'the Oxford of Belgium' as it was described by *The Times* in August 1914, was the scene of one of the worst atrocities of the German invasion. On 25 August, five days after the occupation of Brussels, German troops began setting fire to streets and buildings from which Belgian partisans – or 'franc-tireurs' – were supposedly operating. Over the next few days, the world-famous university library of 230,000 books was destroyed, along with 1,100 other buildings. More than 200 Belgian civilians were killed and the town's population of 40,000 was forcibly evacuated. M. Derez, 'The flames of Louvain: the war experience of an academic community', in *Facing Armageddon: the First World War experienced*, ed. H. Cecil and P. H. Liddle (London, 1996), pp. 617–22; J. Keegan, *The First World War* (London, 1998), pp. 92–3; Haythornthwaite, *World War One source book*, p. 374.

There we met an old priest and talked for a little with him. He described the wanton destruction of the library, part of the deliberate German plan to intimidate Brussels; day after day the systematic enemy had set fire to a specified number of buildings and afterwards, as we saw, had tidied up the ruins in a neat wall of rubble along the pavement. With a fierce glint in his eyes the old man went on to picture the Germans leaving Louvain a week or so ago – the men sometimes dragging transport wagons because horses were dead, 'dogs with their tails between their legs'.[22]

At Tirlemont we were well into the afternoon and at the end of our map. We drove on blind, not only for lack of this guidance but because the snow had begun to fall again. Huddled in our open car, which in those days had no windscreen-wiper, and in the gathering gloom, we found it hard to keep the road in the face of the snow. By this time the signs of the German retirement increased along the roadside in the useless jetsam of war – here and there a bony horse which had fallen dead, a lorry on its side in the ditch, a horse wagon with a wheel collapsed, once even a heavy piece of artillery.

Darkness had fallen when a long climb brought us under big trees at the top of a hill. The snow had given over and below us in the hollow we looked down upon the lights of a considerable town. We drove slowly downhill until on the outskirts we came to the lighted windows of a small general shop. I sighted picture postcards in the window and made Dickie stop. Here, I thought, I can read the name of the place on the cards and we needn't make fools of ourselves by being lost – but the cards hung against the glass, black rectangles upon the light within. As I opened the door a bell jangled and a girl came forward from behind to serve me – one glance at my khaki uniform and with a startled cry she was gone again. I picked up a card from the counter: the name upon it was Aachen. I called out in German, 'Don't be afraid, I only want to buy an *Ansichtskarte*',[23] and she reappeared; I could only pay her with a small French note.

Meanwhile our party at the door had also been discovered. A stout old German citizen was standing on the pavement staring open-mouthed at our car with its strange badge. When I asked him politely for the name of a hotel where we could spend the night he whipped off his hat and clicked his heels at attention, and when I asked him if he could direct us to it he jumped on the running board, refusing to take a seat, and still tried to stand at attention, hat in hand, as we drove on into the town. In the hotel, in better days obviously a good one, we encountered the worst and the best type of reception which we were henceforward to expect from the vanquished Germans. The hotel staff were

---

[22] As potential leaders of local resistance in Catholic Belgium, priests were common victims of German firing squads. In fact, in the wake of the invasion, Cardinal Mercier, the archbishop of Malines and primate of Belgium, emerged as the ultimate symbol of national resistance to German occupation. Mercier's pastoral letter of Christmas 1914, *Patriotism and endurance*, was a godsend for the Allied cause and, because of the neutrality of Benedict XV, he even came to be seen as 'a kind of "anti-pope"' in many Allied countries. Keegan, *First World War*, p. 92; J. F. Pollard, *The unknown pope: Benedict XV (1914–1922) and the pursuit of peace* (London, 1999), p. 95.

[23] Postcard.

horribly, slimily obsequious, they hated us with smirking faces and absurd politeness. The hotel guests, as we walked through the big dining-room full of them, were very well-bred people: they simply looked through us, they didn't appear to see us at all – and for that we gave them a mark for good manners. We were ravenously hungry and ordered the best dinner on the menu from a cringing waiter. Nothing really answered its description, the soup was ditch-water, the fish had been pickled a long time, the steak a microscopic strip of leather, the sweet mere whitewash spread on damp sawdust; the acorn coffee was worse than in Brussels and when the waiter, seeing our wry faces, hastily substituted tea, that was hot water with nettle leaves floating in it. Worst of all was the bread, out of which we picked little chips of wood – no wonder that digestive disorders had increased alarmingly in Germany long before the war ended! They had done their best, we were sure, and their best was almost uneatable.[24]

Next morning we rose betimes, for I insisted on looking round the town for an hour before we drove on. This, after all, was Charlemagne's capital of Aix-la-Chapelle. We visited first his strange cathedral, in which for centuries, legend ran, the body of the great emperor sat in a hidden vault upon his throne, the imperial crown upon his head, orb and sceptre in his hands, waiting to rise again and reclaim Europe. Then we toured on foot some of the older streets. In one of them we came upon an excited group of women at the doorway of a dairy-shop. We stopped and they fell silent; then one of them invited me to go inside. At the counter I found a woman in tears and asked her trouble. This, she explained, was one of the two or three depôts in Aachen which supplied milk for babies, the only people in Germany who for the past year had been allowed a milk-ration. And an hour ago a French officer had come in and commandeered the whole of today's supply: it was wanted, he had said in a parting shot, for the pet dogs of his regiment![25] The women outside were mothers waiting in vain. I was furiously angry, but what could I do? We had seen no sign of French or any other troops and could not spare time to look for them. Yet something must be done at once. I asked for a sheet of paper, which was brought, and I wrote upon it, in block letters, in English, in near-French and in German: 'Milk in this shop is reserved for infants only; any soldier found removing it will be most severely punished.' And to make matters worse, I signed my name and wrote below it: 'town major, Aachen, British Army of the Rhine', with the date. What came of it, if anything, I shall never know.

[24] A combination of Allied naval blockade, poor wartime harvests and bad management of the German war economy led to food shortages and malnutrition. In addition to the notorious 'turnip winter' of 1916–17, German civilians had to endure greatly inflated food prices and over 10,000 types of *Ersatz* (or substitute) food. H. Strachan, *The First World War: a new illustrated history* (London, 2003), pp. 208–15.

[25] French bitterness towards Germany was rooted in the defeat of the Franco-Prussian War in 1870–1. However, this was sharpened in 1914–18 by the experience of a further invasion, partial occupation, wholesale devastation and by the sheer scale of French wartime losses. In total, France suffered more than 1,350,000 killed, almost twice the number of fatal casualties suffered by Great Britain. *Statistics of the military effort of the British Empire during the Great War 1914–1920* (London, 1922), pp. 237 and 352; Winter (ed.), *The experience of World War I*, pp. 206–7.

Then we drove away until we came into Düren, half way from Aachen to Cologne. Here at last was the first sign that our men had passed that way. At the entrance of a large public building hung the sign 'Advance Headquarters, Army of the Rhine'. Something at last ought to be done about our stolen journey and I went in and sought the APM's office. He looked up as I reached his table and flung his pencil down upon his blotting pad:-

'What the deuce are *you* doing here?' (I had heard him ask that on a previous occasion at Cassel). 'Where's your permit?'

'Haven't got one, sir – yet. Can I have a pass, please, for Cologne?'

'No, you can't. We've got nobody there except a few police, and we don't know yet what's going to happen.'

'I'll take a chance, sir, if you'll give me a permit.'

He demurred for quite a time and then he gave me one for us all.

'It's your own affair, mind', he said, 'You're not to come back on me if anything goes wrong.'

I thanked him and extracted a smile at last. We drove on, with the gigantic twin spires of Cologne Cathedral growing plainer every moment against the eastern sky.

I had only once been in Cologne before, as a schoolboy on my first holiday abroad, but the venue of our hotel had stuck in my mind – the *Grosser Kurfust*. And there it still stood, an ugly Victorian building in the shadow of the cathedral. We went in and booked rooms. The booking clerk was barely polite, so we changed our rooms to better ones, for which, of course, we had no intention of paying. The hotel porter was almost openly contemptuous, so we had to assume the overbearing airs – not easy, I hope, to the average Englishman – of the conquering hero. It was an uncomfortable start, but then, as the APM had warned me, we only had the background as yet of a handful of military police. The advance guard of cavalry, we found, had actually ridden in that day, dismounted as a demonstration before the cathedral and passed over the Hohenzollern Bridge to make sure of the opposite bank of the Rhine.

After a rather stiff evening meal in the dingy, over-decorated dining-room, we four went out for a stroll in the streets. We wandered along the river bank until we came to what used to be called the *Bridge of Boats* and made as if to cross. A British military policeman – MFP[26] in red on his brassard – stopped us and examined our permit. 'I shouldn't if I was you', he said, 'There's none of our chaps over there, only a German policeman.'

We thanked him but walked over, stopping in the middle to look down into this grand, swirling river, the goal reached after such fabulous years of bloodshed. At the far end a figure stepped forward and saluted; the feeble light of a street-lamp touched the spike on his helmet and the spread-eagle badge on the front of it. *Treu und Fest*.[27] We spent a few minutes talking to him, a stout Prussian NCO with no truculence in him now. He spoke with rising indignation about the Kaiser.

---

[26]   Military Foot Police. C. Messenger, *Call-to-arms: the british army 1914–18* (London, 2005), p. 516.
[27]   Loyal and steadfast.

'I've served his family for twenty years', he said 'and my father before me – and now that man has run away – far better if he had stopped a bullet! It makes me downright ashamed, it hurts me here', and he thumped his chest a little melodramatically.[28] His humiliation seemed to us to be genuine, his self-pity was all too Teutonic. He calmed down and advised us seriously to go no further into the dark streets. We turned back and went to bed.

The rhythm of drums and bagpipes skirling woke us. It was a most dismal daybreak, with rain falling steadily, but who could have eyes for anything but a Scottish battalion marching up a German street beneath our bedroom windows? We dressed in a scramble, drank a cup of acorn coffee and went out into the cathedral square. Everyone was making for the approach to the huge Hohenzollern Bridge. Round the apse of the great church a crowd of German civilians was packed tight on the pavements. The roadway and the long, gradual slope to the Bridge, which springs from this point, was kept clear by British military police, foot and mounted. We pushed our way through to a solemn policeman on the corner of the approach; he looked at our cap-badge and relaxed into a grin. 'Hullo, YM! No, it's closed – but slip up, quiet as you can, into that little bulge near the top. There's a newspaper chap there now – nobody'll bother you.'

We walked up the slope and squeezed ourselves into a small embrasure which breaks the line of the wall. An official photograph in the Imperial War Museum, clear enough considering the rain and the wretched light, shows the three of us standing with the war correspondent, Philip Gibbs.[29] It shows also another small group, standing fifty yards further up, which was indeed the centre-piece of the picture. For this was composed of Lord Plumer and his immediate staff at the saluting-base for the army's march across the Rhine. We kept very still, for we had no wish to lose our unique stage-box view of a historic event.

The massive archway leading on to Hohenzollern Bridge is fitly guarded by a pair of gigantic bronze equestrian figures, the last Hohenzollern emperors – on the left the Emperor Frederick,[30] on the right his haughty, humiliated son, William II.

---

[28] Kaiser Wilhelm II's abdication was announced – without his permission – on 9 November 1918 by Germany's newly appointed liberal chancellor, Prince Max von Baden. Within twenty-four hours, Wilhelm had gone into exile in Holland where he died at Doorn in 1941. H. Herwig, *The First World War: Germany and Austria–Hungary 1914–1918* (London, 1997), pp. 445–6; Bourne (ed.), *Who's who in World War One*, pp. 304–5.

[29] Philip Armand Hamilton Gibbs (1877–1962) covered the war on the Western Front from 1914, having already served as a war correspondent in the Balkans. In January 1915 he was accredited as one of only five official war correspondents attached to GHQ, his pieces being published in the *Daily Telegraph*, the *Daily Chronicle* and internationally through the *New York Times*. Resentful of the heavy censorship to which his dispatches had been subjected during the war years, Gibbs took his revenge in *Realities of war* (1920), which was highly critical of the British high command and of Haig in particular. Despite his reaction, Gibbs was appointed KBE for his wartime services in 1920 and he emerged from the war as Britain's most celebrated war correspondent. *ODNB*; Bourne (ed.), *Who's who in World War One*, p. 105.

[30] Frederick III (1831–88), a liberal and an Anglophile, became emperor while dying of cancer and reigned from 9 March to 15 June 1888. His relations with his son and heir were notoriously strained. F. H. Hinsley (ed.), *The new Cambridge modern history*, IX: *Material progress and world-wide problems 1870–1898* (Cambridge, 1970), p. 293; C. Cook and J. Paxton (eds.), *European political facts 1848–1918* (London, 1978), p. 19.

Kaiser William, head high in his famous eagle helmet of the Guard Cuirassiers, holds his field-marshal's baton stiffly out in his right hand, in exactly the position, I suddenly realized that morning, in which a British horse-gunner salutes with his coiled whip. And now the commander of the Army of the Rhine stood at the foot of the Kaiser's pedestal, his hand to the peak of his cap, a profoundly humble, upright man with the huge burst bubble of vanity as his background. For the next few hours these two together, the living and the image of the good-as-dead, were to salute a victorious British army. It was not at all difficult to share the thanksgiving of Plumer. I could not help trying to picture the rage and despair, could he have seen the sight, of the other, already an exile in the sham-majesty of his Dutch Castle of Doorn.

The entry into Cologne and the crossing of the river were superbly stage-managed. After the ordeal of a winter march from the Scheldt the Army of the Rhine had been halted short of the city for a rest and entire refit. If the German population had expected to witness the arrival of a 'contemptible little army', as their emperor had once tried to persuade them, they were quickly disillusioned. What they did see was much like a king's birthday parade at Aldershot. The men, even on this wretched wet day, were as smart with blanco and boot-blacking as if they had just been inspected, horses and mules were in brand-new harness, the cords round the guns freshly pipe-clayed, even the mule-drawn field kitchens which came past with each battalion were polished bright and actually smoking – you could almost smell the pork and beans.[31] The regimental bands had been sent out from home and the regimental colours of each unit. Everyone in uniform, it goes without saying, saluted the colours and the German civilians had been ordered to remove their hats.[32] Later in the day I heard of an incident at the bottom of the slope to the Bridge. An elderly German who attempted to defy the order felt his hat whipped from his head and for the next few moments could not discover its whereabouts: then he found that a British policeman was standing at the salute upon it in the streaming gutter.

The 29th Division, which had made its name in Gallipoli as well as at Ypres,[33] headed the procession which seemed interminable. Simultaneously the Canadians were crossing the Bridge of Boats a quarter of a mile further up stream, with General Monash, their commander,[34] taking the salute. At a short interval in front of each battalion its band marched to the saluting point, turned inwards to face

---

[31] A staple of British army diet. Brophy and Partridge, *The long trail*, pp. 133–4.

[32] The clear desire to humiliate the inhabitants of Cologne may have been fuelled by the fact that the city was part of the federal state of Prussia, which was seen as the mainspring of German aggression and militarism. D. G. Williamson, *The British in Germany, 1918–1930: the reluctant occupiers* (Oxford, 1991), p. 20.

[33] This was assembled early in 1915 from battalions returning from garrisons in India and the Far East. It was the only regular division to participate in the Gallipoli campaign and thereafter served on the Western Front. Part of the Second Army, it arrived in Cologne on 9 December 1918. A. F. Becke, *History of the Great War based on official documents. Order of battle of divisions part 1. The regular British divisions* (Uckfield, 2007), pp. 122–4.

[34] Again, some confusion is evident here. Sir John Monash (1865–1931) commanded the *Australian* Corps on the Western Front from June 1918; his *Canadian* equivalent from June 1917 was Sir Arthur Currie. Bourne (ed.), *Who's who in World War One*, pp. 66 and 209.

Lord Plumer, standing at the Union Jack flagstaff, halted and played its men past with their own regimental march; it then fell in at the rear and marched away silent, while its place was taken by the band of the next battalion. This manoeuvre allowed the only intervals in the marching column – the only short space of rest in which Plumer lowered his saluting arm. It was plain that he intended to honour not only the colours or the mounted colonel but every man who had fought under him and now passed before his eyes. Apart from this significance, his gesture was a sheer feat of endurance which stirred our admiration.

When the New Zealanders followed on,[35] moments of delay were noticeable. We were told that some of their officers, who had sworn if they ever reached the Rhine to relieve themselves into it, had kept their promise.

It is unwise to push fancy too far, but, looking back on that day after more than forty years, I am convinced that no more fitting symbol of the fate of nations at the time could have been found than the march over the Hohenzollern Bridge. A few days earlier the retiring German troops had crossed it, a long procession of horse and foot and baggage, the units mixed, their ranks disordered by the long retreat, as photographs show which I bought in Cologne (though they were not displayed in the shop windows). Then, at the due interval behind this host which was trying to put a brave face upon failure, came a screen of British cavalry in good order, a sight which we had missed by a few hours on the day before. These were but the heralds of the main body which was now to hold the semicircular bridgehead covering Cologne.[36] A great many of these men who marched so steadily by, without any demonstration of triumph or hatred, had been in and out for months, for years, of the waterlogged trenches of the intolerable Ypres Salient: now they were marching into another salient, to face not the bombs and bayonets of the enemy but the prospect of a defeated, hungry civil population across the boundary in unoccupied Germany.

I found the spectacle of that day in Cologne infinitely more significant and stirring than the Peace Procession I was to watch go by many months later in a London street.[37] For by that time the world was officially at peace. It was indeed

---

[35] Formed in Egypt in March 1916 from veterans of Gallipoli and newly arrived reinforcements, the New Zealand Division saw extensive service on the Western Front. Although part of the Third Army in 1918, it joined the Army of Occupation and was disbanded in Germany in March 1919. F. W. Perry, *History of the Great War based on official documents. Order of battle of divisions part 5A. The divisions of Australia, Canada and New Zealand and those in East Africa* (Malpas, 1992), pp. 43–7.

[36] The terms of the Armistice of 11 November involved the advance of the British Second and Fourth Armies to the German frontier and the occupation of the left bank of the Rhine by 'the Allied and United States Armies of Occupation'. Bridgeheads on its right bank were also occupied at Mainz, Coblenz and Cologne, which were identified as 'the principal crossings of the Rhine'. Cologne and the British sector was held by Second Army which was renamed the British Army of the Rhine on 2 April 1919. *Statistics of the military effort of the British Empire*, p. 724; Becke, *Order of battle part 4*, p. 87; A. Rawson, *British army handbook 1914–1918* (Stroud, 2006), p. 343.

[37] London's massive Peace Procession – or 'Victory March' as it was also billed – took place on Saturday 19 July 1919, which King George V proclaimed a public holiday throughout Great Britain. It occurred three weeks after Germany had signed the Treaty of Versailles and featured more than thirty military bands (or 'two to every thousand troops') and contingents from many Allied countries. *Times*, 11 July 1919, p. 10, 12 July 1919, p. 9, 21 July 1919, pp. 7 and 13.

struggling in the toils of peacemaking, the intrigues and delays of Versailles;[38] it was launched also into a sea of troubles as perplexing as war, the frustrations and rivalries and scurvy manoeuvres of individuals, classes and nations, the sufferings of the maimed and the anxieties of the unemployed which were part of the price of victory. Somehow, I felt, the very postures of the chief figures in that London procession typified a disunity of the Allies which promised trouble to come: in the years to follow the trouble came and is not yet ended in our own day. The immense procession was led by General Pershing at the head of the Americans (for national jealousies had ordained an alphabetical order) – a gay, self-confident figure, standing up in his cowboy stirrups to set his fine horse caracoling as he waved to the applauding crowd.[39] At the head of the French troops rode Marshal Foch, the supreme commander of the final phase,[40] an impassive, exhausted picture of a man, his face set grimly, riding a horse which looked, like its master, as if it were carved out of wood. Next in order Sir Douglas Haig headed the contingent of Great Britain; he sat, relaxed in his saddle, the very type, I thought, of a gentleman hacking home, tired but contented, after a long day with hounds.

None of the moods typified by these men – the flamboyancy of the American, the exhaustion of the Frenchman, the quiet satisfaction of the British leader – were apparent in the great column which we saw hour after hour crossing the Hohenzollern Bridge in the rain. This was no pageant organized by tattoo experts in the War Office: it was the march of an army still on active service. Its organization and equipment was faultless and first-rate, but every workmanlike detail of it – except the colours and the regimental tunes which lifted men's hearts and added the sense of history – was designed for instant use and not for show. The unbroken rhythm of thousands of pairs of boots, more than the beat of drums,

---

[38] While the Paris Peace Conference was opened on 18 January 1919, after much diplomatic wrangling between the principal Allied powers the Treaty of Versailles was not signed until 28 June. Four further treaties with Austria, Bulgaria, Hungary and Turkey were signed between 10 September 1919 and 10 August 1920. Z. Steiner, 'The peace settlement', in *The Oxford illustrated history of the First World War*, ed. H. Strachan (Oxford, 1998), pp. 291–304.

[39] Dubbed 'Black Jack' Pershing on account of his advocacy of the US army's African-American soldiers, General John Joseph Pershing (1860–1948) commanded the American Expeditionary Force in France from June 1917 to the end of the war. A formidably experienced soldier and a cavalryman by background, he had served in the Indian Wars, in the Spanish-American War of 1898 and he had commanded America's Punitive Expedition into Mexico in 1916. Bourne (ed.), *Who's who in World War One*, pp. 231–2.

[40] Ferdinand Foch (1851–1929) was one of France's leading military theorists prior to the war and he distinguished himself as a corps and then as an army commander in 1914. Despite a fall from grace after successive failures as an army group commander in 1915–16, Foch was appointed as the French army's chief of staff in May 1917 and became the French representative on the Supreme War Council nine months later. However, on 26 March 1918, and with the need for a unified Allied command more apparent than ever, he was appointed supreme commander of the Allied armies on the Western Front. Five months later he was made a marshal of France, in which rank he co-ordinated the counter-offensives that brought about Germany's defeat. A devout Roman Catholic who drew considerable strength from his faith, Foch's contribution to Allied victory in 1918 largely stemmed from his calmness, courage and his ability to delegate to subordinates. *Ibid.*, pp. 93–4; R. Holmes (ed.), *The Oxford companion to military history* (Oxford, 2001), pp. 305–6.

marked the progress, boots which had slogged the unending weary miles of France and Flanders for four years to this decisive conclusion. The parallel marching columns across the two bridges were linked along the banks of this most historic river by a line of heavy howitzers, their ugly snouts trained high to fire, if need be, over the heads of our infantry into the country beyond; a neat pile of shells in gleaming brass cases stood beside each piece, guarded by a sentry with a fixed bayonet. It was hard to realize what was happening in the minds of the silent crowd of civilian spectators, for this was the denial of every promise made to them, the final failure of their utmost effort, the end of hope but not of suffering. It was the most grotesque inversion of their proudest national song –

> Lieb Vaterland, magst ruhig sein...
> Die Wacht, die Wacht am Rhein![41]

Mixed with our elation, in some moments, I found, overwhelming it, was the most poignant remembrance of those who had received the promise but had not lived to see this day of fulfilment. I suppose that every one of us that day had his own gallery of friends in mind, the faces and the voices of the fallen he was never to forget. They now stood out clear and behind them was the nameless host of the dead, the comrades of the 'old sweats' who were this moment marching by. I reflected that I myself, as a ubiquitous camp-follower of their toils and their ease, must have set eyes upon unnumbered thousands of those dead men and have exchanged words, smiles, a wave of the hand with many hundreds of them; they had no names for me but some of their faces were not forgotten.

The mortal liabilities in the balance-sheet of war are so impersonal, as its assets are too often illusory, mere book-entries which conceal the bankruptcy of faith, hope and charity. What does it mean when the history book dismisses a battle in one sentence as a 'holocaust', or an official communiqué reports that 'the enemy losses were heavy' or ours (as if to reassure anxious women at home) were 'slight'? What can the words convey when one's pen slides over a sheet of paper to write down figures like '60,000 casualties on the first day of the Somme' or 'nearly a quarter of a million buried in Flanders'? These losses are not covered by glib phrases about 'the heroic dead', nor atoned for by the bugles on Remembrance Day or the perfect gardening of the Imperial War Graves Commission. It is not enough to say, however truly, 'the lost generation' of the First World War crippled the leadership of our own country or that France, a smaller population which suffered twice as many casualties, was 'bled white' at Verdun[42] and has never since recovered. Ultimately the wastage of war has to be broken down into its component parts, its personal tragedies – the empty chair in

---

[41] 'Dear Fatherland, be assured...the Watch, the Watch on the Rhine'. From 'The Watch on the Rhine', an anti-French, nationalist song that originated in the Franco-German tensions of the 1840s. It became hugely popular in imperial Germany.

[42] The strategic purpose behind the German offensive at Verdun in 1916 was crudely attritional. In the words of Erich von Falkenhayn, then Germany's chief of the general staff, its primary goal was not so much to capture ground but to 'bleed the French Army white'. Bourne (ed.), *Who's who in World War One*, pp. 88–9.

the miner's cottage, the lost last heir of a family which had served its neighbours for centuries, women whose hearts broke as they opened a telegram, fatherless children and the children who might have been born, men deprived of their limbs or their reason, half-living men who still linger, out of sight and so out of mind, in places likes Queen Mary's Hospital at Roehampton.[43]

By the afternoon the last unit had marched over the Bridges, the British through the big suburb of Köln-Deutz into the neat villages of the countryside beyond, the Canadians further south to cover Bonn. Beyond them, on higher reaches of the Rhine, the French had occupied their own bridgehead before Coblenz, and over the immense fortress of Ehrenbreitstein, 'The Broad Stone of Honour', had run up the Tricolour; the biggest flag I have ever seen, covering what looked like an acre of sky. Further up still the Americans were in occupation of Wiesbaden. The Watch on the Rhine was set.

These crossings, with men marching for hours to music, were workmanlike but they could not help being, they were meant to be, a spectacular demonstration of strength. In Cologne itself the occupation was complete but unobtrusive by comparison. A military governor had been appointed and a proclamation in his name had been posted up in public places but scarcely anyone had yet seen him. Outside the Headquarters of the Army of the Rhine in the imposing Dorn Hotel facing the cathedral, sentries marched up and down and were relieved with the super-ceremony of Buckingham Palace, to the undisguised admiration of German spectators. Once in passing I saw a civilian 'try it on' with the army commander himself as he came out to get into his car. The man deliberately walked across the entrance; Plumer as deliberately strode into him and knocked him into the gutter. A proclamation by Plumer himself soon appeared on walls – everyone was to continue at his daily work (if he had any); there were to be no strikes, no demonstrations; there would be no oppression but, equally, no 'nonsense'. Lord Plumer won his way through hostile elements on the Rhine exactly as he was to win it later as governor of Palestine and of Malta – by undeviating justice and humanity which no one could fail to recognize.[44]

The garrison of Cologne used German army barracks, which they found, as our own troops found again in the much more extensive occupation of Germany in the Second World War, much superior to the British soldier's accommodation at home. They soon made themselves popular enough, as they do in any part of the world, and were to be found at ease in the cafés and at shop counters where in the early days astonishing bargains in Leica cameras and valuable watches were to be made. Every day a battalion would 'show the flag' by a route march through the streets and when, after a few months, the Guards relieved another unit

[43] This hospital was founded in 1915 for the care of wounded soldiers, specializing in prosthetics and in the rehabilitation of amputees. With 900 beds, it was the largest military hospital of its kind in Great Britain. www.1914-1918.net/hospitals_uk.htm. Consulted 5 January 2009.

[44] One of Plumer's signal achievements while in Cologne was to persuade Lloyd George to release food for German civilians in the occupied zone. This move was prompted by humanitarian concern and also by a desire to forestall the spread of Bolshevism. G. Powell, *Plumer: the soldiers' general* (London, 1990), pp. 285–6.

they made themselves unpopular with friend and foe alike by insisting that everyone in any kind of uniform, British or German, must salute the column as it went by. In consequence they marched back to barracks with a comical mixed platoon in their midst of recalcitrant Canadians[45] and German postmen, who were locked up for some hours before being dismissed.

All this routine settled down smoothly but not on the first night, when the main body was over the Rhine and the garrison confined to barracks. Again it was the military police only who were to be seen in the streets, where a curfew for all civilians at 9 p.m. was ordered. That afternoon when we met our friend the APM again he invited us to join him in a patrol after dinner to see 'the fun' he fully expected. When the great cathedral bells boomed 9 o'clock, the Hohestrasse, the main shopping street, closed to vehicles and the favourite promenade of men and girls every evening, was still thick with civilians strolling up and down, defiantly. Within a few minutes we were aware that a stream of these people from every direction was setting towards the cathedral square; they poured steadily out of every street, moved on by a strong force of our police from behind. In the square they were marshalled into queues each of which filed past a British policeman, with a German constable beside him as interpreter, and their names and addresses were taken down. It was a long, monotonous process, interrupted at one point by a German lad who made a gallant attempt at get-away. He bolted at great speed for a dark street-opening, amid the cheers of many hundreds of spectators, but at the last moment a policeman's foot shot out and he went head over heels like a shot rabbit and was led away.

In good time next morning we three set about the business of the YMCA for which we had come. The first necessity was the requisition of two buildings – large premises as a centre for troops and a headquarters for ourselves and the many workers we should need. The proper fount for such things was, of course, the town major and we made for his office. The whole street leading to his door was filled with a slowly moving queue, two deep, controlled by police. It was the motliest collection imaginable, citizens of all ages and conditions, here an angry housewife paired with a ragged tramp, next a retired general, by the look of him, with a kitchenmaid, then a priest with a prostitute – unwilling partners in the same adversity of paying five marks for their breach of the curfew the night before.

We pushed our way past the queue which blocked the stairs until we reached the town major's table – and found ourselves facing Captain Bles, an old friend from Flanders. His genial face was now distracted to the verge of hysteria. For Bles, who spoke French like a native, had not a word of German with which to deal with his hundreds of irritable customers. His new appointment as town major

---

[45] The 1st and 2nd Canadian Divisions formed part of the Army of Occupation. Known for their comparatively lax discipline, in 1917 the failure of Canadian soldiers to salute superior officers had caused a certain amount of concern. Plumer, however, took a more pragmatic view, informing a meeting of senior staff officers: 'I don't think there's much wrong with the saluting of the Canadians. Nearly every Canadian *I* salute returns it.' L. MacDonald, *They called it Passchendaele* (London, 1993), p. 82.

of Cologne was a delightful instance of the operation of what Ian Hay,[46] in the early days of the war, had described as the Practical Jokes Department of the War Office. 'Go away!', he shouted at us, 'glad to see you – but go away! Go to the German Billeting Office... take anything you want...but go away!'

We went away. At the Billeting Office I explained our needs to a young German clerk. In excellent English he answered, 'I know exactly what you want – I lived for several years in the YMCA in Tottenham Court Road.'[47] A large hall? – he wrote a name on a chit. A headquarters? – why not the Grosser Kurfust, he said, where we already had three rooms? We didn't want three hundred: I told him it was not only a bit big but much too shabby, and he gave us the name of another hotel.

We saw the hotel, modern, beautifully fitted, facing the cathedral, and requisitioned it out of hand. Every guest was to be out of it, I said, by tomorrow morning, the staff to remain at our disposal. The very unattractive manager, hating us as openly as he dared, raised one question only. One of his old-established guests was an old English lady, the widow of a titled German officer – surely we should not be hard on a fellow-countrywoman? Very well, I said, she could stay until further orders. She turned out to be an elderly adventuress whom we got rid of later with some trouble.

The hall we saw also – too small and too far from the centre of the city. A second visit to the Billeting Office produced the 'Gross Köln', the largest beer-hall and variety-theatre in Cologne. The manager came forward obsequiously: how many seats would the Herr Offizier like for the show tonight? No seats, I said, we were taking the whole bag of tricks. His face fell lamentably – it was very hard, he would be ruined, his staff, many of them with families, would be driven out to starve. The part of the trampling victor of melodrama was a new one to us but we played it as consistently as we could. Nothing, I said, was as hard as the conduct of his countrymen had been in Brussels or Louvain; he must fend for himself now; as for his staff he was to bring me a list at 7 p.m., showing names of his employees and their wives and families. In the upshot I engaged all his staff of waiters who had children, his orchestra and a stranded troupe of Dutch acrobats for ten days at their usual wages; meanwhile they sought, and I hope found, other means of livelihood.

Bills were hastily printed and circulated among the units, the RE painted

---

The pen name of John Hay Beith (1876–1952), a novelist and former public schoolmaster whose book *The first hundred thousand*, which was first published in 1915, portrayed the lighter side of life in Kitchener's New Army. *ODNB*; Bourne (ed.), *Who's who in World War One*, pp. 125–6.

Costing in excess of £100,000, this showcase facility was built by London's Central YMCA after the death of George Williams and was provided with all 'the features of a young men's club – including lounge, swimming baths, shooting gallery [and] gymnasium – besides being thoroughly equipped as an educational and religious centre for men'. Opened in 1888, it was managed and maintained thereafter by the Central YMCA. However, in 1915 it was transferred to the National Council (which had outgrown its pre-war headquarters in Sir George Williams's House, Russell Square) to serve as the headquarters for its war work. Anon., 'The work of the YMCA', *The Times history of the war* (21 vols., London, 1914–21), IX, 179–200 at p. 191; www.ymca.org.uk. Consulted 7 January 2009.

signs for us, a fatigue party helped us to put 'Gross Köln' in order for its new purpose. A few days later it opened with a concert. The little tables in the very large beer-hall were occupied to overflowing, and men drank their tea to the songs of impromptu khaki talent, the blare of a German theatre-orchestra and the tumbling of Dutch acrobats. At intervals during the evening some cheerful 'old sweat' would shout 'Nah them, Fritz, you play the King', and the orchestra stood up awkwardly and gave us the National Anthem: they were rewarded, amid good-natured laughter and applause, by a shower of Woodbines.

There were other large rooms attached to 'Gross Köln', which we brought into use as soon as we could. One was now fitted up as a library, with requisitioned shelving erected by German carpenters, and stocked with a very catholic selection of books. E. W. Hornung, made famous by his authorship of *Raffles*,[48] came up from France to take charge of it. He was a very charming elderly man, who had lost his son in action and dedicated his time for the rest of the war to the service of soldiers. He had run a most successful YMCA library in Arras, where he had a narrow escape when it was destroyed by bombardment. A true scholar, with a gentle gift for friendship, he attracted a constant string of customers, not only to read and borrow books but to listen to his informal talks on literature. We also ran a number of clubs and classes on a variety of subjects and as our YMCA 'director of education' (the army still had no Education Corps)[49] I had the admirable reinforcement of Leslie Hunter,[50] now the bishop of Newcastle. Then there were of course, the visiting lecturers, whose value and popularity we had amply proved in much harder conditions than this. These were now in constant supply in Cologne, thanks to Sir Graham Balfour,[51] the friend and biographer of Robert Louis Stevenson, who directed the educational work of the YMCA from McCowen's headquarters at Dieppe.

To be in Germany and to neglect music is always a wasted opportunity. And here were thousands of our countrymen, most of whom had never been in this home of music before and might never come again after their service was over; they had a good deal of leisure, they only needed, we felt, a little encouragement.

---

[48] Ernest William Hornung (1866–1921) was of Hungarian extraction and was the brother-in-law of Arthur Conan Doyle, to whom he dedicated his first collection of Raffles stories. Hornung's only son, Oscar, was killed in action in July 1915, a loss that led Hornung to devote his energies to YMCA work for soldiers in England and, later, in France and Germany. He published his memoirs of his YMCA work in 1919 entitled *Notes of a camp-follower on the Western Front. ODNB.*

[49] See above n. 5.

[50] Leslie Stannard Hunter (?–?) was ordained priest in 1916 and was curate of St Peter's, Brockley, from 1915 to 1918. *Crockford's*, 1920, p. 763.

[51] Sir Graham Balfour (1858–1929) was a well-known traveller and leading educationist. A cousin of Robert Louis Stevenson, he had lived in Samoa in the early 1890s and, on the strength of his *Educational systems of Great Britain and Ireland* (1898), was appointed director of education for the county of Staffordshire in 1903. Under his direction, the county came to grips with the implications of the Education Act of 1902 and developed a system of educational administration that became a model for the rest of the country to follow. Balfour was knighted in 1917. In October 1918, and having served on the Adult Education Committee of the Ministry of Reconstruction, he succeeded Sir Henry Hadow as the YMCA director of education in France. *Times*, 28 October 1929, p. 19; Anon., *A short record of the educational work of the YMCA with the British armies in France* (n.p., 1919), p. 16.

I went to see the army entertainments officer[52] – and found Esmé Percy, the actor,[53] disguised in the costume of a new *rôle*, that of a captain in a Highland regiment. He had already improvised an agency for concert and theatre tickets, admission free, for troops, and we were able to co-operate with him in distributing them. I recall a night when, seated among spell-bound German men and women, I listened to *Lohengrin* in the Cologne Opera House. Half way through the second act a party of four or five soldiers crashed into the stalls in army boots, pipes in their mouths. The spell was broken and the audience horrified, for this was tantamount to brawling in church. There was, of course, another side to the picture: not all of 'the brutal and licentious soldiery'[54] on the Rhine were Philistines. Those who loved and practised music in any form embraced this golden opportunity, and there are some still living, perhaps, who can date their entry into this kingdom of the spirit back to those days.

It would have been a pity too, if so many men had walked about the streets of the city and passed its Roman walls or the doors of its splendid romanesque churches blindfold, unaware of the treasures at their disposal. Leslie Hunter and I therefore compiled a little guide to Cologne, printed on poor wartime paper and illustrated with such indifferent blocks as we could run to earth. It was a YMCA publication which had some success.[55] Possibly as a result of this I was summoned by the education officer, a colonel, to act as guide to a large outing he was organizing. The Rhine steamers, so familiar to tourists, had been laid up for a long time but he insisted that one of them must be made ready to run, in order to carry his 'pupils' to some of the chief beauty spots up the river. The German engineers and crew had their work cut out to fulfil the order. Some of the machinery was 'properly goommed oop', as an expert passenger said at the first glance; actually he found his German opposite number lubricating it with what looked like tar – proper oil, even for German guns in action, had ceased to flow a year before. It was a bitter January afternoon as we got under way with a party of a dozen officers and about a hundred men on board. Snow covered the Seven Hills and the cold was so intense when we faced the wind that almost everybody crowded into the small saloon after the first quarter of an hour. I had protested at the beginning that I knew nothing about the long history of the Rhine, but there

---

[52] Throughout the war (and in marked contrast to their French, German and Italian counterparts) British army officers played a key *rôle* in organizing and promoting recreational activities for their men. The value of these activities in terms of army morale was fully appreciated at all levels of command. J. G. Fuller, *Troop morale and popular culture in the British and dominion armies 1914–1918* (Oxford, 1990), pp. 114–18.

[53] Saville Esmé Percy (1887–1957) was a prominent stage actor before the war, having performed with several well-known theatre companies in London and elsewhere. Enlisting in 1915, he was commissioned into the Highland Light Infantry and served in Germany with the Army of Occupation in the wake of the Armistice. While in Germany he took charge of the Army of the Rhine Dramatic Company, staging no fewer than 140 plays before returning to civilian life in 1923. *Times*, 18 June 1957, p. 13.

[54] A conflation of the pronouncements of Edmund Burke (1729–97) and Lord Erskine (1750–1823) on the nature of the common soldier. J. M. and M. J. Cohen (eds.), *The Penguin dictionary of quotations* (London, 1960), 80:18 and 155:27.

[55] See Introduction, p. 91.

was no need for the services even of a blind guide. Little could have been seen in any case through the low windows of the saloon, and very soon nothing at all, for they were steamed up by our breath, the only form of heating, and veiled by tobacco smoke. After a while the colonel, shivering on deck in his British warm,[56] could stand it no longer: he prescribed central heating in the form of tea and ordered the steersman to put across the river to Königswinter on the east bank. I knew that tea was most improbable and the fact certain that this place was out of bounds, that is beyond the British zone of occupation. But orders is orders and we landed. The noisy and informal incursion of such a large party in khaki spread alarm and despondency in the little village: was the war starting again? I stopped to reassure the first people we met and by that time the little inn by the waterside had been invaded and almost overwhelmed. There was, of course, no actual tea but the girls worked hard to produce some kind of hot brew and to mobilize every available drinking vessel, cheered on by the good-hearted banter of their guests. We clubbed together enough marks to pay them handsomely.

A good many men preferred to take their ease in the inn, some, I fancy, undertook a noisy fatigue of washing-up. The colonel asked me to conduct a party of walkers to the top of the Drachenfels, one of the most striking of the ruined castles, which was perched on a crag above us. Near the beginning of the ascent, I remember, there is a fine country house, and two of the subalterns in our party determined to see the inside of it. I tried to dissuade them, for we were only on sufferance upon this ground, but they strode up the drive and rang the bell while we looked on. The lordliest of family butlers opened the door – and shut it in their faces, as he had every right to do. We reached the 'Dragon Rock' but it was too cold to linger long, came down, collected our party and boarded our ship. Now it was smiling faces and waving hands and *Auf Wiedersehen*! that we left behind in Königswinter as we set off down the Rhine. I cannot claim that our outing had any educational value – except in its demonstration of good behaviour on the part of both guests and hosts, and that is no small part of true culture – but at least, in the commonest *cliché*, a good time was had by all.

On one of the first days after arrival we three went into a fine-looking restaurant to seek an eatable lunch – for we were not yet on anyone's 'strength' for army rations. As we sat waiting two small children, white-faced and very hungry, flattened their noses against the plate-glass window to watch other people eat. At this a bald-headed business man, lunching at the table next to ours, spread his newspaper on his knee, tipped the whole contents of the plate before him into it, paid his bill and thrust the crumpled newspaper into one of the children's eager hands; unfed himself he strode rapidly away. It was not everyone who shared thus with his nearest unknown neighbour, for Germans, for all their sentimental professions, are too often ruthless towards each other.

---

[56] A short, double-breasted greatcoat. M. Chappell, *The British army in World War I (1) The Western Front 1914–16* (Oxford, 2003), p. 38.

LETTERS

CROWBURY,
HERTFORD
June 5th 1915.

My dearest Mother,

I have owed you a letter for a long time, I fear. I am here, at Crowbury, for the day: I came down this morning and have to get back tonight for our OBM Corporate Communion tomorrow. Rachel is looking much better and David is splendid. He smiles for minutes on end now and makes all sorts of queer noises and chuckles. Rachel and he are staying on here for a bit, and he is to be vaccinated this week probably. I get down as a rule for Wednesday night and for the weekends.

I don't know that there is much real news. We are getting quite interested in Zeppelins in London and people are to be seen staring up at the sky after dark.[1] The last raid did very little damage considering, though not all the facts have been published, I fancy. The damage was in a limited area – Shoreditch, and I hear today that bombs were dropped on Blackheath early this morning. It may be mere gossip. I am providing the household with gas masks but beyond that I don't see one can do much, unless it be to furnish the cellar with comfortable chairs!

As to work – the 'Challenge'[2] makes demands on about two strenuous days a week and the rest I could, without difficulty, devote to something else. I am therefore looking for some war work of *any* kind. I don't want to join the army yet until David is on his feet, though every recruiting office is a temptation. I have been offered a civilian job in Rouen [*sic*]– to run a club for British officers at the Base – but don't feel that a fit man of military age would be in quite a fair position there. If possible I shall get a job in London and write for the Challenge on Sundays. There are several possibilities, for I know people in the War Office and Board of Trade. Like many civilians I am very restless just now.

The OBM gets emptier of older members (about 300 have joined the army and navy) but keeps very full of small boys. We hear often from the members on service and in almost every letter they say how much they think of the club and hope it is going strong. We *must* therefore keep it all going for them as much as for the boys with us now. The 22nd London have been in action again and have had a few casualties.[3] Alec is in a convalescent hospital in France with jaundice, they say, but no one seems to know his address.

The war seems critical enough but very hopeful on the whole. The worst setback is Russia at the moment, though most people have great faith in them in the long run. Italy has started well and Rumania is on the very edge.[4] America? Who knows? Probably they are a good deal more useful to us as neutrals than as allies. The chief point, as far as England is concerned, is that we are waking up. The slacker is going to have a rotten time of it soon.

Did you see the discussion at the Friends' Yearly Meeting? 215 Friends have joined the army and the Society is very worried about its proper course of action with regard to them. Any way they don't seem to be going to turn them out at present.[5]

I don't know that there is much more to say. Lady Lytton has just been in to tea and talked every thing out of my head.[6]

I do hope you are not overdoing yourself again. Love to all,

Ever your loving son

Barclay

---

[1] Zeppelin raids against England commenced in January 1915. A total of fifty-seven raids were made and they resulted in nearly 2,000 casualties. M. Brown, *The Imperial War Museum book of the First World War* (London, 1991), pp. 220–3.

[2] See Introduction, pp. 8–9.

[3] See Introduction, p. 10.

[4] The Russians were being pushed back by the Germans and Austro-Hungarians in Galicia (the Austro-Hungarian fortress city of Przemysl was retaken on 3 June) and the Italians (who had entered the war on 24 May) had crossed the Austrian frontier, making some small territorial gains. Rumania would not enter the war on the Allied side until 27 August 1916. Remarkably, Baron omitted to mention Turkey's frustration of the Allied attempt to force the Dardanelles. R. Gray and C. Argyle (eds.), *Chronicle of the First World War*, I: *1914–1916* (New York, 1990), *passim.*

[5] As patriots and former Quakers, the Barons were naturally interested in wartime developments among the pacifist Society of Friends. In the event, Quaker responses to the war were uneven and one third of all male Quakers of military age enlisted. A. Wilkinson, *Dissent or conform? War, peace and the English churches 1900–1945* (London, 1986), p. 53.

[6] A reference to Edith, widow of the second Baron Lytton, a former Viceroy of India. *ODNB.*

On Active Service
WITH THE BRITISH EXPEDITIONARY FORCE

75 Boulevard de Strasbourg.
Havre
France   Aug. 18th 1915

My dearest Mother,

Thank you very much for your letter. I am here at last. I crossed last night and
had the smoothest passage imaginable. The boat was crammed with officers – a
record load, I believe, and there were only about a dozen civilians. I got on board
at Southampton just after 10 p.m. but we did not start till dawn and got in at
10.30 this morning.

A good deal of yesterday afternoon was spent in getting my passport
stamped at the French consulate in London (by three different men with six
different stamps) and a good deal of this afternoon I spent in getting my papers
and permits to be allowed to exist in Havre at all. The number of papers and
formalities has trebled since I was over before – and the time wasted over getting
things signed is stupendous. They tell me that sometimes men have waited the
best part of a day and a half at the French Consulate for passport *visès* and I came
over with a YMCA worker, a Scotchman, who has had to wait *five weeks* in
London for his military permit to be signed! However here I am.

The officers' club in the Valley is definitely off. I have just been supping
with the senior chaplain[1] who is very savage about it. An officers' club is to be
started in the Town however, and I spent the rest of this afternoon going over the
house which has been taken for it. It is a large house in a good garden, a typical
French house, overdecorated in parts but roomy. The drains are indescribably odd
and would pass no sanitary authority in England. However with a little trouble we
shall make a really good thing of it. A large Institute has also been taken by [the]
YMCA in the town for a club for men.[2] A large number of men get passes from
the camps every day and have nowhere particular to go – with bad results at
times. Don't be afraid that I shan't have enough to do here!

I must not write more at the moment. I hope you will have Rachel and
David next week. Keep them as long as you can: I like to think of them with
you. It was hard work leaving them yesterday. I will write again soon when
there is more to say.

Ever your loving son,

Barclay.

---

[1]   The unity of the Army Chaplains' Department in the BEF was sundered in July 1915 with the
     appointment of Bishop Gwynne as deputy chaplain-general, an appointment that led to the
     creation of parallel 'C of E' and 'non-C of E' branches of the Department on the Western Front.
     The date of Baron's letter and his simple reference to a senior chaplain suggests that the process
     of disaggregation was not far advanced at this stage. M. Snape, *The Royal Army Chaplains'
     Department 1796–1953: clergy under fire* (Woodbridge, 2008), pp. 187–8, 193–4, 196.
[2]   See Introduction, p. 41.

On Active Service
WITH THE BRITISH EXPEDITIONARY FORCE

75 Boulevard de Strasbourg.
Havre
France.   Sept. 28th 1915

My dearest Mother,

I have a bare ten minutes before I go out on my Tuesday journey in a car round
the 'Docks Area.' We have five huts there, one of which is Cinder City, my late
home. I am supposed to keep a general eye on the lot. This afternoon and
evening I shall be at the YM Central Hall in town and one never knows whether
or not there will be time for letter writing.

The news is exciting but so far scanty.[1] You know just as much as we do
here, though you don't see wounded men and German prisoners as we do.
There have been preparations in the hospitals here which hinted to us that
something was up and I have seen one or two men straight from the front who
tell of the small bit of the show which they saw. This week will be an anxious
and, I fear, a very costly one in life. There are rumours as to our casualties but
there is no good whatever in being moved by rumours.

As Rachel may have told you I was asked last week if I would go to our
advanced places up the line and I should love to have gone.[2] What seems to
happen is that a YM man is put into a French village to shift as well as he can.
The army when possible gets his stores up to him and he waits for work. At any
hour of the day or night troops, tired and hungry, may come through and he has
to feed them as well as he can. Serving thousands of men and washing up and
cooking by oneself is very hard work indeed and the life, they say, is very
lonely. But what can we do? We are understaffed for the winter and work
constantly increases.

Dearest love to Rachel, David and all of you.

Ever your loving son

Barclay

---

[1] Baron was writing at the height of the battle of Loos (25 September–15 October 1915), the largest
British offensive of that year on the Western Front, which had commenced three days earlier.
Entrusted to Haig's First Army, the initial attack went reasonably well in its southern sector but
early gains were not exploited and the offensive failed to achieve the intended breakthrough.
British casualties were around 60,000 (compared to 20,000 German) and the battle was to prove
the undoing of Sir John French, the first commander-in-chief of the BEF. T. Wilson, *The myriad
faces of war: Britain and the Great War* (Cambridge, 1988), pp. 251–65; R. Holmes (ed.), *The
Oxford companion to military history* (Oxford, 2001), p. 518; *Statistics of the military effort of the
British Empire during the Great War 1914–1920* (London, 1922), p. 640.

[2] See Introduction, pp. 46–7. This statement contradicts Baron's claim at the beginning of Chapter 2
that the YMCA was not admitted into army areas until 1917.

WITH THE BRITISH EXPEDITIONARY FORCE.
POSTAL ADDRESS   HEAD QUARTERS
YMCA   75, BOULEVARD DE STRASBOURG
C/O ARMY POST OFFICE No. 1   HAVRE
BRITISH EXPEDITIONARY FORCE

May 28th 1916.

My Dearest Mother,

It is a shamefully long time since I wrote to you – in fact I doubt if I have written
since I was home on leave. The days are very full here and pass very quickly –
though not more so, I expect than your own.

On the whole I think our work in Havre goes well. The staff is mostly
very good indeed and never shirks work. It is not easy to get really first-rate
men naturally but some of the most unpromising turn out really useful workers
before they go home. The real difficulty is that as soon as a man who is only
out for three months has got into full swing it is time for him to go home
again. The ladies on the whole stay out longer than the men and some refuse
to take leave until they are really worn right out, for continuous work in a
camp is very hard when it means facing the continual smoke and noise of
crowds of soldiers, the mud and wind of the winter and the heat, dust and flies
of the hot weather.

I often wish you and the 'girls' could be here. You would all simply *love* it
and be most useful. If the war goes on a few years more, perhaps one or other of
you could do three months with us! Not that I suppose that the war will go on for
years more, but I see quite clearly that even if peace came tomorrow we could not
leave our work here this year. So much has passed through here and so much
must pass back through here again (not to mention the vast establishment of men
and goods and buildings at a base like this all the time) that it will take a great
time to clear the place up and leave it tidy for the French.

I can't give you any details naturally but I should like to show you some of
it enormously. The real difficulty I foresee when the war is over is the impatience
of men to get home – both soldiers and our own workers. Everyone will be
simply 'fed up'. The strain and excitement will be gone. The fear of death will no
more hang over our men as it does now. In this restless and homesick crowd after
the war the YM simply must go on working.[1] And with such workers as will be
able or ready to stay behind instead of going home. However our hands are full
enough at the moment and the future will provide for itself.

I am watching the building of two new YM huts (in addition to the 20 we
have in Havre already) and shall have to staff and open them within a week or ten
days. There is no standing still. The more I go on with this job, the more I am
certain that it must be gone on with. There are half a dozen of us men especially
exempted for YM work: the rest are a floating and very mixed population. It is
vital, I feel, that the half dozen should stay to supply the slender permanent

element among short service clergy, medically rejected men and ladies. Any feeling of difficulty I had about not joining the army has gone, for hardly a day passes but officers and men tell me how urgently they want us here.

The APM (head of the Military Police and an official of extraordinary powers under military law as we all are) tells me I am to stay here in charge and that the general wishes the same. The authorities have been watching us very carefully, demanding reports and returns on all sorts of subjects and the APM has several times lately said to me 'How is it that I don't see your people about the town?' or 'How is it that your ladies never seem to ask for passes to go to Trouville or elsewhere for the day, like the coffee stall ladies[2] here?' To which the answer is 'Because we have no time for promenading here or in Trouville.'

I *do* feel often that one lives too comfortably at our Headquarters where we have a marvel of a housekeeper, but when I see our Stores staff come in to supper after a tremendous day and our half dozen lady chauffeurs who have been on their cars, driving, cleaning, repairing from 9 a.m. to 10.30 p.m.[3] I think that good food and a proper chair pays. My own work is some days actually very heavy and continuous with scarcely a moment's quiet, and on others much slacker – but the real burden of it all the time is the anxiety of keeping such a big scattered business in running order. I have got three or four first class men at headquarters now, Pilkington tried to do it alone and completely broke himself in the attempt, but even so the ultimate responsibility is mine.

There is never a day without trouble actual or impending in some camp. It may be shortage of staff or a misunderstanding with the military authorities or some personal irritation between workers themselves. We are a very mixed crowd and the very best of us don't always hit it off with others. It calls for constant tact and more judgment than I sometimes have. I spent two hours last night for instance straightening out a personal misunderstanding at No 1 Camp. That meant removing two ladies to the Bakeries – five or six miles away, and incidentally moving a man on from the Bakeries to Annexe J in order that the man now at Annexe J may be free to move five miles away to Remounts to take the place of a leader who goes tomorrow.[4] And *his* second man in turn wrote me an indignant and rather foolish letter (he is a *very* young parson) to complain that he had not been relieved before. That means a visit to Remounts this afternoon and a thorough 'strafing' for the young parson from me. So that one part of this unwieldy machine depends on another and one can't move in one place without calculating the effect on other places.

This may seem dull and trivial work – it *is* occasionally – but unless it is constantly done and done right the spirit in huts gets wrong and work is spoilt badly. Soldiers are the first to know whether the staff of a hut is going right or not. If it is they will come to us for every conceivable – and inconceivable – kind of help and advice. If it is not we are worse than useless to them. The social, intellectual, spiritual impetus in many a camp here has to come *entirely* from the YMCA hut. (I know that is the sort of thing that rather offensive YM advertisements are always saying – but if you were here you would see that it is mere truth.) And so we have to live publicly and privately on a level which is very hard to reach and maintain. There are plenty of failures and some astonishing successes.

I feel sometimes as if not the least of the uses of the YM is as a mission to the clergy of all denominations. I have seen idle and backboneless and pompous ministers turned into respectable men here in three months – with a new biceps and a totally new idea of service and of the meaning of the Gospel of Christ for hungry men. One of our ladies the other day said to me 'I used to think I led a healthy and useful life' (she is the wife of a country gentleman with plenty of money) 'until I came here. Now I know that I have never done a stroke of work for any one in my life. I can never go back to pottering about the village and opening country bazaars.' That is a common enough case and no doubt you have seen it happen to women doing war work of any kind. If only this new thing can last after the war![5]

Sometimes I look around our Headquarters dinner table – crammed as it is at 1 o'clock, with 25 or 30 noisy people and wonder if we shall ever meet again after the war. A lady who is 'somebody' at home in her own place sits next to old Burr, late London 'bus driver, a canon of Newcastle cracks uproarious jokes with a Baptist straw hat merchant's son, an Australian tradesman's daughter carries on a most solemn argument with the principal of Aberdeen University.[6] (These are actual cases I happened to notice yesterday.) And all without the faintest sign of self consciousness about 'solving the Social Problem' or any such stuff. We are simply one because we share the same work, the same hopes, the same fatigues every day together. It makes one hope.

But this letter is getting dangerously long and dull. I have told you nothing about the visit of the Princess Victoria[7] to us last week (I had three days of trotting round with her, got a stiff neck with bowing, and spent half a day in bed in a state of collapse.) Other news there is of course but some I cannot tell you and the rest I must defer. We don't know really much more than you do at home but we like to write imperiously, some of us (I censor letters and therefore know) as if we were in the inner councils of the commander in chief!

The wrist watch goes perfectly and is a great boon.

Thanks very much for the paper with Father's excellent speech.

Thanks again and again for letters which are very welcome.

I am *so* glad you found David so splendid. He *is*.

When is Father's mayoral photograph coming?

Dear love to all,

Ever your loving son

Barclay.

[1] Baron's fears were well founded. Indiscipline was rife among impatient British soldiers awaiting demobilization in France in the months following the Armistice. R. Holmes, *Tommy: the British soldier on the Western Front 1914–18* (London, 2004), p. 347.

[2] See Introduction, p. 42.

[3] This appears to be a reference to the female drivers of the YMCA's visitation scheme for the relatives of badly wounded soldiers. See Introduction, p. 70.

[4] Baron's reference to Bakeries and to Remounts (both the responsibility of the ASC) underlines the size and the complex organization of the BEF's base areas. *Statistics of the military effort of the British Empire*, pp. 181–4.

[5] The exigencies of war saw a 'feminization of the work force' in several belligerent countries, including Britain, France and Germany. However, expectations that this would permanently change patterns of work and family relations proved illusory. Pre-war patterns of employment were largely restored after the war; in Britain, for example, a smaller percentage of the female population was employed in 1921 than had been the case a decade earlier. G. Braydon, 'Women, war, and work', in *The Oxford illustrated history of the First World War*, ed. H. Strachan (Oxford, 1998), pp. 149–62; J. M. Winter (ed.), *The experience of World War I* (London, 2006), pp. 173–5; Wilson, *Myriad faces of war*, pp. 714–22.

[6] A reference to D. S. Cairns, who was in France at this time. See Introduction, p. 78.

[7] Princess Victoria Alexandra Olga Mary (1868–1935) was the fourth child of King Edward VII and a younger sister of King George V (who made no fewer than five visits to the Western Front during the course of the war). A spinster of a rather delicate constitution, her genuine philanthropy marked an otherwise undistinguished life. *Times*, 4 December 1935, p. 19; J. M. Bourne (ed.), *Who's who in World War One* (London, 2001), pp. 104–5.

ARUNDEL HOTEL,
VICTORIA EMBANKMENT,
LONDON, WC

Sunday[1]

My dearest Mother,

Here we still are – and no positive news of my permit yet! It is very aggravating
to think that I might have stayed on in Devon with David and you. William and
Freda[2] met Rachel and me for lunch today and we spent the afternoon in
Kensington Gardens. We all went to see Gerald du Maurier in 'The Old Country'
last night [3] – a very charming sort of a play. We had not been in long before the
raid started. Rachel and I had just gone to bed when guns began. So we got up
and joined the rest of the hotel which was wandering about in various states of
attire. People's calmness was quite absurd. Rachel dressed fairly well but put on a
hat under which her hair hung down in pig tails behind. I put on an overcoat and
a pair of slippers and stayed to brush my hair rather nicely. We went out into the
street and strolled about. After a few minutes I went up to fetch my cigarette case
as it seemed likely to be a longish job. We heard the guns a long way off and then
nearer and saw the sharp stab of shrapnel bursting in the sky and the glare of a
bomb falling. There was a longish interval of silence and then the searchlights
near us lit up and raked the sky. We were not quite sure if we saw a Zepp or not.
Another burst of distant firing and then silence, except for the trams which ran
unconcernedly the whole time, and the bell of a fire engine. We heard rumours
that a Zepp was down but did not then believe it.

Freda and William *saw* the thing fall, we found today, and are very envious.
If they come again tonight we have promised to meet them if possible to share
the honour of seeing the whole drama!

I may get off tomorrow or Tuesday or next week or next month. I shall go at
the first possible moment, as things are rather extra busy in Havre just now.

The Londons had a bad cutting up last week and did marvels.[4] Mrs
Woodward had a long letter about it from Wooder who is one of their chaplains.[5]
He was burying their dead for 14 hours and also had to do the work of an
ordinary officer owing to the casualties. Willie Newton,[6] who is adjutant of the
21st London, has been seriously wounded.

I must not write more as I have to go to Bermondsey tonight. Rachel is
rather tired and is resting.

I will write a line before I go.

With love to you, Father and Muriel[7]

Ever your loving son,

Barclay

1   Undated. In view of its contents, probably Sunday 8 October 1916.
2   Baron's sisters. Freda was the eldest and Vera, the youngest, was nicknamed 'William'.
3   Gerald du Maurier (1873–1934) was a leading theatre manager and stage actor who was knighted in 1922. Dion Calthrop's play *The old country* was first performed at Wyndham's Theatre in September 1916, with Du Maurier in the part of James Lane Fountain. *ODNB*; *Times*, 4 September 1916, p. 11, and 12 April 1934, p. 17.
4   In the first week of October 1916 the 47th (London) Division was involved in severe fighting on the Somme. Its 142nd Brigade, which included the 21st and 22nd London Regiment, suffered heavy losses in an attack near Eaucourt l'Abbaye on the day this letter was written. C. McCarthy, *The Somme: the day-by-day account* (London, 1995), p. 133.
5   This is a reference to Clifford Salisbury Woodward (1878–1959), who was ordained priest in 1903 after training at Wycliffe Hall, Oxford. A lecturer at Wycliffe Hall and chaplain of Wadham College from 1910 to 1913, he maintained strong links with Bermondsey, having visited the OMM as an undergraduate and having been one of its residents while serving as a curate at Bermondsey parish church from 1902 to 1905. After his spell at Oxford, where he had been active in the Oxford pastorate, Woodward returned to south London in 1913 when he became rector of St Saviour with St Thomas, Southwark. Following a wartime ministry in which he was noted for holding public prayers in his parish during Zeppelin raids, he was commissioned into the Army Chaplains' Department in 1916 and won the MC while serving with the 47th Division. Woodward's citation read: 'He tended and brought in wounded under very heavy shell fire, and continued this gallant work for thirty hours without stopping. He showed an utter disregard for danger, and gave confidence and relief to many.' However, in October 1916 Woodward was wounded and returned to England. Convalescing in Oxford, he reflected how 'I little thought in my undergraduate days that I should live to be carried into Oxford in pyjamas, or become an inmate of a ladies' college, but, thanks to Fritz and his little whiz-bangs, I have achieved both distinctions.' Woodward went on to become bishop of Bristol in 1933 and bishop of Gloucester in 1946. *Crockford's*, 1913, pp. 1677–8, and 1920, p. 1677; Church Missionary Society Archives, University of Birmingham, XCMS ACC/18/Z/1 Army Book of L. H. Gwynne, p. 273; *Times*, 15 April 1959, p. 15; B. Baron, *The doctor: the story of John Stansfeld of Oxford and Bermondsey* (London, 1952), pp. 30 and 161.
6   William G. Newton was another stalwart of the OBM and would later become a leading architect. Baron, *The doctor*, pp. 167 and 196.
7   Muriel was the second of the three Baron girls.

YMCA WITH THE BRITISH EXPEDITIONARY FORCE.
HAVRE ADMINISTRATIVE DISTRICT

HEAD QUARTERS: POSTAL ADDRESS
75, Boulevard de   YMCA
Strasbourg   C/O BAPO 1.[1]
HAVRE.   BEF

Barclay BARON,
General Secretary

13/10/16

My Dearest Mother,

Thanks very much for your letter just arrived. You *do* seem to be busy every day, but the great variety of things – serious and comic – must make life very interesting for you.

I am glad you are meeting Miss Lena Ashwell again. Her last tour here while I was away was a triumphant success. We have one of her parties here now and another, I have heard from her secretary today, is due on the 28th. The men are tremendously keen about these concerts and there is no shadow of a doubt as to the good her work is doing.[2] Miss Ashwell is a good speaker and a really good woman.

There is not much particular news here. Charlie Thompson is lying wounded in hospital in Havre just now.[3] He is getting on all right, I think. He is now an officer of course. He rose very quickly to be sergeant major and was then pressed to take a commission. I have just wired to the OBM about him as they seem very anxious. I saw Newton in hospital in London just before I came away – with wounds in both arms and both legs, only of much consequence in the left arm. He is adjutant of battalion and has done very well indeed. David Woodward is chaplain of the same battalion.[4] Also saw Basil Henriques home wounded after taking his 'tank' into action: only very slight wounds in the face.[5]

Here we are very short of staff but things are gradually improving. There is the usual crop of small crises – several breakdowns of workers, one secretly engaged couple whom I have to give good advice to(!), some cases of square pegs in round holes, some private quarrels and a certain number of grousers – but it all comes out pretty straight in the end with patience.

This is going to be a heavy winter for us just because it is going to be so for the men. Up the line our places are more and more besieged by men and it is hard to keep them staffed. Single workers have to wrestle with thousands. You can guess how the work at the front has developed when I tell you that this time last year about half the goods passing through our Stores at Havre were for us, the other half for the huts in the Armies at the Front. Today 9/10 almost exactly of the goods through Havre are for the Armies and 1/10 for Havre (and Havre is a good deal bigger than it was then). Last Sunday our few men at the

Stores unloaded 160 tons of goods in the day off transports, and the value of goods for the armies handled by us in Havre is 2,000,000 francs a month now. These are some figures out of many – *not* for publication but of interest. I should like to get up to the front this winter – I often long to pack a bag and go off at a moment's notice – but I expect I shall have to stick here. It is not easy to shuffle off a job like this when one has been in it a year and more and knows the ropes, which are many. We are always badly wanted at the base and someone has got to stay.

I had a glorious last weekend with Rachel and David at Woolacombe but it seems a very long time ago now. One gets caught by the old daily job very soon again. It is full of variety and I could want no work much more interesting – which, I shouldn't wonder, is what you may say of yours.

My love to Father, Freda and Muriel – all busy as they can well be, no doubt.

Ever your loving son,

Barclay.

---

[1]   British Army Post Office. The army's postal service was the responsibility of the postal sections of the Royal Engineers. Their task was prodigious; by the end of 1916 more than 10 million letters and 100,000 parcels were being handled each week. On the Western Front, where the service was generally quite efficient, mail was channelled through a system of postal depôts and army, base and divisional post offices. A. Rawson, *British army handbook 1914–1918* (Stroud, 2006), pp. 157–8; C. Messenger, *Call-to-arms: the British army 1914–18* (London, 2005), pp. 436–9.

[2]   See Introduction, p. 44.

[3]   Charlie Thompson was one of Baron's fellow workers at the OBM. B. Baron, *The birth of a movement 1919–1922* (London, 1946), p. 4.

[4]   See above p. 223, n. 5. At this stage of the war it was common for two Anglican chaplains to be found in each brigade of an 'English' division; this meant that two infantry battalions shared the same chaplain. It seems likely that Woodward was responsible for the 21st and 22nd London Regiment, two of the four battalions of 142nd Brigade. Snape, *The Royal Army Chaplains' Department*, p. 218.

[5]   Basil Lucas Quixano Henriques (1890–1961) was educated at Harrow School and at University College, Oxford. While at Oxford he was heavily influenced by Alec Paterson and became involved in the OBM. Very much part of Britain's liberal Jewish establishment, Henriques found his vocation in social work among immigrant eastern European Jews in the East End, work that he saw as aiding their assimilation. He opened his first boys' club in March 1914 and enlisted in The Buffs (East Kent Regiment) in 1915. In 1916, and by now an officer, Henriques transferred to the Machine Gun Corps (Heavy Section), subsequently renamed the Tank Corps, and participated in the first tank attack around Flers that September. He returned, much decorated, to his pioneering work in the East End after the war where, as a social worker and a magistrate, he became a prominent local figure. *ODNB*; *Times*, 4 December 1961, p. 15; Rawson, *British army handbook*, pp. 119–20.

YMCA WITH THE BRITISH EXPEDITIONARY FORCE.
HAVRE ADMINISTRATIVE DISTRICT

HEAD QUARTERS: POSTAL ADDRESS:
75, Boulevard de   YMCA
Strasbourg   C/O BAPO 1.
HAVRE.   BEF

Barclay BARON,
General Secretary

Dec. 20th 1916.

My dearest Mother,

It is a terrible long interval since my last letter to you. The days are wonderfully busy now – as busy almost as yours. We are rather short handed again on account of people ill, people leaving and some new red tape which has temporarily blocked my applications for passes for workers. The other day I found myself saying aloud 'Bound with red tape about the feet of war' and recollected with a start that I was parodying Tennyson's 'Bound with gold chains about the feet of God'![1]

Work steadily increases. I began to think that Havre had about reached its limit of new work but four or five new huts are in immediate prospect. One of these – 35 miles away in the middle of a huge forest – is now being built and I am off this afternoon in a car to see how things are going there. This is the most absorbing work I have ever found, outside Bermondsey, and indeed it is so much a continuation of ten years in Bermondsey that I feel it is a true part of it. The same spirit is needed for both and this is just the OBM on a huge scale.

Thank you so very much for Eden Phillpotts's book[2] (which I ought to have acknowledged a long time ago) and for the delicious illumination of T. E. Brown's 'Garden.'[3] I am writing to the 'girls' but shan't have time today.

I sent off a very little parcel a few days ago and hope you will get it all right. It is just some little things made by French wounded. Nothing valuable (for money is scarce this Christmas) but rather interesting.[4]

But now I must be off to the police for a motor pass etc.

Love to all at home,

Ever your loving son,

Barclay.

---

[1]   From Tennyson's 'Morte d'Arthur'.
[2]   Eden Phillpotts (1862–1960) was a popular novelist, poet and playwright whose best-known novels and short stories were centred on Dartmoor. *ODNB*.
[3]   T. E. Brown (1830–97) was a clergyman, poet and former master at Clifton College. *ODNB*; *Times*, 30 December 1960, p. 11.
[4]   The First World War generated vast numbers of wounded and the French army's non-fatal casualties ran into millions. The manufacture of knick-knacks such as boxes, picture frames and embroideries by such victims of the war was widely held to have economic and therapeutic value. N. J. Saunders, *Trench art: a brief history and guide, 1914–1939* (Barnsley, 2001), pp. 34–6.

YMCA WITH THE BRITISH EXPEDITIONARY FORCE.
HAVRE ADMINISTRATIVE DISTRICT

HEAD QUARTERS: POSTAL ADDRESS:
75, Boulevard de   YMCA
Strasbourg   C/O BAPO 1.
HAVRE.   BEF

Barclay BARON,
General Secretary

21/12/16.

My dearest Mother,

I don't know quite when this letter will reach you – for the post is a little upset at the moment. C'est la guerre!

I must not attempt to write a real letter tonight as I am in the throes of Christmas correspondence; it is nearly midnight and I have to be on the Quay tomorrow morning at 6.30. All I will say tonight is to wish you and all at home a very happy Christmas (yes, why not *happy*?) and a happier New Year.

In front of me as I write lies a very beautiful Christmas card from the YMCA round about Ypres. It just bears the legend 'Words fail us!' and that is merely the truth this Christmas. That sentence seems to me to cover all our sorrow and also all our strange and deep exaltation of spirit at this time. These are unmistakeably terrible days but also unspeakably grand. I often say, from the platform, to soldiers 'The war has shown us the Devil in men – in ourselves as well as in our enemy. War has also shown us, what many of us never suspected, God in men also! Let that be clear, as it becomes every day clearer to me, and what is there not possible for our chastened world in the future?'

It is going to be a strange Christmas Day – blood and crime and mud that drowns men body and soul – and a little child in the midst of us, the new life born again in the hearts of men in distress. I was never so hopeful about us all as now. What I feel (and *everyone* seems to feel the same) is that between Blighty and France there is a strange difference. At home men and women, from all one hears and reads, are caught by the horror of the war and the poverty that is to come, because they have not the same sort of excitement which keeps us going out here, even at a distant base like this. Even here one sees enough of wounds and death and almost worst disasters such as men being 'fed up' and losing their souls. But still one feels something great in it all. I think you have a much harder task at home – trying always to be cheerful and steadfast. My own trouble sometimes – nay, often – is rather that I am *too* happy in my work and have to ask myself and others who feel the same in our little community (how like the OBM it is in this as in other things!) whether one *ought* to be happy at all at such a time.

But what a rigmarole! I must really not run on to another sheet. A happy Christmas again with all my love – and let us thank God together that we live in this awful earthquake through which the still small Voice seems sometimes to speak so clear.[1]

Ever your loving

Barclay.

---

[1] An allusion to the fourth and final verse of 'Dear Lord and Father of Mankind' by the American Quaker John Greenleaf Whittier (1807–92).

YMCA WITH THE BRITISH EXPEDITIONARY FORCE.
HAVRE ADMINISTRATIVE DISTRICT

HEAD QUARTERS: POSTAL ADDRESS:
75, Boulevard de   YMCA
Strasbourg   C/O BAPO 1.
HAVRE.   BEF

Barclay BARON,
General Secretary

21/1/17.

My dearest Mother,

Many thanks for several letters. Things with you seem as busy as ever. I hope very much that the National Mission in Bristol is taking hold: I feel much afraid that on the whole it is rather a failure after all the expectation there was.[1] It is supposed to be going on among the troops in France all this month but I see and hear nothing much of it. Offers of help that we made here were just coldly refused by the chaplains which seems to me a great pity.[2]

Great changes are going on in our work at Havre. My two best men at Headquarters have been taken for very big and difficult jobs at the front – Macdonald as YMCA secretary in the 3rd Army and Reade in the 4th. This means that they must create out of practically nothing an organization for masses of troops in the awful shell-smashed mud of the fighting area. Materials, transport, staff are all practically non-existent for them.

We have a great scheme on hand to connect Havre with Abbeville and so on to the armies – a chain of close communication for men and stores. I feel that I shall soon move from here and get further up – probably to Abbeville (though this is *entirely unofficial*). I want to reorganize things there on the lines of this place and I believe I could do it. I shall have some of my best men and women up very soon – among them, I hope, Vera and Will Clift![3] There are some difficult problems there, partly as usual in connexion with the ladies (I have had my fair share of these in Havre) and there is an immense amount of new work to be done all round that district and one of the most interesting in the whole war area.

I think I have been here long enough and ought not to settle down too much. One difficulty is to find a successor but I think I have got the man. He is starting tomorrow to take over a big lump of my work.

Before I move – if I do – I shall come home for a fortnight's leave. I begin to feel that I need a breathing space. Life here is of course a continual scramble from one thing to another for seven days a week. Today I have given myself the slackest day for months.

Rachel writes me splendid accounts of David and his doings and sayings. He is becoming a ripping boy and I long to see him tremendously. I hope he will get down to see you before long: you would enjoy him so much, I know.

When William has decided anything about France I shall look forward to hearing very much. I do hope for her sake and ours she will come. At Abbeville she would be a great help and if she were here first for a month or so she could get into all our ways.

Dearest love to all,

Ever your loving son,

Barclay

PS Do go and see Miss Grace Inskip, one of the finest women we have ever had in Havre. She is back now at Clifton Park House.

---

[1] The National Mission of Repentance and Hope was launched by the archbishops of Canterbury and York in the autumn of 1916. Led at home by the bishop of London, A. F. Winnington Ingram, the mission was inspired from several quarters in the Church of England and, though variously understood even among leading churchmen, it essentially aimed to capitalize on the opportunity presented by the war to address both church and nation to their fundamental religious needs. However, in view of its inherent confusion, sombre tone and uncertain impact, it was widely criticized by churchmen and secular commentators alike. D. Thompson, 'War, the nation and the kingdom of God: the origins of the National Mission of Repentance and Hope, 1915–16', in *The church and war*, ed. W. J. Sheils, Studies in Church History, 20 (Oxford, 1983), pp. 337–50; S. P. Mews, 'Religion and English society in the First World War', Ph.D. dissertation, University of Cambridge, 1973, pp. 216–44; A. Wilkinson, *The Church of England and the First World War* (London, 1978), pp. 70–9.

[2] A statement that indicates ongoing tensions between Anglican chaplains and the YMCA at this stage of the war. The National Mission on the Western Front was in fact carefully prepared by Bishop Gywnne and his senior chaplains from June 1916. Planning was preceded by a visit from the archbishop of Canterbury, Randall Davidson, that May and its chosen 'Messengers' included G. A. Studdert Kennedy, the celebrated 'Woodbine Willie'. Museum of Army Chaplaincy, Amport House, Andover, 'Proceedings of ACGs' Conferences', 6–7 June 1916, 17–18 August 1916, 28–9 November 1916; L. H. Gwynne, *Religion and morale: the story of the National Mission on the Western Front* (London, 1917), *passim*; D. F. Carey, 'Studdert Kennedy: war padre', in *G. A. Studdert Kennedy by his friends*, ed. J. K. Mozley (London, 1929), p. 125.

[3] A personal friend of Baron's. Barclay Baron to Jane Baron, 5 June 1914.

Barclay Baron
YMCA
c/o Town Major
Peronne
BEF
16/4/17.

My dearest Mother,

I am so sorry not to have written before. Life has been very crowded during the last week and spent in many places. At the moment I write (while waiting for breakfast) at Austin's headquarters in Amiens, where I have been made completely at home by his lieutenant, Brough.[1] Austin[2] is the supervising secretary of 3rd, 4th and 5th armies and is at present at home on leave after a spell in hospital with frost-bite and other legacies of the winter out here. Today I move my quarters to above address.

There is so much to say that it is hard to begin. I came here on my first arrival last Thursday week with McCowen. This is a fine city with a glorious cathedral. Do you know it?

On Good Friday (as was I think fitting), I had my first sight of the unspeakable desolation of the Somme battlefield. After a few miles of green and fertile country one gets into a land which is surely the biggest and ghastliest rubbish heap in history. As far as the eye can see the rolling hillsides are crossed by the white scars of trenches, once held by the Boche, now flattened and smashed by our gunfire. The whole surface of every field is literally turned inside out. The stones of the subsoil lie on the top: shell craters join one another. Woods are black and torn tangles of tree stumps and bare splintered branches. Coils and forests of rusted barbed wire straggle everywhere – in the distance like belts of russet bracken-fern. Some of the villages we pass through are just little piles of brick dust and ashes with here and there a solitary rafter standing on end. A kitchen range now stands for a man's home, a heap of white stones, three feet high, for his village church. Everywhere empty shell cases, shattered wheels, tin helmets and the tatters of sandbags round some bombed dug-out fill in the detail of the landscape. And singly in the middle of this forlorn country or in groups by the roadside white wooden crosses mark where our men or the enemy's lie.

As I caught my first sight of Mametz Wood with its tortured branches against the white storm clouds of April, and, as I stood beside Raymond Asquith's grave, I felt I was treading sacred ground – bought by the glory of England at a great price. In one village – now wiped off the map – I saw a tall fragment of the church wall and on it the life-sized, white figure of Christ upon the Cross. That was the only possible symbol – on this Good Friday – for the country in which it stood.[3]

In the afternoon I walked through the dead streets of Péronne. Not a whole house in a sweet old French town. Not a tree that the Germans have not hacked to death. Not a bridge or cross-road left without its bomb. We have been given a very fine house there for a YMCA – a real palace, and next door to it a house for our own billet. In the big building the Germans took up all the floor boards before they left, smashed every mirror, chopped beautiful woodwork with axes, bayoneted the few remaining pictures. There is not a single pane of glass of course and the top storey is too blown to pieces to be any use. In the garden there is a big bomb crater and a fine fruit tree – just budding and not yet dead – lies over on its side, sawn half way through and pushed over. In our billet the middle part of the staircase has been torn out and at present we enter from next door. All this can be made good enough for an excellent headquarters. I sent two men to get it ready– the first civilians into Péronne. They have laid floors from the mass of wreckage of other houses all round, covered the windows with canvas instead of glass, propped dangerous corners, boarded the shell holes in the walls. Tonight I hope to settle in.

This will make a fine centre from which to run all my work. The general[4] has asked for a YM Officers' Club in the town and I have secured an excellent house (minus the top storey which is mere matchwood now). I also hope to secure the municipal theatre for a cinema hall. The end wall is completely blown away and all the galleries wrecked but we will soon have that patched up. I am taking our cinema expert out today to survey it. Other work in Péronne itself is in prospect of which more later.

I can't tell you details of all our places in my area. There are about 9 or 10 running now but some of these are now too far back and must be shut for new ones to open in the rear of the advance. Huts are now hopeless: I am simply running up marquees which are easily moved and am contemplating horses and caravans to move with the troops. One new place opened last week – and sold out every ounce of stock in the first two hours. Another starts today. Four more have been asked for by the army and we cannot cope with the rapidity of the demand. Our job up here is quite on a different footing to the Base. I knew it was indispensable work for the army at Havre but not all the greater brass hats thought so. Up here one can walk into the offices of the army and be eagerly received, treated as an officer who has as real a job as any other in the field. As for the men – the appearance of my car with a red triangle on it in a new village causes quite a flutter: they all want to know how soon the YM will open. This is the sort of thing the YMCA at home is always saying in its rather nauseous advertisements but after all it is only sober truth. It is a tremendous joy – this job – but also a tremendous responsibility. However I am feeling very fit and have some fine men on my staff.

More later – Breakfast is sending a most seductive smell from the next room. It will be a very busy day for me. Good-bye for the moment.

Dearest love to all.

Ever your loving son,

Barclay

PS One enters Péronne by a wooden RE bridge, labelled in large letters
'Bristol Bridge'. Draw your own conclusion as to the kind of troops in the
town.

---

1   Joseph Brough had worked as a YMCA secretary in Nottingham and Burma since 1907. *Year book
    of the National Council of Young Men's Christian Associations of England, Ireland and Wales*,
    1914, p. 96.
2   William Austin commenced YMCA war work on the outbreak of war, working at Cardiff (August
    1914–January 1915) before serving in France (January 1915–August 1917) and in Italy (August
    1917–February 1919). *Year book of the National Council of Young Men's Christian Associations
    of England, Ireland and Wales (incorporated)*, 1921, p. 142.
3   Such reflections on the survival of wayside crosses and of crucifixes in derelict churches were
    commonplace among soldiers on the Western Front. M. F. Snape and S. G. Parker, 'Keeping faith
    and coping: belief, popular religiosity and the British people', in *The Great World War 1914–45*,
    II: *The peoples' experience*, ed. P. Liddle, J. Bourne and I. Whitehead (London, 2001), p. 414; M.
    Snape, *God and the British soldier: religion and the British army in the First and Second World
    Wars* (London, 2005), pp. 42–4.
4   Rawlinson.

29, RUE CAUMARTIN
PARIS LE *21/5/17.*

HOTEL ASTRA
PARIS
ADRESSE TÉLÉGRAPHIQUE
ASTRATEL-PARIS
TÉLÉPH. LOUVRE 11–25

My dearest Mother,

You will wonder at my strange address perhaps!

I planned anyway to come to Paris this week to see about renewing my passport at the British consulate and yesterday a YM car from our Abbeville headquarters called at Péronne and I heard that McCowen, my chief, was to be in Paris today – so at short notice I decided to come at once. I left Péronne at 7 last evening and arrived (with a broken back axle – not my car, thank goodness!) at Amiens at 11 in a heavy thunder storm. I ate an egg at our Station Hut and boarded the 1.30 a.m. for Paris: it started of course nearly an hour late. In company with two French workmen, two Belgian soldiers and two of our Guards officers I dozed and woke and talked and dozed till we reached Paris at 6 this morning. It rained all night, I think. Once I woke to hear the nightingale singing gloriously at a wayside station where we stopped (we stopped at *every* station I imagine) and once I stuck my head out of [the] window and got a whiff of lilac in bloom. The wet green woods early this morning were a joy after the desolation of the Somme and I had an eager talk with the Guards officers about the English countryside and English village pubs and the sounds and smells and green hedges of home. They knew of course many of the places I know in my present 'diocese' in France.

At this hotel I found McCowen's chauffer (a Sussex vicar, Jacomb Hood)[1] and then went out for a shave and shampoo to wake me up. McCowen arrived about 9 from Marseilles[2] whence he started at 4 yesterday afternoon. A busy morning. McCowen at the embassy, I at the consulate where I got my new passport without any trouble except having to be photographed again. It is now 5.30 and I am waiting for my car from Péronne which was busy in Amiens this morning and is due here tonight. We have to buy various motor parts which can only be found in Paris – if here. My driver by the way, Arundell,[3] is vicar of Cheriton Fitzpaine near Crediton and a very delightful man. Tomorrow we may have to go to Havre for new tyres (these Yankee things won't stand the roads at the front which are appalling).

Work is very pressing and extremely complicated for reasons which I cannot explain in a letter.[4] Sufficient to say that our plans have to be altered almost hourly. Telegrams, telephone messages or despatch riders bring me orders for new work suddenly and marquees, tons of stores, equipment and men have to be got on the move at once. Transport is exceedingly difficult to get for the army wants all it has just now and we are allowed none of our own. However we scratch along and work gets done. In the last six weeks I have opened 12 new places, all in front of Péronne: when I arrived on Good Friday we had nothing nearly as far up as Péronne itself in our army area. Some of these have already shut and been transferred elsewhere. Our old places are all gradually shutting but even these plans are difficult. At one for instance where I was on Saturday the one man left there had taken 3,000 francs on Thursday and on Friday had had so little to do that he spent the afternoon on the old battlefield of last July in the middle of which his hut stands (on sticks in the mud) burying the dead of last summer's offensive who still lie there. I need not describe to you what that means. We were crossing that deserted and ghastly ground – Ginchy, Combles, Trones Wood, Mametz – for some hours and on the sultry thunder afternoon of Saturday the whole air was heavy with decay, a sickly putrid breath. Soon I hope we shall be able to abandon it: we hang on as long as there is work for us.

The new places are most interesting but I may tell you very little about them. Two have been heavily shelled lately and ten days ago I was under fire for the first time. An interesting experience but I don't thirst to repeat it as I shall no doubt have to before long. I was working on the railway all day, with a party of men, unloading 20 tons of stores from trucks and reloading lorries. At noon Fritz put two shells into the centre of the town from long range. The second missed my car by 5 yards – literally no more. I was just out of it and round the corner when the shell burst and a man shouted 'Your car's hit!' I bolted up the road to it and found all serene and no one hurt. All went well during the afternoon but just as I was collecting a fatigue party with a Scotch corporal to erect a marquee on a chosen 'safe' site Fritz woke up again. Boom (seven miles away) – crackle (like tearing a huge sheet of calico across the sky) – crash – and a fountain of black earth and iron went up just behind our site on the hillside. At regular intervals of two minutes he kept it up, always in a different place. I was standing on the open ground talking to the Transport officer. Each time the 'crackle' began we threw ourselves flat and the earth pattered round us like thunder rain after the explosion of the shell. Two men were killed in that twenty minutes and the Scotch corporal remarked quietly 'Ye'll no be wanting the fatig pairty the nesht, sorr', 'Lord, no' said the Transport officer 'It's too hot for that.' So we retired with more determination than dignity, I fancy, for I remember we all picked ourselves up at least once from the mud on the way back. It is an uncanny and indescribable feeling. One is not exactly afraid but one would just give the world to be somewhere else at the moment. There is a fascination about the sound of the shell coming towards you. You see nothing. Where will it pitch? – over there or just here? Heaven knows.

Another of our marquees had two very narrow shaves last week from the same gun – a big naval gun a long way behind the Boche line – but the two old Scotch ministers in charge, though I could see the strain on them, have stuck it out well. One man's nerve at the first place went a few days ago and I have moved him.

As usual the most picturesque and interesting things in my day's work I can't tell you about. So I will say no more for the moment. Very many thanks for letters and the paper with Father's fine speech. Dearest love.

Ever your loving son,

Barclay.

---

[1] Francis Edward Shaw Jacomb-Hood (?–?) was ordained priest in 1904 and in 1914 was rector of Iping-cum-Chithurst, Kent. Unfulfilled in his YMCA *rôle*, he obtained a temporary commission in the Army Chaplains' Department in 1918. His wife also served as a YMCA 'Voluntary Worker' at Abbeville from April to September 1917. *Crockford's*, 1920, p. 785; YMCA Archives, University of Birmingham (hereafter YMCA), K47 Transcript list of ladies who served in France and overseas.

[2] Marseilles was the British army's base in the south of France, being a vital link to the Mediterranean, Malta and the Suez Canal. It was via Marseilles, for example, that the Indian Corps began to arrive in France in September 1914. P. Mason, *A matter of honour* (London, 1976), p. 412.

[3] Wilbraham Harris Arundell (?–?) was ordained priest in 1902. He became rector of Cheriton-Fitzpaine in 1912. *Crockford's*, 1920, p. 40.

[4] Here, and with proper circumspection, Baron seems to be alluding to the impending movement of Fourth Army to the Flanders coast and its implications for the work of the YMCA. A. F. Becke, *History of the Great War based on official documents. Order of battle part 4. The Army Council, GHQs, armies, and corps 1914–1918* (Uckfield, 2007), p. 104.

WITH THE BRITISH EXPEDITIONARY FORCE

[Stamp] YMCA
21.vi.17
4th ARMY

Postal address
APO S.76.

My dearest Mother,

It seems a very long time indeed since I wrote to you. Thank you very much for long and most interesting letters. One written 'down to love' almost made me homesick for the moment. But often all we are [*sic*] too busy here to cherish feelings of that sort much and must just keep on keeping on. What a glorious rest you must have had at Tintagel! I only wish Father would go and do the same somewhere out of reach of business. I am sure he needs it and that in the long run it would pay.

There is not much news really here. The heat has been terrific but a series of immense, short and sudden thunderstorms have broken the weather at last. This heat has made work very trying some days, and besides I have been much hampered by the state of my cars. My new Dodge had to go to Paris for repair and is pronounced irreparable. A mechanic who originally put the engine together in America forgot to secure a small split pin by turning the ends over: this dropped out and loosened a nut and without our knowing what was wrong a deep cut was soon scored in one of the cylinders. There are no more cylinders in France and I doubt if we shall get what we want even from New York to which a wire has been sent. That left me with an ancient Ford, one of the most noted 'dud' Fords in France. It takes hours of work to keep her on these awful roads in running order. Arundell, my Devonshire parson driver, meanwhile went to Etaples to fetch up the YMCA 'reserve car' – which turned out to be an even more 'dud' Ford. Yesterday morning as we were rounding a corner with this one the steering went hopelessly wrong and Arundell had to choose between a collision with a fast military car or with a ruined house. He chose right (there wasn't much time for hesitation) and we charged through a hedge, carrying away a small tree, and buckled up the front axle. I abandoned the wreckage – not without some blasphemy I fear, for it meant abandoning also an 80 mile round of work for the day – and walked home. Arundell spent the rest of the day getting her towed in by a workshop breakdown lorry and got home at 10 p.m. soaked to the skin and absolutely ravenous. I am just off now on the other old 'bus: one back wheel is very dicky and we shall have to go slow or we may be landed through the wind screen. I am going today to see what can be done for the men in a big wood in the way of getting supplies of biscuits etc. up at night for one of our workers to give away. The further end of the wood is still in German hands and our part is constantly and heavily shelled. A hut or marquee is out of the question for it would be seen and smashed, but I think a little shanty or dug-out may be quite easy to arrange. It would be a great boon to fighting men. I have also been making enquiries about another village close to the line where the same sort of thing may be done. As you know from the official news in the papers this part of the front is pretty quiet now:[1] it may wake up at any time of course. All the same we are not idle. When I arrived ten weeks ago we had six huts. Not one of these is now open. At the moment we have just twenty – all new and all except one in front of Péronne – and have been asked to start others. Our weekly takings then were 30 to 40 thousand francs – now they are 120,000 and could be easily four times that were it not for the strict limit per man which we have to impose on account of difficulty with the food supply.[2] We get customers very largely straight from the trenches for I have got a row of marquees strung out at roughly equal intervals all along the front about 3 to 4 miles behind the line. Much of the work is very interesting but unhappily I must not tell you about it in detail. Some is very hard slogging for the hut-workers, but we should all like to be more busy still, and will be when the time comes.

My headquarters are still in the same place which suits us well on the whole and is very accessible as things go here. I wish you could have seen this house when we took it over and then see it now. It is quite comfortable now as things go and we have a fine little garden, all of our own planting – peas, beans, potatoes, radishes, lettuces and a few flowers. We have had two loads of salad already from it. The roses are lovely everywhere now and we always have some on our mess-room table– for one just walks into any garden and picks flowers among the heaps of bricks and broken bedsteads and charred rubbish. We have cleared dozens of barrow loads of stinking rubbish from our back yard into our neighbour's (his house is ruined beyond repair, his fruit trees cut down and his premises suited only to be an incinerator). Also we are getting on, I think, in our battle against flies. The rooms are all decorated with fly papers supplied – as much as margarine or tough beef or cigarettes – to us in rations by the army. The town is getting certainly more sanitary – and needed to be so. All our water is 'chlorinated' and sometimes tastes quite vile: no tea or lemonade can mitigate the iodoformy flavour. However life is good and not less so because it is simple. One does appreciate a meal in a hotel occasionally – with a bottle of French wine. Those chances are few and precious.

But now I must get off or the day's job will not get half done. Dear love to all. I owe William and Freda letters. Also I will write to you again soon.

Ever your loving son,

Barclay.

---

[1] At this point Baron is writing from the vicinity of Péronne, already vacated by most of Fourth Army. The Messines offensive had commenced in Flanders, eighty miles to the north, on 7 June. Holmes (ed.), *Oxford companion to military history*, p. 580.

[2] In 1917, a world shortage of food, which was exacerbated by Germany's renewed submarine offensive against Allied and neutral shipping, led to increased government control over the distribution and consumption of food in Britain and even meant that rations had to be cut for British soldiers on lines of communication in France. Inevitably, this problem was also reflected in the quantity of foodstuffs available to the YMCA. B. J. C. McKercher, 'Economic warfare', in *Oxford illustrated history of the First World War*, ed. Strachan, pp. 119–33; Messenger, *Call-to-arms*, p. 445; Wilson, *Myriad faces of war*, pp. 513–16.

On Active Service
WITH THE BRITISH EXPEDITIONARY FORCE

26.8.17.

My dearest Mother,

I have neglected you very shamefully for weeks and weeks. I seldom get time for letters beyond Rachel's one which I never miss every day and a few business ones. It is difficult to sit down and write a decent letter – for lately I have been getting home, pretty tired, at 12 or 1 at night and leaving in the morning as soon as the necessary routine of correspondence and ration 'incidents' etc. is done. Thank you ever so much for many long letters. Your last about the Salisbury Plain tour made great reading and one feels very proud of all that you and Father are doing. It is almost comic to think of the whole family doing YMCA work in odd places.[1] I don't know much about the YM in England but I am very glad to be in it here: it is a service which has made as definite a place for itself in the army as anything else.

Dr John Kelman of Edinburgh is here with me now for a week – one of the two or three greatest and truest men I have ever known.[2] Really human – a Scotch minister who is a wit, a glorious preacher, a fisherman, shot, rider, footballer, a friend to every man he meets. He just captivates everyone. The special point of his four months with the YM now (he was with me at Havre last year on a previous four months' YM work) is that he is speaking to soldiers about America and the war. He and Ian Hay, the novelist, were sent out together by the British Foreign Office to do propaganda work in USA before they came in as Allies. His special mission was to get into the German cities everywhere, and speak.[3] It was a sporting venture and he had a very great time. Chicago, Milwaukee, Cincinnati – all the cities where German is more spoken almost than English: these were his hunting ground. He spoke to chambers of commerce, dinners, churches, once in a court of justice between two cases, once out of a caravan at night during a pro-German celebration, in bars and railway trains, wherever he got a hearing. And he was in Chicago when war was declared by America. It is a great story he has to tell and he tells it here to breathless audiences of officers and men straight out of the line.

Two days ago he and I were asked by the army commander[4] to meet him at HQ. Sir Douglas Haig had written to him about Kelman (for he had stayed at GHQ and returns there in a few days). The general (I obviously can't give his name but his is one of the best known names in the army) was extraordinarily affable to us, talked for an hour about all manner of things (YM included – he asked me a lot of questions) and asked us to lunch. Kelman unfortunately leaves tomorrow and I am to drive him to a town near that most famous and battered city in the British line. He has promised to come back to me later, for this is an extraordinarily interesting piece of the front. Yesterday morning at 4.30 he had the time of his life when he was taken by an officer to the front line – not trenches for there are none. It was just a question of doubling from shell hole to shell hole in open country only a hundred or so yards from Fritz. He came back tired and with his trousers torn to rags but full of keenness about the men he had talked to up there.

Today is Sunday – a fact which I have remembered: I literally don't get a chance to do so many Sundays – for we are no less busy on one day than on another. I took Kelman up to a camp early to take a big Church Parade of his own countrymen in the open. I sat among them on the sandy grass and heard him deliver an inspired and most inspiring address. Then I came up to where I now am to relieve a worker who has been overdone (we are less than one man per YM here at present) and has been suffering from an abcess [sic] in his mouth and neuritis in his leg. He went off to see the doctor some miles away and I have been carrying on for him.

(At this point I interrupted my letter for half an hour to climb the dune behind us to watch shells bursting. First they were a mile over our heads and beyond. Not much damage – though I saw a haystack just lifted and tossed to the winds. Then Fritz shelled short of us and for the last ten minutes he has been pretty near us. One just now was just over the hill which I had been standing on and the watchers on the dunes scattered or fell flat double quick. All day the shells have been screaming over and now and again one wonders where the next will be. The only thing is to carry on and be busy. The effect of shell-fire on me is to make me restless and very wide awake – and I think this is the usual feeling.)

This is a very lovely landscape – very gentle and brilliant in its light and shade. From a high dune one can see no hill of any sort in any direction – just broken sand with green woods and very red and white cottages shining in the sun. The slender spires of village churches show for many miles over the trees. Far off in front one can see the ruined houses and blasted woods that we got so very accustomed to on the Somme, but at present the country round us is peaceful and curiously sweet. This is of course a very different life to ours at Péronne. Here one can dine in a hotel and shop next door – there are [sic] nearest shops were 30 miles away. But war is much more lively here and every moment is uncertain by day or night. We have one man alone in each of our marquees – for staff is terribly short – and it would be foolish to deny the strain on him often, especially at night. Our own HQ is of course a long way back though not out of range of guns: air raids occur every fine day – once last week three times in one day. The one at night was a marvellous spectacle for a very heavy thunder storm was on behind the many searchlights, rockets and guns to the west of us – a heavenly and human firework display which beat anything you will ever see at the zoo on a Bank Holiday.

I am immensely fit, though all of us are tired. Reinforcements will come soon I hope. The tantalizing thing is that I have marquees and all equipment for five more places – and no men to work them. The army is *very* keen and gives us everything. Men implore us to come up to new places (some must be cellars underground: this I am now in is the furthest limit for marquees and no one pretends it is safe) and we can't go yet, but we will.

Dearest love to Father and the 'girls': I *may* take leave next month. It depends on the progress of the war and consequent work.

Ever your loving son,

Barclay.

PS The men are wonderful! I can't say how wonderful they are. It is just an honour to be here.

---

[1] In 1917, Baron's parents and his sisters Freda and Vera led a concert party on a 'mission of good cheer' around the YMCA huts on Salisbury Plain. At their concerts, the lord mayor of Bristol took the opportunity to make some rousing speeches. For instance, as an accomplished surgeon in his own right, he reminded an audience at Fargo Hosptial 'that there was not one single advance in surgery which could be traced to the discovery of a German. The Hun...was never an explorer, in any sense, but always an exploiter.' Barclay Josiah's enthusiasm for the Red Triangle no doubt facilitated the erection of a mock YMCA dug-out in Bristol for fundraising purposes and he certainly presided at the opening of the city's YMCA 'Dug-Out' centre, a permanent structure that was heavily adorned with sandbags. YMCA, K19 Photographs illustrating the war emergency work of the YMCA Salisbury Plain Area. Western Division, pp. 62–5.

[2] John Kelman (1864–1929) was a minister of the United Free Church. A liberal evangelical, he had enjoyed an influential ministry in Edinburgh prior to the war, particularly among the students of Edinburgh University. Although ill health prevented him from serving as a Presbyterian army chaplain, he worked with the YMCA in 1916–17 and also made a speaking tour of the United States, receiving an honorary DD from Yale in 1917. He was also appointed an OBE in 1917, being among the first to be appointed to this newly instituted order. *ODNB*; *Times*, 4 May 1929, p. 7.

[3] In the early years of the war British propaganda work in neutral countries was actually the responsibility of the War Propaganda Bureau, a secret body directed by C. F. G. Masterman (see above, Chapter 2, n. 25) and based at Wellington House. Its work in the USA, which was orchestrated by the novelist Gilbert Parker, was intended to counter German propaganda and involved the distribution of vast quantities of literature, artefacts, posters and film as well as the organization of correspondence programmes and speaking tours. In 1917 work of this kind passed into the hands of a new Department of Information and, in 1918, it was taken over by the new Ministry of Information. Bourne (ed.), *Who's who in World War One*, pp. 198–9; Wilson, *Myriad faces of war*, pp. 731–9.

[4] Rawlinson.

33 Onslow Gardens
SW
5.x.17.

My dearest Mother,

As you have heard from Rachel I arranged to stay over to the end of this week in case air-raids went bad. Mrs Smith[1] became very jumpy and I thought I had better stand by if possible. Of course as soon as I had made arrangements to stay the wind rose and the floods descended[2] and raids were clearly 'off'. However I have been very glad indeed of the few extra days in London with Rachel. I got my papers all fixed up yesterday morning without the least trouble and take the 1.40 boat train tomorrow (it varies in time every day). I was at Charing Cross yesterday for a few minutes enquiring about trains just as the boat train left. The platform was bustling with brass hats, one of whom disentangled himself and stepped over to me and shook hands. It was Sir Henry Rawlinson our army commander. He asked me if I was travelling: I told him Saturday. 'Mind you come and see me when you get back' he said most genially and moved on. I was glad I had gone to the station. It means a lot to our show to be in real touch with the army commander who is the head of the whole brass-hat hierarchy and not easily got at through the mass of officials round him. I lunched with him (Kelman got me there, having a personal introduction from Sir D. Haig) but hardly supposed he would remember me again.

This has been a fine leave, in unbrokenly glorious weather. It poured the day I landed but has scarcely rained since. Rachel and I have been about together all the time. The weekend at home was perhaps the jolliest part and the Sunday walk to Failand just one of the perfect things one likes to remember at odd moments long afterwards.

We are both itching to hear what has happened today about the mayoral election. Probably we shall hear from you in the morning. If it is another year – as I expect – I do hope you and Father won't wear yourselves to shadows over it. It will be a momentous year, whether peace comes or not. Rachel is reading Smuts's great speech here at the moment.[3]

William came here after school yesterday afternoon with a nighty in brown paper. I got tickets (excellent seats) for 'Trelawney of the Wells'[4] and took her and Rachel. We ate at Gattis and then walked over to the theatre. A very charming play – Irene Vanbrugh and Dion Boucicault[5] – and we most thoroughly enjoyed it. William came back with us to our hotel and stayed the night and I saw her off by Underground early this morning. She seems very fit but has been rather harassed by the raids, I think. London has thoroughly 'got the wind up' about raids.[6] The papers print columns every day about it and the sight of the crowds sitting in the passages of tube station[s] from 5 p.m. onwards is extraordinary. I am not sure that people are behaving very well over it. The rush that carried me off my feet into the Piccadilly Tube the other day with a panic stricken old lady dangling round my neck was something very like a panic. I comforted the old lady and found her a tin dustbin to sit on in the bowels of the earth and then wandered round the passages looking for Rachel whom I had appointed to meet outside the Tube at the very time when the alarm was given. The upshot of the thing was that we missed each other and I got back to a scratch lunch at 3 p.m. Naturally raids aren't nice things and I could well have done without them for a bit. I suppose I shall find them more frequent and more violent than ever when I get back, and it [is] a little disappointing not to have found a rest from them even in England. However the Boche is beat if we can only behave ourselves properly now.

Please tell Gwen[7] I will bear in mind the request in her letter though I may not get a chance to carry it out. My love to all at home – Father, Muriel, Freda and Gwen. I enclose a 'pome' for Freda about her fellow creatures.

I shan't be home for Christmas I fear – perhaps not before Peace comes if it don't delay too long. The winter will be an absorbing and very hard time but I wouldn't miss it up the line for anything. We shall be urgently wanted by troops everywhere.

Good-bye – and take care of your dear selves.

Ever your loving,

Barclay.

[1]   A nurse employed by Rachel Baron's invalid mother who seems also to have helped Rachel Baron.
[2]   An allusion to Matthew 7:26–7, to the foolish man who built his house upon sand.
[3]   Jan Christian Smuts (1870–1950) was a lawyer by training who had fought with the Boers against Britain during the South African War of 1899–1902. However, in the aftermath of the war he became a strong advocate of South Africa's place within the British Empire and, when the First World War broke out, he played a key *rôle* in the creation of the new South African Defence Force. He participated in the invasion of German South-West Africa (Namibia) in 1915 and, in 1916–17, he commanded (albeit with limited success) British forces in East Africa. In 1917, after heading the South African delegation to the Imperial War Conference in London, he was invited to join the War Cabinet by Lloyd George. On 4 October 1917 Smuts gave a much-publicized speech in London on the improvement of the city's air defences and on the necessity of air raids against Germany, 'an enemy who apparently recognizes no laws, human or Divine, who knows no pity or restraint'. Bourne (ed.), *Who's who in World War One*, pp. 268–9; *Times*, 5 October 1917, p. 9.
[4]   Actually *Trelawny of the 'Wells'* by Sir Arthur Wing Pinero (1855–1934). First performed in 1898, the play helped to establish the career of Irene Vanbrugh. *ODNB*; *Times*, 6 April 1910, p. 10, and 24 November 1934, p. 17.
[5]   Irene Vanbrugh (1872–1949) and Dion Boucicault (1859–1929) were leading figures in the British theatre, close associates of Sir Arthur Wing Pinero and had been married since 1901. *ODNB*; *Times*, 26 June 1929, p. 18, and 1 December 1949, p. 7.
[6]   The First World War saw the advent of strategic bombing, with south-east England being subject to over 100 German air raids in which 350 tons of bombs were dropped and more than 1,400 people killed. While Zeppelin raids had occurred from January 1915, by mid-1917 the threat of these airships had been eclipsed by that of the two-engine Gotha bomber. Based in north-west Belgium, carrying a bomb load of 1,000lb and capable of flying at 12,000 feet, these aircraft first raided towns in south-east England on 25 May 1917, killing ninety-five people and wounding 260. In June, London was hit by a similar raid in which 162 people were killed and 432 wounded. Partly because of these losses, by the autumn of 1917 British air defences had improved to the extent that German bombers had been compelled to operate mainly at night. Although heavy losses among the attackers saw the end of raids on England in May 1918, they caused much consternation among the civilian population and were a major spur to the creation of an independent Royal Air Force in April 1918. A. Smith, 'The British experience of bombing', in *The Great World War 1914–45*, II: *The peoples' experience*, ed. Liddle, Bourne and Whitehead, pp. 29–40; W. Murray, *War in the air 1914–45* (London, 2002), pp. 73–8; Winter (ed.), *The experience of World War I*, p. 190.
[7]   A friend of the Baron family.

[Stamp] POSTAL ADDRESS:
YMCA
APO S.4,
BEF

18.xii.17.

Dearest all,

I am so sorry that I can't write a separate letter to each of you. Life is divided
into five minute spells here just now – with interruptions every two minutes
by the telephone. I won't worry you with an account of all the jobs I have to
do or see done. I will just tell you that I am responsible now for eighty
'centres', scattered in the abysmal mud of this battered country for many,
many miles – more than I can cover in a day of continuous running, without
stops, in a car. Each one is a little colony in itself, with its own distinctive
life, its workers (two by rights but sometimes only one nowadays) and
orderlies (four by rights but often none at all in these days) and its crowds –
never ending queues in some places by day and night – of soldiers. Each
centre is – or ought to be – the church, town hall, public library, general store,
sometimes hotel for sleeping, often the only thing remotely like home, in its
own district. Of course these YMCAs vary enormously in character. One may
be a well-built hut, well painted, lighted, heated – with pictures on the walls,
a proper stage, books, a piano, a gramophone – everything a soldier wants.
And another (there are about 20 of such) is a few bent sheets of corrugated
iron dug into the mud and covered with sandbags, shelled day after day,
bombed at night. Here two men will live, cook and sleep (one of these men is
over 60 and others are often parsons who have never been 'up against' real
life before). Here they serve thousands of soldiers who walk straight out of
the trenches down that amazing line of duckboards across the endless waste
of mud. In one place (or rather seven such places) I have two men – one a
fine Bristolian named Hill[1] – who tramp from dug-out to dug-out, in constant
danger, keeping the show running. In the famous City itself – the most
famous place in England's war,[2] I have a man who never leaves. He sits in his
dug-out, deep under the ruined walls and has done so for 15 months
unrelieved – sometimes cut off by bombardment and gas for days at a time.
The town major of the place (the sort of military major whom the British
army appoint in every village we occupy) has just got the DSO[3] for 12
months continuous service. Our man, I am glad to say, is about to be
decorated: no one deserves it more. In another place two men have been
working day and night – literally – giving up their own beds to the first comer
(colonels and privates take them alike), getting up from the mud floor at all
hours of the night to serve cold and hungry men. At another a mere boy
provides hot tea and stuff to eat to every man who comes wounded into a
dressing station: three days ago he came to me to say that he was not busy

just now – might he go into the front line as a stretcher bearer? At his own risk I let him go.

I have not time to tell you of all the work and sacrifice which men make in the YM in this tough place. I don't want to tell you either of the carpet slipper parsons who won't face draughts or shells. There are not many but they make me sick.

It needs all this fine work and the great compensation of the glorious spirit of the British army – 'fed up' to the last ounce but as unconquerable as ever – to make the job worthwhile. For it is hard and patient slogging for me every day (Sunday passes unnoticed almost) from 8 a.m. to 1 a.m. next day. Meals come when and how they can, but I am very fit. I have never enjoyed life so much as now.

But the postman waits at my elbow. I have just talked about us out here I see. What about you all? A Happy Christmas (why not? it can't perhaps be a 'merry' one) to you. I wish I could peep at you for five minutes on the 25th, but it can't be done.

God bless you all,

Ever your loving,

Barclay

[1]   Unidentifiable.
[2]   Ypres.
[3]   Distinguished Service Order. Instituted in 1886, officers were appointed companions of this order for meritorious service or for gallantry short of that deserving the Victoria Cross. Holmes, *Tommy*, p. 582.

[Stamp] YMCA
27.12.17

4th ARMY
APO S.4.

My Dearest Mother,

I have long owed you a letter in return for several of yours. I am afraid I sent you a poor letter for Christmas but we were all very hard pressed then and time simply flew. And I sent you no sort of Christmas gifts at all – for our few shops in this dilapidated town[1] have little variety and are *very* expensive: the simplest things are about 400% above normal prices. I suppose when people have clung to their little businesses for three years at the risk of their lives (for this town has had and sometimes still has a rough time) they feel entitled to exorbitant profits. I will try however to pick up something really interesting and characteristic to send home to you. Tell father that the next Boche helmet I find (I have passed lots and never bothered about them) I will save and send to him.[2]

Christmas is over with all its festivities, its happiness and its real tragedy. We did all we possibly could to help the crowds of men up here but we are very few and scattered and the men are everywhere. All our places were packed with men. The most needed were those (and there are many) to which men on their way to and from the line can go. I wish I could give you a glimpse of one or two of these, for it would tell you more of the war than Beach Thomas or Philip Gibbs can convey in the columns of the 'Daily Mail' or 'Chronicle'.[3] I was on the road after dark on Christmas Eve delivering a load of turkeys and puddings to some of our outlying places. It was bitterly cold but not freezing. Underfoot the snow had turned to slush and the mud was over one's boots. The car skidded from side to side and on and off the vile pave[4] in the centre of the road: driving by night here needs not only skill and a quiet mind but lots of luck. Men muffled up to the eyes were sliding about on the greasy duck-boards which cross the miles of mud – singing, cursing or just too 'fed-up' to do either. In some of our draughty and shrapnel splintered marquees they were drinking hot cocoa by the light of some solitary candle – silent on the whole but sometimes joking in a quiet sort of way. This candle and the array of odd goods like a badly stocked village grocery (for stores have been very short lately) would have looked poor enough to your eyes but it is all a matter of comparison. The alternative to some men was the long tramp up the duck-boards towards that perpetual carnival of flash and flare, rocket and shrapnel spark and bursting shell and the hell of noise which is perpetually drawn across our horizon on one side night and day. To others the only other choice was a dug-out – some sheets of bent corrugated iron buried under sandbags in the mud – with not even a candle to light their supper – for candles just now are more precious than their bulk in francs.

And yet we wished each other a happy Christmas – and somehow kept it. And yet we laughed and talked of home. And yet we sang the Christmas hymns – *how* men sang them! And yet in this misery and stupidity and pitifulness and terror, amid sickness of body and mind, never far from sudden death, – Jesus was born again in the hearts of men. I was standing in freshly falling snow under a struggling moon in our yard at Headquarters when the clock struck midnight and Christmas came in. In the one church which is still whole enough for use here a few Belgian peasants and perhaps a few British soldiers were, I think, worshipping at the only midnight mass of the Church's year. In our yard also I felt the Presence near.

Next morning I made my Christmas Communion in the little chapel of which I enclose a picture.[5] It is the 'grenier'[6] at the top of a Belgian house, now used as a soldiers' club. You climb by a ladder out of the billiard room to it – and find one of the most beautiful chapels I know. 'Tubby' Clayton (one of the old crowd from Oxford – a friend of the OBM) is in charge. B. K. Cunningham of Farnham, for some years past one of my special saints, celebrated.[7] The altar hangings came from *Southwark*. So strangely do the old friends meet – both seen and unseen – at the altar on Christmas Day.

The guns do not pause. Now and again the anti-aircraft opens and I look out to see how near Fritz is likely to be in a minute. There is a war on up here – and our part in it is as vital as any man's: it is just not to falter in our task of cheerfulness and love and willing service.

Dearest love to all,

Ever your loving,

Barclay

[1]   Poperinghe.
[2]   German helmets were widely sought as battlefield trophies. However, by this stage of the war the spiked German *pickelhaube* (made of leather with metal fittings in its pre-war form) had given way to the more practical, but less prized, *stahlhelm* (or 'coal-scuttle' steel helmet) which was issued from early 1916. J. Brophy and E. Partridge, *The long trail: soldiers' songs and slang 1914–18* (London, 1969), p. 131; D. S. V. Fosten and R. J. Marrion, *The German army 1914–18* (London, 1988), pp. 32–3; P. Haythornthwaite, *The World War One source book* (London, 1992), p. 198.
[3]   William Beach Thomas (1868–1957) had written countryside features for the *Daily Mail* prior to the war. Despite having been arrested for an unsanctioned visit to the front, Thomas was selected as one of the first official war correspondents with the BEF in January 1915. He went on to write highly patriotic pieces for the *Daily Mail* and *Daily Mirror* and was knighted for his services after the war. Bourne (ed.), *Who's who in World War One*, p. 286.
[4]   'PAVÉ: The stone-block roads of northern France and Belgium.' Brophy and Partridge, *The long trail*, p. 131.
[5]   See Illustration 16.
[6]   Attic or garret.
[7]   Bertram Keir Cunningham (1871–1944) was recognized as the leading clerical trainer of his day, being the founder of Farnham Hostel and the mentor of an elite band of clergy known as 'the Farnham Brotherhood'. At this point, Cunningham was the principal of the chaplains' school of instruction which had opened at St Omer in February 1917. Snape, *The Royal Army Chaplains' Department*, p. 230.

[Reverse of postcard]

Christmas Greetings
FROM
TALBOT HOUSE CHAPEL
35 RUE DE L'HÔPITAL
(100 yards from the Square)
SERVICES

CHRISTMAS EVE	CHRISTMAS DAY
EVENSONG, 6 p.m.	HOLY COMMUNION, 6.30, 7.30, 8.30 a.m.
	CHORAL COMMUNION, 11.30 a.m.
HOLY COMMUNION, 6.30 p.m.	EVENSONG AND CAROLS, 6 p.m.

Offertories will be sent to the Army Ordinands Fund.

TALBOT HOUSE was opened on 15 December 1915, to provide a Parish Church and Institute for Troops in the Town. The Chapel was first made by the Queen's Westminster Rifles. The hangings came from the Bishop's Chapel at Southwark. The 14th MMG presented the 'stained glass' windows, and various other gifts came from the Guards, the RFA, RE and RAMC, etc., besides many personal memorials.

P. B. CLAYTON, *Chaplain.*

26/3/18

My dearest Mother,

Excuse handwriting! I am sitting up in bed (it is late) close to the boiler in the kitchen. Three of us are sleeping here now for the cover is good. The rest of the family (a dozen or so) I sent out of the town several nights ago to one of our huts about a couple of miles out. They were shelled out of that this afternoon and I gave orders for them to move to another camp two miles further back still. Meanwhile the faithful remnant have elected to stay with me here – and I couldn't want better companions.

As you will have guessed I have so far missed the main battle area again– to my great disappointment. Our people there have had a terrific time. They hung on as long as it was possible.[1] Lyne, late of this place, the secretary of one army, got all his men away safe and salved a large amount of his stuff, I hear. Macdonald,[2] the secretary of the other army and one of my old Havre staff, got all his men away after tremendous struggles but lost all huts and stocks – i.e. every single one of the dear old places started so joyfully and with such labour last Spring is in enemy hands. You will have read in the papers how the battle has swung round about our old HQ in that town which all of us who knew it remember with a very real affection.[3] McCowen (who rang me up tonight from the base to give me orders for all emergencies here) says that Lyne's and Macdonald's work has been 'a real achievement'. I am sure it has: they are two good men.

Compared to their difficulties we have nothing here to complain of. I won't pretend that I am not having a very anxious time. All my places are under fire – some heavily at times. HQ itself has ceased to be a health resort: at the moment we are being shelled and may expect a restless night. This has been the case at intervals – most uncertain – for days and I am keeping all workers away unless they have genuine business. My sub HQ[4] (I was there for some hours this afternoon) has fared worse. The little town is empty – save for police – and YM! The most beautiful town hall is in ruins and the other things of interest all more or less damaged. Our men are all safe but *very* tired. They have been helping to clear civilian refugees etc. but are now condemned for the time to merely awaiting events – a trying proceeding. I took them extra food today (the ration dump has gone) and news (telephone cut and no signal office open).

So far only two places of mine have been badly hit. One – my newest and biggest – is untenable. The fine new cinema hut was hit by an 8" shell and one end smashed: the roof and walls are riddled with literally hundreds of shrapnel bullets. Next day the billiard hut was hit direct and absolutely spread over the camp in small pieces: the table itself was hardly to be found at all. Workers had *very* narrow escapes but only one orderly got a scratch. One worker at another camp – an Australian YM man whom I did not know – was killed last week.[5] I have sent a man to replace him. Otherwise all well at present. Most of the staff are behaving *splendidly* – a few have 'wind up' badly and have to be sent back a bit. When you remember what physical crocks many of them are when they come out this is not at all surprising.

However this is all very small news compared with the real battle of our *wonderful* troops against the maximum strength of the enemy. The first witnesses of the battle have given us scraps of news. They cannot say much for what they have seen is incredible and indescribable. No such slaughter has surely ever been since men began to kill each other. It is useless to write of this fighting and I will not try. There is a fine tenseness of feeling here, but I have seen no consternation or down-heartedness. There is no hysteria – only a sort of solemn eagerness: I hope this is so at home too.

This is an anxious time for us all. After all I am only in a side show just now but I feel the responsibility of the safety of a couple of hundred men widely scattered and hard to reach in emergency. It is up to me to keep them where they are as long as they can be of service, to take what precautions for safety can be taken and to withdraw them at the right moment if necessary. However I sleep well (as far as alarms and excursions permit), eat well and feel well and that is nearly half the battle.

I know that you remember me at home in these days especially.

Dearest love to all of you.

Ever your loving son,

Barclay.

---

1   This refers to the retreat of the British Fifth Army in the area of the Somme during the first phase of the German spring offensive ('Operation Michael') which broke on 21 March 1918. The second phase ('Operation Georgette') would hit Second Army on 9 April. J. Keegan, *The First World War* (London, 1998), pp. 424–31.
2   See Introduction, p. 31.
3   Péronne.
4   In Bailleul.
5   Probably T. Trueman. See above, Chapter 3, n. 57.

YOUNG MEN'S CHRISTIAN ASSOCIATION
WITH THE BRITISH ARMIES IN FRANCE
THE SECOND ARMY AREA

11.9.18

My dearest Father and Mother,

The scene is the YMCA at B,[1] that charming and friendly little town where until last April I had my sub. Headquarters. The Grande Place where in those days the windows of the Falcon Hotel looked out over the gay market to the beautiful Spanish-Flemish belfry of the Hotel de Ville opposite with the tower of the splendid brick church behind, is now an indescribable heap of ruins. All that remains of the Falcon is a pile of bricks two feet high crowned with the white litter of a couple of dozen dinner-plates – some still unbroken. The Spanish belfry is merely a red mound: before we were forced to evacuate in that wild week of retreat in the Spring it had been hit full-force by a 15 inch German shell, and the familiar and well-loved silhouette of the little town as one approached it from the north was spoilt already for ever. The whitewashed piers which once held up the roof of the church still stand. Splashed red, where shell splinters have gashed the bricks underneath, they still look somehow splendid today in the sun with an inky thunder-cloud behind.

Grass grows among the rubbish in the Grande Place. In the centre is a huge shell-hole in which lies the ragged remains of a German military wagon: the mule-team, blown to pieces by our gunners some weeks ago, lies round the edge of the crater. The long ears and brown face of one mule stand up fantastically at one corner of this shapeless and pestilential heap. The sickly and obscene smell of death greets one at many corners of the town.

In the Petite Place, near the ruins of the Palais de Justice, the YMCA is open and very much alive. You will enter it by a door or a window or a shell-hole in the wall or through the next house or the next but one – as you please. The front door which is the proper if unusual way to go in, leads you into a wrecked convent school. If you go straight ahead you will arrive in the back garden. There are no flowers there now – only two graves. One has a big cross of rough wood over it – 'Kapt. Karl Krieger d.136 Rgt.' and twelve of his men whose names in small letters appear below.[2] The other at present is marked merely by a piece of a biscuit-box with the legend in pencil 'Traffic control of the – th. Division. Died in the execution of his duty' and the date. In other words he was blown to pieces in the Square two days ago while standing on point duty. Very likely his name is not known.

Turn to the left through the wrecked house and you will enter a big room, part of the convent school. It is thick in brick dust and plaster and the end wall which for five months faced the British batteries a few miles away, is gone. A clearing has been made at one end and this is stacked high with YMCA stores, cases upon cases marked with our familiar Red Triangle. Go down the cellar stairs in the corner and you find yourself in the YMCA itself. A big room with a stone floor. Plenty of light and air for the shell which removed the wall of the room upstairs performed the same service for the cellar. At the far end is another pile of cases, the counterpart of those upstairs – except that these contain German hand-grenades, machine-gun ammunition, fuses and signal rockets. A few fallen beams make a barrier between these and the space in which troops are served with cigarettes, biscuits, tea and many things, in which also two YMCA workers (one a surveyor from New Zealand, the other a commercial traveller from the Gold Coast) and an orderly (once an Irish-London monk)[3] eat, sleep and make their home. It is the most improbable combination of place and people in the world, but we are too accustomed now to such things to pay any attention to them. All that matters is that this, beyond shadow of doubt, is the most popular spot for miles among men who live in muddy hovels and tramp over muddy roads under shell-fire, uncertain [of] their food beyond the inevitable 'iron ration' of biscuit and bully-beef, uncertain also of life itself.

Opening out of this main cellar in two directions are other smaller cellars running out for a long distance under the houses on two sides of the Square. I have walked – with difficulty – through them all as far as one can go. There is practically no light in the best of them, none at all in most. The floors are covered with mattresses taken off French beds and strewn with an amazing collection of rubbish – for here, under hourly fear of British shells and gas, the enemy made his wretched home for five months. Grenades and cartridges, even a few rifles lie ready to hand by the beds. French books – school books from the convent mainly – and a few German novels and newspapers provided some of such miserable recreation as the Boche can have had. I picked up a few newspapers which make interesting reading, some tools and oddments and a German steel helmet – one of several – camouflaged with patches of colour in the latest manner. I was lucky to pick up no vermin: my driver did not entirely escape!

In one of the rooms of the house upstairs we found the cupboards which had contained the goods of the convent – broken open and ransacked. Statuettes, devotional books, fragments of vestments etc. lay strewn on the floor. I picked up a little girl's sampler worked in brightly coloured wool – a pathetic relic which I have sent to Rachel. I also disinterred from the brick dust a purple maniple embroidered with white passion flowers.

The maniple I send to you, Mother, and the Boche helmet to Father. And this letter is just to go with them to explain them to you.

We are in the throes of moving everything forward, our HQ included.

Dearest love to all,

Ever your loving son,

Barclay.

Note: The maniple, as I expect you know, is worn over the left arm by the priest at the celebration of the Mass. I believe it represents the towel which our Lord hung over his arm when he was washing the feet of the Disciples. This one is only a machine-made thing and has been stripped of its lace trimming, I fancy.

[1] Bailleul.
[2] The details of this grave are puzzling. The 136th Regiment was originally part of the German army's 30th Division, an Alsatian division which did not serve in Flanders until *after* the BEF recaptured Bailleul from the Germans in October 1914, during that autumn's dramatic 'race for the sea'. In April 1915 the regiment was transferred to the newly created 115th Division, a division that saw no action in the vicinity of Bailleul in the last year of the war. United States War Office, *Histories of two hundred and fifty-one divisions of the German army which participated in the war (1914–1918)* (London, 1989), pp. 388–91, 606–8; M. Gilbert, *First World War* (London, 1994), p. 90.
[3] Conscription affected some junior members of religious orders and the army appears to have treated them sympathetically. For example, two groups of Rosminian brothers were allowed to serve together in the RAMC and Francis Drinkwater, a Roman Catholic chaplain, met one of these groups serving with the 90th Field Ambulance in September 1918. In light of such treatment, it is unsurprising that another religious should have been posted to act as an orderly with the YMCA. St Chad's Cathedral, Birmingham, FHD/A5 Francis H. Drinkwater, War Diaries 1915–18, 24 September 1918. I am grateful to Nigel Cave IC for information on this subject.

YOUNG MEN'S CHRISTIAN ASSOCIATION
with the British Expeditionary Force

Organizing Secretary:
OLIVER H. McCOWEN.
Assistant Organizing Secretary:
Z. F. WILLIS.
Supervising Accountant:
ARCHIBALD MURCHIE.   Headquarters for France:
Assistant Supervising Accountant: YMCA
JAMES B. GILROY   APO S.1.
Director of Stores & Transport: BEF
W. S. DUNNING.   *Address reply to:*
Equipment for Sports & Entertainments: R. St JOHN READE
R. St. JOHN READE.
Indian Work:
S. K. DATTA.

[Undated][1]

My dearest Mother,

I have neglected you scandalously lately in the matter of letters but I am having a few hours breathing-space today – away from my own area as you see by the address – and am getting off a few private letters. I write a fair number of business ones but beyond my daily scratch to Rachel have let my other correspondents down badly.

    We have been having a very hustled time lately. Nearly all my centres have had to move up behind the retiring Boche. As everybody wants to move everything up at once, of course transport becomes a tremendous difficulty and there is great delay. I have just completed moving my HQ forward: this – with stores and equipment – is over 20 3-ton lorry loads which with lorries at the rate of one a day and that often cancelled at the last minute owing to military emergencies means a certain amount of worry! We settled into a convenient house with land and big sheds attached in one of the last habitable villages towards the line. The next village is still under fire almost daily and ours has had practically every house hit. We set to work and repaired the roof ourselves (laying tiles on a steep roof in half a gale of wind provides minor thrills, I find) and repaired every window with 'Vitiex', a wine and gelatine concoction which gives the general effect of frosted glass (real glass is out of the question.) We moved any amount of debris, fitted up our garage and got our tons of equipment stowed and in order. This done, the owner (who said he wasn't coming back yet) demands, through the French Mission, to return *at once*! There is nothing for it, therefore, but to move all over again. After much difficulty I have secured a house a hundred yards away which will suit us well. The roof is reasonably good but not only are there no windows but also no doors and a shell hole in one wall which you can walk through without stooping. This means a lot of work of all hands to make the place habitable.

Our HQ staff is unavoidably a biggish one – myself and two assistant secretaries, stores manager and assistant ditto, accountant and assistant ditto, equipment manager, Chinese YMCA secretary and his business secretary (we have 15 Chinese YMs in our area), three motor drivers, the local hut leader, never less than two visitors and besides these the orderlies – 4 men for HQ, 2 for stores, 2 for equipment, 1 soldier driving Chinese car, one French mechanic – and last but not least John Wood,[2] the old family butler who presides over the kitchen. These people take some housing but there is also a lot of material – the office files, typewriters, books etc. of my own office where three of us work at our own desks, the stores office, equipment office, Chinese office, accounts office (in which when I left yesterday for instance there lay over 100,000 francs takings of the past week). All this affair is cumbrous but all essential to work. It takes a lot of moving but we hope to have to move it at intervals towards the Rhine all the winter. Next time it will have to be housed under canvas or in a cellar for there is nowt but the wilderness in front of us.

Work is very interesting just now and may become frantically so at any moment now. I am taking two days away from my area at the moment nominally to see McCowen, my chief, on business but just as much because I am really very tired and want to be ready to plunge into what may soon come to us.

Leave is much overdue for me and provides a great puzzle. I had hoped to get home and be with Rachel and David for the tail-end of the summer. Then came the Boche retirement and a sudden increase of work for us. Then an Army Secretaries' Conference which I had to attend two days ago – for it had to decide a complete re-organization of our work in the army areas (I needn't worry you with the details but it is an entirely new plan which will make the whole difference to our effectiveness and close touch with the army).[3] I then thought I might dash home in the bare three weeks between that conference and the general secretaries' conference on Oct. 17th and 18th. I *can't* dodge that for I have been the representative for all the Army areas for four months now and have to give an account of my stewardship.

Unhappily Rachel can't easily have me till after the 4th when she and David meet at Bournemouth: that makes too much of a rush to make leave good. Moreover we stand on the edge of big things on the front just now and I don't want to be out of it when they come. So I have put off leave – for the second or third time – till after Oct. 18th anyway. I am afraid Rachel will be very much disappointed.

And how are all of you? I have spent all this paper talking about myself!

Love to all.

Ever your loving son,

Barclay.

[1]   The contents of this letter (and especially its references to the wholesale German retreat and the movements this entailed) strongly suggest that it was written towards the end of September 1918.
[2]   Unidentifiable.
[3]   A reference to the creation of a new tier of divisional YMCA secretaries in the autumn of 1918. See Introduction, p. 53.

[Copy made by Barclay Baron's mother.]

26-10-18

I write from my new HQ where I am sleeping the night. We are still very much in the progress of moving and I live mostly on the road between the new place and the old just now.[1] I feel it is very hard to write letters or to post them (for our post-office has been on the move) and still harder to get any. I have not had a single letter of any kind for a week. The budget which will arrive as soon as we trace our lost mail will be staggering.

This has been an amazing week because its experiences have been so new. I have been seeing quite a strange aspect of the war and only wish I could give you a complete picture of it. On Wednesday I went up to a town in the desolated area to meet McCowen by appointment [and] found him among the ruins of a huge building which used to be an old YMCA – now full of signs of Boche habitation and with him drove to the gates of the great city which has lately been delivered.[2] We had especial authority to enter and got passes made out at the gates. Inside we passed up long boulevards just like Paris, all gay with flags like a holiday. Men took off their hats to us, women smiled and waved and one cannot stir without a crowd of children who insist on snatching one by the hand and even on being kissed. It was less than a week since the German troops (who had ruled supreme for over four years in the whole life of the city) had marched out in silence and British bands had played our own men in. Even after days of rejoicing which had gone before the feeling in the town when we first saw it was indescribable. We found one restaurant open and lunched at a price – and then came on here to a neighbouring town. At once I ran into old acquaintances and found I was in the nick of time – a few hours before things were officially in full swing. The feeling among our own men was extraordinary also. Every officer we met smiled and nodded whether one knew him or not. Men waved to us in the street. I even saw a staff officer waving and laughing to some men on the back of a lorry. A brass band came up the long avenue – a really noble street of trees and fine houses – at the head of a British battalion in marching order with tin hats on. The men were singing. There were flowers in their buttonholes and flags stuck into the barrels of their rifles. One man carried a huge French tricolour. It was a complete picture and symbol of victory and I confess that I nearly made a fool of myself. Laughter and tears were in the faces of many of us, I think. After the years of suffering and waiting France here feels herself delivered: one feels the whole world's freedom coming steadily, irresistibly, now at last. That does not mean that 'all is over bar the shouting'. The heavy roll of heavy guns not many miles away by day and night cure one of any extravagant ideas of that. And then there is the dark side under this amazing sensation of deliverance and joy.[3] I have talked to many French people here, for they are all ready to talk. Each one of them has some new story of the Germans but all the stories are hideously alike. The four years they have endured under German military rule will never be forgotten here; hectored, threatened, fined, arrested, imprisoned, pillaged at every turn, kept without a single letter from relatives during the whole four years, without news, shot at if they stirred from their houses after 4 in the afternoon, not allowed more than a kilometre from their doors, with brutal officers and verminous soldiers billeted on them – this was every one's lot. I have seen the civilian prison (our new YM is next door) where they were sent on the slightest provocation or none at all. I have seen a little of the wanton destruction of machinery, roads, bridges, railway stations. Every single metal door handle, knocker, letter box and the ornaments inside the houses have been taken away to be melted: most beautiful works of art have gone to make the driving band of some German shell. Every woollen mattress in the town has been emptied of wool and filled with straw (I am sleeping on one tonight). The gas works were blown up, the electric dynamos stolen so that there is no light, the drinking water cut off on the night the enemy evacuated. This was all organized destruction and pillage. Besides that every householder can tell you of the behaviour of Germans in their houses – the insolence of officers and men, the insults to women. There are tragic tales which cannot be repeated – they are devilishly bestial! Several things every one seems agreed upon. For instance German officers lived well: they had meat ad lib and all kinds of luxuries. But their men were badly treated and hated their own officers.

British prisoners were specially harshly treated and it was a very serious offence to show them any kindness. A girl yesterday told me how the lady next door had thrown some food out of [a] window to an Australian prisoner working in the road: this lady was fined 2,000 marks and sentenced to four months imprisonment. This is a common type of story. The Spanish consul here told me he had seen two famished British prisoners fighting in public for the possession of a beetroot. And the civilians themselves suffered hunger. A wealthy man told me with terrible emphasis that he had often been hungry and that he could not describe the state of some of the poor. He said he had seen German soldiers steal the flour sent by the American Relief Committee[4] and substitute stuff made of chestnuts and full of black vermin. He had seen a poor family rub a little piece of bad bacon – grand comme ça (he held up a match box as he spoke) on their black bread to make it eatable and put the bacon aside to serve the same office at the next meal. And I think the Boche was very short of food himself, it is only fair to say. Life in these towns is starting again, but it will take a long time. All machinery in the great factories has been removed or destroyed, all railway bridges and canal locks blown up, all horses, carts and motor vehicles commandeered. There is no traffic in the streets but our own army lorries and cars, no food except our army rations for civilians. The shops look open at first sight but if you look in the windows closely you will see that they are making a brave show with almost nothing. I see candles for sale in windows at 2 frs each, a 1½d bar of chocolate for 2 fr 50.c. Coffee sells sometimes – if you can get it – at 75 frs a kilo (2 lbs)! One of our YM men asked a French interpreter a day or two ago to drink a glass of wine with him in a restaurant: the wine was vin ordinaire, worth about 1.50 a bottle and the glasses were small [and] when he asked for the bill it was 8 frs a glass! I drew some army rations yesterday at a way side ration dump and found a crowd of civilians hanging round: the staff sergeant told me that they walked miles to see meat – they hadn't tasted it for years. One could multiply instances but this will give you an idea of what invasion has meant in France. People in England simply don't realize the war until they have seen the miles of hideous ruin and the forest of graves behind us, have listened to the stories of civilians around us and to the roll and grumble of the guns along the line ahead of us. I wish to God every striker in England could be pushed through this country and lie in this mud and taste this unspeakable bitterness which the French know so well. He would – if he was a sensible man – go away quietly to work or to shoot himself in a corner hiding.[5]

But don't let me get on the rant. The joy is overcoming the misery of it for the moment.

We *know* that we are saved now President Wilson's latest note just thrills every man here as it surely must do all at home because it is *our* will, *our* purpose [and] *our* hope. The king of Prussia shall never do this thing again.[6]

---

[1] By this point, Second Army had advanced deep into Belgium and its headquarters were based in the French town of Roubaix. Becke, *Order of battle part 4*, p. 81.

[2] A reference to Lille, which was occupied by elements of Fifth Army on 17 October. *Ibid.*, p. 119.

[3] Conditions in occupied France were closely akin to those in occupied Belgium, its population of more than 2 million being subjected to the same requisitioning of food, goods and raw materials. While the taking of hostages (including the bishop of Lille) began in autumn 1914, forced labour and deportations commenced in 1916. While resisters of all kinds were subject to summary trials and executions, it was indicative of the depth of German paranoia about partisan activity (a legacy of the Franco-Prussian War) that at least sixteen French pigeon fanciers were executed for not surrendering their birds. A. Becker, 'Life in an occupied zone: Lille, Roubaix, Tourcoing', in *Facing Armageddon: the First World War experienced*, ed. H. Cecil and P. H. Liddle (London, 1996), pp. 630–41; M. Atack, 'The experience of occupation: northern France', in *The Great World War 1914–45*, I: *Lightning strikes twice*, ed. J. Bourne, P. Liddle and I. Whitehead (London, 2000), pp. 533–50; S. Audoin-Rouzeau and A. Becker, *1914–1918: understanding the Great War* (London, 2002), pp. 54–64.

[4] The Commission for Relief in Belgium extended its activities to occupied France in April 1915 and, by January 1916, conditions were such that its supplies were effectively keeping its population from starvation. Following America's entry into the war in April 1917, control of the CRB passed to the Spanish and Dutch. H. McPail, *The long silence: civilian life under the German occupation of northern France, 1914–1918* (London, 1999), pp. 67–88.

[5] Although 1917 had seen an escalation of industrial unrest, this was abruptly halted by a sense of national crisis induced by the German spring offensive of the following year and calm generally prevailed until the end of the war; indeed, in October 1918 a government report described the mood of organized labour as 'abnormally tranquil'. Nevertheless, the obvious defeat of the German spring offensive was followed by strike action in certain industries and occupations, disturbances that were widely deplored even by elements of the labour movement. Naturally, those with experience of the front line often had little sympathy for the occupational grievances of civilians. Wilson, *Myriad faces of war*, pp. 519–30, 653–9.

[6] Thomas Woodrow Wilson (1856–1924), a Democrat, was elected president of the United States in November 1912. Although he sought to keep the United States out of the war, gaining re-election in 1916 on the basis of his policy of neutrality, German provocation eventually drew the United States into the war on the Allied side in April 1917. Wilson's vision of a new world order (based on disarmament, national self-determination and an international association of nations, a vision that he articulated in his Fourteen Points of January 1918) did much to boost Allied morale and earned him immense popularity abroad. The note to which Baron refers formed part of a diplomatic exchange between Wilson and Prince Max von Baden on the subject of peace terms, an exchange that failed to divide the Allies or to mitigate the terms of the inevitable Armistice. Bourne (ed.), *Who's who in World War One*, pp. 306–7; H. Herwig, *The First World War: Germany and Austria – Hungary 1914–1918* (London, 1997), pp. 442–3.

GENERAL SECRETARY: POSTAL ADDRESS:
WALTER ASHLEY   HEADQUARTERS   YMCA HEADQUARTERS,
ASSISTANT SECRETARY: HOTEL CONTINENTAL   RHINE ARMY
REV. P. R. H. BACK   COLOGNE.

May 3rd 1919

My dearest Mother,

Many thanks for your Easter letter: I hope it isn't too late to answer it. I have been travelling so much since I left home that it is not easy to remember the order of events. I crossed with Sir Arthur Yapp, McCowen and others who were on their way to the Inter Allied YMCA conference at Versailles.[1] I did not intend to go, although I am one of the delegates from the British YMCA in France, but at Boulogne I decided – in spite of urgent jobs up here – to go to Versailles for one day in order to see some of the members on various business. I stayed Friday night in Paris (which is nearly as crowded as London) and went on to Versailles on Saturday. There were about 70 YM delegates there in the Hotel Suisse (since commandeered for the German peace people in addition to the Hotel des Reservoirs). They represent of course all the armies – British, French, American, Italian, Portuguese, Checo-Solovak [sic], Indian, Chinese etc. John Mott,[2] head of the American YM was in the chair: I had hardly met him since Oxford. I was able to do some business with several people. I cut one of the sessions on Saturday afternoon and walked in the Park at Versailles and the Trianon with Arthur Reade and Paterson of Havre. We had tea in a cafe in the park and a most interesting talk about YM future and other things. The Palace at Versailles (you probably know it) seems to me to represent the very worst side of the Old World. It is gilded and overdecorated at every turn, a huge and monstrous barrack, smelling of the pompous luxury and vice of Louis XIV and the rest. There are acres of battle paintings and thousands of noisy Yank tourists. It was interesting to visit the Hall of Mirrors in which the Peace is to be signed – we hope – in a few days now. The Park is great in the stately French manner. What pleased me best were the trees and basins of water round the Trianon and the deserted gardens and farm yard of the Petit Trianon with its pathetic ghost of Marie Antoinette. It was a lovely Spring evening as we walked back through the Trianon gardens. The Tulip trees were wonderful masses of snow and wallflowers out in the beds. Round the little Temple d'Amour, once the playground of Watteau shepherdesses,[3] we picked cowslips and violets in the grass.

Next morning – Easter Day – I went to the early service at the tiny English Church of Versailles. Besides YM delegates, English, American, Indian etc. – of various denominations (for at conferences inter-communion is natural and usual now) there were half a dozen staff officers attached to the Peace Delegation – no one else. It was a very quiet service. Immediately after breakfast I went into Paris and that afternoon took the Paris–Cologne Express. I had time to see a picture exhibition at the Petit Palais (it is an *extraordinary* joy to get among pictures again: the very smell of their varnish nearly intoxicates me at first!) and saw some really grand sculpture by the great Yougo-Slav [*sic*] artist Mestrovic – one of the new men.[4] I also pushed into the Louvre for half an hour – through dense parties of American soldiers taken round by brazen-lunged American YM guides.

The journey up was the most luxurious I have ever made – for I was told that every seat on the train was booked until May 3rd and had to get on the wagon lists by a sheer wrangle (a signature to a document in French composed and typed by myself and a rubber stamp at the bottom worked wonders! – added to 5 francs to the attendant). I had a whole compartment with a comfy bed, an armchair and a lavatory to myself and slept like a top. It is a 16-hours journey.

Up here I had a busy few days and then pushed off again via Paris, where I stayed half a day, to Dieppe. From Dieppe I visited Havre, Rouen, Havre again and then back to Dieppe to clear up my office there finally. On May Day I took a car to Abbeville (after having packed and cleaned things half the night) and train to Boulogne where I met other workers: we all travelled up by the military train from Boulogne to Cologne and arrived yesterday evening. So now I shall sit down for a day or two before I face another railway journey! There is a heap of work to do up here and I shall have to get round all our 65 YM centres in Germany if I can in the next ten days and write a report on the whole job for my chief in London.

I have been summoned to an OBE Investiture on May 15th and as that is the day I am due to be in London anyway to have a pow-wow with Holmes from France and McCowen (my chief) at our HQ, I shall come and get the job over. I hope Rachel can come up to town. I can get her a ticket to see the Investiture. I expect to be in England a week or so and hope that Muriel could be ready by then to come back with me – say on May 20th as she suggests herself. I had a talk with Arthur Reade at Havre. He is very short of ladies and work is going on merrily there still: he was delighted at the idea of Muriel coming to Havre and is a delightful soul who would do anything for her. Holmes who is in charge in France now (at Dieppe) also said as I left 'We shall do anything you want, B.B., for a sister of yours' – so I don't think there will be any difficulty.

Muriel tells me that she has heard from Miss Bridge and arranged an interview with Mrs Ian Malcolm in London. It is then only a question of passport (easy) and a uniform.

I am delighted to hear that you are going to visit the grandchildren at Bournemouth: it ought to be delicious there in fine Spring weather and they are all looking forward to your visit.

Dearest love to all,

Ever your loving son,

Barclay.

1   See Introduction, pp. 72–3.

2   John Mott (1865–1955) was a leading figure in the Student Volunteer Movement for Foreign Missions (established in 1888) and was a co-founder of the World's Student Christian Federation (created in 1895). A tireless and much-travelled promoter of the student movement and of overseas missions, he played a major *rôle* at the World Missionary Conference in Edinburgh in 1910. Prominent in the YMCA since his student days at Cornell, he became general secretary of the International Committee of the YMCA in 1915, undertaking work for prisoners of war. However, he became general secretary of the National War Work Council after the United States entered the war in 1917, receiving the Distinguished Service Medal in recognition of his efforts on its behalf. His international contacts also gave him a *rôle* in international diplomacy. Although he rejected President Wilson's offer of being appointed the US ambassador to China, he was involved in US relations with Mexico and served as part of a special diplomatic mission to Russia in 1917. www.nobelprize.org/nobel_prizes/peace/laureates/1946/mott-bio.html. Consulted 16 December 2008.

3   A reference to the pastoral paintings of Louis Watteau (1731–98) and to the bucolic recreations of Marie Antoinette. www.oxfordartonline.com/subscriber/article/grove/art/T090852pg2. Consulted 16 December 2008.

4   Ivan Meštrović (1883–1962). A pre-war sculptor of international standing, Meštrović spent the war in exile but returned to his homeland, now Yugoslavia, in 1919. www.oxfordartonline.com/subscriber/article/opr/t118/e1727?q=Mestrovic. Consulted 16 December 2008.

On Active Service
WITH THE BRITISH EXPEDITIONARY FORCE

BAPO 1
22.5.19

My dearest Mother,

Muriel and I are sitting in different corners of the Common Room at Havre HQ
writing letters. We had a beautiful crossing last night, tea at 6 on board and
came off about 8. There was the usual passport business which is tiresome but
we had an excellent breakfast at HQ and felt very fit afterwards. I took Muriel
round the seafront after breakfast and to see Miss Royce at the Officers' Club.
Then we came back to HQ and fixed up about her room.[1] It is in this Boulevard
about 200 yards up – a very nice large room with two windows, lots of
cupboard room, a writing table etc. The home is spotless and Madame and her
daughter delightful people: there is another YM lady in the home already. Then
we changed some money at our Accounts office and it was lunch time.

Lunch outside in our 'garden' at HQ with some very jolly people. After
that I took M for a walk to two or three of the camps on top of the hill. We had
tea in the garden of one with two old workers whom I know well. Then on over
the hill to Sainte Addresse by the cliff. The whole of that end of Havre is a
wonderful mass of blossom now – chestnut, hawthorn, lilac, wisteria, laburnum
etc. There has been a thunder shower since tea and the air is very clean and
fresh now.

I hope to spend a day or two showing Muriel round and introducing her to
people: the camp in which she will probably work is not yet full for about two
days [sic] with English troops. Some Colonials have been in it and the Colonial
YM is just handing over the hut to us again.

I feel sure M will be happy here. We have met lots of nice people already
and work will be interesting.

Love to all,

Ever your loving son,

Barclay.

---

[1]   In the interests of propriety, female YMCA workers did not live in the camps in Le Havre but were
billeted in the town. See p. 104.

APPENDIXES

Appendix I

Ashbrook
Coleraine
Ireland
Aug. 11. 1916

Dear Mrs Baron,

By this post I have taken the liberty of sending your little son a book of verse which some one was bound to send him sooner or later, and I wish to be first. I send it now David has been known to me these last three months, for early in May I was allowed the pleasure of seeing his photograph, and his mother's too, and it is one of the few regrets of my stay in Havre that when one evening his father did me the honour of writing me to help him choose the frame for the series of photographs now hanging in his office I pleaded other work – which was quite true – and did not go. And he forgave me, as he has forgiven me other and more serious offences since. For now that I have begun I cannot help going on to tell you that one of the chief events of the most memorable months of my life was that I learned to know your husband and was admitted to share his friendship.

As I dare say you know he carries a load of no ordinary responsibility – too heavy perhaps for one so young as he is. For over 100 workers are under his control. They are of all sorts and sizes – and shapes – and ages: from all sorts of churches and classes and from many different lands, of extremely various and varied dispositions. And the one bond that binds them together is the bond of their common loyalty to him. They may criticize him – and indeed I have one or two criticisms to offer myself – but they trust him absolutely. Even when I remember his quite unusual gift for quickly and accurately estimating the abilities of the strangers who are flung at random to him from London, I never cease to marvel at the dexterous grace with which he manages that fortuitous concourse, and how with such obviously imperfect instruments the work goes forward harmoniously and with constantly increasing efficiency. At Headquarters he has created his own atmosphere, and has made it the brightest and happiest of places, where witty and mirthy talk goes along with earnest discussion. One may see many a smile, but never a frown. It was a joy to hear him morning and evening pray for a blessing on 'this household', pray in that reverent voice of his. At first sight it seemed a big stretch of the good old word to make it embrace that big circle of separate individuals, changing almost every day, but I felt it was the right word for there was the unity of a household in those who dwelt and knelt there – the unity of a common purpose and a common consciousness. I know at least of one who cannot think of the YMCA at Havre without a certain tug at his heart strings.

It was thus I had grown to admire and respect him – but during the last few weeks I came to know him better and deeper still. He brought me up to Headquarters and I slept there and from 8 in the morning, when we met for prayers, till far into the night there were few hours when I was not in his company. He dropped into the habit of coming into my room and sitting and resolving the endless problems connected with the working of that large base; and unconsciously he would go on to speak of his work in Bermondsey, and of the ideal to which life has been consecrated by him – and by you too. It was the revelation of an extremely attractive personality. If I were to speak in the language of the goldsmiths I would say it was 24 carat gold – all gold and all finest gold. Whether an admixture of alloy might not have been serviceable in this rough and tumble world, who knows! There he is and I would be the last to suggest a change.

At the same time a little tincture of selfishness might do no harm. His work in connection with the Military Authorities requires inexhaustible patience and tact, he alone can do it. All the little odds and ends that lesser men can do should be left by him to lesser men. When I first knew him much of the censoring fell to him, from the moment I became censor I saw to it that not a moment of his time was frittered away on work so mechanical. Similarly he should be deterred from lecturing at night. It takes too much out of him. There were times when his eyes seemed very weary. I can see him still on one awful night in the opening week in July, when the first flood of wounded men came pouring into Havre, he went out and in among them as they lay on stretchers in rows of hundreds, so erect and bright, with a word and a smile for each, though he had been on duty without a break for 20 consecutive hours. I am a long way older than he is and need sometimes to admonish him and hope you won't think I am wrong. Of course, if you take out all the quixotry you will not have him the man we know – and why should I hesitate at the word? – and love.

A letter he wrote to my parish before my return will make it possible for me to rejoin him at Havre later in the year. I hope so anyhow.

Meantime, please forgive such a long letter. As if you did not know it already! But I could not help it.

Believe me, dear Mrs Baron

Yours faithfully

William A. Wilson

Appendix II

The edge of the storm

In the New Year of 1914 I found myself firmly committed to an unexpected venture – the editorship of a new kind of Church of England weekly newspaper, *The Challenge*. The true begetter of it was the Rev. George Newsom,[1] later to be a canon of Newcastle. He had just completed a strenuous campaign which had raised the money to build King's College Hostel in Vincent Square for theological students, and now his restless energy sought another outlet. The new weekly was not to reflect the views of any one party or section of opinion in the Church of England, as the three other church weeklies of the time in varying degrees did.[2] It was to eschew ecclesiastical politics and aim at engaging the interest in religion of laypeople, especially the younger generation of men and women: in the event it was to have a limited but genuine success in this. It was to be edited and largely written by laymen and to be illustrated, an innovation then a little shocking to some minds.

Newsom, once possessed with the idea, lost no time in collecting round him a small advisory committee. The original members of this were an elderly lawyer who had devoted all his leisure for many years to Oxford House in Bethnal Green, Edwyn Bevan,[3] a distinguished student of church history, William

---

[1]   George Newsom (1871–1934) was appointed 'vice-principal, chaplain, and lecturer on the Greek Testament' at King's College, London, in 1897; six years later he resigned as vice-principal and was appointed to the chair in Liturgical and Pastoral Theology. Reader at the Temple Church from 1902 to 1912, his years at King's were also marked by his creation of a largely self-governing hostel for theological students in 1902, of which he served as warden until 1916. After a stint in the Army Chaplains' Department, he was appointed vicar of Newcastle-on-Tyne, rural dean of Newcastle and a canon of Newcastle Cathedral in 1916. He was appointed a chaplain to the king in 1920 and died as master of Selwyn College, Cambridge. *Times*, 16 February 1934, p. 19.

[2]   The Church of England weeklies at this time were the Anglo-Catholic *Church Times* ('which had a circulation larger than that of all the others put together'); the High Church *Guardian*; the 'vaguely central' *Church Family Newspaper* and the evangelical *Record*. F. A. Iremonger, *William Temple* (Oxford, 1948), pp. 180–2.

[3]   Edwyn Bevan (1870–1943) was the son of a wealthy gentry family. A liberal evangelical, he was active in the SCM, the London Society for the Study of Religion and the Society of Jews and Christians. A trained archaeologist and distinguished classicist, he had also travelled widely in India and had a strong interest in Indian affairs. Although he served for a time in the fashionable 28th London Regiment (Artists Rifles), his war was largely spent in propaganda and intelligence work, for which he was appointed an OBE in 1920. Two years later, and due to a decline in his personal fortune, he was obliged to seek paid employment and became a lecturer in Hellenistic history and literature at King's College, London. A prolific scholar, he was the recipient of honorary degrees from St Andrews and Oxford and was elected fellow of the British Academy in 1942. *ODNB*; *Times*, 19 October 1943, p. 6.

Temple,[4] at that time rector of St James's, Piccadilly, Alec Paterson (who brought me into the picture as the likely editor), Archie Turner,[5] well known to the Student Christian Movement for his forthright and highly unconventional views, and Ethel Barton,[6] whose fiery faith in the paper was to rescue it at certain moments when mere men hesitated. It was Ethel Barton who founded The Challenge Book and Picture Shop soon afterwards, a risky venture which succeeded in raising to some degree the abysmal standard of popular so-called 'religious art' and which kept alive the name of our paper after it ceased publication in the early 1920s.

We rented a very modest office on the edge of Fleet Street, but not one of us had the smallest experience of professional journalism. We trusted that a practical sub-editor would be able to show us the ropes and advertised for one in the trade papers. As we ought to have foreseen this brought up our stairs a stream of the failures who haunt Fleet Street. The melancholy individual the committee selected let us down ten days before publication and I sent at once for another applicant, a grocer's assistant in Gravesend who edited his parish magazine. I had taken to JB,[7] the man, his cheerfulness, his air of energy, self-reliance and commonsense, at our first interview and my confidence in him was now justified up to the hilt.

For several months I had been hard at it helping to raise capital for our project in private interviews and speeches at meetings and conferences. This first wave of propaganda brought us enough money, it was decided, for a start to be made and we were bold enough to announce the first issue for the first of May. The advisory committee met weekly and had to make many decisions. I remember a session at which we discussed advertisements, how we were to set about attracting them and what categories we should admit or reject; patent medicines, matrimonial agencies and one or two other kinds were ruled out. Edwyn Bevan, who was rather deaf, was meanwhile doodling on a piece of writing paper but when his opinion was asked pulled himself out of his abstraction with 'I don't mind, so long as we don't advertise baptismal trousers for total immersion', and then relapsed again.

4   William Temple (1881–1944) was the son of Bishop Frederick Temple of Exeter, later bishop of London and archbishop of Canterbury. After a distinguished academic career at Rugby and Oxford (where he was president of the Oxford Union, became a fellow of Queen's College and was drawn into the orbit of the OBM) William Temple was ordained in 1908. Already a convinced socialist, he was heavily involved with the SCM and also with the WEA, becoming its president in 1908. Appointed headmaster of Repton in 1910, he moved to St James's, Piccadilly, in 1914. During the war he served as editor of *The Challenge*, as secretary of the National Mission of Repentance and Hope and as chairman of the Life and Liberty movement. Appointed a canon of Westminster in 1919, he went on to become bishop of Manchester (1920), archbishop of York (1929) and archbishop of Canterbury (1942). Hugely and uniquely popular in the latter *rôle*, Temple's episcopal career was primarily marked by his contribution to ecumenism and to Christian social thought. *ODNB*; *Times*, 27 October 1944, p. 2.
5   Possibly Archer Turner, who had been curate of St Andrew's, Earlsfield, since 1910. *Crockford's Clerical Directory*, 1927, p. 1555.
6   Ethel Barton (?–?) served as secretary to *The Challenge*, in which capacity she introduced Willam Temple to his future wife, Frances Anson. Iremonger, *William Temple*, pp. 197–8.
7   James Benson (?–?). According to Iremonger, 'the only trained journalist on the staff [who] served the paper with selfless loyalty'. Iremonger, *William Temple*, p. 184.

At another meeting we compiled a list of eminent churchmen representing every Anglican school of thought, from whom we would invite a note of encouragement for publication in our first number. One of these must obviously be Charles Gore,[8] and Temple, who happened to be staying with him at the coming weekend, promised to bring back his communication. At our Monday meeting Temple turned up crestfallen. What had happened? The bishop had grown impatient as our plans were put before him: what was the point of adding to the church weeklies, each worse than the last?

'In a nutshell', Temple had replied, 'we are out to produce a *Christian* church newspaper.'

'My dear young friend', said Gore with characteristic penetrating gaze over the top of his spectacles, 'the notion is too chimerical to be entertained.'
That was final: content to watch our effort critically, he wrote us no message.

At last the fateful moment was upon us. J. B. and I spent forty-eight hours at a stretch correcting proofs and making up our first number, harried at intervals by Charles Clarke,[9] our advertisement manager, who wanted 'special positions' on our best pages. He did succeed in covering our entire front page with enormous splashes of red and black (for we used two colours in the early months) advertising Stephens's inks; his plan was to introduce on the front of our second number the figure of a little man, the familiar trade mark of another firm, cleaning up the mess, with the legend 'Zog it off.' This was too much, however, for the stomachs of the advisory committee.

Newsom contributed an able leading article to the first issue, and right away letters of appreciation began to flow in: we reckoned that we had got off to a good start. The committee appeared to be too exhausted to meet in the following week and I was left to my own devices. My heart and my home were still in Bermondsey, and I found a text there for that week's leader. In Charles Booth's enormous survey (seventeen volumes) of *Life and labour in London*[10] I had often studied the appalling map of poverty in inner South London and had been struck by the fact that only two small points in it were coloured yellow, which stood for 'well-to-do'. These were Lambeth Palace and the bishop of Southwark's house at Kennington, an encumbrance since turned to other use. Being very careful to repudiate any personal attack on the occupants of these two spots, whom I regarded as victims, like many another, of an outworn tradition, I drew the contrast with the Franciscan ideal, frankly impracticable in its entirety but far

8   Charles Gore (1853–1932), a longstanding associate of E. S. Talbot and Henry Scott Holland, was renowned for his liberal Anglo-Catholicism (he was the editor of *Lux mundi*) and for his relative radicalism on social issues. A founding member of the Community of the Resurrection, Gore became a canon of Westminster Abbey in 1894 and was appointed bishop of Worcester in 1901; he was translated to the new diocese of Birmingham in 1905 and to Oxford in 1911. Despite his keen sense of humour, Gore's manner could be acerbic. *ODNB*; *Times*, 18 January 1932, p. 14.

9   Possibly Charles Philip Stewart Clarke (1871–1947). An alumnus of Clifton College, Clarke was vicar of High Wycombe and in 1914 published *Everyman's book of saints*. *Who was who, 1941–1950* (London, 1952), p. 220.

10 Actually, *Life and labour of the people in London*. Charles Booth (1840–1916), chairman and founder of the Booth Steamship Company, commenced his monumental survey of social conditions in Tower Hamlets in 1887; it was published, in seventeen volumes, fifteen years later. *ODNB*

more likely to win men's respect for the ministry of the Gospel. A spate of letters from readers followed, a good many (I guessed mostly from younger people) applauded but not a few were pained, some quite abusive and demanding the return of their annual subscription to our 'socialist rag'. I laid the cream of this correspondence in both kinds before the committee at its next meeting and it was taken seriously. One or two members were genuinely dismayed – wasn't it too early to court controversy and could we really afford to lose subscribers? At last I got hot under the collar and remember retorting rather recklessly, 'If we're never going to say anything we might as well change our name to *The Tin Trumpet.*'

The Challenge settled down quickly into its stride with the aid of willing helpers like Albert Mansbridge,[11] the founder of the WEA. At last I was able, on 25 July, to get married to Rachel Abel Smith in Southwark Cathedral. It was entirely fitting that the wedding should take place in the mother church of South London, for I had first met my wife in Bermondsey, where she worked regularly in the Time and Talents Settlement, founded some twenty years earlier by her mother with Lady Susan Truman[12] and others. When our happy married life ended, over forty years later, with her sudden death she was still working regularly in the place we both loved.

The wedding was a gay occasion a little out of the common. It took place on a Saturday afternoon to allow our Bermondsey friends to attend, which they did in surprising numbers. Added to these was a large contingent of our West End relations and friends, some of whom appeared to be venturing for the first time into the 'dangerous' parts of London. I remember witnessing the alarm of one well-dressed party when a couple of porters climbed on to the running-board of their big car to wish them luck as it drove slowly through the refuse of the Borough Market. Meanwhile, in the fashion of the time, pedlars were selling at the doors of the cathedral crêpe paper handkerchiefs printed in gold and gaudy colours with our life histories and messages of goodwill.

At the reception afterwards in the cathedral chapter house it was entertaining to watch the fusion of our guests, top-hat and cloth cap coming together, [and]

---

[11]   Coming from a Congregationalist background, Albert Mansbridge (1876–1952) was confirmed in the Church of England at the age of fourteen. He later became a licensed lay reader, a Sunday school teacher and a temperance activist, although his youthful ambition to be ordained was never realized. As a young man Mansbridge was deeply involved in the co-operative movement and in university extension work; a protégé of Charles Gore, he benefited from the bishop's patronage after the WEA was formally inaugurated at Oxford in 1903. Inevitably, the fledgling movement (which built on a foundation of university extension dating back to the 1870s) attracted the support and interest of radical churchmen such as R. H. Tawney and William Temple, as well as that of Barclay Baron, who taught a course for the WEA at the National Gallery. In turn, Mansbridge was active in the Life and Liberty movement, he founded the Church Tutorial Classes Association in 1917, he contributed to the lengthy deliberations of the National Mission's committee on Christianity and Industrial Problems and he published a study of Charles Gore and E. S. Talbot in 1935. Despite a serious illness in 1915, Mansbridge sat on the Adult Education Committee of the Ministry of Reconstruction from 1917 to 1919 and continued to champion its cause until his retirement in 1945. *ODNB*; *Times*, 25 August 1952, p. 8; A. Wilkinson, *The Church of England and the First World War* (London, 1978), pp. 86–8.

[12]   Unidentifiable.

the frank appraisal of differing fashions by the ladies. When the bride cut the wedding cake the West End gaped with astonishment to see it simply disappear under a wave of Bermondsey boys before they had a proper view of it. The last thing I saw in the room before we drove away was a fastidious old uncle, Sir Charles Fremantle,[13] sitting on the floor in his faultless wedding kit, his bearded face wrinkled into a smile, while Fred Brent's Bermondsey baby played with his gold watch-chain.

A honeymoon calls for no comment, except that ours had a very odd ending, reflecting in tiny miniature the disruption of an age. As we drove away from South London it happened that the eyes of the whole British world were bent upon it: the Australians were playing England in the last test match of the series at Kennington Oval. E. F. Benson[14] has described dramatically how he sat, one among thousands, intent upon the game, but found time like others to buy an early evening paper as it was hawked round and to glance at the headlines between overs. The murder of an Austrian archduke and his duchess,[15] a most unsporting event, was stale news long ago, but somehow the Germans did not yet seem disposed to let it be: you could never quite tell what these foreigners were up to! It was a little cloud like a man's hand passing between you and the sun, gone in a moment and out of mind. Everywhere at home sensible people were about their business, as we to our wedding, with a sidelong glance at the foreign news but not yet a tremor of foreboding. The chancelleries of Europe, for all we knew, may have had another tale to tell, but it did not concern us.

At the inn at Balmacara, a plain stone cube put upon the side of the road leading to Kyle of Lochalsh, we had not a care. We lazed and walked together over the heathery hills and saw the sun go down behind the peaks of Skye across the sound. I tried to paint a bit one day, but a cloud of midges, the plague of Scotland, drove me to strip and wash all irritation away under a little waterfall among the rocks.

We had arrived by boat from distant Fort William: the thread of railway which had brought us thither out of England now seemed as good as severed: the place we were in was timeless and deliciously remote. Letters from home were very

[13] The third son of the first Lord Cottesloe, Sir Charles Fremantle KCB (1834–1914) was deputy master and comptroller of the Royal Mint from 1868 to 1894 and served as the British representative on the board of the Suez Canal Company from 1896 to 1903. A magistrate for Middlesex, London and Westminster, he had married into the Abel Smith family in 1865. *Times*, 10 October 1914, p. 11.

[14] Edward Frederic Benson (1867–1940) was the third son of Edward White Benson, headmaster of Wellington College and a future bishop of Truro and archbishop of Canterbury. He was also the elder brother of the colourful and influential Roman Catholic convert and priest, Robert Hugh Benson. Author of no fewer than ninety-three books, including the Mapp and Lucia novels, E. F. Benson's reminiscences are considered to be exceptionally vivid evocations of his own times. *ODNB*; *Times*, 1 March 1940, p. 11.

[15] A reference to the assassination of the Archduke Franz Ferdinand (1863–1914), the heir apparent to the Emperor Franz Josef, in the Bosnian capital of Sarajevo on 28 June 1914. The twin murders, the result of a plot hatched by extreme Serbian nationalists linked to the Serbian military, sparked a diplomatic crisis that plunged Europe into war five weeks later. J. Bourne (ed.), *Who's who in World War One* (London, 2001), p. 97; H. Strachan, *The First World War: a new illustrated history* (London, 2003), pp. 9–10.

few and contained nothing but family news, newspapers were hard to come by
and we did not bother to peruse them. We were more content and self-contained
than we were ever to be again, in those few days before July slipped into
August, 1914.

And then, in a strange fashion for us, the news was out. In the middle of the
night I woke to the sound of several horses trotting down our road, upon which
at any hour traffic was an event rare enough for notice. Quickly out of bed, I
leaned through the wide open window. The moon shone bright across the sea and
cast upon the road the sharp shadows of three riders. They had come to a halt at
our front door and were calling out loudly in Gaelic – I guessed for whisky, which
after very few minutes was brought out to them. I called to them for news and one
looked up to me with four tremendous words in Scots: 'That war started
yesterday.' I repeated them over my shoulder to my wife but I think that neither
of us for the moment found any words to say. Meanwhile the men, still sitting
their horses, presented an extraordinary sight. One was wearing a slouch hat,
turned up at the side with a badge that glinted under the moon, another a pair of
puttees over his farm breeches, the third a bandolier: they were ghosts out of the
last war – and that had ended in South Africa over a dozen years ago! Their
glasses were empty and they turned their horses in a scuffle to go on, but before
they went they told me that they had fought with Lovat's Scouts[16] and were still
reservists; they were going to report at Kyle, hoping to be needed again. So,
'Best of luck!'

Our honeymoon had been snapped in two; we must go home. But that was
much easier to say than do. First thing after breakfast I went to the village post-
office, some way off, to send a telegram. The postmaster, most taciturn of Scots,
said that no unauthorized person was now allowed to send a private message by
wire. Argument had no effect, I went back to the inn. The northbound morning
steamer came in sight but did not put in at Balmacara: she passed us by far out,
leaving nothing but a thin trail of smoke over the sea. When we saw her return
on the following day, steaming south, she ignored us again. I could see through
my glasses that her deck was crowded – we were told with naval reservists,
fishermen from the Outer Isles. Three days later we were to see these men again,
passing northwards. They had reported at their bases and been told that the
Admiralty could not deal with them yet: they had better go home and wait to be
called.

Meanwhile we stood by impatiently, our bags packed ready to go. And every
means of going was withdrawn. There was no railway within reach, no car in the
village. On the first afternoon I met a gunner officer in uniform, rounding up all
suitable farm horses for cavalry remounts or draught purposes: there was no

---

[16] Among many such units raised during the Boer War (1899–1902), two squadrons of volunteers
     were recruited for service in South Africa by Lord Lovat 'from among the ghillies and stalkers on
     his Beaufort estate'. As a Yeomanry unit, Lovat's Scouts were mobilized as part of the Territorial
     Force in August 1914. T. Pakenham, *The Boer War* (London, 1979), p. 438; E. A. James, *British
     regiments 1914–1918* (Heathfield, 1998), p. 24.

likelihood any more of a trap to take us on a long drive. On the second day rumour reached us of a naval battle up the coast and I set out at once to walk to Kyle for news. Attempts at taking a bee line landed me in bogs and I reached the village late in the afternoon. There was a busy picture at the little port, where Lovat's reservists, now swollen to several dozen, still hung about waiting for orders. The people there confirmed the rumour. Firing up the coast had been distinctly heard during the night. No less than nineteen of our ships were down. Admiral Jellicoe[17] was dead. They were expecting the wounded to be landed any minute and were as ready as they could be to deal with them. I walked home soberly but quite unconvinced.[18]

On the next morning a grizzled boatman at Balmacara suggested that if he rowed us out into the bay and hung about, the southbound boat could not choose but slow down enough to take us aboard. We set out with our luggage, in company with a very old lady, also stranded, who assembled round her not only many bundles and string bags but, I well remember, a green parrot in a cage. The bay was choppy and we spent an uncomfortable hour of waiting. At last the boat was in sight …[19] a crate with two pigs in it; the bottom of the crate broke away and the pigs splashed into the quiet sea. To our surprise they swam sturdily, without cutting their throats with their front trotters according to an old wives' tale, until the pursuing boats caught them and hauled them, loudly squealing, on board.

With the first light the weather changed, clouds hid the moon and it began to drizzle. We reached Fort William at last, wet and hungry, on a miserable grey morning. The hotel breakfast, when it came, was shoddy. We boarded the train bound for Edinburgh in pouring rain. In pouring rain, somewhere among the hills, our engine refused to go further on the Highland Line and we sat several hours waiting for a relief to come. All the best engines, they told us, had gone to haul troop-trains. 'It'll just be that war', we murmured to ourselves.

Edinburgh in time for a late dinner, and a hotel bedroom overlooking Princes Street. Once again the sound of footsteps, this time of marching men, brought us out of our beds to the window. This time we saw the first prisoners of war, I suppose, whom anyone had seen in Britain. They were German fishermen, some contriving to step awkwardly in their high sea-boots, under guard of kilted soldiers. They had been sighted, we heard next day, by our fleet on the eve of the

[17] John Rushworth Jellicoe (1859–1935) was appointed commander of Britain's Grand Fleet on 4 August 1914. Given the responsibility this entailed, Winston Churchill, then First Lord of the Admiralty, pithily observed that Jellicoe was 'the only man who could lose the war in an afternoon'. Although this was not Jellicoe's fate, the Grand Fleet's failure to destroy Germany's High Seas Fleet at the battle of Jutland in May 1916 was held against him. Jellicoe was appointed First Sea Lord at the end of 1916 but was dismissed on Christmas Eve 1917 for his mishandling of the U-boat war. Bourne (ed.), *Who's who in World War One*, pp. 144–5; P. J. Haythornthwaite, *The World War One source book* (London, 1992), p. 331.

[18] The first shots of the Anglo-German naval war were fired off Harwich on 5 August 1914. At this early stage in the war, Jellicoe's Grand Fleet was operating with impunity off the coast of Norway. P. G. Halpern, *A naval history of World War I* (London, 1994), pp. 27–8.

[19] Material missing.

declaration of war, fishing suspiciously close to the Scottish coast. Taking no chances, the navy brought them on board and sank their fishing fleet.[20] Years afterwards when I began to tell a young naval officer the tale he stopped me with, 'I know because I was there.' 'And if war hadn't been declared after all?', I hazarded. 'Damned awkward for us chaps', he said with a merry laugh.

Next day we reached London: our honeymoon was over. Besides memories of the greatest happiness it has left me ever since with two causes of wonderment – why did so few among us have any presage of the immense catastrophe which was at a stroke to change our lives, and in a very second place, how had it been possible, within the confines of our small, well-charted island to be, in a twinkling and for nearly a week, completely lost to the wide world.

I sat down to my desk in *The Challenge* office as if pretending that I had never left it. J. B. was cheerful and self-possessed as ever, the small staff were about their own familiar business. But it would never be quite the same again. Even the outward aspect of things altered every hour. Outside the newspaper offices in Fleet Street crowds stared at headlines, jostled to look at photographs. In the outfitters' windows the gay sports shirts had given way to officers' tunics and khaki ties: the whole world seemed bent on going khaki. Old friends looked in, trying to look comfortable in uniform; others, when you rang them up, were not there, gone no one knew quite whither. Elderly city men, like Wells's Mr Britling,[21] were demanding brassards to wear and buying manuals on company drill, sure that if they were armed with these the country would be safer. Posters were beginning to appear, bearing Kitchener's face with piercing eyes, his pointing finger and the legend 'I want YOU' – enough to scare any chicken-livered passer-by into suicide or joining-up. There was much inevitable confusion beneath a mask of purposeful calm.

And in our tiny, sequestered world on the third floor, with a glimpse of the roaring Strand, what was there we could do, anything relevant, anything which might support not hinder the church's cause in crisis, encourage any Christian soul? Press day was tomorrow and here, right at hand, there was this week's leader to be written, to be put on paper against time, the final, last-minute contribution, but also the key-word of the issue. The staff would soon be going home and then I must sit down and write, sit half the night, if need be, writing and tearing up and rewriting those two columns to which many eyes would probably turn first of all. What were 'we' to say? What was worth saying? What had not been better said already?

In the exact three months between its first publication and this sudden, shattering blow which knocked everyone's concerns sideways, *The Challenge*

[20] Several German trawlers were searched and sunk in the North Sea by the Royal Navy on 4–5 August 1914. Apparently searching for the Grand Fleet, at least one of these, with some carrier pigeons on board, was intercepted some hours before war actually broke out. J. S. Corbett, *History of the Great War based on official documents. Naval operations*, I (London, 1920), p. 37.
[21] A reference to H. G. Wells's enormously popular novel *Mr. Britling sees it through* (1916), which took as its theme the impact of the war on the home front. *ODNB*

had found its place and won a limited but faithful core of readers. Its finances were, of course, precarious (that was nothing new in Fleet Street) but its function had been made plain beyond our expectation. And now we were confronted with a fresh opportunity, if we but knew how to take it. We had no doubt that we could, and must, add our own infinitesimal weight to the great shoulder which the whole nation was putting to the wheel of warfare.

Surely one of the most pregnant words in our language is 'steady', which has risen so often, so instinctively in an Englishman's throat at the moment of crisis. There was urgent need for it now if the Christian cause was not to be betrayed. From the outbreak of war, there was need, for instance, to confront the hysteria which fed itself, dewy-eyed, on each fresh atrocity story, which drew an outburst of anger when a friend hummed *Jesu joy of man's desiring*[22] – that man Bach was a German, which caused not a few congregations to cut all German tunes or hymns like Gerhardt's 'O Sacred Head, now wounded'[23] out of their worship. These were but symptoms of a deep disorder. It was proving much too easy to revive the attractive cult of tribal deities, the Kaiser's 'good old German God', our own imperial Jehovah: both could find ample sanction in the Old Testament, so long as you were careful not to turn the pages of the New. The membership of the Universal Church, always divided, was now locked in a savage struggle between two parties, plainly defined by national boundaries such as its Founder had sternly refused to recognize; it was the church militant indeed, as anyone could see, but its warfare was not all for the Kingdom of God. The way forward had never seemed more dark and difficult, whether for the saint or the simplest believer, but it would be desperate if the church itself, destined to outlast this and any other human conflict, were willing to forget, even for 'the duration', the things that belonged eternally to its Peace.

These concerns belong to the highest theme of all. It takes the tongue of men and of angels to proclaim it – and even then it is nothing worth without charity,[24] the scarcest gift in wartime. What could an obscure organ, twenty-four pages a week printed on ever-worsening paper, do about it? Far more powerful engines of the press were in full blast stoking up the fires of hatred. Lord Northcliffe's propaganda machine, officially sponsored, was backing the stories so many people thirsted to hear and repeat in the early stages (though they had a surfeit of them before the end) – the Belgian babies on the lances of Uhlans,[25] the French

---

[22] From Johann Sebastian Bach's cantata *Herz und Mund und Tat und Leben* (1723).
[23] A reference to J. W. Alexander's 1830 translation of Paul Gerhardt's hymn. Paul Gerhardt (1607–76), a Lutheran minister, based his hymn 'O Haupt voll Blut und Wunden' on the medieval 'Salve Caput Cruentatum'. Perennially popular, it was played at the funeral of Frederick William I of Prussia and was first translated into English in 1752. T. B. Hewitt, *Paul Gerhardt as a hymn writer and his influence on English hymnody* (New Haven, 1918), pp. 88–90.
[24] An allusion to 1 Corinthians 13:1.
[25] Lancers. The German army of 1914 possessed a formidable mounted arm and could field more than two dozen regiments of Uhlans alone. Given their reconnaissance *rôle* and their distinctive weaponry, the Uhlans in particular were both vanguard and symbol of the German invasion. Haythornthwaite, *World War One source book*, p. 200.

priests tied to the clappers of swinging bells, the clumsy 'Lusitania medal'[26] (the Royal Mint sold casts of it for war funds – I still have one), which, it was proved afterwards, the German government had never issued or even seen. No story, it was claimed, did more to fill the recruiting stations than the disgusting account of 'corpse factories', and even when the cumbrous word *Kadaververwertungsanstalt* was correctly translated and the legend seen to be a lie, it was never withdrawn. Almost every one of us was convinced that the hideous battle, once joined, must be fought to a finish at any cost – but surely not that of snatching up the weapons of slander and falsehood which in the hands of our enemy we so fiercely condemned! Was it not possible-

> To honour, while you strike him down,
> The foe that comes with fearless eyes?[27]

Such were some of the primitive weapons in the armoury of 'ideological warfare' (a grim tautology not then invented) and they had a keen cutting edge. There were other arguments apparently much more reasonable, more falsely philosophic, more subtle which inflicted deeper wounds on men's minds and hearts. The upshot of them tended to be that we were engaged in a selfless crusade, pure white against sheer black, high civilization versus barbarism unredeemable. 'Christian fellowship' with such people was now shown up as a sentiment without substance; we must never consort with them in any form again. Crystallized in a current phrase, 'there is no good German but a dead German'. There were, of course, many of us who knew from our own experience that this was fundamentally untrue to begin with, it was not nearly so simple as that. Now we must make our voices heard as best we could, not so much in common fairness to our enemy as for the rescue of the ultimate ideal for which we had gone to war – the freedom of the human spirit everywhere.

Not to make too much of too little, *The Challenge* soon had a good many pens, Temple's among them, writing in simple terms about the ethics of the business. But we remembered that we had never set up to be a philosophical or theological journal nor intended now to become a mere propaganda sheet; we wanted to be a weekly newspaper popular enough to attract the normally thoughtful layman and occasionally the sceptic. So we cast our net fairly wide for news paragraphs and

---

[26] The sinking of the passenger liner *Lusitania* off the Irish coast by a U-boat in May 1915 (a sinking that resulted in the loss of nearly 1,200 civilian lives) was a propaganda coup for the Allies and did much to antagonize public opinion in the United States, from whence the *Lusitania* had sailed. An exculpatory medallion of the sinking was privately produced in Germany, depicting the stricken liner carrying munitions. This mendacious artefact was naturally seized upon in Great Britain, where copies were made and sold in aid of St Dunstan's hospital for blinded servicemen. *Ibid.*, pp. 50, 375.

[27] From Newbolt's poem 'Clifton Chapel', first published in *The island race* (1898). Like Baron, Henry Newbolt (1862–1938) was an alumnus of Clifton College. There, and especially from the pulpit of the chapel, Newbolt found that 'the ideals of chivalry...service, self-sacrifice, courage, justice, and an attitude to good and evil based on the Christian ethic, were being propagated as the contemporary way to live'. P. Dickinson (ed.), *Selected poems of Henry Newbolt* (London, 1981), p. 13.

short stories connected with the war – the sufferings or successes of church people, training for various kinds of voluntary service, work for the welfare of troops or refugees and so on. We had no need, of course, for any regular war-correspondent and could not afford to pay expensive agencies of news.

We were fortunate, however, in securing one regular contributor who produced with the strictest punctuality a series of unusual weekly articles. He was himself an unusual character and something of a 'mystery man', a small, vivacious grey-haired parson and a very practised journalist in a popular vein. Officially he was the secretary of a rather quiescent Church of England society, which gave him leave of absence at the shortest notice for operations, so he more than hinted, with the British secret service. There was a touch, I thought, of the *Boy's Own Paper*,[28] almost of the who-done-it about some of this. One Wednesday morning, I recall, his infallible article did not arrive as usual by the first post, together with photographs of his own which seemed to cover all Europe from an inexhaustible reservoir. Before the day was out his article was put into my hands by a messenger. It was written in pencil, not typed as normally, in a hand which I knew was not his. This time there were no photographs with it, but instead a cryptic note to apologize – the text, he said, had been dictated on the telephone to a friend, under great difficulties, to be passed on to me. When he next came to *The Challenge* office he half-told me a story about a French post-office almost in the enemy lines but still with a workable telephone, a quick dictation and a still quicker get-away before the Germans took over. I did not know what to think of this, but the article was very printable and already published.

His weekly line for us was a graphic thumbnail sketch of one of the countries at war; he was specially informative about the Balkans, probably because most of us knew so little. He provided excellent snapshots, right on the point, and nearly always chose an alliterative title like 'Turkey in the Teuton toils'. I gave these articles pride of place on the right-hand middle page facing the leading article, because readers looked for them and liked them. They had the authentic marks of first-hand information, but at moments I still had doubts. I do not know what eventually became of this little man, intriguing perhaps in more senses than one. I can only say that when, a year later, I was applying for a passport to France, which involved a certain amount of interrogation, I found my friend, not wearing his clerical collar at the time, quizzing me across the table. And when, a year later still, I heard him give a lantern lecture, one of a series which went down well enough, to our troops at a French base, I enjoyed tripping him up gently afterwards over some dramatic exaggerations – for his subject was the Republic of Andorra, where, as if to his personal affront, I had been a rare early traveller myself.

There was another type of news, though it could be no more than a precarious trickle, which I took much interest in compiling. Newsom had studied in

---

[28] The *Boy's Own Paper* was originally published by the Religious Tract Society and ran from January 1879 to January 1967. Famous for its adventure stories and jingoistic tone, its more distinguished contributors included Jules Verne, Robert Baden-Powell, G. A. Henty, Arthur Conan Doyle and R. M. Ballantyne. *Times*, 11 January 1967, p. 10, 14 January 1967, p. 9.

Germany, as I had myself, and had remained a close student of German thought, especially in theology. In wartime he still had access to some current German newspapers and serious periodicals: he never told me the source but I don't doubt that it was legitimate. We combed these together for any material from the other side which would support our case for fair-thinking – in short for signs of what Germans had thought or said or done that was 'decent'. Of course we found them here and there, in sufficient quantity to warrant the conjecture that there would have been many more if an official veto or an editor's blue pencil had not stopped them from reaching print. As everyone knows, the same sort of censorship, for security reasons or in deference to public opinion, hinders free expression in wartime on our own side. Here was a manifesto from a body of professors or scientists pleading that charity and truth should be maintained above the battle, or a church reaffirming its faith under agonizing test. Here was a simple instance, authenticated with names, of a German soldier risking himself for the sake of Allied wounded or being as conspicuously generous to a prisoner of war as our own men so often were. I do not remember how we commented on the famous 'Christmas truce' of 1914, which broke out spontaneously between the opposing armies at some points in the front line – a fantastic event which perplexed and infuriated the commanders on both sides and which, if it had not been sternly checked, might have grown into a 'mass movement' to bring the war to an end![29] But I did contribute a fiction of my own to our Christmas number which was published a few days before the 'truce' and oddly anticipated it. It was the simple story of two wounded men, a Londoner and a Bavarian, who stumbled upon each other in a Flemish wood on Christmas night and improvised the festival of peace and goodwill together. These things were small enough crumbs but worth rescuing, we felt, from the rubbish bin of hatred. They were also enough to earn us some cries of 'pro-German' and the loss of a few subscriptions.

The Challenge, then, was standing on its feet, not without the hindrances and anxieties common to every periodical at the time, and was operating freely in its own corner of a vast field of opportunity. Before a busy year had passed the staff had received a most valuable reinforcement in C. B. Mortlock,[30] well known

---

[29] Despite Baron's enthusiasm, the much-romanticized Christmas truce of 1914 was largely fuelled by pre-war, barrack room custom in the British army and by a mutual desire to bury the dead. M. Snape, *God and the british Soldier: religion and the British Army in the First and Second World Wars* (London, 2005), p. 188; M. Brown and S. Seaton, *Christmas truce* (London, 2001), p. 69.

[30] Charles Bernard Mortlock (1888–1967) moved from a Somerset living to St Mary-le-Bow in 1915 and seems to have undertaken some editorial duties at *The Challenge*. He joined the Army Chaplains' Department in 1916 but resigned his commission due to ill health the following year. Although he held two successive curacies in London parishes, he devoted most of the inter-war years to his rising career in journalism. A staunch Anglo-Catholic, he was remarkable in that he had learnt to fly while an undergraduate at Cambridge and his taste for outdoor pursuits was reflected in his appointment as assistant editor of *Country Life* in 1918. However, he found an even more congenial post at the *Church Times* in 1919 (where he wrote under the pseudonym of Urbanus) and was appointed ecclesiastical correspondent of the *Daily Telegraph* in 1921. He also wrote as a ballet and theatre critic for a number of newspapers and magazines. In his later years he served as vicar of Epping, rector of the city parish of St Vedast, Foster Lane, and subsequently as canon and treasurer of Chichester Cathedral. *Times*, 1 November 1967, p. 12; Iremonger, *William Temple*, p. 184.

today as an able parson-journalist, whose inside knowledge of persons and procedure within the Church of England I could not hope to equal: I was grateful for such a colleague. There was voluntary help forthcoming from other quarters, and one day I told Newsom that I believed I had done my job, at any rate that another was calling me. He pressed me to stay on a little longer – the service of *The Challenge*, he said, should be reckoned essential in its own kind as the picture of the war and the mood of men took on ever more sombre colours. I agreed and stayed, but finally, with a farewell from the committee and the staff which was affectionate and very moving, I went.

Other editors, of course, were forthcoming, a whole succession which for a time included Temple. *The Challenge* saw the war out, rather exhausted but with its faith intact, and began to face up to the problems of a period of tragic peacemaking. Then, like many another contemporary starved of capital, it slipped out of the ranks of British newspapers. I shall never regret our effort or believe that it was wasted.

INDEX

WEA (Workers' Educational Association): 8, 268
Wells, H.G.: 272
Westoutre: 170
Whitley, J.H.: 109
Wiesbaden: 208
Wilcox, Alfred: 33
Wilhelm II, Kaiser: 27, 185–7, 194, 202–4, 273
Williams, George: 124
Wilson, William: 14, 108, 263–4
Wilson, Woodrow: 15, 256
Winter, Denis: 16
Withers, Cecil: 33–4
Wood, S.H.: 192
Woodward, C.S.: 222
Wulverghem: 55
Wycliffe Hall: 5
Wytschaete: 35

Yapp, Arthur Keysall
background: 18–19
drives YMCA war work, 22–3, 37–9
on playing cards and drink, 65–67
on YMCA relations with churches, 81
on British generals and soldiers' welfare, 92
on national significance of YMCA army work, 93
on YMCA and practical Christianity, 94
manages Food Economy Campaign, 96
appointed KBE, 96
defends YMCA trading practices, 98

YMCA (Young Men's Christian Association)
and Soldiers' Christian Association, 18, 82, 97
and officers' clubs, 11, 31, 42, 101, 107, 214, 216, 231, 260
and Talbot House, 12
and female workers, 17, 39
and writing tents, 18, 39
National Council, 19, 22, 37, 66, 82
pre-war image of, 19–22, 66, 96
pre-war state of, 20–1
and sports, 21, 90
War Emergency Committee, 22–3, 24, 65, 76, 83, 87
Scottish National Council, 22
policy on huts and marquees, 23
War Emergency Fund, 23, 97–8
wartime finances, 23–8, 97
free distributions of stationery, 24, 118
free distributions of refreshments, 24
fundraising, 24–6, 55, 97, 231

American YMCA, 26, 69, 72, 83–4, 257
trading profits and War Office levy, 26–7
benefactors and benefactions, 27–8
shortage and composition of male workers, 28–32
relations with churches and army chaplains, 29–30, 42–3, 45, 74, 76, 80–1, 83–6, 90, 94, 96, 124–6, 131, 133
Ladies' Auxiliary Committee, 32
female workers, 17, 32–3, 39, 104, 228
casualties among workers, 33
courage and dedication of workers, 34–5, 173–4
in Paris, 37
in Burma, 38
Young Soldiers' Club: 42–3, 113–16, 123
uniform for workers, 52–3
army, corps, divisional and brigade secretaries, 53, 253
as an aid to discipline, 58, 89
as an aid to morale, 58, 89, 92, 166, 238
libraries and lecturers, 59–61, 68, 90, 111, 115, 165–6, 193, 211, 238, 275
Educational Committee, 60
and Scheme of Reconstruction, 62, 64
and Army Education Scheme, 62–3
Universities Committee, 63
problems with transport, 64–5
maternity home at Le Havre, 65, 112
Indian YMCA, 66, 71, 257
number of centres, 67
and internment camps, 69
Employment Bureau, 69
wartime headquarters at Tottenham Court Road, 69, 210
Snapshots from Home League, 69–70
inquiry service for missing soldiers, 69
visitation scheme, 70
and Indian troops, 71
and Chinese labourers, 71, 182–3, 253
and Portuguese troops, 72
and Belgian troops, 72
Canadian YMCA, 72–3, 83
French YMCA, 73, 257
religious publications, 74, 130
and 'family prayers', 74, 131
and religious revival, 75, 129
Religious Work Committee, 75
War Roll Scheme, 75–6, 77
disputes over loss of evangelical identity, 80, 82–3, 96–7, 123–4
and Jewish soldiers, 81
and post-war church reform, 86–88
Religious Work Sub-Committee, 87

Church of England Record Society
COUNCIL AND OFFICERS FOR THE YEAR 2007–2008

Patron

The Reverend Professor OWEN CHADWICK, O.M., K.B.E., D.D., D.Litt., F.B.A.,
F.R.Hist.S.

President

Professor D.N.J. MACCULLOCH, M.A., Ph.D., D.D., F.B.A., F.S.A., F.R.Hist.S.,
St Cross College, Oxford OX1 3LA

Honorary Vice Presidents

Professor D.S. BREWER, M.A., Ph.D., Litt.D., F.S.A.
Professor P. COLLINSON, C.B.E., M.A., Ph.D., D.Litt., D. Univ, F.B.A., F.A.H.A.,
F.R.Hist.S.

Honorary Secretary

M.F. SNAPE, B.A., Ph.D., Department of Modern History, University of Birmingham,
Edgbaston, Birmingham B15 2TT

Honorary Treasurer

A.G. RYRIE, M.A., M. Litt., D.Phil.
Department of Theology and Religion,
University of Durham, Abbey House, Palace Green, Durham DH1 3RS

Honorary General Editor

Professor STEPHEN TAYLOR, M.A., Ph.D., F.R.Hist.S., Department of History,
University of Reading, Whiteknights, Reading RG6 6AH

Other Members of Council

NIGEL ASTON, M.A., D.Phil., F.R.Hist.S.
The Rev. ADREW ATHERSTONE, M.A., D.Phil.
The Rev. NICHOLAS CRANFIELD, M.A., D.Phil., Ph.D.
MATTHEW GRIMLEY, M.A., Ph.D.
The Rev. Canon JUDITH MALTBY, B.A., Ph.D., F.R.Hist. S.
HELEN PARISH, M.A., D.Phil., F.R.Hist.S.
MICHAEL SNAPE, B.A., Ph.D.
D.L. WYKES, B.Sc., Ph.D., F.R.Hist.S.

Executive Secretary

Miss M. BARBER, M.B.E., M.A., F.S.A., 13 Tarleton Gardens, Forest Hill,
London. SE23 3XN

North American Secretary

Dr ROBERT G. INGRAM, Department of History, Ohio University, Bentley Annex, 411,
Athens, Ohio 45701–2979. U.S.A

'The object of the Society shall be to advance knowledge of the history of the Church in
England, and in particular of the Church of England, from the sixteenth century onwards,
by the publication of editions or calendars of primary sources of information.'

Membership of the Church of England Record Society is open to all who are interested in
the history of the Church of England. Enquiries should be addressed to the Executive
Secretary, Miss Melanie Barber, at the above address.

PUBLICATIONS

Forthcoming Publications

THE CORRESPONDENCE OF ARCHBISHOP LAUD. Ed. Kenneth Fincham and Nicholas Cranfield

THE DIARY OF JOHN BARGRAVE, 1644–1645. Ed. Michael Brennan, Jas' Elsner and Judith Maltby

THE DIARY OF THOMAS LARKHAM 1647–1669. Ed. Susan Hardman Moore

THE 1669 RETURN OF NONCONFORMIST CONVENTICLES. Ed. David Wykes

THE SERMONS OF JOHN SHARP. Ed. Françoise Deconinck-Brossard

THE CORRESPONDENCE OF THEOPHILUS LINDSEY. VOLUME II. Ed. G.M. Ditchfield

THE PAPERS OF THE ELLAND SOCIETY. Ed. John Walsh and Stephen Taylor

THE DIARY OF AN OXFORD PARSON: THE REVEREND JOHN HILL, VICE-PRINCIPAL OF ST EDMUND HALL, OXFORD, 1805–1808, 1820–1855. Ed. Grayson Carter

THE JOURNAL OF DANIEL WILSON, BISHOP OF CALCUTTA, 1845–1857. Ed. Andrew Atherstone

ANGLO-CATHOLIC COMMUNICANTS' GUILDS AND SOCIETIES IN THE LATE NINETEENTH CENTURY. Ed. Jeremy Morris

THE CORRESPONDENCE OF ARCHBISHOP LANE WITH WILFRID PARKER. Ed. Garth Turner

Suggestions for publications should be addressed to Professor Stephen Taylor, General Editor, Church of England Record Society, Department of History, University of Reading, Whiteknights, Reading RG6 6AH, or at s.j.c.taylor@reading.ac.uk.